ZDENĚK JINDRA
IVAN JAKUBEC
ET AL.

THE ECONOMIC RISE
OF THE CZECH LANDS I.
FROM THE 1750s TO THE END
OF WORLD WAR I

CHARLES UNIVERSITY
KAROLINUM PRESS 2024

The Economic Rise of the Czech Lands I. From the 1750s to the End of World War I
Zdeněk Jindra, Ivan Jakubec et al.

KAROLINUM PRESS
Karolinum Press is a publishing department of Charles University
Ovocný trh 560/5, 116 36 Prague 1, Czech Republic
www.karolinum.cz
© Zdeněk Jindra, Ivan Jakubec, 2024
Translation © Phil Jones, 2024
Copyedited by Scott Alexander Jones and Michael Stein
Set in DTP Karolinum Press
Printed in the Czech Republic by Karolinum Press
Layout by Jan Šerých
First English edition

A catalogue record for this book is available from the National Library
of the Czech Republic.

Authorial team led by Professor PhDr. Ivan Jakubec, CSc.
and Professor PhDr. Zdeněk Jindra, CSc. (†)

Authorial team:
PhDr. et PaedDr. Jiří Dvořák, Ph.D., PhDr. Jan Hájek, CSc.,
prof. PhDr. Ivan Jakubec, CSc., prof. PhDr. Zdeněk Jindra, CSc. (†),
JUDr. et PhDr. Antonín Kubačák, CSc. (†), doc. PhDr. Petr Popelka, Ph.D.
Doc. PhDr. Michal Pullmann, Ph.D., doc. PhDr. et JUDr. Jakub Rákosník, Ph.D.
Doc. PhDr. et JUDr. Jan Štemberk, Ph.D.

ISBN 978-80-246-3806-5
ISBN 978-80-246-4023-5 (pdf)
ISBN 978-80-246-4067-9 (epub)

The original manuscript was reviewed by doc. PhDr. Jana Englová, CSc. (University
of Jan Evangelista Purkyně in Ústí nad Labem) and prof. PhDr. Aleš Skřivan, CSc.
(Charles University, Prague)

CONTENTS

FOREWORD

The first part of this study of the economic development of the Czech crown lands over the last 250 years is based on the book *Hospodářský vzestup českých zemí od poloviny 18. století do konce monarchie*,[1] published under the aegis of the Institute of Economic and Social History of the Arts Faculty of Charles University and the Karolinum Press. Some passages have been edited from the English version. Given the use of footnotes, the book might be seen as occupying a place somewhere between university textbook and research monograph.

The book is intended for foreign students, researchers, and anyone interested in economics under the conditions of Central Europe. From the reign of Maria Theresa and Joseph II, via the Congress of Vienna and to the First World War, Europe underwent a profound transformation. The same is true of the Austrian Monarchy itself, from the Silesian Wars, its ascent to become one of the five Great Powers responsible for redrafting the map of Europe at the Congress of Vienna, to its decline into a second-class power and an internally unstable, dualist Austria-Hungary. Many of these secular changes took place in the economic sphere and form the subject of our study.

The authors are leading experts in the economic history of the Czech crowns lands in the eighteenth and nineteenth centuries and include representatives of universities and research institutes from Bohemia and Moravia. Given the broad scope of the subject matter and the expertise of individual authors, certain chapters include contributions from more than one author.

Four chapters are devoted to the period lasting from halfway through the eighteenth century to 1918. Chapter 1 examines the economic, institutional, and legal bases of developments in the social, demographic, ethnic, and cultural spheres. The rest of the chapters outline developments in the primary, secondary, and tertiary economic sectors. The concluding chapter looks at events during the First World War. A selected biography is attached, intended to provide pointers to anyone looking to expand their knowledge of this topic. Most of the tables and graphs are embedded in the text. Schematic maps indicating the surface area of the Austro-Hungarian Monarchy,

---

1   Jindra, Z., and Jakubec. I. a kol. *Hospodářský vzestup českých zemí od poloviny 18. století do konce monarchie*. Praha, 2015.

the scope of the chambers of commerce and trade, the development of the leading engineering firms, and the railway network of the Czech lands are contained in an appendix.

Though the aim is not to provide a single interpretation, the different approaches taken by individual authors, depending on their areas of expertise, in no way undermine the integrity of the work as a whole. For the sake of clarity we have left certain overlaps and repetitions in the text. The authors would like to thank the Karolinum Press for publishing this book in English, the translator for his patience, and the proofreaders for their helpful suggestions.

BIOGRAPHICAL DETAILS

Professor PhDr. Ivan Jakubec, CSc. (b. 1960)
Charles University, Faculty of Arts, Institute of Economic and Social History ivan.jakubec@ff.cuni.cz. Specialises in the economic history of the nineteenth and twentieth centuries and the history of technology, transport, and infrastructure. He has recently begun researching travel during the period of the Protectorate of Bohemia and Moravia.

Emeritus professor PhDr. Zdeněk Jindra, CSc. (b. 1931–2023)
Charles University, Faculty of Arts, Institute of Economic and Social History. Specialises in business history in the nineteenth century and first half of the twentieth century, the economic aspects of the First World War, and the history of the company Krupp, Essen.

1. SOCIOECONOMIC, INSTITUTIONAL, AND LEGAL FOUNDATIONS

ECONOMIC FOUNDATIONS

BASIC TERMS AND PROBLEMS EXAMINED

The material conditions of the citizens of the Czech crown lands during the nineteenth century were primarily affected by the following factors: fundamental demographic changes; industrialisation and the revolution in technology and manufacturing (the Industrial Revolution) in the secondary sector (trade and industrial factory production), along with the swift and sustainable economic growth that resulted; radical changes to the primary sector (agriculture, mining, forestry, etc.); and—somewhat ignored by historians—fundamental transformations to the tertiary sphere (i.e., the wide range of services ensuring communication and the smooth running of the economy, state institutions, and society as a whole). These changes saw the establishment of a market-based capitalist economy and a newly structured bourgeois civil society. However, historical research into these changes has raised a host of questions and problems that are still being discussed to this day.[2]

This chapter will not analyse in detail economic and historical terms, which have recently been dealt with comprehensively by the *Oxford Encyclopedia of Economic History*. Instead, it will focus on specific aspects of the developments that took place in the monarchy and the Czech crown lands.

The cornerstone and main sources of economic development during the course of industrialisation are urban trades, crafts, and factory-based industry (i.e., the secondary sector of a national economy, as opposed to a traditional agrarian society, which is based on the primary sector of land and countryside management). The most trusted measure of economic development is an ongoing, irreversible, and significant rise in gross domestic product (GDP) per head of the population. Industrialisation can therefore be characterised as a long-term, sustainable increase in the part played by the industrial (secondary) sector of the national income of a country. This

---

2   Cf. the relevant entries in encyclopaedias of economic and social history.

expansion is accompanied by structural transformations within industry itself, which are manifest outwardly in a change to the relative importance of
individual industrial branches (i.e., an uneven growth rate). In this respect,
it is possible to speak of a historical exchange of positions between leading
or strategic industries. At the end of the eighteenth and the start of the nineteenth centuries, the textile industry was the economy's driving force. In the
second half of the nineteenth century, its role was taken over by coal, iron,
and steel as a consequence of the railway boom, and at the end of the nineteenth century the vanguard comprised electrical engineering, the chemical
industry, the internal combustion engine, etc.

The most important factor accompanying industrial revolution is sustainable and self-sustaining, relatively high *economic growth*, the main driver
of which is (unlike the classical production factors of land and natural energy sources in the form of human, animal, hydro, and wind power in agrarian societies) productive (i.e., investment and operating) capital, and over
the course of time, especially in the twentieth century, human capital (i.e.,
higher levels of education, knowledge, and skills amongst workers).

Economic growth. What essentially and outwardly best characterises an
Industrial Revolution is the fact that there is sustainable and significantly
higher economic growth in the country in question, leading to the extraordinary compression, acceleration, and deepening of the process of industrialisation. Economic growth, which significantly increases the production
capacity of a national economy, also featured in the preceding agrarian society. However, such growth was negligible, slow, and highly unstable, interrupted by long periods of stagnation and decline. "We can therefore say that
the main sign of a successful Industrial Revolution is the institutionalisation
of (economic) growth".[3] Said growth is (leaving aside short-term cyclical
fluctuations) sustainable and significantly higher and faster than at any time
previously.[4]

Theoretically speaking, sustained and faster economic growth can be
expressed in three ways: (1) linearly as a gradual, smooth increase in production capacity; (2) using a discontinuity model that isolates significant
quantitative breaks or short periods of accelerated economic development;
and (3) by plotting a gradually accelerating upward trend in which economic
tempo gradually increases while deviations from this trend are short-lived
and progress is at core permanent and irreversible. The second model is
applied more to Prussia and Germany 1847–1873, and can be compared to

---

3   Buchheim, Christoph. *Industrielle Revolutionen. Langfristige Wirtschaftsentwicklung in Großbri-
     tannien, Europa und in Übersee.* München: Taschenbuch, 1994, p. 11.
4   See the entry Economic growth, in: Mokyr, Joel (ed.). *The Oxford Encyclopedia of Economic History,*
     Vol. 2. Oxford: Oxford University Press, 2003.

the "take-off" phase as posited by Walt Whitman Rostow. In the Habsburg Empire, France, and other countries, the course of the industrialisation process and economic growth is closer in reality to the third model, and all that is left to debate is the precise moment when the entire process began. The American historian David F. Good traces things back to the pre–March Revolution period (*Vormärz*, the period preceding the 1848 March Revolution in the states of the German Confederation): "Data on the growth of the social product and documents on the technical transformations in key industrial sectors indicate that permanent growth began in the Western region of the (Habsburg) Empire after the Napoleonic era."[5]

In national and international statistics, economic growth is measured by the sum of all values created by the citizens of the country in question, in all sectors of the national economy (i.e., by the appreciable increase in the real gross domestic [national] product [GDP]). At the same time, this relatively accurate indicator of the economic, especially industrial, level of the country in question does not so much operate in absolute figures, such as relative annual per capita increases, since not absolutely every increasing national product counts as economic growth. We deem economic growth to be an increase that is higher than the parallel growth of the population. In principle, it represents the greater potential of labour forces. In this respect, the difference between advanced and less advanced industrial countries resides in the extent to which these potential human resources are genuinely and rationally used in the economy or deployed in the most progressive sectors of the economy (secondary and tertiary). This perspective is directly applicable to the protracted industrial process in the Habsburg Empire.

Market economic transformation. The primary sector (i.e., agriculture, forestry, and mining – the Agrarian Revolution), aims to intensify and rationalise performance in these spheres in order to provide the secondary and tertiary sectors a surplus of accumulated capital and abundant supplies of alimentation and raw materials, as well as a reserve army of labour to develop industry and services.[6] In a broad sense, radical change in the primary sphere refers to transforming feudal social and legal ties between the land and the peasantry in the form of emancipating the peasants and commercialising property and market relations, partly on a bottom-up basis in the form of bourgeois revolutions, and partly on a top-down basis in the form of legal decree and reform. This, in turn, saw peasants purchasing their freedom and ceding parts of their land. The Agrarian Revolution is there-

5   Good, David F., *Der wirtschaftliche Aufstieg des Habsburgerreiches 1750–1914*, Wien, Köln, Graz, 1986, p. 61.
6   Cf. Bairoch, Paul. *Die Landwirtschaft und die Industrielle Revolution 1700–1914*, in: Cipolla, Carlo M., and Knut Borchardt (eds.). *Europäische Wirtschaftsgeschichte*, Vol. 3, pp. 297–332.

fore an important precondition for industrialisation, and either wholly or partly precedes the Industrial Revolution or, at the very least, accompanies it. Fundamental changes are associated with this process. Firstly, the land must become a freely marketable commodity, which presupposes the abolition of the fideicommissum (inalienable and indivisible properties with hereditary succession), the abolition of municipal or communal ownership of land, and the entry of an unsuccessful husbandman into bankruptcy proceedings. Secondly, serfs and villeins had to be turned into free, *sui juris* citizens stripped of all feudal duties and benefits.

In a narrow sense, the Agrarian Revolution involved a transition from a triangular planting system to crop rotation, to the stabling of livestock and the cultivation of fodder crops (clover and alfalfa) and root crops (potatoes and sugar beet), the introduction of fertilisers, the improvement of tools and machines, and finally the application of science to large-scale agricultural production. The Agrarian Revolution increased demand for iron, machines, and means of transport, while producing a multiplication effect (i.e., it in turn drove an increase in the production of iron, the creation of agricultural machinery, the development of the food and chemical industries, etc.). All of this then establishes a close correlation between the Agrarian and Industrial Revolutions.

Changes (revolutions) in communications and services[7] include a qualitative transformation in transporting large numbers of people and goods across land and water (networks of roads, canals, and railways; steam navigation; etc.), rapidly disseminating news and information (the telegraph and printing press, etc.), expanding other utilities and institutions of the tertiary sector, ensuring the exchange of goods (wholesale and retail), circulating money (banks, savings banks, and stock exchanges), managing insurance operations, etc. The importance of this sector resides in the fact that modern means of communication and services are an important part of the infrastructure essential to operating the national economy as a whole and its individual sectors and regions. In Central Europe, where industrialisation was delayed, three factors were important for accelerating economic growth: (a) the railway, which, with its multiplication effect (on metallurgy, engineering, mining, construction, etc.), from 1840–1880, was the driving force behind the Industrial Revolution; (b) the creation of joint-stock moveable banks[8] capable of compensating for insufficient short-term investment and operating capital with loans and short-term credit, and later through shares

---

7   Cf. Hartwell, R. M. *Die Dienstleistungsrevolution*, in: Cipolla and Borchardt. *Europäische Wirtschaftsgeschichte*, pp. 233–260.
8   Cf. Gill, B., *Bankwesen und Industrialisierung in Europa 1730–1914*, pp. 165–194; Vencovský, F., Jindra, Z., Novotný, J., et al. *Dějiny bankovnictví v českých zemích*. Praha, 1999.

in an enterprise; and (c) greater state participation in the economy.[9] The state performs an important function by creating a basic framework for economic activities and by managing public institutions through enforcing the law and the constitution; overseeing the activities of the administrative authorities, municipal and parliamentary representatives; providing education for its citizens; supplying energy and water; regulating healthcare; etc.[10]

The *change of demographic regime (the great transition or demographic revolution)*[11] accounts for the explosive population growth (which took place in England from the mid-eighteenth century and in Western and Central Europe from the nineteenth century onwards) and connects it to the Industrial Revolution, since people, as the main productive force, are a decisive factor in economic growth as well as being the users and consumers of the fruits thereof. This transformation involves a transition lasting several decades from the centuries-old "old demographic regime" of agrarian society (high birth rates of from 35-50 per thousand of the population, high mortality rates of 30-40 per thousand) to the "modern demographic regime" of industrial society (average, subsequently low birth rates of 20-30 per thousand and a decreasing mortality rate, especially infant mortality, of 15-20 per thousand). In the advanced countries of Western Europe, this transition was completed between 1880 and 1913, but in the Habsburg Empire, only its Western region, specifically the Czech lands, comes close to conforming to this trend. The sluggish and uneven course of the demographic revolution in the Habsburg monarchy in comparison with the West was reflected in the somewhat lower numerical increase in the population, slower migration from the countryside to the cities, the insufficient capacity of the domestic market and hence the low level of internal trade and the slow progress of industrialisation.

The *concept of the Industrial Revolution* has been subject to extensive debate over the last fifty years and has generated hundreds of publications.[12] Issues particular to the Habsburg Monarchy and the Czech lands can be summarised in the following points.

---

9   Cf. Supple, B., *Der Staat und die Industrielle Revolution 1700-1914*, in: Cipolla and Borchardt, *Europäische Wirtschaftsgeschichte*, Vol. 3, pp. 195-231.

10 Regarding the issue of institutionalism, cf. T. Veblen, J. R. Commons, J. K. Galbraith, D. North in *Theorie des institutionellen Wandels. Eine neue Sicht der Wirtschaftsgeschichte*. Tübingen 1988.

11 Cf. Cipolla, Carlo M. *The Economic History of World Population*. London: Penguin Books, 1962.

12 Purš, J. *Průmyslová revoluce: Vývoj pojmu a koncepce*. Praha, 1973; Myška, Milan. "Průmyslová revoluce z perspektivy 70. a 80. let." *ČsČH* 89 (1991): 533-546; Komlos, J. "Überblick über die Konzeptionen der Industriellen Revolution." *VSWG* 84 (1997): 461-511; Mokyr, J. (ed.). *The Oxford Encyclopedia of Economic History*, Vol. 1-5. Oxford: Oxford University Press, 2003; Hahn, Hans-Werner. *Die industrielle Revolution in Deutschland*. München, 1998; Paulinyi, Á. *Industrielle Revolution: Vom Ursprung der modernen Technik*. Reinbek bei Hamburg, 1989 (Czech *Průmyslová revoluce: O původu moderní techniky*. Praha, 2002).

While in England the prerequisites for industrialisation (the Industrial Revolution) were basically in place by the mid-eighteenth century, in the Habsburg Empire progress was stifled by a number of factors: an economy based on serfdom, the absence of a centralised state unified in terms of both religion and nationality, and a protracted struggle to secure the integrity of the state (the wars with Turkey, the Wars of the Spanish and Austrian Succession, and the wars with revolutionary and Napoleonic France and with Prussia over hegemony in Germany). This meant that enacting the basic legal and institutional regulations for the transition to a bourgeois industrial society was more difficult and took far longer, with breaks and setbacks. A mercantile policy aimed at assisting the process was only later initiated and up until 1740 enjoyed only limited success. It was only in the second phase of Habsburg mercantilism from 1740–1790 that Maria Theresa, Joseph II, and Leopold II passed a series of measures and reforms facilitating the development of a capitalist market economy (placing restrictions on guilds and privileges, granting of subsidies and export premiums to self-employed tradespeople; abolishing internal tariffs; constructing roads and regulating rivers; opening the Vienna Stock Exchange in 1771; eliminating relationships based on serfdom; introducing the Land Registry; converting peasant benefits and services into monetary leases from 1781–1789; enacting education reforms; founding the Czech Learned Society; etc.). However, the relatively free movement of market forces was enforced in defiance of the Metternich absolutist regime. Progress was particularly apparent in the Czech lands and Alpine provinces. (a) At the turn of the eighteenth and nineteenth centuries, a new class of factory owners arose from the ranks of wholesalers, craftsmen, court Jews, private bankers and moneychangers, members of the nobility, and immigrant specialists and entrepreneurs. (b) In the textile industry there was a rapid expansion of the workshop production method and the domestic system characteristic of advanced proto-industrialisation. (c) Gradually, a symbiosis was reached between inventors and entrepreneurs that put down roots in universities, polytechnics, and learned societies, and starting in 1810 found support in the legal protection of inventions. (d) Signs of greater capital mobility were clear in the activities of many private banking houses, in the opening of the Austrian National Bank in 1816 (with branches in Prague in 1847, Brno in 1853, and Olomouc and Opava in 1854), and in the foundings of savings and insurance systems. While the older literature tended to downplay the institutional basis of the economic progress achieved prior to the revolutions of 1848, cliometric research from the 1980s (J. Komlos et al.) has demonstrated the limitations of these traditional judgements. The reforms enacted from 1848–1859 represent the culmination of this gradual trend toward liberalisation. However, as far as the economic development of the Western part of the monarchy was concerned, they did not represent a crucial turning point but at most accelerated economic growth and ensured its irreversibility.

In addition, the course of capitalistic free competition ran neither smoothly nor for very long in the monarchy. This was for several reasons. Firstly, economic liberalism was forced to assert itself against the backdrop of suppressed political liberalism (Baron Alexander von Bach's absolutism or neo-absolutism). Secondly, liberalism was shown to be weaker than nationalism in the multinational Habsburg state. Thirdly, unlike the huge economic boom enjoyed by Germany during the 1850s and 1860s, the Habsburg Monarchy experienced only a short upswing during the 1850s, which was buffeted by Austria's neutrality in the Crimean War and defeat in the Italian Campaign of 1859, followed by the deflationary politics pursued by Plener and defeat in the war with Prussia in 1866. From 1859–1866, economic growth was so attenuated in the monarchy that not even the subsequent sharp upswing and "founders' period" or *Gründerzeit* of 1867–1873 was sufficient to compensate. In reaction to the crisis of 1873, state regulation was reintroduced with the tacit support of businesspeople. This was not restricted simply to a switch over to protectionism. Amendments passed in 1883 and 1907 to the liberal Trade Regulation Act of 1859 placed restrictions on trade. In addition, the high taxation of joint-stock companies saw Austrian economic policy become an "international rarity".[13] This policy contributed to the creation of powerful cartels that monopolised the internal market and increased commodity prices.

For more than fifty years, historians have debated precisely when modern economic growth began in the Habsburg Monarchy. Some date the commencement of the industrial age, at least in the western part of the empire, as far back as the pre–March Revolution period (e.g., David F. Good favors 1820), while others regard as decisive the "bottom-up revolution" (1848) and reforms in the form of a "top-down revolution" (1850–1867). The debate then centred on whether modern economic growth in the region was manifest in the form of a definitive break, a "take-off" (Walt Rostow, 1963) or a "surge" (Alexander Gerschenkron, 1965), or whether the rate of growth simply increased gradually. The first case is an example of a discontinuous model; the second is that of an accelerating trend. Attempts to find Rostow's take-off point for the industrialisation process in the Habsburg Monarchy are not entirely convincing, partly because some writers date it at the turn of the pre–March Revolution period and others from 1850–1873. We should bear in mind that in the economically more advanced Germany (in particular in Prussia), the take-off point is posited by Hans-Ulrich Wehler in his last work to have taken place in

---

13 Koren, St. "Die Industrialisierung Österreichs: Vom Protektionismus zur Integration," in: Weber, W. (ed.), *Österreichs Wirtschaftsstruktur: gestern, heute, morgen*, Vol. I (1961): 236.

the mid-1840s, with the "breakthrough of the Industrial Revolution" taking place from 1850–1873. Neither the Habsburg Empire as a whole nor its western region experienced such a strong dynamic of industrialisation, and thus an increasing number of historians prefer speaking, as in the case of France, of a slow but relatively constant process of growth, the beginnings of which can be traced back to the 1820s. However, the question remains as to whether we can regard this process as culminating in all sectors simultaneously (Jaroslav Purš's opinion, at least as it applies to the Czech lands), as in the more advanced Germany (1873). The approach taken by Milan Myška (1996) is more acceptable. Myška regards the Industrial Revolution in the broadest sense as a "complex of economic, social, and cultural changes associated with the growth of the factory system and modern technical civilisation", and in a narrower sense as a "process of technical, productive revolution" that in the Czech lands culminated in the main industrial sectors around the turn of the 1870s and 1880s. This revolution is more dynamic in the Czech lands than in other parts of the monarchy. According to Myška's calculations, from 1841–1880 the annual increase in industrial production in the region was 3.07%, while in Lower Austria the figure was 2.66% and across Cisleithania as a whole it was 2.44%. If we take the broader concept as our base, even on the eve of the First World War, Cisleithania cannot be deemed an advanced industrial region but at best an "industrialised agrarian state" (Herbert Matis, 1996). As late as 1910, 53% of gainfully employed people worked in agriculture and only 23% in industry and trades. The share taken by agriculture of national assets was 27%, and there were only seven towns and cities with over 100,000 inhabitants, indicating a lower rate of urbanisation and suggesting that internal trade was still insufficiently developed. In the Czech lands, this structural transformation was somewhat more pronounced. However, only in 1910 did the ratio of economically active persons turn to 45:39 in favour of non-agricultural sectors, a fact that saw the Czech lands move up to the higher level of the "industrially agrarian", somewhat comparable with Germany, where in 1907 this same ratio had reached the level of 52:35. The monarchy's slower rate of industrialisation was reflected in the structure and lower concentration of industrial production. In 1911, the textile and clothing industries, along with the food industry, accounted for 52% of the total creation of value in industry, while this figure was only 20% with metalworking and 10% with fuel, chemicals, and energy. Registered enterprises were dominated by small and medium firms, with 70%–80% of all firms employing fewer than 100 workers. The only exceptions were in the iron and steel industry, mining, and some engineering plants (e.g., Österreichisch-Alpine Montangesellschaft, Pražská železářská společnost [Prague Ironworks], Prager-Eisen-Industrie-Gesellschaft, Vítkovické železárny [Vítkovice Ironworks], and Škodovy závody [Škoda Works]).

According to Anton Kausel (1979), modern sustainable economic growth can be identified in Cisleithania, including the Czech lands, from around 1825–1830, a period with an average GDP growth rate of 1.11%, and from 1870–1913 with average growth of 2.16%. The last calculations by D. Good (*Journal of Economic History*, 1994) are somewhat higher than Kausel's earlier estimates: according to these, by the end of the nineteenth century the economy of the Habsburg Empire was posting higher rates of growth than most European countries (though it was still unable to draw level by 1914), thanks mainly to high GDP growth rates in the backward peripheral provinces that began to approach the level of the more advanced western regions of the monarchy. From 1870–1910, GDP per capita rose year-on-year in the Habsburg Empire by 1.63% (i.e., at the same rate as Germany and faster than Great Britain, France, Belgium, and Italy—all around 1%), while in Cisleithania as a whole growth was 1.48% and in Transleithania 2%, in the Czech lands 1.54%, in Slovakia 1.85%, and in the territory of what later became Czechoslovakia 1.59%. Along with Lower Austria and Vienna, the Czech lands were among the most economically advanced countries of the entire the Habsburg Empire, on a similar level to Germany.

In Cisleithania, specifically in the Alpine and Czech lands, levels of industrialisation were not far off those of Western Europe. Though their share of the European population was only 5.5%, these regions contributed a very respectable 4.5% to European industrial production. The 3% growth enjoyed by Western Europe was topped by the crown lands of Austria-Hungary, with an annual average of 3.46%.[14]

Ongoing discussion on the Industrial Revolution is linked to several broader issues relating to European, even global, economic development that from the last quarter of the nineteenth century strongly impacted the Czech economy. These issues are known as the "Long Depression", the "second Industrial Revolution", and "organised capitalism".

The **Long Depression of 1873–1896** is part of the broader issue of economic cycles or the subject of "historical economic cycle research",[15] which Czech historiography has yet to examine systematically (except for two studies by Pavla Horská-Vrbová and the book by Vlastislav Lacina on the crisis of 1929–1934). An outline of the economic cycles in Austria from 1850–1914 is offered by the Austrian historians H. Kernbauer and E. März in the anthology

---

14   Rumpler, H. *Eine Chance für Mitteleuropa: Bürgerliche Emanzipation und Staatsverfall in der Habsburgermonarchie.* (Wolfram, H. (ed.), *Österreichische Geschichte 1804–1914, vol. 1*), Wien 1997, pp. 456–457; Jindra, Z. "Výchozí ekonomické pozice Československa. Odhad národního jmění, důchodu a hrubého národního produktu Rakouska-Uherska a českých zemí před 1. světovou válkou," in: Střední a východní Evropa v krizi XX. století. K 70. narozeninám Zd. Sládka, AUC-Philosophica et historica 3–4, Studia historica XLII, Praha 1998, pp. 183–204.

15   Schröder, W. H. and Spree, R. (ed.). *Historische Konjunkturforschung.* Stuttgart, 1980.

referred to above. For a long time, the "Long Depression" itself was viewed by economic historians in the light of the Hans Rosenberg book *Große Depression und Bismarckzeit* (1967). Rosenberg's description of that period would at first sight appear justified and accurate. Even at the time it was perceived as being characterised by a strong downward pressure on prices, interest rates, and profits. However, a glance at the statistics of those years quickly reveals that the Vienna Stock Exchange crash of 1873 had unusually long-term consequences that dragged on until the mid-1890s. (Incidentally, the German word *krach*, meaning "crash" in relation to the start of the deepest global economic crisis of the nineteenth century, was first used in Vienna by Prague journalists, whence it entered general economic history via the Viennese press). However, we should realise that this depression was far more about a drop in values than a restriction of the volume of production in the leading industrial sectors (with the exception of the years of stagnation and recession lasting until 1878–1879). Moreover, agriculture was severely affected by the reduction in production, and this was accompanied by a large agrarian crisis caused by the flooding of Western and Central European markets with cheap grain and food from America and Russia. In the Czech lands, sugar beet and corn producers were also affected by this crisis in the 1880s. The most striking feature of these years was the great "price revolution", which, compared to the fluctuations in business cycles during the rest of the nineteenth century, saw sharp deflation. For this reason, these days we speak more of the "period of great deflation" when analysing those times. Whatever the case, the industry of the Habsburg Monarchy emerged from this twenty-year period of development lagging behind Germany and after a longer delay.

However, the course of economic cycles from 1873–1896 impacted only one side of economic development. From a broader perspective, the last quarter of the nineteenth century was characterised by a general crisis of structural adaptation and a restructuring of the entire economic system. Painful lessons learned from the crisis and the declining profitability of business led the economic bourgeois to a major turnaround regarding a range of other issues. These included:

- a systemic rejection of classical liberal capitalism and free competition in favour of its containment and regulation within what was known as "organised capitalism"
- a shift in internal economic policy towards greater state participation and intervention (e.g., in the war-controlled economy of 1914–1918)
- a retreat from free trade to customs protectionism and to external capital or territorial (colonial) expansion

- remedial measures aimed at the rationalisation of production and its concentration in large enterprises, and finally to its departmentalisation and allocation to cartels
- the widespread deployment of new methods and technology and a shift towards progressive new spheres of production (the second Industrial Revolution)
- a significant increase in the number of white-collar workers (managers, engineers, laboratory technicians, and researchers)
- the concomitant reorganisation of the top rungs of the corporate ladder and a transformation of the function of entrepreneurs (the "managerial revolution")
- an unprecedented rise in the number of shop-floor workers, introducing a "social question", the solution to which was provided by creating mass workers' political parties and trade unions
- the organisation of the professional interests of entrepreneurs and wealthy business circles, partly through political parties and partly through professional organisations such as chambers of commerce and industry as well as professional federations in Austria and the Czech lands (e.g., Industriellen-Club in 1875, Central-Verband der Industriellen Österreichs in 1892, Bund österreichischer Industrieller in 1897, and Verband österreichischer Banken und Bankiers in 1911, along with independent Czech national affiliates such as Spolek českých průmyslníků textilních [Association of Czech Textile Industrialists] in 1902, Spolek továrníků a výrobců hospodářských strojů [Association of Manufacturers of Agricultural Machinery] in 1910, Jednota průmyslníků pro Moravu a Slezsko [Association of Industrialists for Moravia and Silesia] in 1912, and Svaz českých bank [Union of Czech Banks] in 1917).

More research needs to be conducted into these professional associations, though perhaps the study by Eduard Kubů (2000) will point the way forward.

In 2015, Czech historiography saw the publication of a large collective interdisciplinary monograph that attempted to investigate the phenomenon of economic crisis in its specific Central European forms and its territorial, temporal, and sectoral manifestations.[16] Certain entrenched ideas that located the end of the "Long Depression" in the mid-1890s (1895–1896) were now corrected so as to make it coincide with the peak of the economic cycles in 1899–1900 and even 1909–1912.[17]

---

16 Kubů, E., Soukup, J., and Šouša, J. (eds.). *Fenomén hospodářské krize v českých zemích 19. až počátku 21. století. Cyklický vývoj ekonomiky v procesu gradující globalizace.* Praha and Ostrava, 2015, p. 7. Engl. résumé.
17 Hájek, J. "Velká deprese" 19. století a peněžnictví v českých zemích, in: ibid., p. 144.

The lower and middle classes most affected by the crisis and depression turned away from the liberal philosophy of individualism and the principles of *laissez-faire et laissez-passer* and sought salvation in collectivist solutions, mass parties, and state intervention. This shift was soon reflected in new categories of thinking and action, notably in the rise of anti-Semitism, nationalism, socialism, and conservatism. In Austria, this anti-liberal movement was extremely radical in its discourse and objectives. In 1879, Eduard Taaffe's conservative government came to power (1879–1893) and systematically boosted the power of the state in the economy. On the one hand, it imposed higher taxes and more red tape on businesses, while on the other hand it provided small tradesmen with protection "against economic competition" (amendments to trade licensing regulations in 1883 and 1885), supported the peasantry with the Cooperative Act and other measures, and introduced legislation protecting workers' rights. In practice, this policy provided protection for small industrialists and craftsmen (in 1902, 96.6% of all factories and 55% of all employees were included in the category of small factories and domestic production in Cisleithania), put the brakes on economic growth, and freed up political forces that were eventually to contribute to the downfall of the monarchy. It is no coincidence that the nationalist friction between the Czech and German populations of the Czech crown lands flared up in the 1880s and 1890s and that economic nationalism spread as a protest mainly on the part of small and medium businesspeople most at risk from the growing competition of large companies and mass production. It was less the consequence of competition between large companies, which were more easily able to reach agreement (e.g., in cartels).[18]

MAIN FEATURES AND DRIVERS OF THE SOCIAL AND ECONOMIC DEVELOPMENT OF THE CZECH LANDS

The economic rise of the Czech nation grew from very modest foundations laid during the mid-nineteenth century in parallel with linguistic, cultural, and political emancipation. However, over the next two generations it progressed so quickly that by the time we reach the threshold of the twentieth century, we can speak of the creation of a Czech national economy ranging from agriculture, mining, and industry all the way to its own banking system.[19] For the dual monarchy of Austria-Hungary, based—from the Compro-

---

18   Cf. Jančík, D. and Kubů, E. (eds.). *Nacionalismus zvaný hospodářský: Střety a zápasy o nacionální emancipaci/převahu v českých zemích (1859–1945)*. Praha, 2011; Kubů, E. and Schultz, H. (ed.). "Wirtschaftsnationalismus als Entwicklungsstrategie ostmitteleuropäischer Eliten." *Die böhmischen Länder und die Tschechoslowakei in vergleichender Perspektive*. Praha and Berlin, 2004.

19   Mommsen, H. *Die Sozialdemokratie und die Nationalitätenfrage im habsburgischen Vielvölkerstaat*, Vol. 1. Wien, 1963, p. 26.

mise of 1867 onwards—on the supremacy of the Germans and Hungarians, this was hugely significant. The Czechs deserve much of the credit for the economic growth of the monarchy being sustainable and, despite all barriers, becoming the second largest industrial nation in the whole empire and specifically in Cisleithania after the German Austrians. What were the factors that made this possible?

Demographic developments were favourable overall for the Czech lands.[20] In the first century of industrialisation (1819–1913) the population of the region doubled from five to more than ten million while the birth rate fell gradually to 27 per thousand and mortality to 18.7 per thousand. The turn in the birth rate came in 1873, while that of the death rate came approximately twenty years later. This means that the transition to a modern demographic regime continued apace. Nevertheless, it was not yet over by the time the Habsburg Empire fell, and had only fully taken place within the framework of the First Republic circa 1930.[21]

However, the swift rise in the population was not uniformly spread. Numbers rose most quickly in the industrially advanced regions of North, Central, and West Bohemia, Central Moravia, and Silesia, which in 1910 together comprised more than three quarters of the entire population (as opposed to two thirds in 1857). A remarkable side effect of this development was a larger population density on the one hand—for instance, from 1800–1900 the population/km^2 in the Czech lands rose from 58 to 122—and a significant increase in urbanisation on the other hand. During the first phase of industrialisation, the most densely populated regions were North Bohemia, mainly the textile-producing areas where Germans had settled around Liberec and Rumburk, while later on the workforce spread into the new industrial centres around Prague and Brno, as well as to the coalfields around Kladno, Most, and Ostrava. Based on colloquial speech, in 1910 more than six million Czechs and 3.5 million Germans lived in the Czech lands. In Bohemia, the Czechs represented a majority of the population, around 63%, and in Moravia of almost 72%; only in Silesia were Czechs in the minority. The Czech population was also growing at a slightly faster rate, and as a result, from the pre-March Revolution period onwards, their share in the ethno-linguistic composition of the Czech lands continued to increase and that of the Germans to fall. Importantly, regarding the economic rise of the Czech lands from the mid-nineteenth century onwards, the population of the old textile regions in border areas, where the first phase of industrialisation had taken place with a mainly German population, grew more slowly than that of the new industrial regions hosting the technologically younger and, after

---

20 Cf. Srb, V. *1000 let obyvatelstva českých zemí.* Praha, 2004.
21 Kárníková, L. *Vývoj obyvatelstva v českých zemích 1754–1914.* Praha, 1965.

the second phase of industrialisation, key sectors of the food and engineering sectors and heavy industry, populated mainly by Czechs. This trend was also reflected in the census and classification of nationalities by basic types of occupation in Cisleithania (1902). The Czech lands could no longer be deemed an agricultural nation, as had been the case fifty years previously. Although agriculture's share (43%) of the economy was greater than industry (36.5%), the ratio was slowly being reversed, especially if we include the affiliated spheres of trade and transport (46%). Nevertheless, Czech Germans were in a far more favourable position thanks to support from the government in Vienna. They counted themselves among the numerically stronger Austrian Germans, and in weaker moments, they looked to Berlin. During the course of industrialisation, they achieved a far stronger economic status, and also enjoyed support in the state's power apparatus, which was centrally controlled mainly by German civil servants and run along German lines.[22] Despite these favourable demographic and economic developments, the pre-1914 Czech nation found itself in the inferior position of being a "nation without a state".

The **modern social structure of Czech bourgeois society** was formed in the nineteenth century under the influence of the cultural, linguistic, political, and economic emancipation of the Czech nation in parallel with the industrialisation of the Czech lands and the promotion of capitalism. What follows are the characteristic signs of the emergence and composition of modern Czech society.

From an economic and political perspective, the aristocracy, though numbering only a few thousand individuals, continued to remain a powerful group.[23] Strictly speaking, this was a landed nobility, for the most part indifferent to nationality, professing a "provincial (*böhmisch*) patriotism" rather than endorsing expressly Czech or German national objectives. Though the aristocracy's influential position at the top of the social pyramid, like that of the Prussian Junkers, was due in part to the functions it traditionally occupied in the public administration, army, and diplomatic corps, at heart it derived from its vast estates (thousands of hectares), managed partly by the nobility itself, often using modern capitalist methods. In addition, this particular aristocracy, more than any other in Central and Eastern Europe, was engaged early and extensively in workshop production and later in factories and financial speculation.[24] The abolition of statute labour in 1848 did

---

22   Cf. Jindra, Z. "Národnostní složení úřednictva centrálních úřadů v habsburské monarchii a v Předlitavsku k 1. lednu 1914," in: *Pocta Zdeňku Kárníkovi. Sborník k 70. narozeninám, AUC-philosophica et historica, Studia historica LI.* Praha (2003): 71–88.
23   Cf. Županič, J. *Nová šlechta rakouského císařství.* Praha, 2006.
24   See the chapter "Der Grundherr als Unternehmer" in: Salz, A. *Geschichte der Böhmischen Industrie in der Neuzeit.* München, 1913, p. 275; Myška, M., Der Adel der böhmischen Länder. Seine wirtschaftliche Entwicklung, in: Reden-Dohna, A. von, and Melville, R. (ed.). *Der Adel an der*

not represent a blow to the 1,912 lords in the Czech lands at that time, but afforded them many advantages, the topmost being the transformation of many bondmen into farm labourers and the acquisition of 72.3 million florins from repayment of the bond. The aristocracy often used these funds to modernise their estates and to invest in industry, the railways, banks, and financial speculation. At the end of the 1867–1873 cycle, the aristocracy owned 37% of all plants and controlled 41% of all production in the steel and iron sector, in addition to the 30% it already owned (1841) of all mines responsible for around half of all coal in the Czech lands. Even though it had in the meantime gotten rid of almost all the older positions in the textile industry, it was now more active in industrial sectors linked by raw materials with agriculture (breweries, distilleries, starch factories, oil pressing shops, mills, glassworks, brickworks, and sawmills). It was also strongly represented in the new sugar beet industry. Prior to the crisis of 1873, aristocratic entrepreneurs owned 32% of the sugar factories in the Czech lands, 24% in Moravia, and 30% in Silesia. In addition, we should not overlook the fact that, along with the historical landed gentry, many newly honoured factory owners, wholesalers, and bankers lived and worked in the Austrian and Czech economy. Overall, the engagement of the Czech landed gentry in capitalist business activities was far more important than many historians are willing to concede.[25]

A protracted period of industrialisation saw the *peasants, farmers, and the agrarian bourgeoisie* become the most powerful social group in the countryside. An important position was taken by the owners of small and medium-sized farms, firstly by virtue of their power—since in the Czech lands, for example, they managed 43% of all land (at the end of the 1880s)—and secondly because of their role in the Czech national revival. Almost all the fertile regions in the Bohemian and Moravian lowlands (with the exception of the German districts of Žatec, Litoměřice, Znojmo, and Mikulov) were in the hands of Czechs. Of great significance in the economic upturn of the Czech lands in the nineteenth century were the prosperous mill owners and large farmers. Their vast, accumulated assets, which began with cultivating cereals and potatoes, later moved into new crops, especially sugar beet, and also, by the end of the century, breeding cattle. A large part of this expanding agrarian bourgeoisie were—by origin and even more so by conviction—some of

Schwelle des bürgerlichen Zeitalters 1780–1860. Stuttgart, 1988, p. 169–189; Myška, M. "Šlechta v Čechách, na Moravě a ve Slezsku na prahu buržoazní éry." *Časopis Slezského muzea,* série B (1987): 46–65.

25 Myška, M. (*Časopis Slezského muzea,* 1987). A thorough overview is offered by *Schematismus und Statistik des Großgrundbesitzes und größerer Rustikalgüter im Königreich Böhmen.* Prag, 1906; the most recent examination of the relationship between the nobility and entrepreneurship is offered by Popelka, P. *Zrod moderního podnikatelstva: Bratři Kleinové a podnikatelé v českých zemích a Rakouském císařství v éře kapitalistické industrializace.* Ostrava, 2011, p. 112.

the most fervent supporters of Czech nationalism. It is no coincidence that many of the Czech intellectuals and leading politicians (František Ladislav Rieger, Jan Perner, Alois Pravoslav Trojan, A. Strohbach, etc.) who were to draft the first Czech political programme during the revolution of 1848 came from their ranks. After constitutionalism and municipal electoral law were introduced, these wealthy Czech farmers and sugar growers occupied an important position in municipal and district councils (i.e., the lowest level of the local government administration).

A group was forming on the horizon that would become increasingly important, namely the *urban* and *industrial*, as well as (in a broader sense) the business bourgeoisie. Its members were largely rich farmers living in the agricultural interior of Bohemia and Moravia, and to a lesser extent small businessmen and craftspeople inhabiting Czech cities or the suburbs of large German cities. This organic process progressed very slowly at first. Compared to the similar development of the Czech-Bohemian and Austro-German bourgeois it was barely noticeable even after the start of the Industrial Revolution. *"Up until 1848, there was neither a Czech business bourgeoisie nor individual Czechs who could be viewed as modern industrial entrepreneurs".*[26] Indeed, the Czech nation only became mature enough to take on the most arduous task, namely economic emancipation and the creation of its own business class, in the culminating decades of industrialisation. With its origins in villages and amongst artisans, merchants, and other small producers, the Czech bourgeoisie clung to the petty bourgeois features that were its longtime hallmark. Nevertheless, institutional snags and the stiff challenge represented by German competition drove it towards greater entrepreneurship, diligence, and tenacity, and ultimately to an extraordinarily dynamic market penetration. Only in this way did it succeed in rapidly mobilising the necessary investment funds and finding competent and assertive business personalities from amongst its ranks. The capital accumulated in farms and urban craft workshops gradually found its way, via various channels, into Czech commerce and industry (e.g. through trust funds and gratuities for young farmers' sons or the deposits and credit services of Czech mutual savings banks established for this purpose, and finally through the contributions of self-help and cooperative organisations).

The rise of a Czech industrial, commercial, and financial bourgeoisie with its own economic and political interests and demands is uniquely and gradually intertwined with the short period of economic liberalism and the birth

---

26 Kořalka, J. "Die Herausbildung des Wirtschaftsbürgertums in den böhmischen Ländern im 19. Jahrhundert," in: Heumos, P. (ed.). *Polen und die böhmischen Länder im 19. und 20. Jahrhundert. Politik und Gesellschaft im Vergleich.* München, 1997, p. 64.

pangs of the industrialisation process in the Czech lands from 1850–1885.[27] Whether or not we can shift these beginnings to the pre–March Revolution period will only become clear with the sociological survey of the *Historical Encyclopaedia of Entrepreneurs of Bohemia, Moravia and Silesia*, though it would appear likely. The cradle of Czech entrepreneurs consisted mainly of regions populated by Czechs—most notably in Bohemia, less so in Moravia, and only later in Silesia—and this created a special role for the industrial region of Central Bohemia and Prague as the centre of the Czech nationalist political movement. From the very start, a close link to agriculture in terms of finance, raw materials, and markets was important for the investment strategy of a capital-poor Czech business bourgeois. This entailed business activities in the food industry and service engineering (machines for sugar refineries, breweries, and distilleries), or in the manufacture of artificial fertilisers. In these two sectors, investment demands were lower and there was a faster capital turnover and secure profit. Czech construction companies and hauliers capitalised on this, as did sugar merchants operating a consignment system.

We can only speak of the arrival of the first, pioneering generation of Czech entrepreneurs after 1850. The indigenous Czech business class lacked German and Jewish businessmen like the Leitenbergers, Liebigs, and the Prague-based Porges, who had begun to do business in the era of proto- and early industrialisation. We see this in the difference between the power of Czech and German capital in the Czech lands. If we measure this strength at the end of the wave of company incorporations of 1873 (according to the level of paid-up share capital in companies with a Czech or Czech-German name), a total of 25 million florins of share capital in 134 companies (excluding banks) was held in Czech hands, while in the case of the 135 German companies (excluding banks), this figure was 144 million florins. The Czech business bourgeois did not make significant inroads into this disproportion. By 1901, the paid-up capital of Czech joint-stock companies (excluding banks) had risen to 79 million florins, while that of German companies had leapt to 865 million florins.[28]

Indigenous Czech financial capital advanced in leaps and bounds. After the relatively short period of company incorporation, at the end of 1872 four Czech banks headed by Živnostenská banka in Prague, held total share capital of 8.4 million florins, to which we should add approximately half the capi-

27   The roots and beginnings of the Czech bourgeoisie in the rural and urban areas is examined in detailed in Stölzl, C. *Die Ära Bach in Böhmen: Sozialgeschichtliche Studien zum Neoabsolutismus.* München-Wien, 1971.

28   Cf. Horská-Vrbová, P. "K otázce vzniku české průmyslové buržoazie." ČsČH vol. 10, no. 2 (1962): 257–284.

tal of what were known as the Utraquist (mixed Czech-German) banks (i.e., 3.3 million florins. Confronting this total of around 12 million florins stood nine banks owned by Czech Germans with capital of 27.2 million florins, to which we must add half of the capital of the utraquist banks, making a total of around 30 million florins). However, the centralisation of the Czech financial capital had already attained a higher level, since, in addition to a few joint-stock commercial banks, several hundred Czech credit unions had already been created in the Czech lands. Though these credit unions worked with small amounts of widely scattered capital, taken together they had a further 80 million florins under management. Czech banking capital recorded its sharpest growth in the last incorporation wave of 1907–1913, when it even managed to outstrip that of Czech Germans—in 1914, nine German banks held share capital of 124 million crowns, while thirteen independent Czech banks held share capital of 225 million crowns.[29] The practical results of the extraordinarily expansive power of the Czech entrepreneurial sphere and its capital are reflected in the composition of the management boards of the five business and trade chambers in the Czech lands. When established on the threshold of the 1850s, they were dominated by German businessmen, traders, and entrepreneurs. By the mid 1880s, Czechs had taken over the management of three of them, namely the Prague, Plzeň, and České Budějovice chambers of trade and commerce.

Moreover, for the young Czech nation it was very important to have a broadly educated elite, what we now call a *bourgeois intelligentsia*. Access to education, therefore, played a crucial role in the process of national revival. As soon as a universal requirement to attend school had been introduced in Austria and tuition could be provided, at least in state schools, in the mother tongue, Czechs became, during the period of one century, one of the most literate nationalities in the Habsburg Empire, even outstripping the Czech Germans. By contrast, huge efforts had to be made during the second half of the nineteenth century to promote tuition in the mother tongue at the secondary and tertiary level. In this sphere, the Germans, with the most state support, long outclassed the Czechs. The milestones of this huge Czech educational and cultural project, especially as it relates to the training of specialists for the Czech economy, are as follows: the founding of the Jednota k povzbuzení průmyslu v Čechách (Union for Industrial Support in Bohemia) (1833), the opening of the first industrial schools in Prague (1857), the national division of the Prague Polytechnic (1868–1869), a similar division of Prague University (1882), and the establishment of the Czech University of Technology in Brno (1899). All of this made it possible to train hundreds of engineers,

---

29   For more details, see Vencovský, Jindra, and Novotný. *Dějiny bankovnictví v českých zemích.*

technicians, technologists, and jurists, all of whom were to play an invaluable role in the Czech economic ascent, thanks not only to their know-how and organisational abilities, but to the creation of a specialist nomenclature.

The Jewish minority formed a distinct social group. Though small in number, it grew over the years. In 1776, there were 206,655 Jews living in the Austrian lands (excluding Hungary). According to the first census of 1869, this figure had risen to 822,220 and by 1910 it was 1,313,687. The largest numbers lived in Galicia, Bukovina, and Lower Austria (Vienna), and in the Czech lands most lived in Bohemia (85,826 in 1910), with fewer in Moravia and Silesia. They mostly lived in cities (e.g., in Prague [18,986 in 1900, 9.4% of the population, Brno [7.5%], Jihlava [9.4%], Olomouc [7.7%]), and were represented in the districts of Tábor, Čáslav, Plzeň, Znojmo, and Uherské Hradiště. Most were assimilated with the leading nationality: in Silesia (1910) 84% identified as German, and this was likewise the case in Moravia (78%), though in Bohemia this figure was only 48%. Jews increasingly identified with the Czechs as the nation prospered politically and economically. The most remarkable fact regarding the Jewish ethnicity is its unusually strong participation in business. In 1910, the social status of Jews living in Bohemia and Moravia was as follows: 52% worked in commerce, finance, and transport; 19% in industry and trade; 25% in the liberal professions or were civil servants; and only 3% in the agricultural sector. In the main, they can be categorised alongside the bourgeois industrial middle class as urban "independent employees". Few were simple labourers, or navvies, but most made strenuous efforts to be taken on as apprentices or study at university.[30]

We should not overlook the *proletariat*, which grew rapidly in size during the period of industrialisation in the Czech lands. Its share of the population remained unchanged at 25% from 1857–1910, despite the overall increase in the population. In 1910, the proletariat numbered 2.7 million people (not including dependents). At the same time, there was a fundamental shift within the proletariat from agricultural to industrial work. By 1910, the number of agricultural workers had fallen to around two thirds of what it had been in 1857, while the number of industrial workers had increased threefold. This large proletariat was concentrated in a small number of industrial regions, where it worked for large corporations. This was in line with the trend in Cisleithania for a concentration of business activities. According to the census of 1902, of the total number of people working in industry in the Czech lands, 39.5%

---

30   A sound overview of the status of the Jews in the monarchy is contained in Bihl, W. *Die Habsburgermonarchie 1848–1918, Bd. III/2.* Wien, 1980; regarding their great contribution to economic life, see Otruba, G. "Der Anteil der Juden am Wirtschaftsleben der böhmischen Länder seit dem Beginn der Industrialisierung," in: Seibt, F. (ed.). *Die Juden in den böhmischen Ländern.* München and Wien, 1983, pp. 209–268, pp. 323–351.

were based in large factories (employing a hundred or more people), which was far higher than the average for Cisleithania (30.4%). This also involved important changes on a national level. In the old textile regions, which had set the tone of the first wave of industrialisation up to the mid-nineteenth century, a German labour force predominated. However, the newly emerging centres of the food and heavy industries were manned mainly by Czechs, and this was even so in certain areas populated predominantly by Germans.[31]

In conclusion, the restructuring of the social order in the Czech lands was such that by the turn of the twentieth century, Czechs formed a socially differentiated, modern bourgeois society. As the first Slavic nationality in the multicultural Habsburg Empire, it evolved into a Western-oriented and culturally advanced nation that, even within the economic life of the monarchy, enjoyed greater clout than would appear merited by its share of the population. Nevertheless, it still lacked representation in the ministries and business guilds (e.g., in the Austro-Hungarian bank, in consortia for state loans, etc.) that would correspond to its size and political status. Of a total of 6,293 civil servants in all the Viennese ministries and central institutions, a total of 4,772 were German (76%), while only 53 (10.3%) were Czechs. The rest belonged to other nationalities.[32] Inasmuch as two national categories existed in the monarchy—namely the governing and non-governing on the social, economic, and political level, and the privileged, less privileged, or unprivileged in the sphere of law, the constitution, and the administration—prior to 1914, the Czechs belonged to the second category, even though their social and economic power was growing.

The **agricultural base** of the Czech economic upswing during the nineteenth century was prepared by deep-rooted changes that gradually took place throughout the Agrarian Revolution. These included: (a) the transformation of ownership and the commercialisation of agriculture as a consequence of the abolition of serfdom and bonded labour, as well as the implementation of other reforms; (b) the cultivation of fodder and technical crops (sugar beet, potatoes for starch factories and distilleries, and barley and hops for malt and beer production), mostly in the fertile lowlands populated by the Czechs, gradually replaced the three-field system with crop rotation, which had a crucial impact on the intensification of livestock breeding; (c) the introduction of modern tools and machinery into agriculture, first of all in farms, soon to be followed by manorial farms; and (d) the creation of

31   Regarding the initial status of the workforce, see Stölzl. *Die Ära Bach in Böhmen: Sozialgeschichtliche Studien zum Neoabsolutismus*; Purš, J. "The Situation of the Working Class in the Czech Lands in the Phase of the Expansion and Completion of the Industrial Revolution 1849–1873." *Historica* 6 (1963) 145–237; Bruckmüller, E. *Sozialgeschichte Österreichs*. Wien, 1985.

32   For more details, see Jindra, Z. "Národnostní složení úřednictva."

special research institutes, vocational schools, magazines, exhibitions, and special interest groups. All of these changes led finally to the expansion of intensive plant and livestock production, increases in yield and efficiency, and hence a greater accumulation of agrarian capital. In addition, the burgeoning agrarian bourgeoisie was looking for an effective means to more rapidly mobilise and centralise small agrarian capital, and found it in self-help cooperatives set up in the sphere of rural credit (mutual savings banks, credit unions, and thrift institutions) and in the purchase, sale, and processing of agricultural products. At the same time, agricultural research institutes, vocational schools, and magazines were being established and agricultural fairs organised. All of this was visible in the increase of agricultural production (interrupted only by the great sugar beet crisis of the 1880s), which resulted in the accumulation of free agrarian capital to the benefit of young Czech capital in industry and banking.

The paths taken by Czech industrialisation. According to Alexander Gerschenkron,[33] the more backward a country, the more concentrated, comprehensive, and aggressive the process of industrialisation, with all the attendant effects and tensions of this "great spurt". Using this model, we can outline the industrial boom in the Czech lands during the nineteenth century, a boom which was impacted by several factors: (a) the institutional framework for a capitalist market economy began to coalesce in the Austrian empire later and progressed more slowly and intermittently, while retaining many relics of feudalism and absolutism, (b) the breakthrough in technology and production took place later in Austria and the Czech lands than in Northwest Europe and could thus draw on the latter's technological achievements and knowhow, import machinery, capital, and specialists, and attract many foreign entrepreneurs, (c) Czech industrialisation was thus able to proceed in a more compressed form and shorter period and was more a continuous phenomenon, without a clear take-off and, leaving aside the *Gründerjahre* or founders' years (during which start-ups proliferated rapidly) of 1867–1873, without a "great spurt", (d) Czech industrialisation is an original example of the regional course of the Industrial Revolution, in that the modern economic growth that started in the monarchy approximately ten years after the end of the Napoleonic Wars was uneven, and was earlier and deeper in the western reaches of the empire—specifically in selected parts of the Czech lands where conditions were the most favourable—than in its eastern and southern regions.

Industrialisation was accompanied and supported by the following factors. Firstly, the great wave of European industrialisation that spread from

---

33 See Gerschenkron, A. "Wirtschaftliche Rückständigkeit in historischer Perspektive", in: Wehler, H.U. (ed.). *Geschichte und Ökonomie*. Köln, 1973, pp. 121–139.

west to east reached the Czech lands, and over the course of several decades raised the region, in parallel with the emancipatory movement of the Czech nation, to the status of industrial heartland of the Habsburg Empire. Even though around 1880 only 37% of the population of Cisleithania was settled in the Czech lands, almost 54% of the entire Cisleithanian workforce worked in Czech industry and 64% of the horsepower of all Cisleithanian steam engines was deployed here. Even during the proto-industrialisation period, the region had been known for its production of textiles, glass, porcelain, paper, and musical instruments. At the end of the nineteenth century, these sectors were joined by new ones characteristic of the second Industrial Revolution, in particular the production of steel using the Thomas-Gilchrist process, machinery, engines, cars, and artillery weapons, along with the chemical and electrical industries. However, despite the huge increase in output and capacity, industry in the Czech lands continued to be controlled by Vienna, partly in the spirit of monarchic centralism and a command economy, partly by means of the large banks and joint-stock companies headquartered in the capital. And so as the need for investment and operating capital grew and production was consolidated by mega-corporations, Czech industry also fell under the sway of Vienna through low-key modern phenomena such as overdraft banking, the provision of bank loans, and the takeover of shares in a credit institution. This was possible because German-Austrian capital still dominated indigenous Czech capital on the basis of its volume, its longer tradition and experience, its contacts and links with central government authorities, and its relations with the international banking world.

Secondly, the breakthrough in production and technology in the Czech lands between the 1830s and the 1890s did not take place in a unified nation and amongst the members of a simply structured bourgeoisie united in its modes of thinking and acting. This revolution transformed and differentiated two nationalities occupying the region one after the other and living alongside one another, the Czechs on the one hand and the Czech and Austrian Germans on the other. Furthermore, the upper, middle, and lower classes were each affected in a different way. And so at the end of the nineteenth century two distinct, self-contained, unevenly developed national economic systems of different strength came into being, with business strata that rarely collaborated but instead competed for markets and influence on the state administration.

Thirdly, the breakthroughs in technology and production affected the Czech (Sudeten) Germans not only earlier, but at a time when conditions were more favourable than for the indigenous Czechs.[34]

---

34   Cited in Jaworski, R. *Vorposten oder Minderheit?: Der sudetendeutsche Volkstumskampf in den Beziehungen zwischen der Weimarer Republik und der ČSR*. Stuttgart, 1977, p. 17.

It was under these circumstances that the backwardness factor, along with special methods for overcoming it as formulated by Gerschenkron, played a role in the Czech economy during the nineteenth century. Independent states finding themselves in a similar situation resorted to protectionist measures (for instance, "educative protectionism" in Prussia during the first half of the century, replaced in Bismarck's empire by the expansion of cartel protectionism). Either that, or it was possible to support the still fledgling domestic industry directly (e.g., by means of targeted tax relief, lucrative state contracts, and special laws providing incentives to industry as had been practiced from the end of the nineteenth century in Hungary). In the struggle for internal and foreign markets, influence over the public administration, as well as international recognition, the Czech nation without a state was forced to resort to other methods.

The first of these involved political and economic nationalism. Research into the national question in the Habsburg Empire has until recently focused more on its political, ideological, and cultural aspects, downplaying and neglecting the social and economic roots and the influence of national rivalry.[35] Although disputes regarding the language to be used in communication with the authorities were at the forefront of the confrontation between Czechs and Germans (culminating in 1897–1898 in the struggle over the Badeni language decree), in the background were far more sensitive manifestations of economic nationalism that cannot be attributed only to the Czechs. On the capital market especially, Germany economic nationalism was widespread.[36] However, this was not simply the consequence of the superiority of Germany banking capital, but was also about the power deriving from the dominant political status of Austrian and Czech Germans in the state. This status offered the Czech German and Austrian bourgeois plenty of opportunities to discriminate against other competing nationalities. As far back as the 1850s, Czech entrepreneurs had complained of this (valuable sources where these complaints are recorded include the annual reports of the chambers of trade and commerce, which have yet to be researched from this perspective). This was also fertile ground for the rise and spread of Czech economic nationalism, which entered the fray with the slogan "our own to our own",[37] appealed to

35 See the overview of the social and economic aspects of the issue of nationality in: Matis, H. Österreichs Wirtschaft 1848–1913. Berlin, 1972, pp. 383–413. From the Czech point of view, the latest research is contained in Jančík, D. and Kubů, E. (eds.). Nacionalismus zvaný hospodářský: Střety a zápasy o nacionální emancipaci/převahu v českých zemích (1859–1945). Praha, 2011.

36 Examples are given by Rudolph, R. Banking and Industrialization in Austria-Hungary: The Role of Banks in the Industrialization of the Czech Crownlands 1873–1914. Cambridge, London, New York, Melbourne, 1976.

37 See Bráf, A. Národohospodářské potřeby české. Praha, 1904; ibid., České a německé „svůj k svému", 1909, in: Bráf, A., Život a dílo, vol. IV., Praha 1923, pp. 168–210.

people to buy and sell with Czech traders and businesses, called for a boycott of German goods, organised business on the basis of self-help institutions and cooperatives, encouraged the creation of Czech business schools, and supported the creation and growth of Czech banking. The "our own to our own" movement had its German equivalent, though both have only begun to be researched.[38] However, even though the Czech movement received support in the media from university professors (Albín Bráf et al.), it appears to have failed to convince small consumers to change their buying habits or business-men to adapt their decisions. In an effort to meet the autarkic and separatist needs of the Czech economy, Czech politicians tried to obtain money from the state budget and open up the Austro-Hungarian Bank for Czech credit requirements by expanding the competencies of its branch in Prague and acquiring a voice on its board. However, these endeavours met with failure.

Secondly, while increasing its market share, Czech capital found itself in a position formerly occupied in an earlier stage of development by the more powerful capital of the Czech and Austrian Germans. It was forced to find a quick way out of this narrow domestic base in single-minded commercial and capital expansion beyond the Czech lands, especially to less developed peripheral regions of the monarchy in the east and southeast peopled by the Slavs.[39]

Thirdly, in an attempt at the most extensive and rapid capital mobilisation during the diversification of the entire banking sector, Czech banks tried to apply a new business model, the aim of which was to do away completely with the less advanced wholesale activities being pursued in Austria-Hunga-ry as a whole, but especially in the Czech lands. This involved banks opening their own *departments of goods in commission* in order to sell mass consumer items such as coal and sugar, followed by other goods. On the one hand, this corresponded to the system of Central European universal banking that was characterised by a tight relationship between credit institutions and large industry, and on the other was regarded by German financial experts simply as a departure from generally accepted banking regulation. Nevertheless, commission trade with goods had been a well-established practice in Austria since at least the 1880s, and had thrived under the conditions of organised capitalism in which a bank's business department often functioned as the clearing house and syndicate bureau of cartels. These departments earned

---

38 Jančík and Kubů. *Nacionalismus zvaný hospodářský: Střety a zápasy o nacionální emancipaci/pře-vahu v českých zemích (1859–1945)*, ibid. other literature.
39 For more details, see Nečas, C. *Na prahu české kapitálové expanze: Rozpínavost českého bankovního kapitálu ve střední, jihovýchodní a východní Evropě v období rakousko-uherského imperialismu.* UJEP, Spisy FF No. 272. Brno, 1987; ibid. *Podnikání českých bank v cizině 1898–1918: Rozpínavost českého bankovního kapitálu ve střední, jihovýchodní a východní Evropě v období rakousko-uherského imperia-lismu.* MU, Spisy FF No. 295. Brno, 1993.

huge profits and were therefore popular with Czech national banks, which used them in an attempt to boost their market share and catch up with Viennese banks. This business activity reached a peak during the First World War and in its immediate aftermath, when there was a shortage of goods on the market and it was possible to impose inflationary prices on consumers. This type of banking operation was banned in Czechoslovakia only in 1924.

Fourthly, it proved highly effective for Czech capital to combine older business methods with an effective twofold form of expansion: the centralisation of capital (through the merger of small capital in joint-stock companies), and the concentration of production using modern technology and skilled engineers and managers in either new industrial sectors or older but now mechanised sectors. Czech business capital applied these methods by means of investment and credit activities in the food industry (especially the sugar, brewing, and distilling industries), in the associated machinery and metal-working sectors, and in the manufacture of shoes and off-the-peg clothes.

Fifth, the attempts made by the Czechs to establish their own national economy culminated in the creation and development of an independently functioning banking system without foreign capital, which at the outset, lacking sufficient capital and based on a new law of association, was formed partly on the basis of the self-help activities of farmers (financial cooperatives and mutual savings banks) and partly on the basis of savings institutions and the money of municipal traders. It was from such meagre and diffused resources that in 1868 the first Czech commercial bank, Živnostenská banka, was created in Prague.[40]

All of the factors referred to played a role in Czech industrial entrepreneurship that developed fully in the second half of the nineteenth century. Up until almost the 1850s, Germans living in Austria and the Czech lands gave no thought to the economic emancipation of the Czechs. In the process of modern industrialisation, the Czechs were regarded as weak, inexperienced latecomers to the party. The initial phase of the revolution in technology and manufacturing prior to 1848 was almost completely the work of Germans, and took place in mainly non-Czech regions. Often taking its cue from hand-made production, mass factory production started largely in the textile industry, traditionally located in hilly and mountainous borderlands (Krušné hory, Krkonoše, and Orlické hory), on the northern side of the Bohemian-Moravian Highlands, in Northern Moravia and northwest Silesia, as well as around Brno and, to a lesser extent, Prague (i.e., areas mainly populated by

---

40   For more details, see Vencovský, Jindra, and Novotný. *Dějiny bankovnictví v českých zemích*. Regarding the beginnings of the Czech self-help movement, see Stölzl. *Die Ära Bach in Böhmen*, p. 92 et seq.; Hájek, J. "Počátky a rozmach českého záloženského hnutí ve třetí čtvrtině 19. století, Hospodářské dějiny." *Economic History* 12 (1984) 265–320.

Czech Germans). Even though the natural conditions and domestic raw material base (sheep's wool and high-quality flax) had traditionally encouraged the production of wool and linen products, the Industrial Revolution was initiated in the textile industry in the Czech lands, as in England, by means of the mechanisation of the spinning mills of imported cotton. The first such spinning mills, equipped with English machinery, were put into operation from 1796–1799 in Verneřice, Kosmonosy, and Zákupy by the Leitenbergers, a German Bohemian business family. Germans also predominated in ferrous metallurgy, though not completely, as we see from the example of the Moravian metallurgical Homoláč family. However, this is not true of mechanical engineering, as the first industrial entrepreneurs, investors, and technicians were mainly foreigners: English, Belgian, French, or immigrants from Germany.[41]

To the surprise of onlookers at the time, Czech entrepreneurs joined in the industrialisation of the Czech lands in the peak decades of the Industrial Revolution from 1850–1880 (i.e., when the role of the Sudeten-German textile industry as the leading industrial sector was reaching its zenith and Czech entrepreneurs were able to leap on the bandwagon of newly emerging sectors linked with the second Industrial Revolution.[42] This was linked to the important change that took place to the structure of industrial sectors in the Czech lands in the second half of the nineteenth century, the main feature of which concerned the relationship between the consumer goods manufacturing industry and the means of production. According to calculations by František Dudek (arrived at by means of the arithmetic average of the share of individual sectors in the gross value of production, the efficiency of steam machines, and the number of employees), during the 1840s this ratio was approximately 80:20, during the 1880s it was 74:26, and in the industrial census of 1902 it had dropped to 59:41.[43] What had originally been the predominant position of the consumer industry dropped over six decades from four-fifths to just under three-fifths, while the share of heavy industry and metalworking rose significantly only during the last decades of the nineteenth century. This structural analysis also clearly displays the decisive and long-standing position of the three main industrial sectors in the Czech lands, namely textiles and food in the consumer industry, and metalworking in the means of production industry, the order of which also reflects their relative importance. Compared with the traditional course of an Industrial Revolution from

---

41   Cf. Myška, M. *Rytíři průmyslové revoluce: Šest studií k dějinám podnikatelů v českých zemích.* Ostrava, 1997.

42   Cf. Horská-Vrbová, P. *Český průmysl a tzv. druhá průmyslová revoluce.* Praha, 1965; Brousek, K. M. *Die Großindustrie Böhmens 1848–1918.* München, 1987.

43   Dudek, F. "Vývoj struktury průmyslu v českých zemích za kapitalismu." *Slezský sborník* 86 (1988): 252–269.

the mechanisation of the textile industry to an increase in mineral extraction and processing, in the Czech lands we notice a significant modification, with the food industry participating in this process from the very start (i.e., during the pre–March Revolution period).

It is especially interesting to note how the position of the food industry gradually changed within the consumer industry. In the 1840s, textile production predominated. But by the 1880s, its total share had dropped to 33.6%, and in the 1902 census to 24.75%. In the 1840s the food industry, to begin with controlled by aristocratic entrepreneurs, was the second largest sector with a share of 8.25%, which by the 1880s had grown under the leadership of largely indigenous Czech entrepreneurs to 25.35%, only to be squeezed back to a share of 15.9% in the 1902 census by the metalworking industry. Metalworking, in third place to begin with, recorded remarkably steep growth through the course of the nineteenth century. Its share of the total industrial production of the Czech lands rose from 7%–10% during the 1880s and to 14.8% in 1902 (and by the time of the first Czechoslovak census of 1930 it occupied top place).

The fundamental structural transformation of industry inevitably led to just as profound economic and social consequences for the nation. The significant rise of the coal and iron industries paved the way for a transition to concentrated mass production and the completion of modern capitalism, and by the same token to the so-called "high industrialisation" of the Czech lands similar to that undergone by neighbouring Germany from the end of the nineteenth century. At the same time, a significant turnaround was taking place in property relations in favour of indigenous Czech capital. This was especially true of the food industry, which soon became the leading sector in the Czech economic upsurge and played an important role in the creation of gross domestic product in the Czech lands (for instance, in 1880 it comprised an entire third of the value of industrial production in the region). This industry rose hand in hand with the agricultural sector, which not only delivered it raw materials, but was also an important source of financial accumulation and investment. This also explains why the food industry tended to be located in rural regions and reliant on seasonal workers.

From the 1860s onwards, the main agricultural sector was the production of beet sugar, developed largely by Czechs and controlled mainly by Czech capital. As late as the 1850s, it was reliant on a relatively small raw material base and, as in the pre–March Revolution period, associated with large aristocratic estates: in 1858, more than three quarters of all sugar-beet sowed areas in the Czech lands belonged to aristocrats, cultivated at their own expense by the refineries linked with them. Over the following fifteen years, the sugar industry witnessed a boom that led to further substantial changes in this sector.

Firstly, thanks to the tenfold increase in land sown with sugar beet, between 1858 and 1873 the sugar industry received the necessary raw material base for a boom.

Secondly, sugar production in these decades underwent root-and-branch transformation with the introduction of numerous technical and technological inventions, machines, and steam boilers originating from the Czechs or Czech-Bohemian Germans and indicative of the culmination of the technological revolution in this sector.

Thirdly, the investment capital needed for the promising industry was largely mobilised between the petty bourgeoisie in the countryside and in towns and cities, especially by means of cooperative movements, mutual savings bank savings, and shares. In this way, in the lead up to the 1870s, the sugar industry enjoyed first place in the emerging Czech "national industry". Due to low wages and increased demand for sugar both at home and abroad, it was possible not only to make large profits that boosted the production of readily available Czech money and investment capital, but gave this capital (e.g., through the demand of farmers growing sugar for artificial fertilisers and of sugar refineries for plant) an immediate impulse to do business in other modern sectors (chemicals, artificial fertilisers, engineering, and electrical engineering in Prague and Central Bohemia). This was a role analogous to that played by the textile industry during the accumulation of Sudeten German capital and to that played by the modern mill industry at the same time during the expansion of Hungarian capital.

Fourthly, the importance of the young, mainly indigenous Czech sugar industry can be seen in the figures: from 46 sugar refineries in 1853 to 164 in 1873, and from 18,663 employees in 1864 to 40,143 in 1873, as well as in the tenfold increase in sugar production compared with the mid-1850s. This production was easily capable not only of covering the needs of the internal market of the entire monarchy, but also, from 1864 onwards, of leaving a surplus to be exported. It was during this time that the Czech lands became the most important producer and exporter of beet sugar in Europe, after Germany and France.[44]

Besides the sugar industry, other branches of the agricultural sector typical of the Czech lands emerged and proliferated rapidly on the back of the raw materials provided by Czech agriculture: milling, brewing, distilling, and manufacturing malt and starch. Originally auxiliary operations associated with large aristocratic estates, these activities, during the course of the Industrial Revolution, became an independent industrial sector that, with the help of steam power and new production methods and apparatuses, was

---

44   Cf. Dudek, F. *Vývoj cukrovarnického průmyslu v českých zemích do r. 1872*. Praha, 1979.

transformed into factory mass production. In these sectors, so important in the economic rise of the Czech lands, Czech capital also played an increasingly important role.

Within the context of the ongoing mechanisation of agriculture and on the basis of its demand for machinery, the Czech engineering industry was born and grew in a similar way. It is no coincidence that in the 1870s and 1880s, Czech entrepreneurs (Kokora, Ježek, Jouza, Melichar, Pracner, Knotek, etc.) established factories for agricultural machinery in Czech cities (Přerov, Prostějov, Pečky, Brandýs nad Labem, Roudnice, and Jičín) with large agricultural backgrounds, though it should be added that the beginnings of engineering in the Czech lands (in Brno and Liberec and their environs, and in the suburbs of Prague) reach back to the pre–March Revolution period and are not Czech in origin. To begin with, these engineering plants manufactured machines for the textile industry and soon after fixed steam engines for factory operations. However, overall the engineering industry of the Czech lands remained for the next few decades below the level of Lower Austria, where the construction of locomotives, wagons, rifles, ammunition, etc. was concentrated. The first engineering works in the Czech lands were established and for a long time managed by mostly foreign mechanics from England, Scotland, Belgium, France, and Germany, though by the mid-nineteenth century half of them were to be found in the hands of entrepreneurs from the Austrian and Czech lands. Soon afterwards, the first indigenous Czech entrepreneurs and managers (Vincenc Daněk, Emil Škoda, etc.) were to make their presence felt.[45]

Right from the start, **joint-stock companies** were extremely attractive and important for the emerging Czech economic bourgeoisie because they allowed for the immediate pooling of the modest, dispersed funds of the Czech middle classes, thus compensating for their late arrival on the scene. In the pre–March Revolution period, this would have been impossible. In this first phase (up until 1850), there were only eight joint-stock companies in the Czech lands, all of them German. The situation did not change much over the next few years. In 1864, there were only nineteen joint-stock companies registered in the Czech lands, including Společnost buštěhradské dráhy (Buschtěhrader Eisenbahn or the Buštěhrad Rail Company) (1852) and the first German joint-stock banks, Mährische Escompte-Bank (1862) and Böhmische Escompte-Bank (1863). More favourable conditions for joint-stock companies were created only after the codification of trade freedom (1859) and the adoption of the Commercial Code (1862), as well as the Associations Act (1867), since in Austria joint-stock companies were deemed associations.

---

45   Cf. Vrbová, P. *Hlavní otázky vzniku a vývoje českého strojírenství do r. 1918.* Praha, 1959; Smrček, O. "Průmyslová revoluce ve strojírenství." *Sborník historický* 32 (1985): 125–161.

There then followed what was known as the "founders' fever", the proliferation of start-ups that lasted until the crash of the Vienna Stock Exchange in May 1873 and which saw the creation of 351 companies in the Czech lands and 429 in the remaining areas of Cisleithania. At first sight, this would seem to imply an important status for the Czech lands in the Austrian economy. However, in reality, capital power was already highly concentrated in Vienna and German Austria: of share capital totalling 4,146 million crowns, only 500 million crowns was held in the Czech lands, with five times that amount (3,405 million crowns) held by Viennese companies. Joint-stock companies in the Czech lands did business with capital totalling 1.42 million crowns, while Viennese companies had 11.7 million crowns at their disposal.[46]

The traumatic experience of the deepest crisis and longest depression of the nineteenth century was manifest not only in the collapse of many joint-stock companies (by 1882, 188 such companies had gone bankrupt in the Czech lands alone), but saw confidence in the development of the joint-stock model in the monarchy plummet. This was not helped by the public administration's hostile approach to this form of business (see, for instance, the *Aktiengesetz* or Stock Corporation Act of 1899 and the high taxation applied to joint-stock companies). As a consequence, there were still only as many joint-stock companies in Cisleithania in 1912 as there had been in 1873 (i.e., a total of 780, of which 330 were in the Czech lands). This meant that one of the traditional methods of raising business capital was severely restricted and as a consequence Austria lagged behind other states of Europe. Germany, for instance, was home to five times more industrial joint-stock companies than Austria. In addition, the obstacle-strewn development of joint-stock companies in Austria displayed several other idiosyncrasies.

Firstly, regarding the overall level of industry in pre-war Austria, the food industry, based mainly in the Czech lands, occupied first place (34%) among joint-stock companies. It and other consumer sectors accounted for 58.6% of the economy, while fewer joint-stock companies operated in heavy industry.

Secondly, even though many of the large joint-stock companies based their production exclusively in the Czech lands (e.g., the Škoda Works in Plzeň and the Poldi Kladno steelworks), they moved their headquarters to Vienna, where they were in immediate contact with the large Austro-German banks that were financing them, as well as with the government authorities that provided them information and reached decisions on economic policy.

---

46 Cf. Oberschall, A. "Hundert Jahre Aktiengesellschaften in den Sudetenländern (1822–1937)." *Statistische Rundschau – Statistický obzor* 25 (1944); Jindra, Z. "Rozvoj akciového podnikání v Rakousku a v českých zemích do r. 1914," in: Myška, M. (ed.). *Podnikatelstvo jako předmět historického výzkumu*. Ostrava, 1994, pp. 108–119.

Thirdly, within the context of Czech economic emancipation, the ratio of national Czech capital to total Austrian share capital is a point of interest. Austrian statistics and manuals (Compass) only contain indirect data regarding the nationality of capital. This information is gleaned, for instance, from a company's registered office, the people sitting on its board, and company registrations using a German, Czech, or bilingual name. However, even if we include bilingually registered companies amongst Czech firms, the outcome with respect to Czech capital remains underwhelming in both the first *Gründerjahre* or founders' year (lasting until 1873) and during the second wave of company incorporation from the end of the nineteenth century until the First World War. According to these criteria, in 1874 a total of 128 exclusively German companies operated in the industry of the Czech lands with a nominal capital of 252 million florins (of which approximately 150 million was paid up), and 135 indigenous Czech joint-stock companies with nominal capital of around 61 million florins, of which some 30 million was paid up. This means that Czech joint-stock companies, mostly sugar refineries, accumulated considerable assets in a relatively short period of time. Nevertheless, these assets only amounted to one-fifth of paid-up German share capital.[47]

The rise of indigenous Czech share capital visible from the 1890s onwards was not overwhelming, though neither was it negligible. The painful losses caused by the great crisis and depression of the 1870s had not yet been offset, and one could not yet speak of the indifference and timidity of Czech capital. However, its late arrival on the scene and its sluggish development meant it remained fragmented and dispersed. And so at the start of 1901 we find 123 Czech joint-stock companies with capital of around 123.9 million crowns (1 million crowns per company on average) operating in the Czech lands, as opposed to 155 German companies with capital of 918.6 million crowns (5.9 million crowns per company on average). On the one hand, the expansion of Czech share capital could no longer be ignored, especially in the Czech lands, where the majority of Czech companies operated (84). These had already moved beyond the narrow boundaries of the agricultural industry and had put down roots in engineering, metalworking, chemical and electrical engineering, the production of porcelain, glass, and ceramics, as well as the leather, paper, and construction industries. On the other hand, the gap between Czech and German industrial capital in the Czech lands gradually narrowed from the 1870s onwards. In 1874, the ratio was 30:150 million florins (i.e., 1:5 in favour of German-Austrian capital), while in 1901 this ratio was now 89:376 million crowns (i.e., 1:4.2 in favour of German capital). In addition, the continued dominance of the combined Sudeten German and

---

47   Purš. *Průmyslová revoluce: vývoj pojmu a koncepce.* Prague 1973, p. 451.

German Austrian capital in the Czech lands was secured by the affiliates of Viennese banks established there and boosted by several joint-stock companies of the German Empire operating there.

The **emergence and growth of national banking** is one of the most important phenomena of economic development in the Czech crown lands in the nineteenth century, though it was not until the third quarter of the century that it made its presence felt. In the early, pre-1848 phase of industrialisation, industrial credit was still in its infancy, and financial transactions, mainly based around state loans, were controlled in the Czech lands and the rest of Austria by private bankers. Especially worthy of attention in this respect are the two Prague bankers Lämel and Zdekauer, who, despite being German by birth and language, displayed a certain sympathy to the Czech revivalist feelings during their time spent at the Association for the Promotion of Industry in the Czech Lands (founded in 1833) and indeed afterwards. The finance industry was still weak and represented by a few small savings banks. However, these were not important in terms of the country's industrialisation, and in addition were controlled by the Czech landed gentry and the German-Austrian aristocracy. The Austrian National Bank, founded in 1816, was equally passive as regards the funding needs of entrepreneurs in the Czech lands. This did not matter too much, since business requirements were still modest (factories were small and mostly owned by individual businesspeople, while the light consumer industry that predominated did not place high demands on investment and operating capital) and for the most part could be met without resorting to bank loans: (a) from a company's own profits (self-financing), (b) by means of loans from family members (family capital), (c) through the importation of registered or operating capital in the case of foreign entrepreneurs, and (d) through the passive involvement or direct participation of the nobility in business.

It was the liberal era and the new Trade Regulation Act, or *Gewerbeordnung* (1859), and the subsequent economic boom generating greater credit requirements that triggered the first wave of modern joint-stock banks in the Czech lands. In the case of Sudeten-German banks there was a delay of ten years after the establishment of the first commercial banks in Vienna and almost fifteen years in the case of the Czech lands. The foundations of modern banking in the Czech lands were laid in the 1860s, and its network proceeded to spread in two directions. The first was carried by strong agricultural interests and involved the provision of long-term credit by means of mortgage banks (following the model of the Crédit Foncier de France, 1852), while the second met the short-term credit needs of expanding industry, commerce, and transport, then leading to the creation of a movable-asset based, universal type of commercial bank (following the model of the Parisian Crédit Mobilier, 1852). The first mortgage banks, established in the Czech lands on a public law basis with guarantee and under the supervision of the crown land, were in Prague (1864), Opava (1869), and Brno (1876). However, they suffered hefty losses during the crisis and depression of the 1870s and lost a great deal of their relevance in the years to come because of the emergence of the provincial banks, which took over the railway, municipal, and improvement loans. The largest of these was the Zemská banka království českého (Provincial Bank of the Kingdom of Bohemia) in Prague (1890). With the exception of this bank, the Czechs did not achieve any important positions in the public law bank sphere.

Likewise, the beginnings of movable-asset based commercial banking in Prague were not Czech but more closely related to the older, more powerful centre in Vienna. The first representative of modern banking on the Prague financial market was an affiliate of the Viennese bank Österreichische Creditanstalt für Handel und Gewerbe, opened in 1857. Not even the first commercial banks in the Czech lands from 1862–1864 (the discount banks in Brno, Prague, and Varnsdorf) were of Czech origin. It was only at the start of the boom of 1867–1873 that Czech capital elected to open the first commercial banks, which possessed several very specific features: (a) compared to the decades-long delay in the industrial sphere, these banks were opened relatively soon after the arrival of institutions established by Germans; (b) unlike Viennese and Sudeten German banks they did not enjoy lavish state support or the contribution or participation of foreign capital, private banking houses, and the aristocracy; (c) their capital had been raised in small enterprises and self-help organisations and held in mutual savings banks and cooperatives in the countryside and small towns. With the creation of an independent Czech banking sector, an important feature of the Austrian banking system was established, namely its national diversity as the economic reflection of the multinational composition of the Habsburg monarchy.

The German bourgeoisie in Austria and the Czech lands enjoyed favourable conditions, since on the threshold of the 1850s it already had so much capital at its disposal that it could subscribe millions of florins in the registered capital of the first banks (with the participation of bankers, especially Rothschild, and many aristocrats). By contrast, Czech banking had to be built from the bottom up on the basis of small amounts of dispersed capital. German banks in Austria and the Czech lands were tasked with providing credit to an already healthy German industrial sector, trade, railways, and large (aristocratic) landowners, while the Czechs, given their starting position, had to make personal loans to farmers, to craftmen's workshops, and to small merchants. These tasks could not be taken over by municipal savings banks, which concentrated on charitable activities and the collection and safekeeping of savings, while being largely German. The Czechs, inspired by the ideas of economist Franz Hermann Schulze-Delitzsch and an ambitious campaign of articles and lectures organised by František Šimáček, František Cyril Kampelík, and Filip Stanislav Kodym, resolved this problem from 1858–1868 through creating a dense network of mutual savings banks with tens of thousands of members. Small credit institutions of local importance in villages and small towns were established in accordance with the letter of federal law (as were joint-stock companies) as associations, cooperatives, and societies. These then compensated for the initial lack of Czech capital by means of the cooperative organisation and personal guarantees of their members. They enjoyed extraordinary success. After twenty years of operations, 446 Czech mutual savings banks held a total of almost 80 million florins (equity and loan capital). At around the same time the mutual savings bank movement spread around German districts, but neither the number of institutions nor the level of capital under management ever attained the level of Czech savings banks.[48]

Thanks to the mutual savings banks, the Czechs were able to mobilise the accumulated savings of the middle classes relatively quickly, and in 1868 they used this capital to found the first joint-stock commercial banks (the Záložní úvěrní ústav or Credit Saving Institute in Hradec Králové, and Živnostenská banka in Prague). By the First World War, Živnostenská banka had become the fifth largest banking institution in the Czech lands, with equity of 100 million crowns, and thus the most powerful provincial bank, establishing Prague as a new financial centre, alongside Vienna and Budapest. There were now 13 Czech banking institutions with a total of 1,022 million crowns under management, eclipsing the banking capital held by Czech Germans (829 million crowns) and narrowing the gap on Viennese banking capital (5,280 million crowns). Greater Czech capital strength was now to be felt more than ever before on the Czech market, within Austria as a whole, and even on the foreign capital markets. This changed somewhat the status of Czech banking within the Austrian banking system, highlighting its unique features and developmental tendencies.

Firstly, in line with the general rise of organised capitalism, Czech banks expanded their industrial interests by converting credit companies to joint-stock companies, retaining some of the shares of these companies in their custody and occupying important positions on their management bodies. They also tried to keep track of these companies systematically through special industrial departments and systematically built up their own industrial concerns.

Secondly, closer ties with factories were in many cases reinforced by the development of trading their goods on commission, with all the advantages and concomitant effects listed above.

---

48   Hájek, J., and Lacina, V. *Od úvěrních družstev k bankovním koncernům*. Praha, 1999.

Thirdly, confronted with the small internal market of the Czech lands and the control previously exerted by German business, Czech banks very quickly embarked on ambitious business and capital expansion beyond the Czech borders, partly to the larger markets of the monarchy, especially to areas settled by Slavs and economically less developed provinces (Slovakia, Galicia, and the southern Slavic countries), partly abroad, especially to Russia and the Balkans, under the pretext of cultivating "Slavic solidarity" and under the slogan of "neo-Slavism". This expansion was in line with the general imperialist trend and availed itself of the customary tools, ranging from loans and credit to the purchase of Czech goods and finally to the establishment of banking affiliates and subsidiaries. It would even seem that, prior to 1914, the exportation of Czech banking capital was excessive if we bear in mind, for instance, that after 1905 almost 80% of all of Živnostenská banka's capital investments were located outside the Czech lands and that Ústřední banka českých spořitelen realised up to 90% of its credit and forex trading outside the province.

Fourthly, Vienna's "haute finance" finally acknowledged the strength of Czech capital by inviting Živnostenská banka and another three Czech banks to participate in the lucrative issue of state loans during the reorganisation of a "large Austrian consortium" (1911). However, the quota allocated was very small (approximately 5%) and unquestionably did not correspond to the share capital held by the bank in all Cisleithanian banks (16.4%). The importance of Živnostenská banka was also recognised when, shortly before the outbreak of war, it was the only provincial institution to participate in cofounding the Austrian Control and Audit Bank for Industry and Commerce, which oversaw the actions of leading economic organisations (cartels, syndicates, etc.) and thus represented the culmination of the monopolising attempts made by the Austrian banking giants to establish influence over and a closer relationship with industry.

Fifth, we should not overlook the fact that the Czechs entered World War I with a comprehensive banking organisation stretching from rural mutual savings banks, credit unions, thrift institutions, and regional agricultural exchequers, to medium and large commercial banks, and at its peak (as a substitute for its own issuing bank) provincial banks in Bohemia and Moravia. Over the course of a single generation, this organisation managed to acquire its own experts and management, and by 1914 it had accumulated more than 5 billion crowns ready to be used in all spheres of the Czech economy.

Where was all this to lead? The remarkable emergence and expansion of Czech banking over the course of only fifty years marked the successful culmination of the Czech revivalist movement on the economic scene, by coincidence several years prior to the creation of an independent state and, one might argue, as the precondition of this epoch-making event. The creation of Czech banking also involved a significant turnaround in the history of Austrian banking and in the development of Austrian capitalism as a whole, since despite the consolidated official statistics kept from the establishment of Živnostenská banka onwards, there no longer existed Austrian banks in Cisleithania. Instead, banks were divided into German-Austrian, German-Bohemian (Sudeten), Czech, Polish, southern Slavic, and Italian. Almost as a response to the disregard for and even discrimination against Czech credit requirements (e.g., the rejection of Czech bills and bids), Živnostenská banka, followed by other Czech banks, implemented from the outset a national, economically motivated banking policy that was guided by the principle "Czech capital to the Czech and, by extension, the Slavic economy".[49] They were scrupulous in ensuring that at least a majority of their share capital was Czech, they did not vote Germans to their management boards, they avoided lending to German companies, and they were ready at any time to face down the expansion and domination of German capital. This somewhat strange banking policy, imbued with the ideas of "economic nationalism," that were of course infiltrating Sudeten-German and Viennese banks too, was ample proof for the multinational empire of the "national economic diversification" of its banking industry. This striking feature of the Austrian banking system had no less serious consequences. Long before the military and political disintegration of the monarchy, the competition for markets under the guise of the struggle for the national sphere of influence (for example, under the motto "our own to our own") had led to problems and strains on the Austrian capital market that repeatedly intersected with the attempts being made at integration by the government and court.

INSTITUTIONAL AND LEGAL DEVELOPMENTS

CONSTITUTIONAL AND ADMINISTRATIVE DEVELOPMENTS

During the second half of the eighteenth century, the Holy Roman Empire of the German Nation celebrated one thousand years of existence. From the end of the Thirty-Years' War, it had become a more or less formal grouping of independent states in which the function of emperor was more ceremonial than genuinely policymaking. After a short break in the first half of the 1740s, when Charles Albrecht of Bavaria, an enemy of Maria Theresa, became emperor, the title returned to the hands of the House of Habsburg-Lorraine. The final blow to this grouping, of which the Czech crown lands were an

---

49   *Živnostenská banka 1869–1918*. Praha p. l. [1919], p. 46.

established part, was dealt by Napoleon Bonaparte. Faced with the successes of Napoleon's armies, the Holy Roman Empire began to collapse. Franz II, the last emperor, was aware of the catastrophic threat as well as the fact that the continued existence of the Holy Roman Empire was no longer sustainable. At the same time, he wanted to be considered an equal partner to Napoleon, the emperor of the French. It was for this reason that in 1804 he declared the creation of the Austrian Empire. Franz became emperor of Austria, the first of that name. What was left of the Holy Roman Empire of the German Nation was formally dissolved in 1806. The Austrian Empire included the Czech lands, and nothing was to change regarding the relationship of individual crown lands within the empire. Nevertheless, we might call the creation of the Austrian Empire a legal step confirming the implementation of Theresian and Josephinian centralisation reforms enacting a transition from a personal union to a real union.

After the defeat of Napoleon, Austria attempted to reinstate its position among the German states. These efforts culminated in the establishment of the German Confederation (Der Deutsche Bund) in 1815, which at the time of its creation comprised 41 German states. By 1866, this number had fallen to 34. The president of the confederation was the Austrian emperor. The confederation was important both politically and economically. It was within the confederation that liberal economic ideas based on classical political economics and the integration of the Central European space (e.g., a common currency and unified commercial law) were to be implemented. Many of the measures aimed at economic integration could not be realised, or was so only in part, because of the conflicting opinions and interests of individual states. As the power of Prussia grew, Austria gradually lost its position in the confederation. The turning point in the elimination of Austrian influence in the German regions was the Austro-Prussian War of 1866, which resulted in the demise of the German Confederation and Austria's withdrawal from the region of the unifying Germany.

The conservative forces that came to power at the end of the eighteenth century in the Habsburg Monarchy subordinated all other interests to defeating France and preventing the spread of the ideas of the French Revolution, which they identified as the main danger. The introduction of censorship and a tightening up of the rules governing movement across the borders of the monarchy were intended to slow down the spread of modernising trends in economic, political, and social life. A general reluctance to make any changes reigned. Anything new was scrutinised for any hint of a threat to the existing system. The main aim was to conserve a system that stood on the dividing line between a decaying feudalism, with all the privileges accorded to the aristocracy, and the advancing tide of capitalism based on the principle of equality of opportunity and personal success. Many drafted economic or political measures were postponed for fear of the consequences. The first half of the nineteenth century in the Habsburg Monarchy was associated with absolutism. The state apparatus opposed all innovations that might lead to political change. This approach was reasonably successful until the outbreak of revolution in 1848.

The unfolding revolution generated a host of requirements in the legal sphere, and the state apparatus was forced to react to revolutionary demands with a number of concessions. However, many of these compromises were only temporary. In April 1848, the first Austrian constitution was published. The provisional Pillersdorf Constitution was to be replaced by a new constitutional law that would be debated by the first elected legislature. After the elections, the first Austrian parliament was established in the summer of 1848 to discuss a new constitution. However, negotiations dragged on as various political views and claims asserted themselves. After the revolutionary upheavals in Vienna, parliament relocated to Kroměříž, Moravia, where it continued its deliberations. Conservative forces exploited the growing political conflicts in order to suppress the fledging parliamentarism, and at the start of March 1849 they were successful. The first step was the replacement of the somewhat simple-minded Emperor Ferdinand I (V as Czech king), the last crowned king of Bohemia, with a new figure that would not be "compromised" by revolutionary promises. An event took place unheard of since the time of Rudolf II, namely the abdication of the emperor and the enthronement of his nephew, Franz Joseph I. At the start of March 1849, when the government had already consolidated its position around the new emperor, a new constitution was promulgated, the Stadion Constitution—again by fiat (i.e., imposed and not passed by the legislature)—and the Imperial Diet, which subsequently dissolved. The only tangible decision to be passed by the first Austrian parliament was the abolition of servitude and bonded labour, which opened the way to a civil society based on equality before the law. The new constitution remained for the most part a lifeless corpse and was finally dissolved in the Sylvester Patents in 1851. The Austrian Empire returned to a form of absolutism (1851–1860) often called neo-absolutism or, less accurately, Bach's absolutism (after Minister Alexander Bach).

After Josephinian absolutism, the period of neo-absolutism (1851–1860) represented the second stage in the formation of the Austrian legal order. Regulations were passed that affected almost all aspects of life. As regards economic legislation, the 1850s was highly productive (the exchange code in 1850, the associational patent in 1852, the railway concession act and mining code of 1854, and the Trade Regulation Act of 1859). Most of these legal regulations remained in force until the end of the monarchy as well as afterwards in the territory of Czechoslovakia up until the mid-twentieth century. After the Hungarian Revolution of 1848 was crushed, the western and eastern regions of the monarchy were brought together more closely than ever before. The validity of several older regulations was extended to Hungary (e.g., the General Civil Code) and new regulations were published covering the entire territory. This period lasted until the end of neo-absolutism, and from the beginning of the 1860s onwards the legal order of the western and eastern parts of the monarchy again began to diverge.

Military setbacks in Italy at the end of the 1850s and Austria's ineffective foreign and domestic policies saw the fall of absolutism and the promulgation of the October Diploma in 1860, in which the emperor undertook to restore parliament. At the start of the 1860s, the Habsburg Monarchy embarked on the long path to internal democratisation. This transformation was enshrined externally in the February patent or Schmerling Constitution in February 1861

In the mid-1860s, relations between the western and eastern regions of the monarchy were enshrined in the Austro-Hungarian Compromise (in Cisleithania this situation was sanctioned by Act 146/1867 of the *Reichsgesetzblatt*, which in essence represented part of the December Constitution – Act 141–145/1867). From a legal perspective, the Habsburg Monarchy was divided into two halves that, in addition to the person of the monarch, shared a common currency, foreign policy, and army. In accordance with the emperor's cabinet directive of 14 November 1868, the state was officially called the "Austro-Hungarian Monarchy" (or Dual Monarchy) and the "Austro-Hungarian Empire". Other issues were dealt with by Cisleithania, the official name of which was "The Kingdoms and Lands represented in the Imperial Council" (which comprised 17 kingdoms and lands, including the Austrian Land, the Kingdom of Bohemia, Galicia, Bukovina, Dalmatia, etc.), and Transleithania or the lands of the Crown of Saint Stephen (Kingdom of Hungary). The names are derived from the River Leitha, which formed the border between both regions. Unofficially Cisleithania was known as Austria, though Slavic MPs were opposed to this becoming official, which is why we often encounter the term Cisleithania as an unnamed realm. The part each province was to play in joint affairs was set forth in settlement agreements that were entered into periodically for a period of ten years (Cisleithania's ratio was in the region of 60%–70%).

Unlike feudalism, the new legal order created in the monarchy from the end of the eighteenth century onward was based on the concept of the generality of the law, its universal validity, and equality before the law. The legally enshrined hierarchisation of society associated with the personality or personhood of the law, in which every class in society had its own rights, gradually disappeared. A free citizen was born, who replaced the villein subject to the state. As of 1848, the question of the enshrinement of civil rights formulated by enlightened thinkers became more urgent. The state guarantee of civil rights represented one of the important revolutionary demands. The catalogue of basic human rights was subsequently attached to the December Constitution by Imperial Act 142/1867.

From the seventeenth century onwards, the formation of the rule of law was completely dependent on the sovereign. Provincial assemblies enjoyed only a limited and strictly defined range of activities. From the eighteenth century, the interest of the sovereign in legislative activities grew, and culminated in the period of enlightened absolutism with a "legislative storm" of various different patents. After the unsuccessful attempt at parliamentary government during the revolution of 1848–1849, legislative power was returned to the hands of the sovereign. This state of affairs lasted until the start of the 1860s, when there was a revival of parliamentary life in the monarchy. During the course of the 1860s, the monarchy underwent internal democratisation and the Austrian half of the state saw the creation of territorial self-governance that became in part a response to the increasing demands of individual nations of the monarchy. Self-government was asserted on the level of individual lands, districts, and municipalities. However, the provincial self-governments did not satisfy the demands of individual nations of the monarchy for federalisation or full autonomy.

In the revolutionary years, the old court authorities were transformed into ministries, the number of which fluctuated over the years depending on the changing state agenda. After the creation of the ministries, the economic agenda first lay within the purview of the Ministry of the Interior. During the course of the revolution, a separate Ministry of Commerce was formed (established on 8 May 1848, dissolved at the end of the 1850s, but revived on 4 February 1861). Thus, as the state's economic agenda grew, so too did the number of economic ministries. For instance, in 1896 a Ministry of Railways was established that attended to the development of the state rail network, and 1908 saw the creation of a Ministry of Public Works.

As the number of ministries and other state offices increased, so too did the number of civil servants. In addition to the aristocracy, the upper echelons of the state bureaucracy began to be occupied by educated commoners. Working in the service of the state became a sure source of income and opened the way for upward social mobility. German civil servants overwhelmingly dominated the centralised state authorities. With 507 civil servants (10.4%), the Czechs, who represented 23% of the Cisleithanian population (1910), enjoyed above-average representation. As regards specific economic briefs, Czech civil servants accounted for 6.1 % (Ministry of Commerce), 8.1% (Ministry of Finance), 10.8% (Ministry of Agriculture), 12.9% (Ministry of Public Works), and 13% (Ministry of Railways). On the other hand, the share of Austrian Germans (including Czech Germans) in the ministries was

92.3%, 75.9%, 79%, 80.3%, and 78.8% respectively of all central government officials.[50]

Although the monarchy did not favour the Czech ethnic group or its representatives, there were still many Czechs who occupied the highest positions in the state administration of the monarchy. Let us look at those ministries of the Cisleithanian governments whose activities were linked with the economic and state administration. Firstly, there was Josef Kaizl, Minister of Finance (7 March 1898 – 2 October 1899); Josef Fořt, Minister of Commerce (2 June 1906 – 8 November 1907); Albín Bráf, Minister of Agriculture (19 November 1911 – 1 July 1912); and Otakar Trnka von Laberon, who enjoyed the longest term of office as Minister of Public Works (3 November 1911 – 22 June 1917). Occupying the post of minister did not necessarily mean that the politician in question favoured his ethnic group, although a certain level of support was assumed. Nevertheless, ministers were often reproached for not having sufficiently defended "Czech" interests. Czech civil servants returning to Prague from Vienna after 1918 to offer their services to the republic often faced local and political prejudices regarding their alleged "pro-Austrian" leanings. Even Germans who came from Bohemia and Moravia played a significant role in the operations of the monarchy.[51]

Congruent with the development of legislative activity during the Enlightenment, the publication of individual patents and regulations became more and more important. This in turn led to the creation of official collections of legal regulations, the publication of which was overseen by the state in accordance with the legal principle of *ignorantia legis neminem excusat* or "ignorance of the law is no excuse". In 1780, a decision was taken to publish Collections of Statutes (*Justizgesetzsammlung*), to be joined in 1790 by a Collection of Political Acts (*Politische Gesetzessammlung*) focusing on the regulations of administrative law. In 1848, both collections were replaced by the Imperial Code (*Reichsgesetzblatt*), which continued to be published until the fall of the monarchy. The Imperial Code contained regulations promulgated by the sovereign, parliament, and central bodies of the monarchy and later Cisleithania. Transleithania had its own system for publishing acts (legal articles). Notwithstanding the original plans for the collection of laws to be published in all the languages of the monarchy, the official version was published at the start of the 1850s in German only. Provincial codes were published for individual lands that contained the regulations of the state (e.g., the Bohe-

---

50 For more details regarding the composition of the civil service in the monarchy, see Jindra, Z. "Národnostní složení úřednictva centrálních úřadů v habsburské monarchii a v Předlitavsku podle šetření k 1. lednu 1914" in: Štaif, J. (ed.). *Pocta profesoru Zdeňku Kárníkovi: Sborník příspěvků k jubilantovým sedmdesátinám*, AUC Philosophica et historica / 1999, Studia historica LI, Praha 2003, pp. 71–88.

51 Profiles of the finance ministers are to be found in *100 Jahre im Dienste der Wirtschaft*. Wien, 1961.

mian Governor's Office) and the self-governing bodies, and were valid only in their territories. Translations were put together and the codes published bilingually in German and the land of the province.

STATE ECONOMIC POLICY

Theresian and Josephinian reforms were a significant presence in the sphere of economic law and governance. The Habsburg Monarchy was characterised by an Austrian form of mercantilism called cameralism.[52] Economic opinions of mercantilism spread from France and, in the climate of the enlightened absolutism of the Danube Monarchy, acquired a specific focus. Mercantilism, as the name implies (from the Latin *mercator* meaning merchant or trader), sets great store by trade and a positive trade balance backed by reserves of gold and precious metals. According to mercantilists, the quantity of precious metals it possesses is the measure of a state's wealth. A state was to maximise exports and restrict imports. High-quality goods were to be exported, while only raw materials were to be imported and even then, only when needed. Cameralism advocated state intervention in the economy. The state was to channel and support business activities and to create advantageous conditions for them.

During the course of the first half of the nineteenth century, mercantile ideas gradually began to give way to classical political economics highlighting a liberal approach to economic policy. The state was to refrain from providing direct support for the economy and indeed any participation in economic life. The activities of individuals were deemed most beneficial to economic development. Everything should be left to private initiative and the state should serve purely as the guardian of law and order and security. Ideally, all barriers to the economic activities of individuals should be lifted, with the market being the final arbiter. The founder of classical political economics, the British economist Adam Smith, wrote of the "invisible hand" of the market that acts as a limit on economic activities. However, economic liberalism enjoyed only limited success in the Habsburg monarchy. Many liberal ideas were too revolutionary and threatened what was still an estate-based society. Nevertheless, economic liberalism was strongly reflected on the level of commercial law and asserted its presence forcibly in the 1850s.

By the second half of the nineteenth century, Austria was increasingly influenced by the views of the German Historical School. In the 1840s, its founder, Friedrich List, warned of the inappropriateness of pure liberalism for states whose economic development was lagging. He emphasised that the

---

52 Krameš, J. *Kameralismus a klasická ekonomie v Čechách*. Praha, 1998.

acceleration of economic development would be possible by means of a suitable state economic policy and rational interventions in the form of protectionism. The economic policy of Prussia and the whole of unifying Germany can be viewed in the light of the German Historical School. In 1871, the Austrian economist Carl Menger wrote *Principles of Economics*, thus establishing the tradition of the Austrian School of Economics that ended the dominance of classical political economy. The Austrian School entered into a dispute regarding methodology (*Methodenstreit*) with the German Historical School, which it criticised for a purely descriptive approach that lacked theoretical grounding. The ideas of the Austrian School were personified in the highest places by its adherent Eugen Böhm Bawerk, who occupied the post of Finance Minister of Cisleithania several times.

From the mid-nineteenth century onwards, socialist economic ideas made their way into the Czech lands, though these were by no means linked only with German political philosopher and economist Karl Marx. On the contrary, ideas associated with the cooperative movement proved attractive as a means of overcoming huge economic disparities and creating a way forward to the economic emancipation of the Czech nation, which at the start of the development of capitalism had to deal with a lack of capital and lagged far behind German-Austrian entrepreneurs. The cooperative principle was promoted by František Cyril Kampelík (in the sphere of finance) and František Ladislav Chleborád (consumer cooperatives), among others.[53]

THE CODIFICATION OF CIVIL AND COMMERCIAL LAW

By the latter half of the eighteenth century, there was a growing need for new regulations covering most relationships under private law. The existing regulations, largely dating back to the sixteenth and early seventeenth centuries, would be replaced by new ones addressing the new conditions. After the failure of Maria Theresa to achieve this, Joseph II enjoyed greater success in the codification of civil law with the publication of the first part of the draft Civil Code. Work on the regulation of civil law continued in the years to come, and the gradual suppression of Josephinian ideas was not essentially reflected in codification practice.

The basic private law framework that influenced legal relationships throughout the nineteenth century was the General Civil Code (*Allgemeines Bürgerliches Gesetzbuch*) of 1811. The code marked a turning point. It completely removed the remains of personality law, under which different regulations applied to individual classes, and specified that all the legal relationships it

53 Sojka, M. et al. *Dějiny ekonomických teorií*. Praha, 2000.

regulated would abide by its terms regardless of personal status. The authors took enlightened natural legal theory as their starting point. Underlying the code was its generality and exclusivity. It expressly rejected slavery and servitude (serfdom). It also set forth the principle that ignorance of the law excuses no one. Ownership was based on exclusivity and limitlessness. The outcome was a modern legal regulation that, by virtue of its liberalism, opened the way to the emerging capitalism. The extent to which the regulation was modern is borne out by the fact that it was over a hundred years before it was amended, during the First World War. It remained valid in what became Czechoslovakia until 1950, with some sections remaining in force until 1965. It applies to this very day in Austria.

The General Civil Code also had implications for the relationship between employee and employer, and set forth the conditions for entering into employment, service, and wage contracts. An employment contract thus arose by virtue of the free agreement of two contracting parties: the employee and employer. Though the code set forth employment relationships on the basis of civil equality, the practical consequences of the regulation were substantially less radical. A number of customs remained unaffected. Regulations governing farmworkers as well as rural and urban domestic workers published in 1782 contained many provisions that curtailed personal freedom and created a kind of patriarchal feudal relationship between the farmworker and farmer or the journeyman and master. Furthermore, there was virtually no free labour market, and so the factory worker was highly dependent on their employer. Employment relationships in rural areas were significantly affected by the abolition of serfdom and bonded labour (1848), which represented one of the standout successes of the revolution (for a more detailed analysis, see the chapter on agriculture). In the mid-1860s, new employment laws were passed covering the employment of ancillary workers in private (personal) service who basically worked directly for their employer. The remuneration for such work often took the form of payment in kind.

The civil code was to be followed by a commercial code.[54] The idea was to bring together commerce, bills, maritime law, bankruptcy, and business affairs, and this objective was reflected in the creation of a Court Commission on Justice and Legal Affairs (Hofkommission in Justizsachen) on 18 February 1809. The official in charge was the chairman of the exchange, court councillor Johann Michael von Zimmerl. Only two sections were drafted, covering commerce and bills, but were never approved. In 1842, work on the codification of commercial law was restarted, but not even this second draft, published in 1849, was passed. In 1853, the Ministry of Commerce submit-

---

54   Urfus, V. *Zdomácnění směnečného práva v českých zemích a počátky novodobého práva obchodního.* Praha, 1959.

ted a third draft of the commercial code to the Imperial Council. After it had passed through the committee stage, it was published in 1857. Nevertheless, it was not passed. Codification work within the monarchy was suspended in the same year, because proceedings were initiated upon the suggestion of Bavaria with the German federal states on the creation of a single commercial code that would apply to all member states of the German Confederation.[55]

Basically, three systems of commercial law applied in the monarchy. The first comprised spheres covered by French commercial law (the *Code de commerce*). This involved the southern reaches of the monarchy occupied by Napoleon's troops, as well as the region of Kraków, only annexed by Austria in the 1840s. The second sphere of operations (Hungary and the Kingdom of Croatia-Slavonia) was passed in 1839–1840 and displayed the influence of the Hungarian commercial code. It was only in 1875 that the provisions of commercial law were brought into alignment in both Cisleithania and Transleithania. The third system, which related to the rest of the Austrian lands, including the Czech lands, was not based on any previous codification and comprised a mixture of various regulations and precedence.[56]

On 17 January 1857, a commission met in Nuremberg comprising 25 representatives of the individual government of all 21 states of the German Confederation and began work on an outline of the code. The executive head of the commission was Dr. Franz von Raule, chairman of the Vienna Commercial Court and a native of Trhové Sviny in South Bohemia. The basis of the negotiations was a draft code submitted by Prussia, and account was to be taken of an Austrian draft of 1857. Negotiations dragged on until spring 1861. At the same time, talks were taking place in Hamburg regarding the fifth volume devoted to maritime law. Austrian representatives were active during the talks, even though the volume was never passed by Austria. The commercial code drafted by the Nuremberg commission was gradually passed in all the German states (and remained valid in the territory of what became Germany until the end of the nineteenth century). In Transleithania it became Imperial Act 1/1863 on 17 December 1862. The General Commercial Code entered into force on 1 July 1863. It was divided into four volumes. It governed the creation and existence of business companies (public companies, limited partnerships, partnerships limited by shares, and joint-stock companies) and contractual relationships. Following the economic crisis and the bankruptcy of many joint-stock companies, Imperial Regulation No. 114/1873 was passed, which facilitated the dissolution of joint-stock companies. In 1875, the commercial code was joined by the Stock Exchange Act, and in 1903 by the agricultural produce exchange act. At the end of the nineteenth century,

55   Randa, A. *Soukromé obchodní právo rakouské*. Praha, 1908, p. 11.
56   Ibid., p. 9.

the Commercial Code was joined by an equity regulation (Imperial Government Regulation No. 175/1899) intended to facilitate the establishment and transformation of joint-stock companies in the sphere of industry and commerce. The regulation did not relate to companies involved in the banking, insurance, rail, and steam transport sectors.

The concept of a limited liability company was introduced into Austrian law by Imperial Act 58/1906, which was based on a German model from the turn of the nineteenth and twentieth centuries. Further material pertaining to commercial law was contained in the Cooperatives Act 70/1873 (Imperial Code), which became the basis for the development of the Czech cooperative movement (until then cooperatives had been formed, similarly to the predecessors of limited liability companies, pursuant to Federal Patent 253/1852).[57]

The most important position was gradually occupied by joint-stock companies. The joint-stock company existed prior to 1848 and was formed mainly to do business in the railway and steam transport sectors. It was created on the basis of landowner patents that had to be awarded before such a company could be established. However, joint-stock companies really began to flourish after 1848. It was in that year that the concessionary system began its operations (a special administrative licence had to be obtained in order to create a joint-stock company). The source of equity law was a federal patent (no. 253/1852) and many additional ministerial regulations. Upon being passed, the new commercial code formed the basis of provisions governing joint-stock companies. However, it was still necessary to obtain authorisation to create a joint-stock company, and this was granted by the Ministry of the Interior. At the head of a joint-stock company was the board of directors. Board members were remunerated for their work by *tantième*, or director's fee. A limited liability company became the most popular form of legal entity. It offered the advantages of personal management and limited liability in the event of failure, since a partner was only liable for company losses up to the level of their unpaid deposit. The registered capital was set high at a minimum of twenty thousand crowns. Creating a limited liability company was easier than creating a joint-stock company, and in general the authorisation of the Ministry of the Interior was not required. It was only required for specific business activities (e.g., railway transport).

---

57   Skřejpková, P. "K dějinám obchodu a vzniku obchodního práva." *Právněhistorické studie* 34 (Praha):, pp. 190–191.

THE DEVELOPMENT OF TRADE LAW AND THE COMPULSORY ASSOCIATION OF ENTREPRENEURS

From the Middle Ages onwards, guilds formed the basis of trade organisations, the preparation of new masters, the training of apprentices, and quality control procedures. However, during the eighteenth century their importance dwindled and they began to act as a brake on economic development. During the reign of Charles VI, legislative steps had been taken to support entrepreneurship and curb the power of the guilds. In 1731, the general trade (guild) patent was published, and eight years later general guild articles. However, it was only with the laws passed by Maria Theresa and Joseph II that the foundations of guilds were undermined and the state regulation of production reinforced. Among other things, the guilds lost jurisdiction over their members. Certain cameralist theoreticians (e.g., Joseph von Sonnenfels) became convinced they should be abolished completely. In 1791, a general guild patent was issued that established the institution of guild inspector.

Another measure was the issuance of commercial patents in 1732. The patent established a register of merchants at the commercial college (created in 1724 from the manufacturing commission). These were a mandatory record of all merchants and can thus, with a stretch of the imagination, be regarded as the predecessor of the commercial register. After registering, every merchant received a legitimisation docket. The records were to protect upstanding merchants from the competition of the black market.

Different approaches to trade policy were applied in the Habsburg monarchy during the second half of the eighteenth century. The most conservative system was in Hungary and Transylvania. In the cities the guild system remained in force, unaffected by reforms. Special privileges were issued for new manufactories and factories. At the other end of the scale, the most liberal atmosphere was to be found in the regions of Lombardy and Veneto, as well as in the free harbour city of Trieste.

Liberal ideas advocating free trade were applied in the Commercial Court Commission founded in 1816 (the commission performed the function of the Ministry of Industry and Trade). The commission created a centre of liberal access to business and took action against the remnants of the old guild system. The fact that a liberal approach to business enterprise has become established even in the highest circles is evidenced by an opinion expressed as early as 1816, that "every individual has a natural right to carry out any occupation that they see fit". During the 1820s and 1830s, several regulations were released upon the instigation of the commercial commission that further restricted the authority of the guilds, though they did not yet abolish them completely. This was due to the leniency shown to the guilds by the emperor in the belief that they were a force for conservatism, and out of fear for the political consequences of liberalisation. Though pre–March Revolution absolutism did not hold up the gradual evolution of new forms of business, it placed obstacles in its path. Not only was the influx of foreign experts limited, but so was the possibility of travelling abroad (as journeymen). At the start of the 1830s, a questionnaire was circulated amongst state and trade organisations on the liberalisation of entrepreneurship. Most of those questioned were in favour. In response, in 1836, the commission submitted the Trade Licensing Act, intended to unify the wildly divergent legal norms that regulated business. Though the proposal was still far from enshrining freedom to do business in law and only imposed limitations on the scope of the guilds, it did not go so far as to abolish them. Discussions of the regulation continued at the highest level for five years, after which it was rejected.

The removal of this inflexible system, which was failing to meet the needs of modern business, was one of the main demands of the revolutionary years 1848–1849. The restored neo-absolutism rejected political freedom, but was willing to offer freedom to do business as compensation. The first sign of a change in economic policy was the abolition of the customs border with Hungary in 1850, followed by the removal of most restrictions on exports and imports in 1851. A revolutionary step was the demand that business organisations be established to protect their members' interests. During the first half of 1848, Viennese traders and factory owners came up with a plan to create chambers of commerce. The ministerial council gave a cautious welcome to the plan in October of 1848, under which a provisional instruction was issued on 15 December 1848 to the effect that chambers of commerce and trade be established in all towns and cities where it was required. However, only one such chamber was created under this instruction, and that was in Vienna. The chambers were to function as consultancies for the newly created Ministry of Commerce. The legal basis for the creation of chambers in other regions of the monarchy was established by a provisional act of 18 March 1850 (Bruck's Act 122/1850). The act was adopted at the suggestion of Karl Ludwig von Bruck (1798–1860), then finance minister and later minister of commerce. The chambers were created as mandatory lobbying corporations. In the Czech lands eight chambers were set up based in Prague, Liberec, Plzeň, Cheb, České Budějovice, Brno, Olomouc, and Opava. Burgeoning business activities now at last had a partial platform for political lobbying within the chambers of commerce and trade. The chambers were authorised to give their opinions of the commercial and political aspects of the forthcoming trade licensing code, tax and financial matters, and transport problems (which included an influence on the creation of a railway network). They submitted expert reports, supported technical progress and new forms of business, cooperated with the courts on issues pertaining to the business agenda, and registered firms and federal contracts with the courts. They drafted regular progress reports and submitted them to the state authorities. The importance of the chambers was underlined in the early 1860s, when they were authorised to post their representatives to the provincial councils. In 1873, when direct elections to the imperial council were introduced, a special court was set up for the chambers of commerce and trade. The legal status of the chambers was finally set forth in full in Imperial Act 85/1868, which also set forth the territorial remit of the chambers. The most important feature of the new act was that it assigned additional duties to the chambers, which now took over several of the tasks of the public administration. For instance, the chambers held a trade register and registers of trademarks and designs. There were twenty-nine such chambers of commerce and trade spread throughout Cisleithania. Their number and headquarters remained constant in the Czech lands, though they were spread very unevenly and based more on the obsolete regional borders than genuine economic relations. They continued to function as an intermediary between the state authorities and businesspeople. Conflicts around nationality in the Liberec chamber were resolved by the establishment of a trade and commerce centre in Hradec Králové in 1910 that oversaw the same agendas as the chambers. The centre was created on a federal basis. It provided Czech businesspeople services that they should have been provided by the chamber in Liberec but were not. A similar centre for the Olomouc region was created in 1913 on similar foundations to that in Hradec Králové. The activities of the centres were financed by the Czech businesspeople operating within their district.

The number of representatives of small businesses increased in the chambers along with the democratisation of voting rules. Czechs slowly became the majority in individual chambers (Plzeň in 1882, České Budějovice in 1882, and Prague in 1884). There were between sixteen and forty-eight elected members in two sections, commerce and trade, and sometimes in mining. Each section was divided into election committees of large, medium, and small industry and commerce. In 1901, on the basis of joint meetings, a Centre of Commercial and Trade Chambers was established in Vienna. The competencies of the chambers expanded over the years. Their operations were funded by surcharges to the taxes paid by businesses. The chambers continued their activities up to 1948.[58]

The most important measure in the sphere of economic policy during the 1850s was the systematic preparation of a new draft Trade Regulation Act (*Gewerbeordnung*), which would remove the existing discrepancies between legal regulations and the haphazardness of their interpretation, and adapt le-

---

58   Grulich, P. *Obchodní a živnostenské komory 1918–1938.* Hradec Králové, 2006; Gruber, J. *Obchodní a živnostenská komora v Praze v prvním půlstoletí svého trvání 1850–1900.* Praha, 1900; *Zápas o většinu v pražské obchodní a živnostenské komoře.* Praha, 1905.

gal norms to the needs of modern economic life. In 1854 and 1855, two drafts of the Trade Act were submitted, the second of which met all the basic requirements of economic liberalism. However, it was the draft submitted by minister Karl Ludwig von Bruck, written during the second half of the 1850s, that was passed. The proposal was announced by Imperial Patent of 20 December 1859 and published under Imperial Act 227/1859. It took effect on 1 May 1860. The Trade Regulation Act represented an outstanding legal document for its time. It was meticulously written, and individual sections remained valid in Czechoslovakia until 1965. It ensured business freedom within the context of economic realism and proclaimed the freedom of production and trade.

Trades were divided into unqualified notifiable trades and licensed trades. Having paid the requisite fee, all citizens theoretically had access to every trade without requiring a license or educational qualifications. Trades were further divided into unlicensed, which simply had to be reported to the Licence Office, and licensed. The license was an official permit, and legal requirements had to be met if it was to be granted. Though the Licence Office enjoyed discretion when awarding licences, if an applicant met the conditions specified by law they had to be awarded a licence and the office had to justify its approach in its decision. Every licence holder had to be reliable, a level up from in good health, the condition for a free trade. Special qualifications were specified for certain licences involving education, certification, and local circumstances (representatives of the community in which the applicant hoped to pursue their activities would offer their opinion in such cases). An exhaustive list of licensed trades was given in section 15. The most important included bookbinding, librarianship, public transport (added later), construction work, and weapons production. The trades not listed in this paragraph were free.

The Trade Regulation Act also abolished the old guilds and replaced them with the institution of "societies". Admission to a society was the legal consequence of the taking up of a trade. The societies were self-governing corporations whose aim was to protect the interests of tradesmen and to encourage solidarity. During the 1860s and 1870s, the development of this organisation slowed down. In 1883, there were 2,870 such societies, with only a small number meeting the requirements of the law in full. The rest were what remained of the guilds. The further development of the trade societies would only take place after an amendment was passed to the Trade Regulation Act in 1883.

At the end of the nineteenth century, demands were increasingly voiced that the societies, until now organised on the basis of municipality, should be reorganised along sectoral lines. It was felt that this measure would allow them to protect their interests more effectively. However, these large societies also had disadvantages. One was the sometimes excessively large territory they covered and the remoteness of individual businesspeople from a society's HQ that prevented them from participating at special events. The health and old-age insurance of members was organised under the aegis of the communities. The insurance was optional. Each society offered to establish a sickness fund for its members. The fund was set up by its general assembly and was subject to approval by the governor's office. Old-age insurance was based on the Jubilee Land Insurance Institute of Emperor Franz Joseph I, founded in 1888. The institute insured persons from the poor strata of society.

The district magistrate's offices (municipal authorities) functioned as the trade office of first instance. The second instance was generally made up of provincial land governing offices (in Bohemia, the governor's office).

Up until the great economic crisis of 1873, there were no concerns regarding the effectiveness of trade law. Since the crisis mainly threatened small and medium crafts with limited capital, voices were increasingly heard calling for a review of what was known at the time as "toxic liberalism", which favoured factory production. As long as liberals were in power, these voices had no influence on the state's economic policy. However, things were to change after the arrival of the conservative cabinet led by Eduard Taaffe in 1879. During the 1880s, the government passed a range of economic and social reforms that launched an era of state intervention in economic policy.

An important step was the adoption of an amendment to the Imperial Trade Regulation Act 39/1883 on 15 March 1883. A third category, crafts, was added to the free and licensed trades. Though a license was not needed to operate these crafts, a certificate of competence (i.e., a certificate of apprenticeship or employment in the sphere) had to be submitted. The act did not specify which trades were to be considered crafts, but left that to the government. The government issued a regulation specifying the crafts, which included the commonest occupations, including cobbler, baker, tailor, carpenter, butcher, barber, and glazier among others. The amendment also expanded the catalogue of licensed trades (e.g., gas maintenance and plumbing, equipment for the production and distribution of electricity, funeral parlours, porters, etc.). In the years to come, the range of licensed trades expanded as conditions on the market changed (e.g., travel agencies were added in 1895). In 1907, the number of crafts was expanded to fifty-four. Substantial changes were made in a 1907 amendment that introduced qualified trades for which a certificate of competence was required (e.g., a certificate from a business school).

RELATIONS BETWEEN EMPLOYEES AND EMPLOYERS, SOCIAL LEGISLATION

The state respected contractual freedom in the relationship between an employer and employee. This liberal stance was based on an equal relationship between both parties and the possibility of choosing whether an employee was willing to perform certain work (poorly paid, physically demanding, etc.) or not. The transformations of society attendant upon the emergence and development of capitalism increasingly show that this approach was inappropriate and, especially during the period when capitalist relations were being created, was focused on the maximum exploitation of labour and the minimisation of the employer's payroll and other costs.

Regulations governing the relations between employees and employers appeared sporadically during the first half of the nineteenth century. The longest tradition, stretching back to the Middle Ages, was in the mining industry. To begin with, working conditions and hours were regulated inasmuch as they applied to child labour. A court decree of 1786 stipulated basic hygienic requirements for working children. A court decree of 1842 allowed for the employment of children aged nine and upwards as long as they had attended school for at least three years, or aged twelve and upwards if they were not attending school. Children aged up to twelve could work for ten hours and children aged between twelve and sixteen for twelve hours a day. However, these measures were guided not so much by social concerns as by military considerations, since they made it possible for young, healthy men to perform military service. The 1830s saw the first attempt to introduce sickness insurance for the working class, but the state refused to participate in the system. Under a court decree of 1837, the state instructed factory owners to pay for time spent in hospital in the event of a work-related accident or sickness for a period of up to four weeks.

However, we should first look at the way that terminology changed, since the contemporary concepts of employee and employer were not used back then, nor indeed was the concept of an employment contract. In principle, the law as it applied to this sphere was fraught with terminological ambiguity. Many different and overlapping categories were applied. The lowest status was accorded to unskilled manual labourer. Next came persons in lower services (physical work) and persons in higher services (mental work). A separate category applied to civil servants working on a national and self-governing level, teachers, etc. who enjoyed different arrangements and rights to emoluments. Other categories of employee also existed (e.g., agricultural workers).

Given that most of the population fell into the category of physical workers, I shall examine this group in more detail. The specification of working conditions in trade enterprises was set forth in the Trade Regulation Act. However, the act distinguished between ordinary trades and factory-style enterprises (with more than twenty employees, several trades being operated under one roof, etc.). According to these criteria, employees were divided into labourers and factory workers, and enjoyed different rights.

The Trade Regulation Act left all questions relating to working conditions to the discretion of the contracting parties, except as regards the minimum standards of care for children and juvenile employees in factories. It banned the employment of children younger than ten in industrial enterprises and specified maximum working hours for children up to the age of fourteen of ten hours a day and for children up to the age of sixteen of twelve hours a day. Children younger than sixteen were banned from night shifts, with minor exceptions. The employer's duty to their employees was restricted to the payment of a wage. The wage had to be paid in cash, but part of it could take the form of payment in kind (accommodation and food, but not alcohol). If a period of notice was not specified in the contract, it was usually fourteen days. If a worker downed tools, he could be forced to return to work and still be punished. Strikes remained punishable until the publication of the Coalition Act 43/1870. However, a strike still entailed a breach of contract.

From the 1880s onwards, the state showed greater interest in the sphere of employment and the working conditions of employees. It was in this year that social legislation (known as protective law) was introduced in Cisleithania, following the model of Bismarck's Germany. A new phenomenon appeared in the employer-employee relationship, namely interventionism in the social sphere, which consisted of setting forth working conditions and providing some form of benefit in the event of incapacity for work. These measures, which were aimed at the working class, were intended to head off their radicalisation in the struggle for social benefits.

The protection granted the labouring classes was boosted in an amendment to the Trade Regulation Act 22/1885 (the labourer's amendment) and was the first significant intervention on the part of the state in the employer-employee relationship. The amendment banned children aged twelve and younger from working and shortened the working hours of older children (e.g., children aged twelve to fourteen could work for up to eight hours, while factory work for children under fourteen was significantly restricted). The working hours of adults in factories was reduced in 1885 to eleven hours a day. Another amendment, no. 117/1883, introduced inspections of compliance with the new regulations that covered health and safety, employees' rights, etc. The amendment was extended in the years to come.

Women were another group of factory workers granted increased protection. Women workers were advantageous to employers because their wages were lower than men's. The state's interest in protecting women was related to maternity. In 1906, an agreement on the prohibition of night work by women employed in industry was signed in Bern, and pursuant to this Act 65/1911 was passed, which banned women from working night shifts in companies employing more than ten persons.

Working hours were regulated most in the mining industry. An amendment to the Mining Act (no. 115/1884) restricted the working hours not only of children but also of adults. Children aged between twelve and fourteen could only perform surface work above ground, and not on Sundays and public holidays. Girls up to eighteen years old could only work above ground. A miner's shift was to last ten hours a day. Miners' working hours were further shortened in 1901, this time to nine hours a day. The workers' amendment to the Trade Regulation Act restricted the hours worked by factory workers to eleven, and Sunday became a day off. The provisions applying to Sundays and public holidays in trade enterprises were set forth in Act 21/1895 (an amendment to Act 125/1905). Every worker had the right to twenty-four hours of uninterrupted free time per week. However, the law introduced exemptions for certain trades and periods of the year.

The next step was the introduction of sickness and accident insurance. General sickness insurance for workers was introduced in 1888 (under Act 33/1888). The principle of reciprocity formed the basis of the scheme. Workers' contributions were obligatory. The period of support was set at a maximum of twenty weeks at 60% of an employee's average daily wage. Women were also entitled to sick pay during the first four weeks after giving birth. Accident insurance was first dealt with under private contract law. A more appropriate arrangement was contained in Act 1/1888 on accident insurance. However, the provided coverage only related to large factories and hazardous conditions. Workers were expected to contribute up to 10%, and insurance companies could seek redress from employers if the accident was caused deliberately or through gross negligence.

Only small successes were recorded in the sphere of invalidity and old-age insurance. In 1907, a law was passed on the pension insurance of private-sector employees. The pensions of public-sector workers were dealt with as part of the terms and conditions of employment. The status of public-sector workers was reviewed in Act 15/1914.

However, the achievements of social legislation did not apply to persons working in the agricultural sector (with the exception of seasonal workers operating machines) and those who worked in private service (i.e., in the households of employers and for the latter's direct benefit). Their terms and conditions were set forth in the Farm Workers Act (no. 42/1857 of the crown land law gazette, or *Landesgesetzblatt*, for Prague and no. 11/1866 for Bohemia). These regulations placed high demands on workers and placed them at a disadvantage in terms of wages, which included accommodation and food.

Unemployment insurance developed slowly and was organised at the trade union level. Only very gradually were regulations drafted stipulating rules pertaining to the health and safety of workers.

During the First World War, workers saw a severe deterioration of their employment and social conditions. Working hours rose to thirteen hours a day against the backdrop of falling wages. The legal basis in this sphere was Act 236/1912 on acts of war, which granted extensive powers to the government during times of war. The Trade Regulation Act did not apply to employees working at munitions factories.

THE TAX SYSTEM

Moving through the latter half of the eighteenth century and into the nineteenth, as the role and function of the state expanded, so too did its expenditure. The state took an increasingly active role in the economic sphere, and the pressing question arose of how to cover these costs. The state revenue comprised taxes, fees, monopoly revenues, and customs duties. The answer was thought to be a more evenly distributed and increasingly higher tax burden on the population. The question of tax was at the forefront of the state's activities as an economic agent. In terms of state revenue, direct tax played the lead role. Most important was a land tax paid on yield. During the period of enlightened absolutism, the idea was floated of a flatter tax and a lowering of the burden on farmers. At the same time, the role of the provincial assemblies in approving tax was weakened. With this in mind, the Theresian and Josephian cadastre, which was intended to form the basis for the collection of land tax, was drawn up.

Maria Theresa's letters patent of 1756 made a further difference in the rate of land tax between farmland (*rusticus*) and demesnial or manorial land (*dominicus*). The tax applied to farmland was in excess of 40%, while that applied to manorial land was not even 30%. The reforms of Joseph II began with the release of the letters patent of 20 April 1785, which required an inventory of all fertile land and a determination of its yield, on the basis of which the level of land tax would be specified for each individual landowner. The total amount paid in tax was not to exceed 30% of net return. As a matter of principle, no difference was to be made between farmland and manorial land. This resulted in the swift creation of the Josephian cadastre. However, the increase in the tax burden on the nobility provoked resistance. In 1790, after the death of Joseph, this system, along with the Taxation and Urbarial Letters Patent, which was intended to play a role in reducing the financial burden on the countryside, was revoked and for a short time tax collection returned to Theresian rules. However, this solution proved to be unsustainable.

In 1810, a special court commission was set up to create a permanent and stable tax register. The Napoleonic Wars interrupted its work, but in 1817 it met again. On the basis of a stable cadastre, it set a land tax of 16% of the net yield on the land. In 1849, a surcharge of one third was added to the tax.

A special construction tax was collected in towns and cities, and was the predecessor of the building tax introduced in 1820.

In the second half of the nineteenth century, the structure of state revenues changed. The income from direct taxes gradually fell and indirect tax revenues stagnated. However, income from the newly introduced charges rose. The overall share of tax in government revenue fell slightly. The second most important source of state revenue remained that derived from monopolies. Income from customs duties fell slightly. Depending on their purpose, duties were divided into financial (with the aim of increasing state revenues) and protective, and the latter were then subdivided into industrial and agrarian (with the aim of protecting the economy). Czech historian Milan Myška states that in the 1880s and 1890s, financial duties represented 55.19%, industrial duties 39.37%, and agrarian duties 5.44% of the total revenue collected in the form of customs duties. The state coffers benefitted most from imports of coffee (approximately 33% of revenues), mineral oils (approx. 17%), cotton yarn (around 4%), and iron and iron products (5%).[59] The structure of state revenue is shown in the table 1.

Table 1: The structure of Austro-Hungarian state revenue 1847–1913 in %

Type of revenue	1847	1868	1883	1889	1913
Direct taxes	35.57	35.14	31.12	27.64	28.15
Indirect taxes	16.66	22.08	16.11	15.84	16.84
Revenue stamps, taxes fees	5.26	14.70	20.41	17.25	16.52
Net monopoly revenue	28.14	20.51	16.98	25.37	26.06
Customs duties	14.37	7.57	14.98	13.88	12.43

Source: Myška, M. "Celní politika rakousko-uherské monarchie (se zvláštním zřetelem k hutnímu železářskému průmyslu) 1850 až 1914." *Časopis matice moravské*, vol. 98, no. 118 (1999), tab. 1, p. 50.

After dropping at the start of the 1860s and leaving aside slight fluctuations, the revenue and expenditure of the state budget climbed throughout the period under examination. A sharp rise was recorded in the middle of the first decade of the twentieth century, and between 1904 and 1913, incomings and outgoings almost doubled. The structure of expenditure also changed, with, for instance, the largest item in the 1910 budget comprising railway construction and maintenance on 26.8%. Spending on armaments also increased, reflecting heightened international tensions. Prior to the First World War,

59   Myška, M. "Celní politika rakousko-uherské monarchie (se zvláštním zřetelem k hutnímu železářskému průmyslu) 1850 až 1914." *Časopis matice moravské* vol. 98, no. 118 (1999): 48–50.

the surplus was 12.5 million florins. The following table offers an overview of state budget revenue and expenditure flows.

Table 2: State budget revenue and expenditure flows of the monarchy 1848–1913 in millions of florins

Year	Expenditure in millions of florins	Revenue in millions of florins
1848	256.3	160.0
1859	588.2	503.8
1869	300.0	323.2
1879	454.3	394.8
1889	551.3	562.4
1899	759.0	799.1
1904	897.4	898.9
1909	1,441.8	1,397.4
1913	1,730.5	1,743.0

Source: *Die Habsburgermonarchie 1848–1918, Bd. I, Wirtschaftsentwicklung.* Wien 1973, p. 93.

The system of taxes and other state payments was created by a host of letter patents and regulations based on the need at any one time to top up the state coffers. These were often expedient regulations first issued for a transitional period, which then became embedded as a permanent part of the tax system. At the start of the nineteenth century, the tax system in Cisleithania comprised both direct and indirect taxes. Direct taxes were divided into personal (general earnings-based, publicly accountable corporate earnings-based, rent and interest, pensions and personal income, senior service, bartender) and property (land and buildings). Mining had its own special status. Indirect taxes comprised taxes on sugar, spirits, beer, kerosene, meat, wine, and excise duty (i.e., octroi: a local tax collected on articles brought into a district for consumption). The final amount of tax payable was often increased by hefty surcharges. In general, the tax burden in the monarchy was amongst the highest in Europe. Direct and indirect taxes will be examined in more detail below.

DIRECT TAX

The basis of the property tax was a land and building tax. Prior to the First World War, the revenue from property taxes was around 166 million crowns. The legal basis for the collection of personal taxes for almost the whole of the nineteenth century was a letters patent on earnings-based tax (*Erwerbsteu-*

erpatent) of 31 December 1812. Taxpayers were divided into four classes. The first was made up of factory owners, especially the holders of a provincial trade licence. The second comprised merchants, and the third artists and sole traders. The fourth class included service trades (subdivided into teaching, brokerage, and the importation of persons and consignments). Normal tax rates ranged from 2 florins to 1,575 florins a year. From 1859, a war tax surcharge was added.[60] In 1849, personal tax was joined by income tax (revenue tax), which also taxed earnings from dependent work and the ownership of capital.[61]

As regards personal taxes, the system at the end of the nineteenth century was being criticised for its obsolescence and the uneven distribution of the tax burden. A comprehensive overhaul of personal taxes was carried out under the terms of Act 220/1896, a regulation that replaced the fractured arrangements and renamed several taxes. Some of this tax was earmarked to be used to support small businesses and subsidise provincial finances. Businesspeople were subject to a universal tax on earnings if they did not receive a wage or salary and were not subject to any other personal tax. The tax was assessed on the basis of the economic success of the business, and this was derived from tax returns. The tax was quota based (the sum was stipulated in advance), with the proviso that the set quota was divided up between payers for each year. Taxpayers were divided into four classes on the basis of the last tax paid and their place of business. The total quota for the Czech lands rose by 7% between 1898 (9,029,628 crowns) and 1912 (9,647,107 crowns).[62]

INDIRECT TAXES

These taxes were designed as excise taxes and were applied to certain commodities, the range of which changed during the period under examination. However, in general it can be said that the range of taxed commodities increased. They would include sugar, spirit, beer, meat, kerosene, etc.

Both direct and indirect taxes were subject to surcharges (local taxes) destined for the budgets of self-governing entities. These included crown land (municipal, district, and provincial) and professional administrations (the surcharges of chambers of commerce and trade). The surcharges were usually in the order of tens of percentage points. The issuance of independent local taxes that were not surcharges required a crown land act. The municipalities usually collected a tax on dogs. The tax burden was also increased during a state of war, when wartime surcharges were applied. During the

---

60   Nevšímal, A. V. *Jaké a jak veliké jsou nové daně*. Praha, 1897, p. II.
61   Ibid., p. III.
62   Ibid.

First World War, there was a substantial increase in certain forms of personal tax and taxes on spirit. A new tax on war profits was introduced and selected charges increased.

The economic situation of the Czech crown lands is clear in the following table, which shows their share of direct and indirect taxes. While the direct burden of the Czech lands gradually decreased in 1841–1913 from 40.8%–32.9%, the share of certain indirect taxes doubled from 32.2% to an incredible 59.5%. It is clear from this that from the 1880s onwards the Czech lands collected more than half of the indirect taxes collected. A similar ratio applies to the yield on the tobacco monopoly.

Table 3: Regional development of income taxes (in %)

Direct taxes	1841	1850	1860	1870	1880	1890	1900	1913
A	19.0	21.5	23.1	27.1	27.4	30.5	35.4	40.2
B	35.2	37.6	37.3	40.2	40.9	45.6	48.9	52.6
C	40.8	43.1	44.5	41.9	41.3	37.5	35.5	32.9
D	15.5	13.1	12.7	12.1	12.5	11.7	10.4	9.2

Indirect taxes	1841	1850	1860	1870	1880	1890	1900	1913
A	31.6	29.6	27.4	29.8	21.0	23.3	14.0	15.5
B	47.5	44.6	40.6	40.2	28.8	30.9	20.4	21.6
C	32.2	35.1	40.1	45.8	62.6	49.5	63.0	59.5
D	15.5	15.1	15.7	10.6	6.4	17.6	13.9	16.7

A – Lower Austria; B – Alpine lands; C – Bohemia, Moravia, (Austrian) Silesia; D – Bukovina, Galicia

Source: Sandgruber, R. "Wirtschaftswachstum, Energie und Verkehr in Österreich 1840–1913," in: Kellenbenz, H. (ed.). *Wirtschaftliches Wachstum, Energie und Verkehr vom Mittelalter bis ins 19. Jahrhundert. Bericht über die 6. Arbeitstagung der Gesellschaft für Sozial- und Wirtschaftsgeschichte.* Stuttgart and New York, 1978, tab. 2, p. 82.

At the top of the financial system was the Ministry of Finance, to which all provincial financial authorities reported. Next in line were the district tax authorities, with departments for the administration of direct taxes. These oversaw the district financial authorities, with the revenue department or authority of the regional governorships looking after direct taxes, and regional financial authorities in larger lands and financial inspectorates in smaller lands looking after indirect taxes.

SOCIAL, DEMOGRAPHIC, ETHNIC, AND CULTURAL FOUNDATIONS

TRANSFORMATION OF THE SOCIAL STRUCTURE OF THE CZECH CROWN LANDS

The transition from a traditional society to a modern one is accompanied by a comprehensive transformation of the social structure. This process is often referred to as a society's decorporatisation (i.e., the transformation from feudal society to a class-based society). The standout criterion by which society is classified is no longer family origin and the rights deriving from privilege, but an individual's class within the framework of the economic system.

It should not be forgotten that several stratification criteria operate in every society. In the modern society of the nineteenth-century Habsburg Monarchy, these criteria included family origin, religion, gender, nationality, and class. In economic history, we are mainly concerned with class, though the other criteria should not be overlooked if the social status of the individual in a complex of social relationship is to be expressed accurately.

Social stratification has objective and subjective dimensions that do not overlap completely in ordinary life. The objective dimension refers to a quality ascribed from outside (e.g., being a manual worker receiving a wage, religion determined by parents at baptism, language indicating nationality, etc.). The subjective dimension relates to the degree of personal identification with this ascriptive quality. An individual displays the level of their identification by virtue of the degree to which they accept identical or different cultural models in their everyday lives. Take, for instance, the concept of a labour aristocracy: the best-paid, qualified workers would be categorised as being working class, but in their everyday lives they often follow bourgeois cultural models (clothing, how they spend their leisure time, an emphasis on education, etc.). Someone may be a baptised Catholic and yet not observe religious rituals and duties in their everyday lives. A maid in the service of a German patrician family may have been recorded in a census as speaking German, even though subjectively she felt Czech. And so on.

Social constructivists emphasise one more crucial incongruence between the objective and subjective dimension of social stratification. If we wish to describe the working class of the nineteenth century, it is not enough simply to statistically monitor the growth in the numbers of manual workers. No less important is understanding the experience of the actors we deem workers. Throughout the whole of the nineteenth century, it was by no means exceptional for workers to relate more to the sector in which they worked (building, glove-making, pharmacy, etc.) than their class. It is for this reason that historians still have doubts regarding the existence of a working class in the nineteenth century, or at least regarding the extension of such a class-based concept amongst wage earners. In addition, working-class identity as dreamt of by the Marxist social democrats of the day was undermined by other, sometimes more powerful feelings of group membership, primarily confessional and national.

There is yet another problem. The meaning of a particular concept often shifts dramatically during the course of history, and so two centuries ago actors might have understood the same word completely differently to the way we understand it. For instance, during the first half of the nineteenth century, the Czech word *fabrikant* referred to both factory owner and workers, since both were associated with the *fabrika* (factory), whereas these days *fabrikant* refers exclusively to a factory owner or entrepreneur. Similarly, a statement made by a Saxony industrialist in the 1840s to the effect that he employed at least seven working classes in his business now seems completely incomprehensible.

The traditional pre-modern society was above all a rural society, with a very low share of the population living in towns and cities (as late as 1830, only approximately a quarter of the entire population of the Czech lands lived in urban areas, most of these in small towns). At the top of the hierarchy of rural society, and usually some distance away, stood the landowning nobility, operating outside of the day-to-day life of the villagers. The aristocracy made its presence felt in such a world through the manorial bailiffs with whom the population came into immediate contact. The backbone of a village community consisted of the villeins who worked on the land. The better off were known as peasants, the less well off as cottagers, and the even poorer as small householders. The leaders of the municipality were recruited from the wealthier peasants and embodied in the council of neighbours (councillors), at the head of which stood the reeve appointed by the lord. We also know of cases in which the reeve was elected. As well as other manorial bailiffs, the reeve was the main broker between the nobility and the villagers. On the lowest rung were the cottars and menials working on the farms—that is, if we overlook the existence of the paupers that at that time were mainly old people, widows with children, orphans, and invalids. The village community included freemen (i.e., free peasant families such as millers), along with many craftsmen, tradesmen, and members of the intelligentsia (e.g., teachers, clerks, and the clergy). Their social status derived from their property and freedom. Yet more significant was whether a person worked with their hands or not. In a traditional village community, non-manual work had high symbolic value, and he who did not have to toil in the fields, cowshed or workshop was considered a master, regardless of his assets and income, which in reality might be quite low.

The status of the individual in such a society was determined almost exclusively by family background, gender, and age. In a traditional society, which changed very slowly, older people enjoyed a higher standing in the social hierarchy than we are used to in modern post-industrial societies. This was down to two factors. Firstly, older people were basically "rarer" in Europe's pre-modern societies, where the average lifespan was between thirty and forty years. However, this is to a certain extent a statistical distortion caused mainly by the high child mortality rates and not by the fact that most adults died without reaching the age of forty. Qualified estimates show that persons older than fifty were barely one tenth of the total population of the Czech crown lands during the second half of the eighteenth century. In this respect, the region did not differ significantly from the rest of Western and Central Europe.

Secondly, the relatively high standing enjoyed by older people resulted from the nature of the economic and social organisation. Pre-modern social systems changed very slowly, and so an individual died in a world that did not differ in any fundamental respect from that into which he had been born. Older people had experience that could not become obsolete and so were able to pass on valuable knowhow to the next generations.

During the nineteenth century, religion as a stratification criterion lost much of the significance it had enjoyed during the period after the Battle of White Mountain. A turning point in this respect was the Patent on Toleration (*Toleranzpatent*) issued by Joseph II on 13 October 1781, which made it possible for non-Catholics to *"buy houses and farms, to enjoy the rights of citizenship and mastership, to receive academic qualifications and to participate in civil service"* (Article 7). It did not entail complete equality, since in family law Catholics in particular retained many privileges, even after the adoption of the Civil Code of Austria (*Allgemeines bürgerliches Gesetzbuch* or ABGB) in 1811. Likewise, public manifestations by non-Catholics were limited by the patent (and the restrictions only lifted by the Protestant Patent of 5 April 1861). Nevertheless, as far as economic activities were concerned, religion no longer played a role, and this impacted the way an individual's social status was determined. In spite of the Patent on Toleration, the Czech lands remained Catholic. According to a census conducted in 1900, 96.6% of the population declared itself Roman Catholic: 96.2% of Moravians and as many as 98% of the inhabitants of Silesia with Czech as their vernacular.

In the case of the Jewish faith, even though enlightened absolutism in Austria never intended to go as far as in the case of other Christian confessions, even here a process of gradual emancipation was initiated. Jews obtained freedom of education (with the exception of theological faculties), access to the professions was opened up (with certain exceptions), and they were no longer forced to indicate their faith when outside the ghetto. On the other hand, a special Jewish tax remained in place and the marriage rate of Jews was kept low by artificial means under the terms of the *Familianten*, the laws regulating the number of Jewish families. Jews had to wait until the revolution of 1848 for civil equality. The state was even more repressive in relation to the Roma people, who, in the spirit of the Enlightenment, were encouraged to settle down and adopt the values of the majority.

However, the letter of the law was one thing, everyday life something completely different. Despite attempts at assimilation, Jews adopted a German, Austrian, and later a Czech, identity, which meant that the attitudes of the majority remained negative. Anti-Semitism did not disappear with the modernisation of society. If anything, the opposite was the case.

No less a chasm between the letter and spirit of the law is to be found in the case of another important criterion of status, namely nationality. The Renewed Land Ordinance of 1627 proclaimed the equal rights of Czech and German. The modern institutions that replaced it after 1848 guaranteed formal equality to all "national tribes" of the Habsburg lands. While Article 1 of the April Constitution of 1848 guaranteed "to all national tribes the inalienability of nationality and language", the December Constitution of 1867 expands on this principle and declares explicitly that "all national tribes have equal rights". However, ordinary legislation, especially that relating to education and the language to be used in official relations, retained the privileges of the German language and, by extension, of those who spoke it. Czech was an obstacle to promotion not only in the army or civil service, but to the higher rungs of society, and only the partial Germanisation of an individual could eliminate this handicap. This is why equality of language in official communication (external and internal) and the creation of Czech universities at which all tuition could be in an individual's mother tongue, so ensuring the spread of Czech influence throughout the higher rungs of society, was a central plank of the Czech nationalist programme.

An individual's standing in society was also determined by their gender. Notwithstanding the fact that eighteenth-century enlightenment philosophy had opened up the possibility of gender equality, in practice things were considerably different. The General Civil Code of 1811 explicitly subordinated women to men, took for granted their economic dependency, and in the sphere of the home regarded the woman simply as executor of her husband's instructions, while he, as head of the family, had a duty to represent the family in its relations with the authorities and to ensure it had enough to eat. The later Trade Regulation Act of 1859 speaks a different language when it declares that "there shall be no differences on the basis of gender in respect of pursuance of a trade", though married women required their husband's permission. Even so, very few women tried to set up their own companies in the nineteenth century and all such companies were involved

in what were at that time regarded as typical women's activities (e.g., the production of corsets). We more often find women helping out their husbands as
assistants in running a business or as widows and heirs of companies, even
though—formally, at least—a company had to be represented by a man. For
a woman from the middle and upper classes, paid employment was unthink-
able through almost the whole of the nineteenth century and would have
resulted in social stigmatisation.

The status of men and women was determined in the nineteenth century
by the ideology of separate spheres. The public sphere and professions outside the home were reserved for men, while women belonged to the intimate
domestic sphere, looking after the privacy of the family and the safety of
its children. The level of equality enjoyed by women differed considerably
depending on class. Women from an aristocratic background and the upper
classes inevitably enjoyed the greatest opportunities in society. Even so, they
were forbidden from pursuing certain activities. Under the Association Acts
of 1852 and 1867, they were forbidden from becoming members of political
associations, and during the introduction of universal suffrage between 1906
and 1907 they were explicitly excluded from the active exercise of electoral
law.

A crucial barrier to emancipation and the independent social mobility of
women was the inaccessibility of a formal education. Compulsory general
education was based on the principle of equality between boys and girls.
However, higher levels of education were characterised by discrimination
against women and girls, and it took a painfully long time to deal with this.
Upper schools for girls (the first was founded in 1860 in Písek, the most famous in Prague in 1863) were not yet traditional secondary schools and focused on the management of the family and domestic duties. From the 1870s
onwards, girls could study at boys' schools as private pupils, and starting in
1878 they could sit their school-leaving examinations (something like the
baccalaureate). In 1890, with the creation of the Minerva Girls' Grammar
School in Prague, a separate branch of secondary education for girls was created. Except for the very limited possibilities of studying abroad, access to
university for young women was only partially opened up in the 1890s. From
1896, women could attend the German University in Prague as observers, and
in 1897 the philosophical faculty of the Czech University opened its doors
to women (as regular students), as did the medical faculty in 1900. Unsur-
prisingly, technology and law remained inaccessible to women. Attitudes to
gender at that time regarded the humanities and medicine as better corresponding to the attributes of femininity, which was considered to be natural
for women.

Women's access to the labour market also differed considerably depending on social class. Only working-class women regularly received paid

employment and even then only prior to marriage. After starting a family, even employed women usually stayed at home, unless extreme financial difficulties forced them back to work. According to a survey carried out by the Liberec Chamber of Commerce in 1888, half of all female factory workers in the region were younger than twenty-two, and only 2% were older than thirty-one. In 1880, the factory workforce was made up as follows: women 34.4%, men 63.2%, and children aged up to fourteen 2.4%. The highest proportion of working women was to be found in the textile and food industries, and the lowest in engineering, construction, and metallurgy. Huge wage discrimination between men and women was the norm. Women's pay was on average around 60% of what a man earned. However, this figure fluctuated widely. The most favourable relative figures were reported by the textile industry, where wages were low compared to other sectors. Here, according to data from 1888, the average wage for women was just over 67% of a man's wage. In metallurgy this figure was barely 35%.

In traditional and early modern societies, income stratification took the form of a pyramid, with the base representing the poorer classes. Moving up the pyramid entailed fewer people and more wealth. During the era of high modernity, the number of people in middle-income groups rose, and during the twentieth century the pyramid was transformed into an onion, with relatively small numbers of extremely rich and extremely poor people, and the larger part of the population in the middle class. At the end of the eighteenth and beginning of the nineteenth centuries, the wealthiest classes (with assets exceeding one hundred thousand florins) were the richer aristocrats and top businesspeople, merchants, and bankers. The middle classes were made up of the lower aristocracy, civil servants, peasants, craftsmen, and larger businesspeople, merchants, and financiers. The annual income of this group was in the region of hundreds or thousands of florins per annum. The lower classes had practically no or very few assets and their annual income was perhaps dozens or hundreds of florins a year. This stratum would include the poorer craftsmen: cottiers, menial workers, journeymen. and domestic producers.

On the threshold of modernity, land was still the decisive factor in production, and because of this the bourgeoisie was more inclined to acquire land than seek business profits. Ownership of land was an important status symbol. In the eighteenth century, most land belonged to the higher nobility (62%). The church owned around 12%, the royal cities 10%, the lower nobility 8%, and the sovereign 8%. The domination of the upper nobility is particular to Central Europe, though it can be explained historically. After the Battle of White Mountain, the upper nobility was hugely diminished in terms of numbers in the Czech lands. Both waves of confiscations that followed in the wake of the battle led to the concentration of land in the hands of a relatively small aristocracy. Prior to the Thirty Years' War, there had been approximately six hundred knightly families in the Czech lands. By 1750, this figure was 190. The upper aristocracy was highly exclusive, as we see from the fact that during the eighteenth and nineteenth centuries, its members often refrained from marrying members of the new nobility. It enjoyed many privileges that shaped its exclusive social status: the right to use a nobiliary particle (e.g., von or de) and coat of arms, access to certain court authorities, and the establishment of fideicommissum, and later, in the era of constitutionalism, the right to sit in the House of Lords.

On a theoretical level, the internal structure of the bourgeois can be classified using several criteria. Firstly, we can identify the old middle class, business class and educated bourgeoisie (the *Bildungsbürgertum*). The old middle class represented the descendants of traditional bourgeois families involved in guild crafts or (local rather than supraregional) trade. Their mental horizons did not differ significantly from the rustic environment. Emphasis was placed on the self-sufficiency of the family and the continuity of its appreciating wealth. Conservatism and a distrust of innovation typical of this class. Their supreme goal was the purchase of a sizeable plot of land, since this represented security, and ideally the acquisition of a noble title. The expansion of their assets was not their main motivation, and they usually perceived investments in manufacturing or machine production as too risky a venture. The business bourgeoisie was recruited from the host of successful entrepreneurs of all kinds of origin who managed to establish and run a sufficiently large industrial or commercial enterprise. Expectations notwithstanding, the social status of the first entrepreneurs (unless they were aristocrats establishing manufactories or factories) was by no means clear. If they enjoyed success, the rapid expansion of their assets was viewed with suspicion by traditionalists, and generally speaking it was difficult for them to rid themselves of the stigma of being "workers". In early modern society, in which a lord was still someone who did not have to engage in physical work even though his income might be meagre, this stereotype was an important barrier preventing the first self-made men from improving their social status through business. The educated bourgeoisie was a social group that derived its social status from the prestige of qualifications achieved. Internally it was highly diversified and the sole common denominator was a higher level of formal education. The group included members of the liberal professions, senior civil servants, university professors, judges, etc. Whereas in neighbouring Germany the educated bourgeoisie compromised a relatively closed group displaying features of elitist exclusivity, empirical surveys of the Czech lands (e.g., Brno or Opava) show far greater openness and more frequent crossovers with other social groups (especially with the crafts and business bourgeoisie) by means of intermarriage.

Secondly, if we broaden our perspective to take in political and more general public activities (including associational activities and the like), then following the Bielefeld School we can divide the bourgeoisie into the core middle class (*Kernbürgertum*) and the peripheral middle class (*Randbürgertum*). Members of the first group were recruited mainly from the ranks of medium and large businesspeople and the educated bourgeoisie. This group was characterised not only by the high social status deriving from wealth or qualifications attained, but above all by its public activities in the form of the acquisition of direct influence on the management of the parish or town in which a family lived. Within the framework of the three-class franchise that operated in the municipalities of Cisleithania at the time of regional self-governance, we would find the members of this group mainly in the first and second electoral bodies. In contrast, the peripheral elements of the bourgeoisie (*Randbürgertum*) were concentrated in the third electoral body. This was a very heterogeneous group whose sole common denominators were lower assets and usually the acquisition of fewer educational qualifications. Its influence on the management of the parish was minimal and its social status substantially lower than that of the core bourgeoisie.

Thirdly, a division would be possible based on the level of assets and social status into upper, middle, and petty bourgeoisie. In Czech literature, this classification is the one used most often. The city-based upper bourgeoisie was made up largely of the larger entrepreneurs and the upper rungs of the educated classes. With the gradual commercialisation of agriculture and the deployment of capitalist production methods in rural areas, large farmers also joined the upper bourgeoisie in the latter half of the nineteenth century. Following the economic crisis of 1873, the group became more exclusive. The scramble to create industrial enterprises of the previous decade was peaking, and as a consequence it was far more difficult to introduce new industrial operations and generate the high profits that would guarantee entry to these social circles. The group of industrial large business owners was never very large. At the start of the nineteenth century, it was estimated to contain a total of between four and five hundred people in the Czech lands. At the end of the same century estimates place the number of owners of large companies (employing more than twenty people) at five thousand. However, given the boom in the equity ownership of large companies, this seems unlikely and it is likely that there were more of these significant shareholders. The middle bourgeoisie is not easy to identify. As well as owners of medium-sized companies, we find the technical and economic intelligentsia, whose role had grown firstly because of the need for specialist knowhow in production, and secondly because of the expansion in the managerial class necessary to run larger enterprises. In terms of cultural models, this group was highly heterogeneous. While the lifestyle of its most successful members mimicked that of the upper bourgeoisie that formed its reference group, it was difficult to distinguish its less successful members from the petty bourgeoisie. The petty bourgeoisie represented on the one hand owners of small companies employing up to twenty people, and on the other, individual small producers with no employees whatsoever.

The boundary between the bourgeoisie and the working class, though clear cut in the latter half of the nineteenth century, was not primarily based on assets. It was not unheard of for the standard of living of a member of the working class to be comparable with or higher than that of a less well off member of the petty bourgeoisie. The decisive distinction was symbolic: even the poorest sole trader felt superior to a worker because he was independent (i.e., he was his own boss), while the sign of a labourer was his dependent status within a system of production as a consequence of the wage principle. Generalising somewhat, we can say that during the latter half of the nineteenth century, the wealthier bourgeoisie represent not more than 10% of the population, the petty bourgeoisie up to 40%, and the working class and the destitute comprised the rest of the population.

The working class, too, was highly heterogeneous despite attempts by social democrats to promote a discourse of proletarian identity that would have bridged the categories separating the working class into particular, often mutually isolated groups, and create a more collective identity. Firstly, the working class was divided by sector, and an awareness of sector exclusivity often prevailed over an awareness of the solidarity of all manual labourers in a wage relation. Secondly, the working class was divided into skilled and unskilled, and the model of conduct of these two groups differed significantly. Unskilled workers were mainly recruited from new arrivals from the countryside (i.e., first generation workers). Skilled workers were recruited from the ranks of those who had previously been craft factory workers or even former masters in small-scale production, as well as from families who were descended from factory workers.

Horizontal mobility was typical in the case of unskilled workers. Driven by the profit motive, they moved between different industries and locations. They differed from the poor rural population by virtue of higher income that, as long as household resources were put to rational use, did not exclude the possibility of material betterment. Having said that, their savings quickly dissolved during times when they were unemployed, which in the case of unskilled workers was not simply due to the business cycle but to high levels of job churn. However, this very mobile group was particularly vulnerable during economic downturns, and when things were tough, unskilled workers often found themselves hitting the bottom amongst the destitute and beggars. This meant that women and mothers from these strata were also often to be found working. Migrating fathers were often unable to send money for long periods, and so the household required a second income. As far as cultural models were concerned, the maximization of material needs was valued the highest. Education, on the other hand, came bottom on the list of priorities. This was partly due to the fact that the pressure of work left parents with almost no time for their children, and it was not easy for individuals to break free from their class affiliations and move up within the social hierarchy.

Skilled workers enjoyed more stable employment, and this allowed for a more settled life. However, there were exceptions. Right up until the mid-nineteenth century, print workers, though a highly mobile labour force that regularly migrated across the length and breadth of Europe, enjoyed relatively high wages thanks to their expertise, and had a social status equivalent to specialist craftsmen. However, this was not the norm, and the group disappeared during the 1840s as a consequence of the introduction of machines that rendered their knowhow redundant. The most successful skilled factory workers, dubbed the labour aristocracy, usually kept their distance from the rest of the working class, preferring to adopt bourgeois values, including ways of dressing, better-quality accommodation, leisure time, an appreciation of education, etc. (the process of bourgeoisification or *Verbürgerlichung*).

Thirdly, the working class can be divided according to their place of work into factory workers, small-scale production workers, domestic workers, and agricultural workers, with these groups becoming the nineteenth century successors of the premodern retainers and cottiers. There were minimal links between these groups of workers, and this was reflected in political activism. The organised workers' movement was primarily a matter for factory workers, who were easiest to attract to the cause of social democracy. On the other hand, nationalist parties found support in small-scale production, which is undoubtedly related to the fact that more personal relationships existed between the employer and the employee (the literature sometimes speaks of patriarchal relations), and so antagonism between the two parties to an employment contract didn't reach the intensity that it did in factories. Agricultural workers, geographically dispersed, long remained poorly organised and politically inactive. There were also intermediate groups, difficult to classify, such as the peasant factory workers or the abovementioned domestic servants. A peasant factory worker worked in a factory, but unlike the urban proletariat, also owned agricultural land in the countryside, albeit of a minimum acreage. Nevertheless, this plot of land provided a natural top-up to his wage. The urban factory workers often regarded this group as unfair competition, since its members could afford to offer their labour for a lower price. Homeworkers engaged in piecework were located on the border of self-employed and dependent workers. They were similar to self-employed workers in that they usually owned some of their means of production and as a rule their place of work. However, they were dependent on the sale of their labour to businesspeople (i.e., their suppliers), and so were more like labourers. Many pieceworkers were active in the textile and glass industries. Their standard of living was usually below that of skilled factory workers.

According to statistics from 1915, leaving aside agriculture, half of the working class worked in factories, a third in small-scale production, and just under a fifth of wage earners were dependent homeworkers.

At the bottom of the stratification pyramid were the unclassified, beggars, and the clients of poorhouses. It is difficult to piece together a more precise statistical picture of these groups. In 1830, there was apparently one beggar per 200 inhabitants and one pauper per 25 inhabitants. At the end of the nineteenth century, between 1% and 2% of the population was accommodated in poorhouses. A more accurate calculation of the number of beggars cannot be made, not even using the statistics of those convicted of vagrancy, since not every vagrant was convicted and not every vagrant was a genuine beggar. They were often migrating unemployed who in practice, however, were difficult to distinguish from professional beggars. In addition to its philanthropic dimension, the care of the poor was also an important stratification criterion. It created a group of second-category citizens who did not enjoy full civil rights. When universal suffrage was introduced in 1906–1907 for men, clients of poorhouses were explicitly excluded from this right. Under an amendment to the Right of Domicile Act of 1896, it was possible, after ten years of living continuously in a place, to apply for residency. However, the act excluded people who had lived in a poorhouse during that period.

Membership of individual economic sectors was also a stratification criterion. This is examined in greater detail in another chapter of this book.

DEMOGRAPHIC AND ETHNIC DEVELOPMENTS

Favourable developments meant that at the start of the eighteenth century it was possible to make good the considerable losses incurred during the course of the Thirty Years War. Demographic developments were extensive, with high unregulated birth rates and high mortality rates influenced by wars, epidemics, and crop failures.

Developments were greatly influenced by the plague of 1713–1714, the disease, hunger and famine of 1736–1737, the War of the Austrian Succession, and the Seven Years' War and famine in 1771–1772. These conflicts, which impacted very differently on both a regional and local level, led to the spread of different infections, a decline in agricultural production, the disruption of market relations, and a sharp rise in the price of cereals.

The absolutist state supported population growth, since mercantile and populationist theories (e.g., those of Johann Heinrich Gottlob von Justi and Josef von Sonnenfels) regarded it as a prerequisite for economic growth and greater power. A demographic upsurge increased the capacity of the internal market (i.e., the number of consumers and the labour pool), and had important military implications.

Table 4: Annual population increase in the Czech lands (1754–1810) in percentages

	1754–1780	1780–1790	1791–1800	1801–1810
Bohemia	9.4	10.2	4.6	3.8
Moravia and Silesia	7.3	7.7	2.5	3.6
Czech lands	8.6	9.3	3.9	3.8

Source: Srb, V. *1000 let obyvatelstva českých zemí*. Praha, 2004, pp. 24–25.

From the 1830s to the 1890s, the demographic cycle was characterised by a balanced birth rate and a fluctuating mortality rate, with surges in 1855 and 1866 along with smaller increases in 1872–1873 and 1877–1878. From the 1830s onwards, the population grew steadily and evenly, falling from the 1850s because of the emigration of significant numbers from the Czech lands to Vienna and beyond the borders of the monarchy. This period saw a new population structure take shape in the Czech lands.[63]

The northern regions enjoyed economic and demographic growth, while the south suffered economic stagnation and mass emigration. The new industrial centres reported the highest rate of growth: in central Bohemia (the Prague-Kladno region), South Moravia (Brno and environs), Moravia-Silesia (Ostrava), North Bohemia (Teplice-Most), and West Bohemia (Plzeň and Falknov-Karlovy Vary). These centres were swamped by new arrivals from agricultural regions. In terms of settlement density, factory-produced textile production ran a close second to the most important centres in North Bohemia (the regions of Liberec, Tanvald, Děčín, and Šluknov), West Bohemia (Aš, Kraslice), certain parts of Northeast Bohemia and North Moravia, and Silesia-Opava and Nový Jičín in North Moravia. The old centres of textile production, which were unable to master the transition over to machine production, stagnated and were subject to deindustrialisation (the south Podorlicko Lowlands, the northern Bohemian-Moravian Highlands, and part of the Jeseník Region). The population of the lowlands of the Labe (Elbe) region and the Moravian Vale grew faster than in the old textile centres. In the industrial and agricultural regions of South Bohemia and Southwest Moravia, which lagged behind the rest, the population grew slowly, and some regions even underwent slight depopulation (the region of Central Vltava [Moldau] and

---

63   For more details, cf. Jindra, Z., Jakubec, I. et al. *Hospodářský vzestup českých zemí od poloviny 18. století do konce monarchie*. Praha, 2015, pp. 115–122.

Southwest Bohemia). While textile regions involved mainly in mass production reported low marriage and birth rates and high infant mortality, agricultural regions and new industrial centres were characterised by limited
birth rates, relatively high mortality rates, and lower infant mortality rates.
The agrarian crisis of the 1880s and 1890s set in motion a wave of outgoing
migration from the countryside that saw the depopulation of South Bohemia,
the Central Vltava Region, and the Bohemian-Moravian Highlands.

The new industrial centres continued to exert an attraction, especially
the coal basins (Ostrava and Teplice-Most) and the emerging metropolises
of Prague and Brno. After a period of slow growth in the 1870s and 1880s, the
textile regions experienced a new surge at the end of the century, though
they did not attain the population levels of the new industrial centres such as
those in North Bohemia (Liberec-Jablonec), West Bohemia (Aš, the southern
Ore Mountains, Krušnohoří/Erzgebirge), North Bohemia (Děčín), East Bohemia (Trutnov, Hradec Králové, and Náchod) and Silesia (Opava). The other
textile regions suffered a population decline and emigration (Jeseník, the Podorlicko Lowlands / Lower Adlergebirge, the northern Bohemian-Moravian
Highlands and part of the Podkrkonoší Lowlands / Lower Riesengebirge).
The agrarian crisis of the 1880s and 1890s set in motion a wave of outgoing
migration from the countryside that saw the depopulation of South Bohemia,
the Central Vltava Region and the Bohemian-Moravian Highlands. The 1870s
marked the beginning of a gradual drop in birth and mortality rates that sped
up at the end of the century. Healthcare improved and epidemics became
a thing of the past. Only in the lead-up to the First World War did the drop in
birth rates appreciably outstrip the drop in mortality rates and the natural
population growth slow down.

In the last quarter of the nineteenth century, the mortality rate began
to fall. This, coupled with a drop in birth rates in Western and Central Europe, culminated in the transition from the old demographic model to the
new. From 1867–1910, the population of Cisleithania rose from 20 million to
28 million (in Transleithania the rise was from 15 million to 21 million). At
the start of the twentieth century, barely a quarter of women got married
before the age of twenty-four, while in Central and Southern Europe around
a third were already married by this age. As regards type of family, during
the eighteenth and nineteenth centuries the Czech crown lands followed the
populations of Western and Northern Europe. The western system of inheritance with a sole heir predominated. The biggest shift in the population of
the Czech lands took place in the last third of the nineteenth century and
involved migration from the countryside to industrial centres and abroad.
From the 1830s onwards, between two and three people out of every thousand
left the countryside, more Czechs than Germans, because there was enough
work in the industrialised border regions inhabited mainly by Germans. An

imperial patent of March 1832 permitting immigration did not affect people with military, financial, and legal obligations. Migration both within and without the monarchy was of an individual character. Approximately one-third of the increased numbers of people departed for another region of the monarchy or abroad. Early on, popular destinations were Lower Austria and Vienna, later including the USA, Canada, and Brazil. It is estimated that prior to the First World War 1.2 million people from the Czech lands lived beyond their borders, of which 750,000 settled in the western part of the monarchy, 40,000 in the eastern part, 90,000–110,000 in Saxony, 70,000–110,000 in Prussia, 30,000 in Russia, and 184,000 in the USA. At the turn of the nineteenth and twentieth centuries, based on colloquial speech (*Umgangsprache*), it seems that 100,000 members of the Czech population were based in Vienna. Unofficial estimates put the figure higher, at between 400,000 and 600,000. Vienna was regarded as the Czech land's largest city.

From 1869–1910, the proportion of the population active in agriculture dropped by 14.2%, while it rose in industry by 6% and in commerce and transport by 5.5%. The biggest change was recorded in agriculture and industry in Silesia (down by 16.7% and 8.3% respectively), and in commerce and transport in Bohemia (down by 5.9%).

Table 5: Proportion of the population of the Czech lands active in individual sectors in 1869

	Agriculture, forestry, fisheries	Industry	Commerce and transport	Miscellaneous
Bohemia	50.73	30.76	3.21	15.30
Moravia	57.14	25.23	2.82	14.81
Silesia	51.80	31.06	2.35	14.79
Total	52.29	29.16	3.03	15.52

Source: *Přehled československých dějin, díl II/1, 1848–1918*. Praha, 1960, p. 198.

Table 6: Proportion of the population of the Czech lands active in individual sectors in 1910

	Agriculture, forestry, fisheries	Industry	Commerce and transport
Bohemia	36.60	36.80	9.10
Moravia	45.80	30.10	7.10
Silesia	35.10	39.40	8.10
Total	38.90	35.20	8.50

Source: Lacina, V. *Hospodářství českých zemí 1880–1914*. Praha, 1990, p. 88.

From 1819–1869, the population in the western region of the monarchy rose by 47.7%, and between 1870 and 1910 by 38%. High marriage ages, low marriage rates, high birth rates, and high mortality rates characterise agrarian societies (i.e., the old demographic model). To begin with, there was a divergence of the two tendencies (i.e., gradual mortality and the retention of approximately the same high birth rate with an excess of new-borns). From the end of the nineteenth century onward, both trends converge, and there was a long-term decline in birth rates to the point where these demographic values were perfectly balanced at the end of the interwar period. During the first half of the nineteenth century, we see irregular population growth of 1% interrupted by famine, epidemic, and war, while from the middle of the century onward there is stable growth of 0.8%. The Alpine and Czech lands reported the lowest increase. From 1857–1910, average per-annum growth in the Czech lands was 0.69% and in the Alpine lands and the Austrian Littoral 0.82 %, while in the Carpathian lands the figure was 1.03%. In addition, this region reported the highest rate of emigration. From 1869–1910, the population density increased from 68 to 95 persons per km^2. In the Czech lands, Vienna, Trieste, and certain parts of Galicia, this figure was as high as 120 people per km^2. The urbanisation process in Cisleithania was such that while in 1870, Vienna and Prague, where 5.2% of the total population lived, had populations in excess of 100,000, at the end of the nineteenth century, the number of large cities had risen to seven, with these cities containing 10.8% of the total population.

The birth rate oscillated between 33 and 39 per 1,000, and it was only from the 1870s onward that it began to fall. In comparison with Western Europe, this is still high. Similarly, from 1850–1910 the death rate fell from 32.9 to 21.2 per 1,000. There was a natural increase in the population of between 6.8 and 11.9 per 1,000. During the 1850s, men tended to get married between the age of 30 and 40, whereas at the start of the 1860s this figure had dropped to 24–30. Most women were married by the age of 24, with some leaving it as late as 30.

In the mid-nineteenth century (1843), the vast majority of the population of the Czech lands (81.7%) lived in communities of up to 2,000 people. By 1910, this figure had dropped considerably (57.9%). During the middle of the nineteenth century (1843) only 3.7% of the population lived in settlements with a population in excess of 10,000, while by 1910 this figure had increased to almost one-fifth of the population (18.7%).[64]

The ethno-linguistic composition of the population of the Czech lands is shown in the table below. Official Austrian statistical surveys recorded vernacular speech (i.e., the ability to communicate with those around), but not ethnicity. A slight increase in Czech ethnicity is evident in Bohemia and

---

64   For more details, see ibid., pp. 127–130.

Table 7: Largest towns/cities in the Czech lands (1830–1910) in thousands

Bohemia	1830	1869	1890	1910
Prague	102	158	182	224
Královské Vinohrady (now part of Prague)		5	34	77
Žižkov (now part of Prague)			41	72
Nusle (now part of Prague)		2	12	31
Smíchov (now part of Prague)	2	15	33	52
Liberec	11	22	31	36
Cheb	10	13	19	27
Kutná Hora	10	13	14	16
Plzeň	8	24	50	80
Ústí nad Labem	2	11	24	39
České Budějovice	8	17	28	44
Pardubice	4	8	12	20
Most	3	6	15	26
Teplice	2	10	18	27
Jablonec nad Nisou	3	7	15	30

Moravia	1830	1869	1890	1910
Brno	36	74	94	126
Jihlava	15	20	24	26
Olomouc	12	15	20	22
Ostrava	2	8	19	37
Přerov	4	7	13	20
Prostějov	8	16	20	30

Silesia	1830	1869	1890	1910
Opava	14	17	23	31

Source: Horská, P. a kol. *Dějiny obyvatelstva českých zemí*. Praha, 1996, p. 397.

Moravia, as well as in Austrian Silesia, where the Czechs were a minority. The Jewish population is to be found mainly within the German population (in terms of vernacular language) and to a lesser extent the Czech population. Apart from the borderlands, people of German ethnic origin are to be found in larger town and cities. As industrialisation proceeded, people of Czech ethnicity relocated to the industrial border regions (e.g., to Most in North Bohemia) and the composition of nationalities changed.

Table 8: Ethno-linguistic composition of the population of the Czech lands (1846–1910)

Bohemia	1846		1880		1910	
	absolute	in %	absolute	in %	absolute	in %
Czechs	2,598,774	59.77	3,470,252	62.78	4,241,918	63.19
Germans	1,679,151	38.62	2,054,174	37.17	2,467,724	36.76

Moravia	1846		1880		1910	
	absolute	in %	absolute	in %	absolute	in %
Czechs	1,253,320	70.23	1,507,328	70.41	1,868,971	71.75
Germans	496,492	27.65	628,907	29.38	719,435	27.62

Austrian Silesia	1846		1880		1910	
	absolute	in %	absolute	in %	absolute	in %
Czechs	93,561	20.08	126,385	22.95	180,348	24.33
Germans	222,616	47.77	269,338	48.91	325,523	43.90
Poles	146,870	31.52	154,887	28.13	235,224	31.72

Source: Kořalka, J. Češi v habsburské říši a v Evropě 1815–1914. Praha, 1996, tab. 13, pp. 140–142.

Apart from Russia, Austro-Hungary was the largest state in Europe. In terms of population it ranked second after Germany (leaving aside Russia). The Czech lands represented a quarter of the territory of Cisleithania (26.44 %), of which Bohemia accounted for 17.32%, Moravia 7.41%, and Silesia 1.72%. The Czech population was one-third of Cisleithania as a whole (35.29%), of which Bohemia accounted for 23.50%, Moravia 9.14%, and Silesia 2.66%.[65]

CULTURAL FOUNDATIONS

If industrialisation was to happen, it needed a skilled workforce, and this applied as much to technologists and civil servants as it did to labourers and farmers. Although the latest findings in science and technology were taught in primary school (*Volksschule*), polytechnics and technical schools became increasingly important. The industrial classes (studies) introduced by Ferdinand Kindermann von Schulenstein (1740–1801) in 1777 introduced modern findings pertaining to the crafts and farming to the primary school on a region-by-region basis (classes in textile, lacework, fruit growing, beekeeping, forestry, fisheries, etc.).

---

65   For more details see ibid., pp. 130–134.

Table 9: Austro-Hungary in 1914

Land	Capital city	Area in km²	Population
Bohemia	Prague	51,947	6,860,000
Moravia	Brno	22,222	2,667,000
Silesia	Opava	5,147	776,000
Czech lands total	—	79,316	10,303,000
Lower Austria	Vienna	19,825	3,635,000
Upper Austria	Linz	11,982	864,000
Salzburg	Salzburg	7,153	221,000
Styria	Graz	22,425	1,468,000
Carinthia	Klagenfurt	10,326	406,000
Carniola	Ljubljana	9,954	530,000
Austrian Littoral	Trieste	7,969	938,000
Tyrol with Vorarlberg	Innsbruck	29,285	1,130,000
Galicia and Lodomerien	Lviv	78,497	8,212,000
Bukovina	Chernivtsi	10,441	818,000
Dalmatia	Zadar	12,831	668,000
Cisleithania total	Vienna	300,004	29,193,000
Hungary	Budapest	282,870	18,811,000
Rjeka	Rjeka	20	49,000
Croatia and Slavonia	Zagreb	42,521	2,670,000
Transleithania total	Budapest	325,411	21,530,000
Bosnia and Hercegovina	Sarajevo	51,200	2,076,000
Austria-Hungary total	Vienna	676,615	52,799,000

Source: Österreich-Ungarn 1914, Freytag-Berndt & Artaria, Wien.

During the latter half of the nineteenth century, a network was formed of technical and vocational secondary and tertiary educational institutions focusing on technical subjects and modern languages. After the Bonitz-Exner reforms of 1849, the traditional eight-grade gymnasium or grammar school was joined by the *Realgymnasium*, a type of secondary school representing a compromise between the *Realschule* and traditional grammar school and focusing on science, maths, modern languages, draughtsmanship, and design.[66]

First off, the economic (i.e., agricultural) schools were divided into farming, upper economic and economic-industrial, and higher economic studies

---

66   Efmertová, Marcela C. *České země v letech 1848–1918*. Praha, 1998, pp. 346–347.

(academies). In 1884, these became schools of agriculture, winter schools of economics, secondary schools of economics, and upper provincial economic institutions. In the Czech crown lands, there were 52 farming schools at which Czech or German was the language of instruction, five secondary schools of economics with Czech as their official language, and one upper provincial economic institution with Czech tuition and one with German.[67]

Secondary vocational education was provided by industrial schools, *Real-schule*, and business schools, where teaching was conducted in both Czech and German. The first Czech industrial school was opened thanks to the efforts of Jan Evangelista Purkyně in 1857 in Prague. The transition between secondary vocational school and polytechnic was the work of mining academies (in the Czech lands the academy in Příbram, which became a university in 1904).

In the latter half of the eighteenth century, a genuine attempt at combining university and technical education was made. At the Philosophical Faculty of Prague University, alongside teaching in the technical and economic spheres, positions were created to teach mining sciences (1763–1772) and arable farming (1775–1812). There was a tradition of technical training in Prague. The Professional Engineering School (Stavovská inženýrská škola) had been established as far back as 1707. For almost thirty years (1787–1815) the centre's engineering professorship was linked with the Philosophical Faculty.[68]

At the start of the nineteenth century, Professor František Josef Gerstner submitted plans to reform technical education. His proposal suggested dividing studies into two departments, chemistry and maths, "to which technical subjects would be added in each of the three years".[69] Based on Gerstner's successful proposal, polytechnics were created in Central Europe in Graz (1814, originally only offering classes in science), Vienna (1815), Nuremberg (1823), Berlin (1824), Karlsruhe (1825), Dresden (1828), Kassel (1830), Hannover (1831), Stuttgart (1832), Augsburg (1833), Braunschweig (1835), Darmstadt (1835), Zurich (1855), etc.

In Moravia, technical education was provided by the Moravian-Silesian Professional Academy (Stavovsko-moravsko-slezská akademie) in Olomouc (1724). In 1849, a German technical school (Technische Lehranstalt) was established in Brno (1849), transformed in 1873 into an institute of technology (Technische Hochschule). The Czech Polytechnic in Brno (Česká vysoká škola technická) was only established in 1899 as an expression of the emancipa-

---

67 *Ottův slovník naučný*, vol. 6, Praha 1893, pp. 203–204.
68 Efmertová, Marcela C. "Technické (odborné) školství a další vzdělávací a vědecké instituce", in: Jindra, Z., Jakubec, I., et al. *Hospodářský vzestup českých zemí od poloviny 18. století do konce monarchie*. Praha, 2015, p. 92.
69 Ibid., p. 93.

tion of the Czech technical intelligentsia. It offered comprehensive tuition, especially in the humanities. In 1869, the Prague technical school was divided into Czech and German counterparts.

Universities for agricultural science and commerce were located in Vienna: the Hochschule für Bodenkultur (1872) and the Exportakademie (1898).

After Latin gradually fell out of favour as the language of the sciences at the end of the eighteenth century, it initially seemed only logical that German should take its place in the Czech lands. As the finishing touches were being put to Czech literary language, the way was opened to utilising it to exchange information in the sphere of science and technology. The scientific community was also important in terms of transferring economic, technical, and agricultural innovations. The Prague linguistically Utraquist (bilingual) Royal Bohemian Society of Sciences (Královská česká společnost nauk) (1773/1774) was joined in 1890 by the Czech-language Czech Academy of Franz Joseph I of Science, Letters and Arts (Česká akademie Františka Josefa I. pro vědy, slovesnost a umění), and a year later by the German Society for the Advancement of German Art, Science and Literature in Bohemia (Gesellschaft zur Förderung deutscher Wissenschaft, Kunst und Literatur in Böhmen).

Like the scientific societies, specialist societies established a tradition in the eighteenth century that flourished during the nineteenth century. The Society of Ploughing and Free Arts in the Kingdom of Bohemia (Společnost orby a svobodných umění v Království českém), founded in 1769, was transformed in 1788 into the Bohemian Patriotic-Economic Society (Vlastenecko-hospodářská společnost) in Prague. As well as opening schools for economic civil servants, the society attempted to improve the breeding of livestock (sheep) and arable farming, and to promote the development of hop growing and beekeeping. In general it aimed to encourage progress in farming. A similar organisation was the Moravian Economic Society (Moravská hospodářská společnost), which was founded in Brno in 1770, followed a year later by the Silesian Economic Society (Slezská hospodářská společnost).

Economic and industrial trade fairs can be regarded as the emancipation of Czech industrial products. The exhibition of industrial products made in the Czech crown lands held in 1791 at the summer refectory of Prague's Clementinum, on the occasion of the coronation of Leopold II as King of Bohemia, was the precursor of many such exhibitions during the following century. The highlight of this tradition included the Central Land Centennial Exhibition or Prague Jubilee Exhibition (Zemská jubilejní výstava) in 1891, and the exhibition of architecture and engineering of 1898. The latter was accompanied by technical attractions (the Křižík electrified light fountain, the Petřín lookout tower, cable cars, electric trams, air shows, etc.). The exhibition was visited by 2.5 million people.

2. DEVELOPMENT OF THE PRIMARY SECTOR: AGRICULTURE

THE PERIOD UP TO 1848

The Czech lands retained their agrarian character right up to the onset of industrialisation, and even then, farming and the processing of its products played an important role in the economic structure of the region. More people continued to work in agriculture than in any other sector, though their numbers continued to fall right up to the start of the twentieth century. The basic impulse for changes in farming practices was linked to the development of the internal market (i.e., a growing population needing to be fed), and the development of industry (raw materials).

The biggest changes to farming practices took place towards the end of the eighteenth century. Nevertheless, the King of Bohemia, Holy Roman Emperor Charles VI (1711–1740), continued to make changes to the state policy regarding the serfs, moving from a position of indifference, which left a free hand to the aristocracy, to a more active protection of the peasant population from the capriciousness of their masters. Under the influence of the Enlightenment, agrarian reform moved up the agenda and resulted in real economic progress. After the last major uprising in Bohemia in 1775 (in the towns of Broumov, Smiřice, and Náchod), the Statute Labour Patent was issued in the same year for Bohemia (13 August) and Moravia (7 September). Duties were set forth in more detail, depending on the size of a given farm. The serfs were divided into eleven categories by property, from those who did not own land and did not pay tax but laboured for 13 days a year, to peasant farmers paying 42 florins 45 kreuzer per year who laboured three days per week with a team of horses, and one person on foot working a statutory three days per week (May to September).

Maria Theresa's first attempts to remedy feudal relations involved administrative reforms. The starting point and an important component of these endeavours was a reform of the tax system. This resulted in the first Theresian cadastre (1748–1756) and the second Theresian cadastre (1757). Both of these were inventories of serf-tended land. The Theresian cadastre of 1757 recorded the manorial demesne. The distribution of taxes was uneven. The serfs paid about 50 percent more than the nobleman (the peasant farmer was to deduct around one-third of gross yield in tax). Maria Theresa also made a stab at land reform, and these reforms continued under Joseph II. On 1 September 1781, letters patent were issued governing jurisprudence as it pertained to the serfs (the prohibition of punishment without prior interrogation), and on 1 October of the same year a patent was issued on the abolition of serfdom (personal bondage, vassalage, serfdom, and peonage or *Leibeigenschaft*), followed by many imperial regulations. The patent guaranteed personal freedom; freedom of movement, relocation, and marriage; and freedom to offer a child a craft and the opportunity to study. Upon leaving an estate, the serf was issued a release letter (letter of manumission or affranchisement), and in the event of leaving the country he had to find a suitable substitute or he might be returned and punished. Financial obligations, benefits in kind, and the duties of a bondman remained in force. At the same time as the patent on the abolition of serfdom, a patent was issued relating to the purchase and ownership rights of serfs to property. Peasant farmers could freely dispose of property in their ownership.

Agricultural production in the Czech lands only attained the level it had reached prior to the Battle of White Mountain at the start of the eighteenth century. Up until the middle of the century it remained unchanged. Only in the eighteenth century and later were new strains cultivated, such as clover (to begin with, in Brabant) (1788 Lednice) and alfalfa (1794 Hostěnice), along with industrial crops such as potatoes and sugar beet. Potatoes spread during the "hungry years" of 1771–1772. The increase in demand for crops on the part of the textile crafts saw a rise in the sowing of flax and hemp, as well as the cultivation of the silkworm at the end of the eighteenth century. The middle of the century saw a change to livestock feed. Green fodder was used to a greater extent, to be joined at the end of the century by the waste from industrial potato and sugar processing plants. Within the monarchy, Bohemia and Silesia were the largest wool producers. In 1848, a third of all sheep in the monarchy were to be found grazing in the pastures of the Czech lands.

The traditional three-field system forming the basis of agricultural production underwent important changes and was gradually replaced by crop rotation. The importance of crop rotation was that the most suitable precrop was selected for each subsequent crop and no crop was planted twice in succession. New sowing procedures originated in Flanders and were then perfected in the county of Norfolk in the east of England in the mid-seventeenth century as the Norfolk four-course system: 1. wheat 2. turnips 3. barley 4. clover (or undergrass). From Norfolk the system crossed the English Channel to France and thence to the rest of Europe. Eventually, the process was narrowed down to: 1. clover 2. wheat 3. root crops. Simply put, fallow land in the new system ceased to be the main regenerator of soil fertility and its function was replaced by better fertiliser, better cultivation of the land, and improvements to the composition of crops in the sowing process. This was especially so in the case of fodder plants, mainly red clover and, where suitable, alfalfa, which allowed for the soil to be better aerated and supplied with nitrogen and ensured sufficient green fodder for cattle in the summer and dry feed in the winter. This unprecedented boom in crop production was hugely beneficial to cattle breeding. During the first half of the nineteenth century the cultivation of sugar beet was associated with the new sowing system, firstly in Central Bohemia and later in other convenient locations. In the crop rotation system, the main role was played by root crops and cereals, especially wheat, which produced the highest yields.

The introduction of crop rotation was broadly linked to the development of the agrarian sciences and farming technology. And so, for instance, the land for sowing sugar beet by machine had to be better prepared, and the same demands were made by grain sowing machines. Improved ploughing equipment reduced the number of ploughing operations. Perhaps the real standout progress was made in the harvesting of cereals, with reaping machines first making an appearance in the larger farms at the end of the 19th century. Improved cultivation techniques included the introduction of the deep plough, better soil preparation prior to sowing, machine sowing, extensive fertilisation using manure, and the introduction of fertilisation equipment. As a result, crops were denser and stronger. Improved crop breeding, especially of sugar beet, potato, barley, rye, and oats, must also take some of the credit for the successful application of crop rotation. Regional varieties of cereal gave way to new, refined strains that were more intensive and demanding on growth conditions.

One positive outcome of this new system was increased production capacity at large farms. This was aided by, among other things, the relatively generous financial compensation offered for the release of serfs from their obligations under feudalism. In terms of organisation and production, the manor farm demonstrated the advantages of agricultural production, since it could avail itself of technical progress and new technology. Because it was well capitalised, had professional management, and a large enough area of land to enable the improved utilisation of technology and labour, it could more easily put new management systems and the latest technology into practice. Around the mid-nineteenth century, the manor farm rightfully became the centre of economic progress. During the first industrial revolution, when capitalism was entering the agricultural sector, it was the aristocratic manor farm that was the driver of new progressive directions in agriculture. Several members of the nobility living and working in the Czech lands were ahead of their time in terms of economic perspective, social conscience, opinions, and actions, though they were sometimes misunderstood or rejected. However, their efforts and results won them supporters and followers. The landed nobility, driven by the desire for both wealth and more advanced agricultural equipment, either visited other countries themselves or sent their financial advisors, agricultural specialists, and teachers on study trips. Thanks to them, the Czech lands became acquainted with improved machines and technology, scientific findings, specialist literature, and more advanced economic thinking. In consequence, the manorial farms were the first to introduce new sowing procedures, intensive crop farming, machine fertilisation, soil drainage (see below), new farm machinery and tools, and specially bred crops and animals.

After the abolition of serfdom in 1781, the agricultural sector gradually regained its strength. The landed nobility dealt with the developments affecting their estate by renting out plots of land, replacing payment in kind for bonded labour with cash benefits, setting up industrial enterprises, and reorganising their own practices. The much-anticipated liberalisation of agriculture, increasingly supported by the state, made it possible to sell agricultural products at higher prices and thus to raise cash for the fundamental transformation of the economy.

The manorial farm played an important role in all of this. Naturally, among the aristocrats settled in the Czech lands, there existed differences in wealth and sophistication, as well as ambiguous feelings as regards nationalism, and so it would be appropriate to recall the composition of the nobility prior to the revolutionary year of 1848, since it remained in this form, with minor changes, right up to the First World War. The Czech lands were home to the old upper pre–White Mountain aristocracy (e.g., the Czernin family of Chudenice, the Wratislav family from Mitrovice, and the Sternbergs, Choteks, Waldstein-Wartenbergs, etc.), along with new families who arrived after the Thirty Years' War, such as the Piccolomini, Trauttmannsdorf, Buquoy, Clary-Aldringen, and Desfours families, as well, of course, as the South Bohemian Schwarzenbergs and many others. Both of these groups were consanguineously related, and individual families enjoyed an important, albeit changing, status in the provincial government or at the Viennese court. Of these aristocratic families, the largest ones, based on the number of serfs they owned, were as follows: Schwarzenberg, Waldstein-Wartenberg, Clam-Gallas, Lobkowicz, Kinsky, Trauttmannsdorf, Auersperg, and Harrach (the last three settled in the Czech lands after the Thirty Years' War), and the Czernin family of Chudenice. In the eighteenth century, these aristocratic families were joined by others seeking refuge from the French Revolution and other revolutions breaking out over Europe, such as the Rohan, Beaufort-Spontin, Schaumburg-Lippe, Hohenlohe-Sigmaringen, and Schönborn families, as well as the nouveau riches of bourgeois origin (e.g., the Nádherní, Veith, and Geymüller families) who had been elevated to the status of nobility. One could argue that power in the country was divided between several esteemed aristocratic families, especially the Clam-Gallas, Thurn-Taxis, Colloredo-Mannsfeld, Lichtenstein, Dietrichstein, Harrach, and Windischgrätz families. However, a unique status and extraordinary power was enjoyed by the Třeboň and Orlice branches of the Schwarzenbergs.

During the latter half of the eighteenth century, several progressively minded aristocratic farmers, as well as the Viennese government, became aware of the necessity of boosting agricultural productivity. In addition to the reforms of Emperor Joseph II, the efforts of the Austrian absolutist state focused on supporting science and education, especially in the sphere of agriculture. In 1771, Prague University created a chair of agriculture (arable economy), though during the post–White Mountain period, the first agricultural experts had already been contributing to both the theory and practice of agriculture (e.g., the learned Jesuit Christoph Fischer [1611–1680]). And so following the model of other European countries and upon the instigation of Empress Maria Theresa, the Society for Ploughing and Free Art in Bohemia (Společnost pro orbu a svobodné umění v Čechách) was formed in 1769 and renamed the Patriotic Economic Society in the Kingdom of Bohemia (Vlastenecko-hospodářská společnost v Království českém) in 1789. The society, whose members included the leading scholars of the day, attempted to improve the individual activities of agricultural production. Prior to 1848, the Patriotic Economic Society played an irreplaceable role in the development of agriculture. It operated in many different ways, depending on the resources and abilities of the farmers it assisted. For instance, at the start of its existence it had an important influence on the development of the flax industry. It also improved sheep breeding and the breeding values of livestock, encouraged the propagation of new crops (clover, potatoes, sugar beet, rape, and later maize), introduced crop rotation, improved plant nutrition, introduced stable breeding, monetised products, introduced new tools, and paved the way for experimentation and research.

These endeavours were manifest, for instance, in the introduction of new crops: clover, alfalfa, hybrids, potatoes, and sugar beet. The Napoleonic wars led to a hike in the price of agricultural products, which allowed for a smooth transition over to the three-field system and later to the introduction of crop rotation (which will be discussed in more detail later). During the wars, the sugar industry underwent huge changes. At the start of the nineteenth century, beets acquired the name "sugar" (from the German *Zuckerrübe*). Sugar beet was grown both for the production of sugar (technical sugar beet) and as feed (fodder beet). During the first half of the nineteenth century, sugar beet was mainly grown in Kolín, Čáslav, Plzeň, and Tábor. The sector was given a boost, inter alia, by Napoleon's ban on imports of sugar cane from abroad.

Before 1848, agricultural tools had not undergone any serious development in the Czech lands. Nevertheless, the country was responsible for making remarkable improvements to two types of tool, thus contributing to the technical development of agriculture on a European level. From 1774–1778, Josef Wunderlich revolutionised the operation of the grain-sowing machine. This involved a line-sowing machine with cylindrical sowing unit and a common storage chamber for seed. To begin with, the fourteen-line machine was mounted on two wheels and later on a rigid frame on four wheels. It was only at the end of the 1820s that Karel Kročák in Černovice, Brno, made the first single-line beet-sowing machine. Significant progress was also made in improving the main tilling tool, the plough. In 1827, two brothers named Václav Veverka (1790–1849) and František Veverka (1799–1849) from Rybitví near Pardubice built a new plough with a cylindrical cutting blade (ploughshare) known as the turning plough. The Veverka brothers achieved this by making on-going technical improvements to a tool known as the Hradec Králové hook.

In 1821–1830, the drop in the price of farm produce after the Napoleonic Wars was exacerbated by a precipitous slump in the price of cereals of between 30% and 50%. The market price of animal products fell only slightly. According to Georg Norbert Schnabel, in 1846, 34% of cultivated arable land in Bohemia was given over to rye, 27% to oats, 16% to barley, 11% to wheat, 6% to root vegetables (including potatoes), and 2% to flax and hemp. From the mid-nineteenth century onwards, the difference became increasingly obvious between the barren and fertile regions of the Czech lands, especially those in proximity to the emerging industrial centres (the Labe/Elbe region, the Lower Ohře/Eger region, and the Upper Morava Vale). Prior to 1848, the transfer over from bonded labour paid in kind to financial payments continued most rapidly in Moravia (approximately 75%–80% of the total number). However, not all feudal obligations were removed.

THE PERIOD LEADING UP TO THE FIRST WORLD WAR

THE SIGNIFICANCE OF THE ABOLITION OF SERFDOM

Under a law passed on 7 September 1848, serfdom was abolished in the Czech lands, thus fulfilling the wishes of the peasant folk. Not only serfdom, but all rights of the nobility over the serfs were abolished, and this eliminated the difference between demesne (the land retained by the lord of the manor for his own use) and serf tenures (the plot of land occupied and tended by serfs but owned by the lord of the manor), and the liens were lifted from all fiefs. The law declared everything in rem rights, services, payments in kind, and in cash, applying to all fiefs, whether they ensued from servitude or from the noble's ownership rights or any other legal dominion of the lord over his vassals, to be abolished. For the sake of comparison: in Prussia, serfdom was abolished in 1807; in Tsarist Russia in 1861. Prior to their liquidation, the patrimonial (bailiff) authorities were faced with an extraordinary amount of work consisting of the removal of feudal encumbrances. The outcome of this complex activity was an extensive and complex balance sheet, and the feudal obligations were divided into the following three categories:

(1) Obligations ensuing from servitude, which were redeemed without compensation.
(2) Obligations and benefits from peasant land, for which the lord of the manor was not entitled to full refund but to fair compensation.
(3) Obligations and benefits from the manorial land for which the lord was entitled to full compensation.

Complex principles were set forth in detail governing the estimates of discontinued benefits, wages, and labour for which the lord was to receive compensation. A third of the resulting amount was deducted as an equivalent of the tax that the nobles paid from their urbarial benefits and for arrears. The remaining two-thirds was paid to compensate the nobles so that the serf himself paid half (i.e., a third of the total estimated price of the abolished encumbrances), which was recorded to the debit of the peasant farmland in land registers. The other half was to be paid by the lord of the land. The estimated price was capitalised twenty times over. Half of this capital was then entered on the settlements of the former serfs as a mortgage debt that they were obliged to repay within approximately twenty years in the form of annual instalments not levied by the former lord but paid to the state treasury in quarterly instalments. The other half, taken over by the province, was to be redeemed by annual repayments within forty years at the latest.

At this point the serf's dependency on his lord came to a definitive end. However, his economic links continued. Even after the abolition of bonded labour and serfdom, these legal relationships between the freedmen and the nobleman were governed legislatively through the offices of the state.

After 1848, several provisions restricting a peasant's right to a farm remained in force from feudal times. However, in 1859, with the fall of Bach's neo-absolutism, the shackles of political life were loosened and the demand was increasingly heard for the full and free divisibility of rural farms. Only with the advent of the provincial laws issued in Moravia in 1868 and Bohemia in 1869 was it stipulated that every farm owner was entitled to dispose freely and without official permission of his freehold.

In 1889, a framework law was issued that, inter alia, stipulated the rules pertaining to the distribution of inheritances in the case of medium-sized freeholds. However, of the three historical lands, the implementing regulation was only published in Bohemia in 1907. Under its terms, medium-sized freeholds were deemed to be those whose net cadastral yield was a minimum of 100 crowns and a maximum of 1,500 crowns and that covered at least five hectares of agricultural land. As regards which of the joint heirs should inherit the farm, the act stipulated that if the testator left more than one survivor, the male heirs took precedence over the female, and in the case of the same gender, the older took precedence over the younger.

THE DAWN AND DEVELOPMENT OF CAPITALIST AGRICULTURE

It was inevitable that the revolutionary year of 1848 should impact agricultural production and commerce, since with the relaxation of the rigid feudal system and its economic relations a space opened up for capitalist enterprise, which was based on the free market and wage labour. This brought progress and benefits overall. Capitalism began in England and France in the late seventeenth and early eighteenth centuries, gradually spreading into other countries.

The method and duration of the removal of the feudal system depended on the political and economic circumstances of the country in question and how advanced its system of production was. In 1848, the level of agriculture in Europe was patchy. Most advanced were the western countries, where capitalist practices had begun early. As well as certain parts of France, the whole of the Netherlands, Flanders, and Northern Italy, England had the most advanced agriculture at the end of the eighteenth century. The commencement of capitalist practices was linked to the migration of the rural population to industrial centres, the disappearance of small farmers, and the gradual consolidation of the tenant system of farming. The greatest power was held by the landowners (landlords), while the largest group comprised small farmers, farmworkers, and tenants.

What developments did agriculture in the Czech lands undergo, and what specific influence did capitalism have? Essentially, capitalism developed via the "Prussian road" of agrarian development (i.e., through the transformation and evolution of the feudal estate into a capitalist system that retained traces of feudalism). The manorial farms retained their structure while moving into a capitalist social system and mode of production. The following types of manorial farm existed in the Czech lands: (a) the chamber (or crown imperial), the income from which belonged to the lord; (b) the manorial farms of the secular nobility; (c) ecclesiastical estates; (d) the farms belonging to towns and institutions. The manorial farms of the secular nobility were divided into the *fideicommissum* and the *allodium*. As regards the *fideicommissum* or fiduciary estates, under the law all the assets were passed down to the first-born (the primogeniture, majorat, or seniorat). The aim was to maintain economic and political power by preventing the aristocratic family's estates from being split up. For instance, in Bohemia at the end of the eighteenth century there were 58 fideicommissa with 220 farms and approximately 583,732 hectares of tended land (of which 64% was woodland). And then there were the allodial estates, or independent freeholds.

The switchover from feudal to capitalist estate did not take place without significant organisational changes. These took various forms, depending on the stage of development of the estate and its economy in the production sphere in question, as well as whether the landowner participated directly in the management of the farm (i.e., under the emerging capitalism of a "modern" agricultural enterprise). What was important was that the structure of the organisation and management of production took on a completely different form. The management agenda was no longer based on the old politics of the lords of the manor and judicial power, but instead was based on agricultural production and forestry management. The estate director managed a certain number of farmsteads (latifundia had more than ten, each with an average of one hundred to two hundred hectares of agricultural land). What had been an inflexible, centralised form of management gave way to decentralising tendencies, allowing officials in the farmsteads to take the initiative. The director and administrators managed all production divisions. Some estates also employed foreign experts who designed and implemented changes that had proved expedient abroad or introduced new farming methods. The principles of the market and financial economy of emerging capitalism began to make their presence felt in the management of large estates, and this meant better records needed to be kept.

The economic and political status of the peasantry changed considerably under capitalism, which brought relief from feudal oppression and benefitted, at least initially, the life and working conditions of the former serfs. It created new, favourable conditions for rapid improvements to production even in peasant farms. However, it was not capable of resolving satisfactorily the social standing of the peasant and his relationship with the land. The question of land became increasingly urgent in all ownership categories, since all parties had an interest in acquiring more and more. At the same time, new discoveries and inventions that increased productivity were being used even in small-scale peasant production. This sphere too was influenced, though not to the same extent as the large estates, by the improved cultivation of the land, breeding practices, plant hybridisation, and improved technology and mechanisation. These facts were reflected in economic prosperity. With higher sales of farming produce, market-linked agricultural production increased far more rapidly than previously. At the same time, rapidly expanding industry and transport increased construction activities in villages and helped the development of agriculture.

The social composition of a Bohemian village in the latter half of the nineteenth century displayed considerable diversification and variability. The most common setup was a farm with up to two hectares of agricultural land. At the end of the nineteenth century, 48.3% of settlements were of this type. Farms with up to 0.5 hectares accounted for 15%, and farms with between one and two hectares 18.9%. Almost all of these farms were family based. They possessed only the most rudimentary technology (the most common equipment being cutters and a simple machine for cleaning and sorting grain). They tended not to be self-sufficient, with almost half of the farms supplementing their income from agriculture with wage labour or cottage production. Most farmers with less than two hectares would sublet land, and only 40% of them worked on their own land. During the next stage in the differentiation of the peasantry, the number of these agricultural enterprises increased.

Another group comprised small-scale peasant freeholds, with between two and five hectares of land. In the period under examination, this group represented almost 25% of all such enterprises. The overwhelming majority were family farms, 8.5% of which employed a permanent workforce and 5.4% a seasonal workforce. This group had better equipment. On average, sixty-four out of a hundred of these enterprises used machines (sowing machines, graders, and hay tedders, in addition to cutters). However, many enterprises had only one machine. These farms often suffered from a lack of land, with only 40% of owners tending their own land.

As well as peasant smallholdings, the category of farms with between five and ten hectares included medium-sized farms in the most fertile regions practicing intensive agriculture. Such holdings were capable of supporting a family and during fruitful years even generating a surplus. Most were family based, though more than 25% employed a permanent workforce and almost 8% resorted to seasonal labour. This was a well-equipped category, with more than one machine in regular use.

Farms with between ten and twenty hectares were borderline. Some were owned by medium-sized peasant farmers, while others, especially those in fertile regions, were run by affluent farmers. Fewer of them were family based, though twice as many employed a permanent workforce.

Yet another group comprised farms with between twenty and fifty hectares. These belonged to wealthy farmers and landowners who employed both permanent and seasonal workforces. The family members of crofters and small farmers often worked for them in order to pay for the loan of machines, animal traction, and other services. These farms were best equipped with steam and later electrically powered machines.

Farms with between fifty and one hundred hectares were capitalist agricultural enterprises, of which only 2% were family based. Such farms even employed supervisors and clerks. Almost two-thirds of them used highly efficient technology. The last category listed in the statistics involved agricultural enterprises with more than one hundred hectares of land. These were capitalist estates measuring up to 250 hectares and even larger aristocratic latifundia. All of these businesses employed clerks, foremen, and specialist personnel, and production activities took place without the active involvement of a businessman or nobleman. Approximately 70% of the large estates were fully mechanised.

However, in terms of land held, it was the aristocratic latifundia (estates with more than one thousand hectares) that predominated. At the end of the nineteenth century, 1% of farmers owned almost 30% of all land in the Czech lands. The nobility secured political power in the burgeoning capitalist system mainly by its active participation in public and political life.

What this meant was that, during what was known as the *balancing*, which lasted until roughly 1866 in the Czech lands, aristocratic and other large estates acquired enormous capital from 578,341 persons valued at 56.93 million florins of conventional currency, which was distributed amongst 22,062 persons and corporations, of which 1,231 were former manorial estates. The table below shows that from 1756–1896 the demesnes decreased by 5.3% and the peasant smallholdings increased by 5.3%, mainly at the expense of municipal property. Interestingly, the largest category of peasant land to increase was arable, while in the case of manorial estates, the amount of arable land decreased.

Table 10: Share of peasant land and the land of large estates in the Czech lands, 1756–1896

Annual average	Peasant land in %	Large estate land in %
1756–1757	57.1	42.9
1839	58.5	41.5
1861–1872	62.7	37.3
1896	62.4	37.6

Source: Lom, F. "Československé zemědělství od roku 1848." *Věstník Československé akademie zemědělské* 15 (1939): p. 10.

So the manorial estates began to operate intensively under their own management on stretches of what was usually the best land offering the highest yields and rent. They usually let out the poorer quality land and then, in an effort to acquire some of the differential of the rent, reclaimed it from tenants after it had been cultivated and improved. The process of the concentration of land in the hands of the manorial estates in capitalist fashion continued gradually, and as stated above, was accompanied by a growing fragmentation of peasant farming and thus an increase in the number of smallholdings with a surface area of up to five hectares. The development of capitalism in agriculture is bound up with the changes underway in individual land cultures (i.e., arable land, meadows, gardens, vineyards, and pastures). The fragmentation of peasant farming, exacerbated by the debts incurred because of the *balancing*, was hastened by the lack of cheap credit, an overall increase in capitalist land rents, and a rise in the price of land, which became ripe for speculation on the part of banks. The development of capitalism in agriculture contributed to the regional specialisation of agricultural production.

THE CRISIS IN AGRICULTURE

From the 1840s onwards, the intensity of agriculture as a whole increased sharply. However, the development of capitalist agriculture brought with it unexpected problems. Recurring economic crises caused by overproduction slowed the capitalist boom in agriculture. After the wave of economic upswings beginning in the 1840s, Europe became subject in 1873 to its second protracted agricultural crisis, and the Czech lands were no exception. The crisis was preceded by an industrial, commercial, and banking crisis. Though previously agriculture had suffered crises brought on by wars and natural disasters, this new kind of crisis was hitherto unknown, arising mainly because of overproduction and other economic factors. The integration of the Czech lands into Europe and later the global market meant that the country's industry suffered the consequences of the global economic crisis that had erupted in the USA several years previously. In 1878, the economic crisis was superseded by an agricultural crisis caused by a surplus of grain production in non-European countries. This, along with other agricultural products imported by cheap shipping and rail transport, began to compete strongly with European grain.

In the Czech lands the agrarian crisis unfolded in two stages, the first lasting from 1873–1878, and the second from 1879–1904. The first phase was not as intense and was related to a more general crisis caused by an overheated economy. The symptoms of the crisis in agriculture were caused by the partial decline of the disproportionately developed agricultural sector, a widespread drop in the purchasing power of the population at large, and by years of poor crop yields. The beginnings of the long agrarian crisis were mitigated at the end of the 1870s and the start of the 1880s by a boom in sugar beet and potatoes wrought by an upswing in the fortunes of the sugar industry and distilleries, as well as by an overall revival in other branches of industry. After the crop failure of 1882 and the subsequent importation of cheaper Hungarian grain, the second phase of the agrarian crisis intensified. The price of bread, wheat, and rye fell twice as much as the price of barley and oats. This was most evident in the case of wheat, which offered its growers the highest profits. Livestock husbandry was affected to a far lesser extent. The price of beef and butter fell during the worst phase of the crisis in the mid-1880s, but not by much, and otherwise the price of meat rose. Livestock production enjoyed a boom during the crisis, since by expanding this sphere large farmers and landowners ameliorated the consequences of the crisis, as grain production had became almost unfeasible and unprofitable. A characteristic of the second phase of the agrarian crisis was the outbreak of a beet crisis as a consequence of a severe sugar crisis in the mid-1880s. The entire cultivation of plants was affected and, driven by the beet crisis, peaked around 1894–1895.

Agriculture was forced to adapt to the consequences of the crisis in the Czech lands. There was a shift from plant cultivation to livestock farming, and more fodder plants and industrial crops were grown. Several manorial farms increased soil fertility by means of irrigation, empty land was turned into pastures, respect was paid to natural conditions when modifying the structure of crops, and above all more attention was paid to the management of agricultural enterprises and livestock farming. Milk production was boosted and more attention was given to ground cattle feed and to expanding the ratio of feed crops when sowing. The crisis saw the creation of many sugar refineries, distilleries, starch plants, and other processing plants, and agricultural joint-stock companies were also affected. Above all, production was rationalised. The large estates, especially in fertile regions, were better able to adapt to the changed conditions and ride the drop in profits than small farms. Indeed, during the crisis, several of them industrialised their operations, since they were in a better position to avail themselves of mechanisation than other plants.

The crisis did not really affect the standard of living of the large farmers, while the peasant farmers were hit hard because they lacked capital resources and reserves. Almost all categories of the peasantry found themselves burdened with high-interest loans. During the last quarter of the nineteenth century, debt spread through the agricultural sector. It is estimated that around one hundred thousand farms were served warrants of execution, repossessed, and resold in the Czech lands, and at the start of twentieth century farmers were in debt to the tune of approximately three billion crowns. The agrarian crisis led to the partial depopulation of the countryside and migration abroad, especially amongst the poorest regions of the Czech lands.

When reaching any kind of definitive assessment of the development of agriculture during the period under consideration, the following facts should be taken into account. From 1848–1914, the volume of agricultural production expressed as grain units per hectare increased in the Czech lands by almost 100%. Not only did the consumption of cereals increase, the price of which rose up to the end of the 1870s, but also that of root crops and all kinds of meat. Supplying a growing non-agricultural population forced the industry to make fundamental changes, increasing the area of arable land and moving from extensive to intensive forms of production. Livestock farming, usually a stable sector, also underwent dynamic development. From 1846–1869, the production of beef per capita increased by 50.4%, pork by 24.3%, and milk by 34%. During the second half of the nineteenth century, the production of beef almost tripled and the production of pork rose even more sharply. One should not overlook the significant increase in the production of pork and milk from 1869–1900, which resulted from the development of livestock production during the crisis. The development of livestock farming had a knock-on effect on dairy farming, which for peasant farms entailed processing milk and butter for an ever-expanding and more accessible market thanks to developments in the transport sphere.

AGRICULTURAL PRODUCTION

From 1848 onward, agricultural production was influenced by the internal market in conjunction with the increase in the population. Production needed to be increased, and yet the old three-field system was unable to meet the demand for higher yields in plant and livestock production. It was therefore supplanted by crop rotation. New cultivation techniques and economic systems were introduced, and production technology was improved. Agriculture also experienced its own technical revolution, which is examined in greater detail below. In the second half of the nineteenth century, the second stage of the technical revolution in agriculture began, with the arrival of more powerful machines. However, developments were not identical in all spheres. The new technology was immediately taken up and exploited by the large estates, which had sufficient funds to purchase it thanks to the abolition of serfdom. After centuries of operation, the three-field system was gradually rationalised and wasteland was sown with fodder and root crops, later with imported potatoes, and from the start of the nineteenth century with sugar beet. First the large estates and then peasant smallholdings replaced the improved three-field system by crop rotation. Greater efforts were made to adapt to the natural conditions than before. Regions that were more suitable for production were expanded, and the imprint of agriculture was felt everywhere. Areas specialising in sugar beet, potatoes, hops, grain, cattle, etc. came into being. Other specialisations were created that did not have a direct relationship with the natural character of the landscape but were based on the sensibility of breeders and growers. These included nurseries, winemaking, beekeeping, and livestock farming.

Other new production technologies were reflected in working practices that were often mutually supportive. For instance, the large estates attempted to refine basic materials such as feed, fodder, litter, and manure. Greater care was devoted to preparing land for sowing, cultivation, and harvesting. Harvesting at farms and estates required machine work and greater traction power. A highly productive force involved new methods of land reclamation (drainage by way of underground canals and irrigation) and artificial fertilisers, which were used to a greater extent at the end of the nineteenth century than they had previously. Crucial to the development of agricultural production was the creation of greatly improved farm buildings, providing better conditions for the breeding and utilisation of livestock.

CROP PRODUCTION

The development of crop cultivation as the basic activity of agricultural production also affected livestock production and land rent. From the end of the eighteenth century onwards, crop production underwent significant changes resulting in a transformation of the farming system. It was split into several specialisations (grain, beet, potatoes, and fodder), which impacted on each other. The ratio of industrial plants such as rape, potatoes, barley, chicory, and flax grew significantly, and interdependence on the emerging food processing industry increased.

The Czech crown lands remained the granary of its neighbours. In Bohemia, grain trading centres were established that supplied the neighbouring regions. Such centres were located in Prague, as well as Kutná Hora, Mladá Boleslav, Jičín, Hradec Králové, Litoměřice, Liberec, Chomutov, Plzeň, České Budějovice, and Jindřichův Hradec. It is worth briefly noting the status of individual types of grains. The climate of the Czech lands was best suited to rye. The largest harvests of rye were in the Labe/Elbe region, especially the surrounding areas of Hradec Králové, Brandýs nad Labem, Slaný, and Žatec. Though rye had been very popular, by the time we reach the period under examination here, almost no varieties were known. The most highly prized cereal was wheat, which symbolised the wealth not only of individuals but of entire regions. Even though wheat required more heat and care than rye, farmers used all the resources at their disposal to expand its cultivation. They were motivated by the higher demand and the higher prices that wheat commanded. It was cultivated almost everywhere, aside from certain mountainous regions. Barley was ranked alongside wheat and rye. It was used in the brewing industry as well as by poor people during lean times. It had been grown from earliest times as a spring and winter crop. Best known was Haná-Prostějov flax, which given the right choice of variety, good fertilisation, and proper inclusion in the sowing system, guaranteed good quality and high yields. The last of the main group of cereals was oats, which had been an important foodstuff from the Middle Ages right up to the first half of the nineteenth century in poor mountainous regions, since oat flour was used to make bread and oatmeal. Oats then lost their appeal somewhat, though regained their importance in modern farming because of the quantities of grain needed to feed livestock, above all horses.

It is worth noting the data on the harvesting of cereals. The most important benefit was that overall yields increased. For instance, from 1848–1930, wheat yields rose by 150% (in the case of potatoes, this figure was 470% and even higher for sugar beet). The intensity of agricultural production was manifest most in an increase of yield per hectare, which almost until the eighteenth century had remained on the same level but doubled from 1848–1914. The development of average yields in the latter half of the nineteenth century is shown in the following table.

Table 11: Average yields of the main crops in the Czech lands

Crop	1801–1850		1870–1879		1894–1904	
	q/ha	Index	q/ha	Index	q/ha	Index
Wheat	11.0	100	12.1	110	14.1	128
Rye	9.5	100	10.8	114	11.4	120
Flax	9.0	100	11.0	122	14.1	157
Average of cereals	8.0	100	10.1	115	12.3	140
Sugar beet	150.0	100	175.0	117	252.0	168
Potatoes	50–100	–	72.0	100	84.3	117
Clover	20–30	–	25–35	–	28–40	–

Source: Beran, Z. "Krmivová základna v soustavě českého zemědělství 1750–1938." *Prameny a studie.* 11 (1978): 61, 81.

The growth in yields during the 1880s and 1890s undoubtedly resulted from the spread of artificial fertilisers, mechanisation, and the utilisation of agro-biological findings, most apparent after 1900. These innovations applied to regions growing both beet and cereals. Relatively high yields in mountain regions where crop rotation was still infrequently used required a focus on livestock production and a forage-oriented fodder base, and this was in turn reflected in the yields of cereals. The ratio of cereals to total crop production within the context of the agrarian crisis gradually fell. The areas sown with grain dwindled, while flax flourished.

As well as wheat, barley, rye, and oats, small amounts of millet were also grown that required a warmer climate. Millet served as a tasty food for the preparation of millet purée. It was grown most in the Labe/Elbe region. Greater quantities of maize began to appear, which had previously featured in manorial farms or as an ornamental plant. Maize was most appreciated in autumn, when other green feed was lacking. The grain family also included buckwheat, which required warmer climes and a light soil, and was therefore not as popular.

Protein-rich legumes retained their place in crop production and the nutritional requirements of humans and animals. They occupied an important place in cultivation techniques, and as a typical fallow crop they played a role during the transition from old sowing procedures to crop rotation. The most popular and widespread were peas and lentils, as well as vetch and beans sometimes cultivated as feed, and green beans from earlier practices. Other legumes such as lupin beans, sweet peas, and soybean were rarely grown. Certain species of legume persisted in the foothills thanks to sheep breeding. In more barren regions, they provided an abundance of pastureland and in winter served as a more nutritious straw and grain for feed.

From the mid-nineteenth century onwards, clover became more popular, and more attention was paid both to its seeds and to protecting it from pests. As the most important forage crop, clover was most highly valued by farmers and beekeepers. Before clover, alfalfa was known in Central Europe and the Czech lands as a domesticated plant. Of the root crops, potatoes and sugar beet were the most important. Potatoes came from South America and different species were grown from wild potato or other strains. The potato arrived in Europe at the end of the sixteenth century and was grown in small quantities only in the gardens of aristocratic estates. It was still not deemed a delicacy but was more of a curiosity. From the 1870s onwards, potato seedlings from imported varieties were cultivated in the Bohemian-Moravian highlands, and after the First World War farmers began successfully cultivating domestic varieties.

Besides potatoes, sugar beet was very important. It was already being grown as fodder at the time of the three-field system. In the Czech lowlands alone, around two-thirds of the country's sugar beet was grown in what was in 1890 approximately 17.7% of the arable land, producing yields twice as high as cereal crops as a whole. It was at this time that the optimum possibilities for cultivating sugar beet in terms of yield, sugar content, and technological quality were defined, and so it was cultivated in the natural sugar beet regions. The best conditions were medium, deep clay soil with a neutral to slightly alkaline reaction, good aeration, and good water capacity. The culture and cultivation of sugar beet had a significant impact on the intensity of agriculture in the nineteenth century. The crop required better tillage and fertiliser, and aided the development of the sugar refining industry and the nascent agricultural machinery sector.

The new social and economic relations impacted positively on the cultivation of special cultures, especially hops. Around the 1880s, the cultivation of hops on rods came to an end and use of the Žatec trellises, a world-famous construction for growing hops, spread rapidly. Another important change was the artificial drying of hops by heating, firstly on slat boxes and later on specialist driers. These improvements to the production process were matched by developments that took place in the sphere of the tools and machines used in hop gardens. Most hops were grown in the classic hop growing regions of Bohemia (Žatec, Rakovník, Litoměřice, and in certain parts of Česká Lípa and Mělník). Faced with this competition, the small hop gardens that had been attached to breweries gradually disappeared and new cultivation techniques and farms and manorial estates became the focal points of hop production. Hops continued to be an important agricultural crop only in regions with the most advantageous conditions. Hop growing areas expanded up to the end of the nineteenth century. In 1890, they accounted for approximately ten thousand hectares, though the figure subsequently fell somewhat. In order to protect the individual strains of the Bohemian hop, it was patented.

As far as fruit growing is concerned, this period saw both the number of fruit trees and the range of varieties increase. Fruit growing became highly specialised and only the most suitable varieties were grown in individual regions.

More vegetables were grown too. At the end of the nineteenth century, vegetables were grown over approximately thirty thousand hectares of the Czech lands. However, this area continued to spread, especially around larger towns and spa centres. Certain regions were already known for their vegetables, such as Žatec (cucumbers and turnips), Mělník (onion and garlic), Jičín (cabbage and cauliflower), the warmer regions of South Moravia such as Znojmo, Břeclav, and Kroměříž. The most popular vegetable was cabbage, though other high quality vegetables were also being grown (e.g., celery, carrots, kale, and turnips). These were slowly joined by leeks, spinach, and lettuce, along with tomatoes, peppers, and radishes, and foreign varieties began to make an appearance. The industry was extremely labour intensive.

Plant grading and protection saw improvements to crops. Most newly grown varieties arrived in the Czech lands from the West, but spread rapidly. Czech experts began to focus their attention on crop protection and the fight against weeds.

LIVESTOCK PRODUCTION

Livestock production, which is not directly dependent on the climate and the operation of which is more continuous, is organically linked to plant production. Developments in agriculture only really created suitable conditions for improving livestock breeding and increasing production as late as the latter half of the nineteenth century. The introduction of crop rotation resulted in a close link being established between crop cultivation and the breeding of livestock. A new concept of cattle breeding predominated based on rational foundations and drawing on foreign experience. For Czech cattle breeders, what was most important was the efficiency of dairy and meat production, since the population, and consequently the demand for foodstuff, had been growing during the latter half of the nineteenth century. From 1850–1900, cattle breeding was characterised by a greater number of animals being reared and an attempt to improve dairy and meat yields and to achieve breeding consolidation. Breeding circuits were gradually created in Bohemia and Moravia and breeding stations constructed under professional supervision. In 1871, the Czech Livestock Studbook was established. Cattle breeding benefitted greatly from imports of Alpine cattle, as well as imports from Switzerland, and less frequently from England.

A characteristic of this period was a rise in the volume and intensity of livestock production. For instance, plant production in Moravia during the last three decades of the nineteenth century increased in volume by 87% and in value by only 37%, while the volume of livestock rose by 164% and its value by 204%. The situation was similar in Bohemia. Though the intensity of livestock production rose unevenly in terms of region and individual category of farm, it rose steadily per unit of agricultural land. An important point to note is that these favourable indicators were achieved more by increasing the numbers of farm animals regardless of the actual possibilities of the feed base at the time, and less by means of an increase in average yield.

The quality of cattle was defined by size and live weight. Milk yield was average and the fat content good. On average a cow weighed 400–500 kg and an ox 500–700 kg. Cattle were predominantly mottled red in colour.

Unlike in the past, pig breeding, especially in sties, spread. This applied especially to smaller peasant farms, less so to large estates. During the first half of the nineteenth century, the most popular breed was the Old Bohemian Bristleback. This was a breed known for its fertility and resilience and its strong constitution, though it was late to mature. In the early 1850s, imports of foreign breeds began. The large manorial estates were especially keen on the English Yorkshire pig, and the expansion of the rail network saw cheap Mangalica imported from Hungary and later, pigs from Galicia. Pig breeding was the main source of income for the small peasant farms that predominated in the structure of agricultural holdings.

Sheep farming was still successful in the first half of the nineteenth century. During the 1840s, approximately 40% of heterogeneous hybrids were found on the large estates. In later years it declined in importance and the number of sheep fell over the decades. This was mainly to do with the disappearance of the three-field system and the importation of cheap wool from abroad, which saw the fall not only of the price of wool but also that of sheep. However, goat farming continued to grow in popularity throughout this period, both on small peasant farms and in suburban regions. The original primitive breeds were maintained and the number of goats rose almost threefold over sixty years.

Horse breeding was linked not only to the needs of agricultural production, but also to military and transport requirements. After a slight decline in the number of horses in the 1840s, numbers began to rise again, and this trend continued right up to the end of the century. Imported breeds also featured. The number and ratio of horses to livestock in general was largest in the most fertile regions, where plant production was at its most intensive.

Poultry farming became more and more important but remained restricted mainly to smaller farms. Its expansion was partly down to the regional and provincial breeders' associations and, from the end of the nineteenth century onwards, breeding stations and institutes.

The development of livestock production was linked with other activities that we will examine in brief below. In the livestock sector, it was believed that the quality of a breed was dependent on purity, and this gave rise to the conviction that purity was a guarantee of yield. Throughout this period, cattle were crossbred with imported breeds in an effort to increase the weight of the cow. In the 1870s, two-breed, correctional breeding and composite breeding techniques expanded. The degree of success achieved differed according to both individual breeds and whether they were grown on large estates or peasant smallholdings. More attention was given to fodder, and feed obtained from arable land (clover, root crops, the waste obtained from beet, and the production of beer and spirits) was prioritised. To begin with, fodder was administered in batches, and later the production batch was specified at 1/30 of the live weight of an animal. Finally, at the end of the 1870s normative nutritional batches were introduced in which the ratio of nitrogenous and non-nitrogenous substances was the deciding factor.

Given the lack of qualified veterinarians, individuals with little experience, such as farriers and orchidectomists, acted as vets. Cattle thrush last afflicted the Czech lands in 1879 and swine erysipelas was still widespread up to the First World War. Developments in veterinary care were supported by findings in microbiology, state grants, legislation, and international cooperation, and considerable success was achieved in this field. Technological developments were also influenced by new approaches to livestock production and purpose-built buildings. Thought was put into constructing barns and stables, which were built using steel beams and cast-iron supporting pillars. Automatic feeders only appeared towards the end of the 1880s. Stabling became an integral part of livestock husbandry, and improvements were made in terms of operation and hygiene.

THE INDUSTRIAL PROCESSING OF AGRICULTURAL CROPS

The latter half of the nineteenth century was also important in terms of the processing of agricultural products. This process was dependent on the Industrial Revolution and on economic changes ensuing from the consolidation of capitalism in agriculture. Many factors played a role in the development of individual spheres of agriculture. For instance, new raw materials were used that drove developments in the sugar industry, distilleries, the starch industry, and other spheres. The processing of agriculture products was dependent on science and technology more than ever before. Czech specialists quickly adopted the know-how and experience of more advanced countries, especially as regards the sugar industry, distilleries, and milling. The rapid introduction of new equipment and technology laid the foundations for modern refineries. This was most apparent in the sugar industry. So in the 1861–1862 season, there were 59 sugar refineries in the Czech lands, while only ten years on this figure was now 157, of which 74 were joint-stock companies, mostly farms that had been established during the speculation fever of 1867–1872, even though after the outbreak of the economic crisis the number of refineries fell. These were mainly breweries, sugar refineries, distilleries, and commercial mills, which formed the basis of the agricultural processing industry.

Traditional processing activities, though they expanded in terms of production volumes, lagged behind somewhat in terms of technology. Milk was produced in the same way for a long time. Right up to the 1870s it was treated and processed for butter, curd, and cheeses according to traditional instructions by family enterprises. In the second half of the century, the use of butter churns with a fixed or rotating drum spread. The production of cheeses was divided from a technological perspective into acid-set and fresh cheeses. Butchers and smoked meat manufacturers also slowly divested themselves of restrictions associated with the old guilds. It was only at the end of the 1880s that mechanisation began to replace heavy manual work. One of the most widespread ways of conserving fruit involved drying and cooking plum butter. Vegetables were preserved by souring, as we see from the quantity of sauerkraut that continued to be produced.

This century saw big changes take place in the agricultural processing industry, especially in malting and brewing, where new improved practices were applied, and in distilling, the starch industry, milling, baking, and the storage of grain. In the distilling industry, the production of yeast and vinegar became independent specialist spheres.

THE TECHNICAL BASIS OF AGRICULTURE

The dynamic development of capitalist agriculture and the intensification of production were strongly influenced by the technological base. The main components of this base included the mechanisation and application of chemicals to agriculture. The findings of science and technology were applied more and more. The last quarter of the nineteenth century saw the final stage of the technical and scientific revolution in agriculture, which fundamentally changed its technological base.

AGRICULTURE 1900–1914

At the start of the twentieth century, the trends characteristic of advanced capitalist agriculture, which was driven almost solely by the markets with which it was inextricably linked, expanded and deepened. The main criterion when assessing the success of agriculture became productivity and intensification.

One of the most important and advanced branches of agriculture in the Czech lands was plant production, which was divided into three spheres of activity based around cereals, beet, and potatoes. In several regions, hop growing, market gardening, and flax farming predominated. Plant production was characterised by specialisation depending on production conditions (cereals, potatoes, beet, and fodder), which were interconnected and mutually dependent. The larger farms producing for the market concentrated on crops subject to industrial processing, such as sugar beet, potatoes, flax, barley, and chicory. Intensification in plant production was manifest in an increase in arable land, the liquidation of fallow land, and the expansion of technical crops, mainly sugar beet, potato, barley, and fodder crops. The yields of the four main cereals increased, as the table 12 shows.

Overall, higher average yields were supported by better grassland fertilisation and treatment. Measures to improve grazing land were taken as recommended by agricultural lobby groups. An increase in the production of clover had been recorded from around 1910 onwards. The higher intensity was achieved by better agro-technology and an increase in the production of the seed stock of domestic red clover and alfalfa. The most popular fodder crops at the start of the twentieth century were beetroot, turnip, carrot, and swede. Potatoes grew in importance and at the start of the century covered 14% of arable land, while sugar beet accounted for only 5.6% in the most favourable locations.

The new century brought with it fundamental changes in livestock production. Statistics show a significant rise in the number of units of livestock bred. Extensive cattle-breeding was a feature mainly of medium and large

Table 12: Yield per hectare and the production of the main crops in the Czech lands in quintal per rural dweller 1881–1910

Indicator	1881–1890	1891–1900	1901–1910
Hectare yield in q/ha:			
4 main cereals (what, rye, barley, oats)	12.00	12.10	15.60
sugar beet	21.00	233.60	271.30
potato	69.90	77.70	99.20
Yield in q/rural dweller:			
4 main cereals	8.04	8.62	11.42
potato	9.88	11.78	15.06

Source: Klonov, V. "Vývoj výkonnosti československého zemědělství." *Zprávy zemědělského ústavu účetnicko-správovědného Čsl. republiky* 36 (1938): 6.

farms, which adopted more intensive dairy production methods. It became clear that the state was interested mainly in productivity and quality, as well as supporting and protecting domestic breeders. Of huge importance was the fact that breeding practices were systematically and periodically upgraded by both state legislation and by special interest groups headed by the Board of Agriculture. At the end of the nineteenth century, breeding stations came into being that attempted to ensure that enough purebred bulls and calves were available for breeding. An important aspect of livestock production that became increasingly popular, especially amongst small and medium-sized farmers, was pig breeding. It is worth noting too that, with the exception of sheep, numbers of livestock rose during the first decades of the twentieth century.

The rapid development of the agricultural sciences and new farming systems at the start of the twentieth century saw experimentation in both plant and livestock production. The first crops cultivated empirically by the large estates included potatoes and sugar beet. At the turn of the twentieth century, agricultural production in the Czech lands was still being impacted by the economic crisis of the 1870s and 1880s. The fall in prices caused by the crisis was halted only at the start of the twentieth century, when prices began to rise again. The crisis affected not only cereals, but also potatoes and sugar beet, and this was reflected in the fact that by the First World War the price of sugar had fallen by 50%. There was a shift in production, since the prices of livestock products followed an upward trend. Capitalist agriculturalists, especially landowners and medium-sized farmers, were more oriented toward livestock production. As far as crops were concerned, the focus was on fodder crops and supplying industry.

However, the inescapable fact remains that industry became the keystone of the Czech economy at the start of the twentieth century, and the importance and rate of development of agriculture and forestry began to decline. Like other economically advanced nations in Europe, the Czech lands slowly lost the agrarian character they had possessed for centuries. The region was transformed from agrarian into agro-industrial. This was clear at the start of the century, when a population census revealed that the number of people active in agriculture had dropped and those active in industry, commerce, and trade had risen. Despite all these changes, agriculture continued to play an important role in the economy, not only of the Czech lands, but also of the whole of Austria-Hungary, a fact borne out by production figures and the number of people still employed by the sector.

However, a telling comparison can be made regarding the importance of Czech agriculture for the Austro-Hungarian monarchy. Although Bohemia, Moravia, and Silesia occupied a quarter of the agricultural land of the Austrian duchies, they produced more than a third (35%) of its wheat, almost half (48%) of its rye, and more than half (59%) of its barley. The Czech lands supplied almost half (40%) of the total amount of grain grown in Cisleithania. As regards levels of sowing, these crown lands accounted for almost a half (46%) and were responsible for 32% of potato production and as much as 80% of sugar beet. This intensity was reflected in the agro-industry. For instance, almost all sugar refineries were to be found in the Czech lands, which also produced 44% of the overall production of spirits. More than half of the region's beer was produced here (58%). The situation was similar in the case of livestock farming. Of the total number of livestock in Austria-Hungary, the Czech lands accounted for a third (33%) of the empire's beef cattle, more than a quarter (27%) of pigs, but only 5% of sheep. Another indicator of just how advanced farming was in the Czech lands was the level of its harvests.

Table 13: Harvests of selected crops in the Czech lands and Cisleithania at the turn of the 20th centuries in q/ha

Crop	Czech lands	Austro-Hungary
wheat	17.7	13.2
rye	16.3	13.7
barley	18.9	14.5
oats	12.3	12.5
potatoes	92.0	97.0

Source: Reich, E. *Základy organizace zemědělství Československé republiky*. Praha, 1934, p. 318.

Other indicators deserve a mention. For instance, 80% of the hops produced in the monarchy were grown in the Czech lands, along with three-quarters of all the poppy, flax, and fruit. Even this quantitative data does not do full justice to the importance of the agro-industry in the Czech lands, especially regarding the reputation of their hops, beer, and barley.

With the exception of 1851, between 1841 and 1911/13, the Czech lands reported the highest agricultural production and the largest share of production in Cisleithania, as can be seen in the following table.

Table 14: Agricultural production (contribution to GDP) 1841–1911/13 in florins and in %

Land	1841		1851		1864		1911/13	
	mil. of florins	%	mil. of florins	%	mil. of florins	%	mil. of florins	%
A	150.7	31.9	346.2	38.9	287.9	27.8	431.6	20.6
B	212.2	44.9	325.6	36.6	412.6	39.9	970.2	46.4
C	80.8	17.1	158.0	17.7	262.2	25.3	463.3	22.1
D	28.6	6.1	61.0	6.8	72.3	7.0	227.6	10.9
Total	472.3	100.0	890.8	100.0	1,035.0	100.0	2,092.7	100.0

A – Upper and Lower Austria, Salzburg, Styria, Carinthia, Tyrol, and Vorarlberg; B – Bohemia, Moravia, (Austrian) Silesia; C – Galicia, Bukovina; D – Carniola, Austrian Littoral, Dalmatia

Source: Bachinger, K., Hemelsberger-Koller, H., Matis, H. (eds.). *Grundriss der österreichischen Sozial- und Wirtschaftsgeschichte von 1848 bis zur Gegenwart*. Wien, 1987, tab. 6, p. 21.

In the last quarter of the nineteenth century, the demand for credit rose, mainly in the form of mortgages on land. The number of farmers in debt rose sharply. In 1910, there were six times as many mortgage borrowers, mainly farmers, than in 1868. For small and medium farmers, indebtedness was often a disaster. It put their livelihoods at risk and led to the sale of their holdings. On the other hand, progress was achieved in the sphere of agricultural insurance.

The unprecedented development of production led to a concentration of production and capital, mainly in trade and finance. Businesses became so bloated that mere individuals were unable to control their capital, and the individual ownership of firms gave way to the pooling of capital in the form of joint-stock companies. In 1911, on the instigation of farmers, the Agrarian Bank was formed in Prague, part of the financial and credit system. As in other sectors, financial management was tightened up and farmers found themselves in a closer, more regular relationship with the economic principles and conditions of the entire national economy. Modern intensive farming, availing itself of new machines, tools, fertilisers, chemical soil amelioration, and other technical measures, needed far more capital than previously.

MECHANISATION

It was in this sphere of mechanisation that the most important changes took place. Earlier field tools were soon replaced by improved, purpose-made equipment and an extensive machine fleet. Automation resolved different problems in the agricultural sector to those in industry. Unlike industrial machines, agricultural equipment was often mobile and affected by the weather, and so wear and tear was faster. The efficiency and cost-effectiveness of agricultural machinery is also lower than in industry, since most agricultural equipment is used for a short stretch in the year, whereas in industry it is in operation year-round. The Czech lands were among the most industrially advanced in Austria-Hungary and enjoyed favourable conditions for the development of agriculture. The development of technology went hand in hand with the material and intellectual achievements of Czech society as a whole.

Below we highlight the most important types of tools and machines increasingly used by farmers during the period under examination. Having proved its worth, this equipment was quickly subject to improvements, and its use promoted and spread.

In the latter half of the nineteenth century, new types of soil cultivation tools were developed and old ones improved. This included new types of plough, cultivator, harrow, weeder, and various rollers that made possible a deeper furrow of up to 30 cm, better soil preparation prior to sowing and the suitable cultivation of root crops for the duration of their vegetation. On small farms the ard was used to harvest potatoes. New cultivation equipment appeared: a two- or three-bladed plough for rapid tilling and multi-rake reversible ploughs for rapid re-sowing and stubble tillage. Various kinds of cultivators, tillers, choppers, scarifiers, and extirpators (tillers with V-shaped blades) were used. Ridger ploughs, listers, windrowers, and graders had been used in the cultivation of potatoes since the 1870s. The traditional manual harvesting of beet was replaced by the plough and later the double harvester. At the end of the nineteenth century, a new type of plough was introduced to the Czech lands called the turning plough, which not only turned the soil but also aerated it. This plough came in many types, including the Eckert and Zeithammer ploughs. The rotary tiller, the predecessor of later disc ploughs, was also very popular. Large pivoting and multi-furrow ploughs were made necessary by steam tillage employed on large farms. At the end of the nineteenth century, sixty steam ploughs were already being used in Czech farms.

Sowing machines were also improved and their utilisation expanded, which took the burden off human resources, conserved seed, improved the regularity of seeding, and resulted in higher yields. The sowing machines were constructed for all three types of seeding: broadcasting, continuous line sowing, and dibbling. Line sowing machines helped increase production by as much as 15%, since the grain was uniform and planted more deeply.

Mowers, especially grass mowers, were quickly introduced into small-scale production, and by the end of the nineteenth century almost every medium-sized farm possessed its own mower. However, the basic mowing tool that found its home in the Czech lands in the first half of the nineteenth century remained the scythe. The most important change to take place was the introduction of the threshing machine, which brought to an end centuries of flail threshing. From the 1870s onwards, manual and powered threshing machines (flail harvesters) were used that were made by local craftsmen. Large steam threshers imported from German and England were used on estates. From the 1880s, combine threshing machines with the cleaning of grain were used. During the threshing, grain cleaning mills with fans and mesh were used in addition to fanners (winnower, ventilator, and fans) without mesh. Improvements to machines and tools were made across the board. Prior to the First World War, simple graders were produced for potatoes, onions, and other vegetables. In 1880, production began of pressure steamers. In the last quarter of the nineteenth century, the development of the beet industry saw the appearance of machines for mixing molasses and other fodder, and bone grinders and different pressing devices were put into operation. Combustion engines arrived on the scene later, though really picked up in the twentieth century.

The mechanisation of agricultural production involved big improvements to productivity, a shortening of agro-technical deadlines in crop production, increased production volumes, and all-around better-quality soil cultivation by deeper ploughs, thus increasing fertility. All of this impacted positively on the return to be made from crop production and the rearing of livestock.

CHEMICALISATION AND THE DEVELOPMENT OF SOIL AMELIORATION

Up until the start of the industrial production of artificial fertilisers, cow dung and various types of compost were used to fertilise the land. However, these were not produced in great quantities, since herds were small and there was a lack of housing. Ash and waste from the production of nitrate and potash (potassium carbonate, used to produce glass and soap) were also used. The first artificial fertiliser was lime. Firstly, the land was limed with marl (sedimentary rock), lime, and plaster. At the beginning of the nineteenth century, bone meal was introduced as a fertiliser in England, but only appeared sporadically in the Czech lands until the end of the 1840s. Advances in fertilisation were mostly confined to the large estates. The peasant farms lacked the right conditions, and so their owners focused more on manure, composts, and slurry pits.

However, from 1850–1890, when agriculture took a leap forward, most of the known artificial fertilisers were adopted. These beginnings were linked with the importation of a fertiliser of natural origin – guano – in 1843. Another popular, factory-made fertiliser was Chilean nitrate, discovered by a German, Thaddäus Haenke, at the end of the eighteenth century. However, most important for agriculture was the production and utilisation of industrially produced artificial fertilisers, above all superphosphates. From the 1870s onwards, phosphorus fertiliser was produced in increasingly larger quantities. In 1870, the first factory for phosphorus fertilisers was opened in Kolín. The chemicalisation of agriculture received effective support from experimental institutes and agro-technical stations. Up until the end of the nineteenth century, it was mainly large estates that used artificial fertilisers, though there were instances of it spreading to smaller farms thanks to lower prices and an expanding range of products on offer. Prior to the First World War, the average consumption of artificial fertilisers in the Czech lands was around 500–600 thousand tons (i.e., around 60% of total consumption in Cisleithania). In the 1870s, 1 kg of pure nutrients covered 1 hectare of farmland. By 1905–1914, this figure had risen to 25 kg. The chemicalisation of agriculture directly affected the biological character of production, and so its influence on developments in agriculture and its intensification were fast and effective.

Another technical measure was soil amelioration, which temporarily increased or permanently improved agricultural land and indirectly contributed to the development of agricultural production. Amelioration includes both the regulation of rivers and streams (i.e., increasing the surface of meadows and pastures), and the draining of wet meadows and pastures and fields or, conversely, their flooding. From the 1860s onwards, the technique of tubular drainage was imported from abroad. Amelioration began in regions with the greatest share of wetlands. The first large project in the Czech lands and virtually the entire monarchy was implemented in 1854 on the Schwarzenberg estate near Třeboň. The technique spread slowly and was only used in the larger estates. Right up until the end of the 1870s, medium-sized and peasant smallholdings almost never used soil amelioration, which was made more difficult by the fragmentation of land tenure. Amelioration was also important in that, alongside regulation of watercourses, it balanced the water regime and had a positive impact on the ecology of the landscape.

AGRICULTURAL COOPERATIVES

The idea of an agricultural self-help cooperative movement, having arisen in the West, was first adopted by Czech agriculture in the financial sphere and only then in the production, processing, and marketing of products. The first attempt probably consisted of the contributory financial funds founded in Bohemia after 1750, which to a certain extent represented a rudimentary peasant credit institution. After 1848, the development of the financial sphere was the priority in respect of the on-going development of capitalism within agriculture. Up until then, the mainly natural, self-subsistence economy of farmers had been retreating in the face of a market and financial economy. New farming systems placed greater demands on external material expenses. Agriculture was flooded with new machines and tools. This was one of the reasons why the credit crunch of the second half of the nineteenth century was manifest in agriculture. It was impossible to borrow for less than 12%–15% interest, even with collateral. Loan sharks charging 100% interest became commonplace. Wealthy individuals were always ready to talk up the advantages of credit and were free with their loans. A peasant who needed money and became indebted very quickly learned of the disadvantages of these loans. Tens of thousands of peasants became victims of unscrupulous loan sharks, speculators, and predatory entrepreneurs, and were unable to bear the burden either materially or mentally. Their businesses went into receivership and were sold at auction. The high interest rates bound them hand and foot, and the threat of indebtedness hovered permanently over their property. At the same time, the conditions of such financial institutions as Pražská spořitelna (Prague Savings Bank), established in 1825, or the Hypoteční banka pro Království české (Mortgage Bank for the Kingdom of Bohemia) founded in 1863 in Prague, did not meet farmers' needs. In 1871, Hypoteční banka (Mortgage Bank) was opened in Moravia and in 1869 the Úvěrní ústav pozemkový (Land Credit Institute) was founded in Silesia. Though Hypoteční banka in Prague managed to reduce the interest rate on loans from 6%–4%, in reality the bank served mainly large farmers and manorial estates, and was unable to alleviate, let alone eliminate, the weight of debt on peasant farmers.

During the first half of the nineteenth century, information reached the Czech lands regarding the first positive results of the emerging cooperative self-helps, especially those of England, France, and Germany. As in other advanced countries, first to be formed were credit cooperatives. The leading pioneer of credit and agricultural cooperatives was František Cyril Kampelík (1805–1877), a polymath with a broad outlook. Kampelík expressed his programme with the high-sounding slogan: "What is impossible for one, is easy for all." At the same time he drew on the principles of the German economist Friedrich Wilhelm Raiffeisen. Kampelík's savings banks were intended to spread morality, temperance, and diligence; to improve not only agriculture but also the crafts and industry; and to found new businesses, schools of agriculture, and societies. In addition, Kampelík drew up detailed statutes of collateral savings banks, templates for accounts ledgers, and other practical recommendations. His ideas were ahead of their time and never really took off during his lifetime. However, Kampelík was the first in the Czech lands to point out that the future of the peasantry—and thus of the entire nation— did not depend on foreign assistance but on their own strength and efforts. He is justly considered to be the spiritual father of smaller credit unions, mutual savings banks, and savings cooperatives founded later and known in Bohemia as *kampeličkas* and in Moravia as *raiffeisenkas*.

These were small, unlimited-liability credit cooperatives with an ambit restricted to one municipality or parish. The fact that liability was unlimited represented security for depositors. Care for the shrewd and mobile invest- ment of surpluses or the procurement of loans was entrusted to a central treasury that managed the assets of local savings banks and credit coopera- tives and were also self-sufficient. Credit cooperatives greased the wheels of commerce by providing peasant farmers easy credit with a low interest rate and reasonable repayment deadlines. The credit was then used to purchase operating requirements, livestock, and machinery, and to build and equip farm outbuildings.

Notably, peasant self-help groups grew in strength during the agrarian crisis. Farmers responded by increasing cooperative business, not only in the sphere of capital, but also in the sphere of production. It should be em- phasised that it was the kampeličkas and raiffeisenkas that were successful and spread around the countryside, accepted small deposits, and provided special-purpose and investment loans that were taken up eagerly by small farmers. For instance, in 1912 there were already 3,588 kampeličkas operat- ing in the Czech lands with 343,500 members comprising approximately 60% farmers, 22% labourers, and the remainder largely consisting of craftsmen, tradesmen, or members of other professions. A huge advantage during the rapid expansion of rural financial institutions was the fact they were estab- lished on a bottom-up basis (i.e., individual savings banks and credit unions were the first to appear, with central headquarters only subsequently being created). In this way, typically capitalist enterprises emerged as part of the budding agrarian capital. Kampeličkas and raiffeisenkas were also a great help in consolidating typically Czech self-help associations. In addition to their economic importance, they also performed certain educational func- tions. They taught people how to think and act economically, motivated them to do business, and led them indirectly to act honourably. Kampeličkas sup- ported intelligent saving, discouraged hoarding, and bolstered democracy by teaching people to take account of the bigger picture.

From the second half of the 1860s through the 1870s also proved more favourable politically for the development of non-credit agricultural coop- eratives, in particular the establishment of self-help cooperatives. It was characterised by folk camps and radical opposition to the dual monarchy of

Austro-Hungary, and witnessed a new political awareness spread amongst the rural population and demands grow for greater economic autonomy. It was around this time that the first cooperatives were formed in the sectors of the sugar industry, brewing, dairies, malt houses, and distilleries (most of them in Hradec Králové, the Labe/Elbe region, and Central Bohemia). It was during these years that important cooperative sugar refineries were formed in Moravia, such as those in Vrbátky, Litovel, Kroměříž, and Přerov. The idea that the cooperative principle could be profitably applied to crop processing saw dairy, starch, and milling cooperatives formed, as well as others for drying chicory, etc.

Warehousing, procurement, and sales cooperatives began to spread, making it easier for their members to sell agricultural products, especially grain, while facilitating the purchase of industrial requirements (mainly fertilisers). Their operations tended to stretch over municipalities, sometimes to the entire district. Livestock cooperatives were formed in cattle breeding regions, and later on cooperatives for monetising livestock. During the period under consideration, the agricultural cooperatives in the Czech lands were amongst the most advanced in the Austro-Hungarian Monarchy and bore comparison with the advanced countries of Western Europe.

Table 15: Number of agricultural cooperatives and their members in Czechoslovakia 1905–1918

Type of cooperative	1905	1909	1912	1918
Kampeličkas and raiffeisenkas	787	–	3,588	3,798
Non-credit cooperatives:				
Warehousing, milling and other procurement, and sales	108	128	168	240
Distilleries, starch factories, fruit and veg processing	54	67	81	117
Dairies	–	–	–	–
Flax and weaving	28	41	36	38
Chicory drying	14	25	32	32
Livestock	184	165	174	151
Engineering	45	233	236	169
Power sector	1	2	24	86
Consumer and housing	93	81	113	123
Miscellaneous	42	72	71	59
Total non-credit	569	814	935	1,015

Source: Špirk, L. *Zemědělské družstevnictví v kapitalistické a lidovědemokratické ČSR*. Praha, 1959, p. 260.

Table 16: Number of members of cooperatives in Czechoslovakia 1905–1918

Type of cooperative	1905	1909	1912	1918
kampeličkas and raiffeisenkas	68,000	–	343,544	388,812
non-credit cooperatives	–	71,327	109,344	223,077

Source: Špirk, L. *Zemědělské družstevnictví v kapitalistické a lidovědemokratické ČSR*. Praha, 1959, p. 260.

Interestingly, even prior to 1918, there were areas in Czech agriculture in which some medium and small farmers received everything they needed for their work from cooperatives, and, on the other hand, sold almost everything they produced by means of these same cooperatives. From the last quarter of the nineteenth century onwards, the cooperative ideal has remained vibrant and popular in the Czech agricultural sector, albeit applied unevenly. Somewhat later, credit cooperatives in the Czech lands were among the most developed in Europe.

AGRICULTURAL SCIENCE, EDUCATION, AND OTHER ACTIVITIES

The rapid development of agricultural production on capitalist foundations required a new conception of both general and vocational education and farmers' lobby groups. This was most clearly reflected by small peasant farmers, who made up a substantial part of Czech agriculture, spread over an economically growing number of small- and medium-sized farms. The situation was better for the large estates, since their owners were able to draw on the know-how of highly qualified civil servants and foremen. There was a keen awareness that an economic education touching upon all aspects of farming was the prerequisite for a new, better life and was the driver of agricultural production. This programme, utilised by both professional aristocrats and progressive farmers, included an educational component reflecting the latest scientific findings, training in economics, and specialist literature.

The foundations for the successful development of professional farming were laid by František Xaver Hlubek (1802–1880), a native of Czech Silesia, who was interested in almost all branches of agriculture and achieved European-wide renown. His most important work on the topic is the three-volume *Die Landwirtschaftslehre in ihren ganzen Umfange nach den Erfahrungen und Erkenntnissen der letzverflossenen 100 Jahre* (*Agricultural Science Drawing on the Experience and Findings of the last 100 Years*), which was long the definitive textbook in Central Europe. It examined new forms of progress and recommended, among other things, increasing permanent net income and land rents. The experiments that Gregor Johann Mendel (1822–1884) conducted with pea plants were also important, and enabled the laws of inheritance to be formulated. One of the founders of agro-chemistry in the Czech lands was Professor František Farský (1846–1927), who looked at ways of increasing soil fertility and nutrient content in concentrated industrial fertilisers. His research into substitutes for phosphorus, potassium, and various organic and inorganic nitrogen compounds, as well as his findings on the replacement of nutrients in plant foods, were of lasting validity. This work was later followed up by Professor Julius Stoklasa (1857–1936), the leading Czech agricultural scientist at the turn of the twentieth century. The beginnings of phytopathology stretch back to the mid-nineteenth century. Diseases afflicting cereals and potatoes were examined, among others, by Ladislav Josef Čelakovský and Otakar Nickerl, though at the end of the nineteenth century the best results were achieve by František Sitenský (1851–1924), a lecturer at the Higher School of Economics in Tábor. Animal husbandry was also built on scientific principles. One of the first personalities in this sphere was Karel Milan Lambl (1823–1884), who studied the crossbreeding of English and Czech pigs. From around the 1860s, education in agriculture began to expand. Three types of school were created: lower (peasant), upper farming school, and farming academies. In addition, the publication of agricultural periodicals made a great contribution to progress in the sphere. As well as František Horský, another important figure was Antonín Emanuel Komers (1814–1893), an outstanding economist who improved the management of aristocratic estates, rationalised production, and introduced different types of enterprise. Lobby groups helped raise the level of peasant farming. Of great significance for the development of agriculture was the establishment of Zemědělské rady pro Království České (Agricultural Council for the Kingdom of Bohemia) in March 1873. The council was a special interest group supporting agriculture in the Czech lands and, unlike the Vlastenecko-hospodářská společnost (Patriotic Economic Society), was a public institution. It mediated links with economic associations supporting agriculture. In 1897, the Zemědělská rada pro Markrabství moravské (Agricultural Council for the Margraviate of Moravia) was formed in Moravia and, like its Bohemian counterpart, was divided into a Czech and German division. In Silesia, the Agricultural Council was replaced by the Ústřední hospodářská společnost pro Vévodství slezské (Central Economic Society for the Duchy of Silesia), established in 1895 in Opava.

After 1848, various kinds of economic associations were established, reflecting the economic, social, and cultural elevation of the peasantry and the countryside. They were private and apolitical. The rapid development of capitalist practices in agriculture in the latter half of the nineteenth century supported the boom in business and production, but increased the social differentiation of farmers and countryside. The beginnings of an agrarian party were also associated with the activities of Alfons Šťastný (1831–1913), an economist and theoretician from South Bohemia. The party was formed in Prague in 1899. It attained its greatest power and political influence during the period of the First Republic, especially under the leadership of its chairman Antonín Švehla (1873–1933), who as ministerial chairman took great credit for the creation of a democratic Czechoslovakia.

3. DEVELOPMENT OF THE SECONDARY SECTOR: CRAFT (TRADE) PRODUCTION AND THE FACTORY SYSTEM

GENERAL OVERVIEW AND THE DEVELOPMENT OF KEY SECTORS

Proto-industrialisation precedes the modern industrialisation of the nineteenth and twentieth centuries and is characterised by a growth in non-agrarian production, usually in rural areas. The first signs of this new phenomenon date back to the eighteenth century, and by the latter half of the century cannot be overlooked. Numerical data is difficult to come by, since the public administration at the time collected no statistics. Proto-industrialisation is a modern, classical typological term, the outcome of subsequent interpretations and generalisations carried out by historians in the latter half of the twentieth century (Fritz Redlich, Herman Freudenberger, Franklin F. Mendels, etc., and Milan Myška in Czechoslovakia / the Czech Republic).[70]

The institutional conditions for the rise of proto-industrialisation were created by the Habsburg state's single-minded economic policy of mercantilism. The application of this policy began shortly after the end of the Thirty Years' War, though it flourished only in the second half of the eighteenth century under the governments of Maria Theresa, Joseph II, and Leopold II (1740–1790). The practical impact of this policy on the Czech lands has been described by historian Arnošt Klíma.[71] The mercantilism of the Viennese government involved subsidies paid to selected producers and bonuses to machine builders, the granting of guild exemptions and the removal of internal customs duties (1775), the construction of imperial highways and the conversion of large rivers into navigable waterways, the facilitation of foreign trade, and an influx of foreign craftsmen and entrepreneurs. However, equally important was the strengthening of the institutional framework so as to make it favourable for proto-industrial entrepreneurship, a process enshrined in government reforms that freed up relations between the serfs and the aristocratic landowners (the Raab system, the tax and land reforms of

---

70 Myška, M. "Problémy a metody hospodářských dějin, část 1: Metodické problémy studia dějin sekundárního sektoru." *Učební texty Ostravské univerzity*. Ostrava, 1995.

71 Klíma, A. "Merkantilismus in Habsburg Monarchy in Bohemian Lands." *Historica* 11 (1965): 95–119.

Joseph II, the letters patent on serfdom and vassalage and on certain personal legal freedoms for the serfs of 1781, the transformation of certain operations into cash benefits in 1789, etc.).

In the end, these developments were reflected in the overall economic level of the Habsburg Empire. Around 1800, the western reaches of the monarchy, including the Czech lands, fared well in comparison with countries like France, Belgium, and Germany. Like these countries they followed in the wake of England, which had already experienced the Industrial Revolution. The production of textiles in Brno is often cited as a graphic illustration of the economic progress in the Habsburg Monarchy at that time, since it attained almost the same momentum as Manchester, the centre of the mechanised textile industry in England.[72]

Overall, the eighteenth century, especially during the reign of Maria Theresa, was a period during which the western part of the Habsburg Monarchy experienced significant economic growth and fundamental structural transformations. Mercantilism effected lasting institutional changes that laid the foundations for the development of a capitalist market economy. Conversely, from 1790–1820, active participation in the Napoleonic Wars and the political reaction to the French Revolution had the opposite effect and slowed things down.

It was only after the draining effects of the French Revolution and the subsequent wars with Napoleon over who was to control Europe that the conditions arose in the Habsburg Empire for the full development of modern industrialisation. It was only then that the secondary sector of the Austrian and Czech economy, including all craft and industrial production, underwent the phenomenal, nearly century-long development that, in terms of numbers employed, productivity, and the creation of national assets, elevated it to being the most important link in the national economic chain. A decisive factor in this process was the mechanised factory industry, and for this reason we shall focus on this sector. Deploying a large number of production and propulsive machines, large factors easily covered the largest part of value in the secondary sector of manufactured goods, even though small-scale producers and craft industries never disappeared completely, but with state support maintained an important position in Cisleithania.

The question of when industrialisation actually began in the Czech lands can be answered in two ways. If we focus more narrowly on the beginnings of mechanisation and the period during which industrial and economic growth increases and becomes a sustainable, irreversible phenomenon comparable with the leading industrial countries in the West, then according to Jaroslav

---

72   Freudenberger, H. and Mensch, H. *Von der Provinzstadt zur Industrieregion (Brünn–Studie)*. Göttingen, 1975.

Purš and Milan Myška the beginning of industrialisation is identical to the start of the Industrial Revolution or the technical production transformation of 1825–1830 (i.e., after the Napoleonic Wars). If we stand back somewhat and broaden our perspective on the economic, social, and demographic developments linked with proto-industrialisation (and with its centre of gravity in the countryside, in textiles and ironmongery), then the start of the process of Czech and Austrian industrialisation shifts back to the second half of the eighteenth century, if not to the time of the first manufacturers.

If we wish to describe the industrialisation linked with the development of factory production after 1825, we must accept that, unlike the English discontinuous model, this process in the Habsburg Monarchy is continuous, and there is no clear break between proto-industrialisation and the mechanisation of factory production (the transformation in production technology). On the contrary, both phases overlap. On this basis, the American econometric historian John Komlos[73] identifies three developmental phases during the course of Austrian industrialisation: a relatively long period of proto-industrialisation (lasting until approximately 1795); a short transitional phase introducing the first production and propulsive machines in textile factories (lasting until approximately 1825); and a third and final stage in which mechanised factory production with a higher and sustainable rate of growth predominates. Looking at the irreversible dynamics of this last phase, and freeing our minds of artificial models, it is fair to call this last phase an industrial revolution or transformation in production technology.

When assessing this transformation in modern Czech history, we must bear in mind that industrialisation took place within the diverse economic conditions of the Habsburg Monarchy, in which several antithetical factors were at play, some historical and others natural. First, the protracted and far from perfect overthrow of the feudal past was embedded in the political system and in how the sovereign and court shaped the country's internal, foreign, and economic policy in accordance with the influential interests of conservative and "supranational" forces of the nobility, church, army, and civil bureaucracy. Second, the imperial government from the time of absolutism and again under the Metternich regime of 1815–1848 and Bach's neo-absolutism of 1849–1859, though in practice up to the end of its existence, pursued a two-pronged strategy: to centralise all executive power in Vienna and to maintain its status as a great power in Europe despite the large financial sacrifices. Third, from the period of mercantilism onwards, the limited creation of an institutional and legislative framework for the capitalist development of the country had been subject to these objectives and interests,

---

73   Komlos, J. *Die Habsburgermonarchie als Zollunion: Die Wirtschaftsentwicklung Österreich-Ungarns im 19. Jahrhundert.* Wien, 1986, p. 65.

without the political modernisation and rapid industrialisation of the country ever becoming a nationwide consolidating objective. Fourth, the necessary reforms were only carried out under the pressure of circumstances, conservatively, in a piecemeal and compromised fashion in order to meet the needs of a single, small, privileged stratum of estate owners on the one hand and a large group of small traders on the other, at the cost of industry being subjected to high taxation. Fifth, the Austrian empire as a multi-ethnic commonwealth was confronted in the nineteenth century with a powerful nationalist ideology that operated against the German-speaking centralism of Vienna more as a centrifugal, even destructive, force. Sixth, leaving aside the Hungarians, this applied to Czech nationalism, which from the end of the eighteenth century had received renewed impetus in the linguistic, literary, and political revival and in the latter half of the nineteenth century had established a beachhead in the Czech corporate sphere. Seventh, in addition, the Austrian empire possessed a number of natural deficits. Over the course of centuries it had been created from countries that did not form an ideal geographic whole and so communication was encumbered by various natural barriers (mountain ranges), the main river system in the form of the Danube flowed east, links to the world's seas were limited or arduous (the loss of Silesia and the connection via the river Oder, only a short connection via the Elbe, the Alps separating it from its main seaport of Trieste). Eighth, natural resources that would become important for industrialisation were distributed unevenly between individual countries (the Alpine countries had rich deposits of iron ore, while coking coal was located in the Czech lands), which entailed an extremely uneven and protracted course of the Industrial Revolution in the Habsburg Empire, typically from west to east and from north to south.

Under these circumstances, the Czech lands, along with Lower Austria and Styria, were the most progressively developed regions of the Habsburg Empire right from the start of the industrial transformation. In 1841, though they only represented approximately 19% of the total population of the monarchy, they were responsible for 29.2% of its industrial production: 75% of baize and woollen goods, 42% of cotton goods, 78% of glass industry production, and 75% of the coal produced (excluding Hungary). At the same time, mechanisation was well underway. In 1846, more than 60% of all stationary steam engines of the non-Hungarian part of the monarchy and 64% of their output was to be found in the Czech lands.

In terms of the relatively rapid industrialisation of the Czech lands, being a part of of the Habsburg Empire had its advantages and disadvantages. The second largest European country in terms of area and the third in terms of population size represented huge opportunities for the factory industry in the expanding internal market (in 1775, a customs union between the Czech lands and most Alpine countries, from 1783–1796 a customs union between Galicia and Bukovina, in 1817 Lombardy and Veneto, in 1825 Tyrol and Vorarlberg, in 1851 Hungary, and in 1880 Istria and Dalmatia). On the other hand, domestic trade was long restricted by the relatively low level of urbanisation, poorly developed business capital and entrepreneurship, not to mention the negligible purchasing power of the majority of the population. Foreign trade, subject to various barriers from the period of mercantilism until at least the mid-nineteenth century (import quotas and prohibitions, high customs duties, the taxation and banning of exports, etc.), tended to lock the country within itself and severely hampered technical progress and industrialisation. The Czech lands possessed the ideal conditions for the development of the leading sectors of Austrian industrialisation, namely textiles and ironmongery, followed by the food industry, partly thanks to their long commercial tradition cultivated in the textile and ironmongery manufactories, and also thanks to domestic raw materials (flax, wool, iron ore, wood and mineral coal, vegetable dyes, sugar beet, and other agricultural products for distilleries, breweries, and the starch industry), and finally thanks to their more favourable and closer connection to the markets, communications, and technological production facilities of the more advanced Saxony, Prussia, and the Western world in general. Nevertheless, in the mid-nineteenth century, one of the insurmountable barriers to faster economic development was the surviving feudal relationship between the landowning nobility and the serfs, the negligible purchasing power of the population, and the lack of domestic capital and business credit ensuing therefrom. Although certain highly placed officials, especially at the court chamber in Vienna, took a more liberal approach to factory production, overall the political climate of the Metternich government was not kindly disposed towards the unlimited development of industry.

On the other hand, one of the peculiarities of industrialisation in the Czech lands was that the local aristocracy became more directly involved in business than any other European country (alongside bourgeois entrepreneurs). According to research carried out by Milan Myška, aristocratic entrepreneurs during the proto-industrial era were strongly represented in textile production. Though they withdrew somewhat during the industrial era, they nevertheless retained a relatively strong position in metallurgical engineering, mining, and the sugar industry. The aristocracy also made clear its interest in economic development by forming Česká spořitelna (the Bohemian Savings Bank) (1824), Jednoty pro povzbuzení průmyslu v Čechách (the Union for the Promotion of Industry in the Czech Lands) (1833), and from the 1840s–1860s by purchasing shares in railway companies and the first commercial banks in Vienna and Prague. The multinational composition of the population of the Czech lands was reflected in its industrialisation. Both Czech and German speakers participated, and up until the mid-nineteenth century it was fuelled mainly by German and Jewish capital, before national Czech corporate and bank capital adopted a more important role.

The commonest symptom of the long-term transformation of the economic structure of a country under the influence of industrialisation is a drop in the number of people working in agriculture and a corresponding increase in the population working in trades and industry, or in commerce, transport, and services. At the start of industrialisation, when we have only partial data on factory production, information of this type from the statistics compiled at that time are all the more welcome. They are not always precise, but they suffice for the purpose of illustration:

Table 17: Percentage of people working in agriculture of the population as a whole

Year	Austria	Czech lands
1756	–	78
1790	75	–
1846/50	72	64

Source: Good, David F. *Der wirtschaftliche Aufstieg des Habsburgerreiches 1750–1914.* Wien, Köln, Graz, 1986, p. 49.

These figures give us a rough indication of the situation in the second half of the eighteenth century, when the agricultural sector was still dominant and when, therefore, even proto-industrial production often took place in rural regions and in cottage industries. However, there is a small shift at the turn of the century when the first factories appear, which, with the boom in mechanisation, squeezed the agrarian sector to less than two-thirds and even less than half in the Czech lands. All this was taking place at the same time as the population was growing (from 1817–1845 by 1% on average per annum, which is high historically speaking), and the productivity of agriculture itself was increasing, which now was forced to supply the market with a larger number of agrarian products working with a smaller number of workers and capital. When a regular ten-yearly census began to be taken in the monarchy in the 1860s, we receive even more detailed data on these trends (cf. the chapter on demographic developments). This shows that the structural transformation of the Habsburg Monarchy lagged behind that of the advanced Western economies, as can be seen from an international comparison around 1910.

While in the advanced economies of the West the proportion of the population active in industry and mining on the threshold of the twentieth century was 36%–47 %, in Cisleithania it was only 23%, and even lower in Transleithania at 17%. The transformation of the structure of employees proceeded very slowly, especially when compared with Germany, where the proportion

Table 18: A comparison of the three main economic sectors in selected countries

Country	Year	Agriculture, forestry, fisheries	Industry, mining	Commerce, transport
Cisleithania	1910	53.1	22.6	9.9
Transleithania	1910	64.5	17.1	6.5
Bohemia	1910	39.1	39.2	21.7
Moravia	1910	48.8	32.1	19.1
Silesia	1910	37.1	41.7	21.2
Great Britain	1911	8.9	47.2	22.5
Germany	1907	35.2	37.5	12.4
France	1911	41.0	35.9	9.8

Source: Lacina, V. *Formování čs. ekonomiky 1918–1923*. Praha, 1990, p. 13; Čechy, Morava, Slezsko: Horská, P. "Pokus o využití rakouských statistik pro studium společenského rozvrstvení českých zemí v 2. polovině 19. století." *ČsČH*, vol. 20, no. 5 (1972): 650.

of industrial workers rose by 30% from the 1860s onwards, while this figure was only 22% in Cisleithania. In Silesia and Bohemia, the development of industrialisation was as fast as in Germany, and its tertiary sector outstripped Germany's and matched that of Great Britain.

The quantitative indicator most often used to indicate industrial growth is the extent to which individual sectors or large corporations were kitted out with machines and propulsion units, their aggregate production expressed in units of weight, and less commonly, the value of production or business turnover. This data as it applies to individual production spheres is shown below. Even so, it would at this point be useful to point to one statistical aggregate demonstrating the industrial boom of Austria-Hungary in the nineteenth century (i.e., coal, pig iron, and steel, which were the main raw materials serving industry and reflecting the economic clout of the Habsburg Monarchy compared to other countries in the lead-up to the First World War). It is clear from the table that with a share of 3%–3.3% of global extraction and the production of what was strategically the most important raw materials, the Habsburg Empire ranked with Tsarist Russia at the bottom of the Great Powers, and outperformed Russia only in terms of production per capita. The only exception was coal, though more than two-thirds of what was extracted was the less valuable brown coal, which the monarchy produced more of than any other country in Europe, aside from Germany. However, its production of pig iron and steel was far lower than that of Germany, which moved up to first place in Europe and second place in the world.

As regards the extraction of anthracite and lignite, the Czech lands were important not only for the Cisleithian region but also the Transleithian region of the monarchy. The coal production of the Czech lands was indispensible to

Table 19: Average annual yield of basic raw materials 1898–1909

Country	Coal			Pig iron			Steel		
	total in millions of tonnes	kg per capita	% of global production	total in millions of tonnes	kg per capita	% of global production	total in millions of tonnes	kg per capita	% of global production
USA	316.6	3,681	37.2	18.9	220	38.7	15.5	182	42.9
Great Britain	240.2	5,554	28.2	9.2	214	19.0	5.3	?	14.9
Germany	146.4	2,450	17.2	10.0	169	20.6	8.6	146	23.9
France	34.2	873	4.0	2.9	75	6,0	1.9	50	5.4
Russia	19.1	155	2.2	2.7	22	5.6	1.9	16	5.4
Austria-Hungary	28.2	629	3.3	1.6	35	3.3	1.1	24	3.0

Coal production is shown as 0,5 t anthracite = 1 t lignite (brown coal).

Source: Kološek, J. "České hospodářské a kulturní potřeby ve státním rozpočtu rakouském." *Naše doba XIX* (1912): 653 et seq.

the monarchy. Naturally, we must also take into account the distribution of sources of raw materials in individual regions (lands).

Table 20: Coal extraction in Cisleithania 1840–1910

Regional share of total production of anthracite in %					
	1840	1860	1880	1900	1910
A	5.9	2.8	0.7	0.5	0.5
B	91.3	91.6	94.3	88.8	89.7
C	–	5.6	5.0	10.6	9.8
D	2.8	–	–	–	–

Regional share of total production of lignite (brown coal) in %						
	1840	1850	1860	1880	1900	1910
A	46.7	55.5	42.9	23.2	15.8	13.7
B	48.2	40.8	53.0	74.6	81.5	83.9
C	–	–	0.6	0.1	0.4	0.1
D	5.1	3.7	4.5	2.2	2.3	2.3

A – Upper and Lower Austria, Salzburg, Styria, Carinthia, Tyrol, and Vorarlberg; B – Bohemia, Moravia, (Austrian) Silesia; C – Galicia, Bukovina; D – Carniola, Austrian Littoral, and Dalmatia

Source: Sandgruber, R. "Wirtschaftswachstum, Energie und Verkehr in Österreich 1840–1913", in Kellenbenz, H. (ed.). *Wirtschaftliches Wachstum, Energie und Verkehr vom Mittelalter bis ins 19. Jahrhundert. Bericht über die 6. Arbeitstagung der Gesellschaft für Sozial- und Wirtschaftsgeschichte.* Stuttgart–New York, 1978, tab. 6, p. 85.

Over time, the Czech lands also became indispensible to the monarchy in producing pig iron. This was thanks to the dephosphorisation process (the "basic process") invented by Sidney Gilchrist Thomas, which was first used outside of Great Britain in 1879 (Kladno), as we see from the table 21.

Table 21: Production of pig iron and steel in Cisleithania 1831–1910 by region in %

	1831	1841	1860	1880	1900	1910
A	65.5	59.9	57.5	61.8	38.5	34.5
B	32.4	33.4	37.3	36.8	61.0	59.2

A – Upper and Lower Austria, Salzburg, Styria, Carinthia, Tyrol, and Vorarlberg; B – Bohemia, Moravia, (Austrian) Silesia

Source: Sandgruber, R. "Wirtschaftswachstum, Energie und Verkehr in Österreich 1840–1913", in Kellenbenz, H. (ed.). *Wirtschaftliches Wachstum, Energie und Verkehr vom Mittelalter bis ins 19. Jahrhundert. Bericht über die 6. Arbeitstagung der Gesellschaft für Sozial- und Wirtschaftsgeschichte.* Stuttgart–New York, 1978, tab. 6, p. 85.

Of the five largest iron and steel companies in Cisleithania, three were to be found in the Czech lands (Vítkovické horní a hutní těžířstvo / Witkowitzer Bergbau- und Eisenhütten-Gewerkschaft / Vítkovice Upper and Metallurgical Mining; Pražská železářská společnost / Prager Eisen-Industrie-Gesellschaft / Prague Iron and Steel Company ; and Österreichisch-Alpine Montangesellschaft). The most important companies outside of the Czech lands were Österreichisch-Alpine Montangesellschaft and Krainische Industriegesellschaft.

Other indicators can be used to measure the economic development of the Habsburg Monarchy. As regards energy sources, the nineteenth century was the century of steam, and so it makes sense to examine the modernisation of Austrian industry using data on the use of steam turbines. An international comparison again reveals the level attained by Austrian and Czech industry.

Table 22: A comparison of the output of steam turbines in industry 1841–1902 (index: HP per 1,000 of the population)

Year	Great Britain	Germany	France	Cisleithania	Czech lands
1841	19.6	0.7	1.1	0.2	0.3
1852	25.5	3.2	2.1	0.6	1.0
1863	31.8	12.4	5.9	2.4	4.2
1876	54.7	24.1	11.6	7.0	12.0
1880	68.0	37.2	14.5	7.9	15.0
1885	68.4	39.9	18.2	11.3	22.0
1890	84.5	44.3	22.6	16.7	34.0
1902	180.2	82.5	51.2	32.3	60.4

Source: Purš, J. *Průmyslová revoluce: Vývoj pojmu a koncepce*. Praha, 1973, pp. 631–633.

The first attempts to build a steam engine were made in the Czech lands twelve years after the Watt double-acting engine was patented (1784). Conditions were far from ideal. The country was at war and contact with England was constrained by the continental blockade. Czech ironworks had huge problems in making the parts for these engines at a time when engineering as a sector was only beginning to emerge in the workshops that the first mechanised textile factories had established to repair their spinning machines. Additionally, construction of the first steam turbines was linked not only with the names of technicians such as František Josef Gerstner and Josef Božek from the polytechnic institute in Prague, but also Count Jiří František August Buquoy, who made available his ironworks in Hořovice and provided substantial funding. The first steam turbine producing factories, which began operations in the Czech lands in the 1820s, were established or managed largely by foreign specialists and entrepreneurs, mainly from England and Germany. The statistics relating to utilisation of the first steam engines in the Czech lands show that, of the total of eighteen machines with an output of 330 HP deployed in the western part of the empire from 1816–1829, most (twelve) were imported from abroad and two-thirds (twelve) were operated in Bohemia, Moravia, and Silesia, though with a somewhat lower output (142 HP in total). By 1834, the year of the first surviving official list of steam engines, the number of engines operated in the Czech lands with a minimum output of 390 HP had risen to forty-four. This is a telling sign of the rapid mechanisation of industry and the emergence of steam navigation, followed swiftly by the introduction of steam-powered trains. According to the list dated 1846, there was a total of 799 steam engines with an output of 25,171 HP being operated in the western region of the monarchy, of which 491 were stationary (used in industry) with an output of 6,312 HP, 68 with an output of 5,574 HP were used on steamboats, and 240 with a maximum output of 13,285 HP powered locomotives. In industry, 52% of steam power was deployed to produce textiles, followed by mining (18%), the iron and steel industry (9%), and miscellaneous sectors. From that time onwards, the use of steam power in Austria and the Czech lands increased inexorably, at a faster pace in the Czech lands than even other parts of the monarchy:

Table 23: Steam turbines in Cisleithania by region 1841–1902

		1841	1852	1863	1875	1902
Alpine countries	number	60	155	676	2,427	–
	HP	792	1,885	11,348	44,281	261,802
Czech lands	number	156	473	2,012	5,956	–
	HP	1,845	6,689	32,076	101,086	602,981
Galicia, Bukovina	number	1	15	129	570	–
	HP	16	1,944	2,416	8,487	55,703
Carniola, Austrian Littoral, Dalmatia	number	7	28	63	207	–
	HP	166	360	1,126	3,425	24,511
Cisleithania total	number	224	671	2,880	9,160	–
	HP	2,819	10,878	46,966	157,297	944,997

Source: Sandgruber, R. "Wirtschaftswachstum, Energie und Verkehr in Österreich 1840–1913", in Kellenbenz, H. (ed.). *Wirtschaftliches Wachstum, Energie und Verkehr vom Mittelalter bis ins 19. Jahrhundert. Bericht über die 6. Arbeitstagung der Gesellschaft für Sozial- und Wirtschaftsgeschichte.* Stuttgart and New York, 1978, tab. 14, p. 89.

It is equally interesting to observe the uneven progress of the revolution in production technology from one sector to another and to note its over-all dynamic, interrupted only by recurring cyclical fluctuations and crises. This progress saw significant shifts between small-scale and large-scale production, between consumer and heavy industry, as well as in the sectoral structure of the industry as a whole. According to Myška, the replacement of handicraft and manufactories by mass production in mechanised factories took place in individual sectors with a certain time lag and over differing periods of time.

Fig. 1: The course of the revolution in production technology (the Industrial Revolution) in the main industrial sectors of the Czech lands

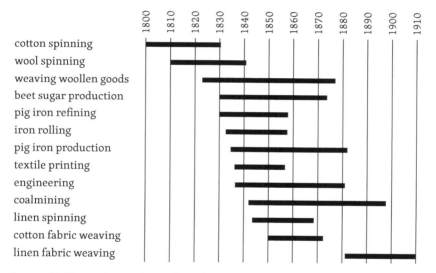

Source: Myška, M. "The Industrial Revolution: Bohemia, Moravia, and Silesia" in Teich, M. and Porter, R. (eds.). *The Industrial Revolution in National Context*. Cambridge, 1996, p. 253.

Just as it had in England, the revolution in production technology in the Czech lands began in the textile industry, first with the introduction of ma-chines for spinning cotton and wool. However, it then diverged from the Eng-lish model, with another consumer sector, beet sugar production, soon joining the revolution. Only then was it time for the modernisation of metallurgical iron production, the introduction of the domestic manufacture of machines, and the mechanisation of coalmining and other sectors. František Dudek at-tempted to plot the long-term structural changes from the 1840s onwards. He merged miscellaneous data by calculating the arithmetic averages and was thus able to reveal in detail a fascinating aspect of the Czech economy, namely that for the whole of the last century of the Habsburg Empire's existence, the initial structure of its industry remained intact. This was based on the earlier and easier (from the point of view of investments and markets) expansion of the production of consumer goods and was determined by the prevalence of light over heavy industry in respect of employee numbers, technological equipment, and production value. The sectoral structure at the start of the Industrial Revolution was described as the "textile industry, food industry, and metal industry" in descending order of importance. However, after the commencement of the second Industrial Revolution, from the 1880s onwards the qualitative sequence was now "metal industry, textiles, and food industry" (though only realised in full after 1930). The predominance of the consumer industry declined from its original three-quarter share to less than three-fifths at the start of the twentieth century. This was because the significance of the textile industry dwindled, to be joined from the 1880s onwards by the

Table 24: Development of the sectoral structure of industry in the Czech lands 1840–1902

Industrial sector	Arithmetic average of ratios in % per		
	no. of employees, machine output and production value		no. of employees and machine output
	1840s	1880s	1902
Textiles	53.90	33.60	24.75
Clothing	–	1.55	4.50
Food	8.25	22.35	15.90
Wood processing	–	3.70	5.20
Papermaking	1.90	2.90	2.65
Glass, porcelain, ceramics	2.20	4.60	2.90
Leather	3.70	0.60	0.50
Footwear	–	–	2.75
Printing	–	0.60	0.50
Other consumer industries	–	1.00	0.20
Metalworking	7.00	10.00	14.80
Mining	–	12.90	12.50
Construction materials	1.20	0.90	3.80
Chemicals	–	2.00	1.50
Construction	–	0.10	4.75
Power	–	0.20	2.30

Source: Dudek, F. "Vývoj struktury průmyslu v českých zemích za kapitalismu." *Slezský sborník*, vol. 86, no. 4 (1988): 259.

food industry. However, the share of heavy industry and new production sectors (the metalworking, mining, construction, chemical, and power industries) grew significantly. At the same time, the production of glass, porcelain, ceramics, and paper stagnated, while the footwear, wood-processing, printing, and clothing industries rose. All of these changes are clear in the table 24.

In 1902, the metal and mining industries occupied second place in terms of employees and mechanised output behind textiles and clothing, and the food industry fell to third place. On the basis of this data, Dudek estimated that in the long term, the development of industry in the Czech lands took place in its two basic groups – the production of consumer goods and the manufacture of means of production – in the following ratios:

Ratio	1840s	1880s	1902
Production of consumer goods: Manufacture of means of production	80:20	74:26	59:41

The industrialisation of the Czech lands was uneven, not only regarding sector, but also in terms of territory. Luckily there are plenty of resources available showing how the large industrial sectors came into being and were differentiated (Prior to the First World War there were a total of thirteen: North Bohemian brown coal; North Bohemian textiles; Liberec-Jablonec, with its thriving glass production; Northeast Bohemian textiles; the Plzeň region; the Brdy Mountains; Kladno; Prague; Mladá Boleslav and surrounding areas; North Moravian textiles and with it Jeseník, Ostrava, and Brno). We can only make reference here to this literature.[74]

People living in the Habsburg Empire (and elsewhere) at the time had little idea of the cyclical development of capitalist economics until they felt the impact of the cyclical crisis when the Industrial Revolution in the main sectors was reaching its peak in Austria. And so if mention is made at that time of a crisis, this refers to a sudden stock market collapse as the consequence of previous speculation with securities (this was how the crisis of 1873 was written about in Czech and Austrian newspapers). At most, this collapse would be linked with its knock-on effects on business (i.e., with poorly performing bank loans and a collapse in sales of goods). The paralysis that overtook entrepreneurial activities, the huge increase in unemployment, and the gap that opened up between supply and demand (i.e., overproduction) were only appreciated subsequently. Since on the face of it sales were most affected, economists at that time deemed such phases to be business crises.

74 Cf. Mrázek, O. *Vývoj průmyslu v českých zemích a na Slovensku od manufaktury do r. 1918.* Praha, 1964; Kárníková, L. *Vývoj obyvatelstva v českých zemích 1754-1914.* Praha, 1965; more detail is contained in *Průmyslové oblasti v českých zemích za kapitalismu,* Vol. I, 1780–1918. Opava, 1987.

Pioneering work was carried out in this sphere by the French economist Clément Juglar in 1862.[75]

For the pre-March Revolution period, when in Austria and the Czech lands the agrarian economy prevailed despite the emergence of industrialisation, these were still old-fashioned crises. The cause of these crises (as in the agrarian society as a whole) can be found in the agricultural sector (crop failure, potato blight), in climatic and demographic disturbances (severe winters, flooding, epidemics), and in external phenomena (war, continental blockade, etc.). It is no wonder, then, that the revival of economic life after the Napoleonic Wars and state bankruptcy of 1811 lasted more than ten years. It was only in the mid-1820s that stagnation gave way to an upswing, which apart from agricultural prosperity was based mainly on the extensive mechanisation of the cotton and wool industries and the development of the iron and steel industries. From 1826–1830, the average annual increase in production in these three sectors was 5.2%, an irrefutable sign of the forthcoming revolution in production technology. This promising development was somewhat undermined in the first half of the 1830s by a cholera epidemic introduced to Austrian from Asia. Its continuation was subsequently ensured by two new sectors—the sugar beet industry and engineering—along with railway construction. However, in the year before the 1848 revolution, the economy again faltered under the influence of potato blight, a rise in agrarian prices, and the spread of pauperism.

The first harbingers of authentic cyclical development can be seen in the western regions of the monarchy only in the 1850s, when the leading sectors began to acquire the contours of an industrial factory structure. At the end of 1849, the boom underway was favourably impacted by a number of internal and external factors, namely the discovery of gold deposits in California and Australia, the consolidation of state power in the wake of the revolution, the liberalisation of agrarian conditions after serfdom was abolished, and the liberalisation of the Austrian market and trade. Unfortunately, however, the Crimean War came along and the neutrality of the Viennese government, the cutting-off of the textile industry (employing the greatest number of people) from oriental markets, as well as the general loan the state was forced to take out in 1854 due to the government's financial straits, reduced capital credit to factories. And when the war ended and the economy picked up again, it suffered another blow, this time in the shape of the first global economic crisis, which arrived in the Czech lands via Hamburg in autumn 1857. Worst

---

75   Juglar, C. *Des crises commerciales et de leur retour périodique en France, Angleterre et aux États-Unis.* Paris, 1862. Regarding the issue of the crisis in general, cf. the most recent publications Kubů, E., Soukup, J., and Šouša, J. (eds.). *Fenomén hospodářské krize v českých zemích 19. až počátku 21. století. Cyklický vývoj ekonomiky v procesu gradující globalizace.* Praha and Ostrava, 2015.

hit were home-based industries, though textiles, iron and steel, engineering, and sugar refineries also saw a drop in output and workers laid off. However, under the conditions of the still nascent Austrian industrialisation process, we can view this as only a partial crisis caused mainly by external factors, in contrast to parallel developments in Prussia, where cyclical economic developments were underway that began with a bubble that was burst by overproduction. Equally unfavourable economic development afflicted Austria in the following deformed cycle that ended with a short crisis in 1866, the year of the Seven Weeks' War. The development of a coherent economic cycle was prevented by a number of external and internal factors: military losses in Italy, Denmark, and Germany; the deflationary policy pursued by Minister of Finance Baron Ignaz Plener, restrictions on imports of American cotton during the American Civil War, and a decline in railway construction. The indices calculated by the American historian Richard Rudolph (1880 = 100) illustrate clearly the extent and depth of the stagnation at that time: the metalworking index in 1859–1863 increased from 71 to just 73 points, textiles in 1857–1865 fell from 60 to 37 points, mining stagnated in 1857–1867, and the railway network expanded in 1861–1865 by only 771 km, almost half the figure of the previous five years. It is no wonder that the literature records that this period saw the Austrian economic lag so far behind the West—especially Germany—that it never really caught up again.

The monarchy experienced its first full economic cycle, lasting seven years, in 1867, again stimulated by a number of positive factors: the end of the crisis in foreign and internal policy (the Peace of Prague signed between the Kingdom of Prussia and the Austrian Empire, and the Austro-Hungarian Compromise establishing the dual monarchy of Austria-Hungary), the "miraculous" harvests of 1866–1867 and 1867–1868 that had the effect of reducing market prices, increasing exports of grain and sugar, reviving the fortunes of rail transport, and spurring construction of new track. The economy of the Habsburg Empire and the Czech lands experienced rambunctious development, without doubt the most rapid and intense boom in its history, which in the two years prior to the great Stock Exchange crash on 9 May 1873 became a veritable *Gründerzeit*, or founders' period, and saw the speculative creation of dozens of banks and other enterprises, the subsequent failure of which was paid for by hundreds of brokers and thousands of credulous investors. The Viennese crash of 1873 was a global news story, firstly because it overlapped with the recently opened fifth world's fair, the Vienna World Exposition, and secondly because it marked the start of the deepest economic crisis in the nineteenth-century world.[76]

76 Kubů, E., Soukup, J., and Šouša, J. *Fenomén hospodářské krize v českých zemích*; Neuwirth, J. *Bank und Valuta in Österreich-Ungarn 1862–1873, Bd. 2*. Leipzig, 1874; Wirth, M. *Geschichte der Handels-*

To summarise: After two imperfect economic cycles, the Austro-Hungarian economy matured at the peak of its Industrial Revolution (and as confirmation of the culmination thereof) into a normal nine-year economic cycle from 1867–1875—as is customary, we determine its boundaries by means of the timing of its troughs. If the period of expansion is merged with the following years of recession into a single cycle, we can distinguish a further five economic cycles in the Austro-Hungarian economy up until the pre-war period, each lasting seven years on average: two five-year cycles in 1876–1880 and 1881–1885, an eight-year cycle in 1886–1893, a seven-year cycle in 1894–1900, and a nine-year cycle in 1901–1909. A cycle that looked to be nicely shaping up in 1910–1912 was interrupted by the Balkan Wars and eventually by the outbreak of the First World War.[77]

The crisis of the 1870s reached its nadir in 1875, though many sectors only climbed out of the depression three years later. When assessing the entire period from 1873–1895, it must nevertheless be borne in mind that, of these twenty-three years, fifteen were years of growth and only eight involved economic decline. The very short cycles in the latter half of the 1870s and first half of the 1880s indicate that, relative to the very deep and widespread crisis of 1873, the Austrian economy experienced a disproportionately long and arduous depression and stagnation (with low or negative annual growth), which in the Czech lands, with their large agrarian production, was intensified first by the corn crisis and then by the severe sugar crisis. During the 1880s, the agricultural and forestry production index reveals a distinctly stagnating tendency, though the secondary sector grew more rapidly and from that time on became the decisive factor in all subsequent economic booms. In particular, the last two economic cycles before the First World War featured extraordinarily high growth, which was 3.2% from 1894–1898 and rose to 6.6%, 4.1%, and 4.8% respectively during the three boom years of 1905–1907. Economic growth at this time was driven by industry, the production volume of which rose by almost 58% from 1894–1907, while agriculture and forestry (the primary sector) expanded by only approximately 28%. The rate of growth also changed within industry, with heavy industry rising more rapidly than the production of consumer goods. Cisleithania gradually began to catch up with the industrialised countries, and the Czech lands headed straight for the status of predominantly industrialised region. It is

krisen, 3. A. Frankfurt 1883; Verhandlungen des Hauses der Abgeordneten des österreichischen Reichsrathes, VIII. Session 1876, Beilage 445; Mendel'son, L. A. Teorija i istorija ekonomičeskich krizisov i ciklov, tom II. Moskva, 1959; Matis, H. Österreichs Wirtschaft 1848–1913. Berlin, 1972.

77   There is an interesting essay on the historical development of cycles in Austria in Schröder, W. H. and Spree, R. (eds.). Historische Konjunkturforschung. Stuttgart, 1980; P. Horská. "Ekonomické cykly v českých zemích 1879–1914." Hospodářské dějiny–Economic History 1 (1978): 33–88.

not by chance that this period is sometimes called Austria-Hungary's second *Gründerzeit* or speculation fever.

For the moment, however, let us return to the previous period. The term "great depression", especially as applied to the quarter of a century from 1873–1896 of the social and economic history of Central Europe, was first used by Anglo-Saxon historians on the threshold of the great economic crisis of the 1930s. However, it became a widely debated issue only after the publication of a book by the German historian Hans Rosenberg,[78] which devotes a lot of space to Austria. In Rosenberg's opinion, it is a mistake to view this period as a long-term cyclical depression. Industrial production quantitatively grew, but at a slower rate than the rapid boom preceding the crisis of 1873, and was forced to confront problems with sales, lower prices, a decline in liquid investments and loans, and ultimately lower capital return. For this reason, the leading German historian Hans-Ulrich Wehler prefers to describe this period as the "great deflation".[79]

We also have to bear in mind that Rosenberg used the term "great depression" in its broadest sense, including significant changes and new phenomena that affected the economic structure and the political and ideological climate of the time. The growth rate in agriculture slowed down to the point of crisis, and as a result this sector lost its predominant position in the economy. Within industry, the rate of growth fell. Problems in the consumer sector were accompanied by an increase in heavy industry, as well as technologically progressive sectors linked with the second Industrial Revolution. There was pressure from entrepreneurs for a reduction in production costs, especially wages, accompanied by an emphasis on maximum profits by increasing productivity, rationalising the production process, and improving company management. This then intensified the trend for the concentration of production and capital, which eventually led to a transformation of classical capitalism into a higher form of organised capitalism characterised by the increased participation, if not the direct intervention, of the state in the economy (e.g., interventions that benefitted small sole traders in the Austrian laws of 1883 and 1884, or the nationalisation of railway companies by the Austrian state in the 1880s and 1890s). In addition, the "great depression" was not a purely economic phenomenon but affected people both socially and psychologically. As a consequence, business confidence was low until almost the end of the century, dominated by a climate of crisis, large losses, and incessant complaints regarding "bad prices", the "pitiful state of businesses", and "unfair competition", and these resentments spread through society creating a climate of pessimism, discontent, and intolerance. This in turn encouraged ex-

---

78 Rosenberg. *Große Depression und Bismarckzeit.* Berlin, 1967.
79 Cf. Wehler, H. U. *Deutsche Gesellschaftsgeschichte, Vol. 2.* München, 1995.

tremism, both left-wing and right-wing (calls for the rejection of economic and political liberalism; grumblings about "bank and Jewish capital"; the stirring up of class warfare, religious and national disagreements; the creation of unions and employer's organisations, workers', and bourgeois parties; the reinforcement of conservatism; the consolidation of economic and political nationalism; modern anti-Semitism; etc.). Entrepreneurs sought protection in collectivist measures—on domestic markets through the restriction of an individualistic system of free competition by means of cartel agreements, and on foreign markets through the replacement of Manchester-inspired free trade by tariffs (protectionism), all with the assistance of a strong state that in the interests of protecting the economic system attempted to resolve the "social question" through a carrot-and-stick policy (the suppression of the workers' movement and social legislation). All these important changes show that, whatever word we use to define the period from 1873-1895, this quarter of a century represents a genuine turning point in which the first phase of industrialisation was transformed into the second, more extensive, and classical capitalism (i.e., a liberal, individualistic system of free competition based on the "invisible hand" of market forces) and was replaced by a higher type of organised capitalism or a system involving the pooling of resources, collective measures, and regulation of the market by means of the "visible hand" of large corporations, specialised management, and a pliant interventionist state.

An important driver of this transformation was the process of economic concentration,[80] which operated over the long term on four levels. Production was concentrated in large corporations and concerns. Enterprises were merged in cartels and interest groups. Tariffs and other protectionist measures were introduced allowing large corporations and cartels to control the domestic market and, with the aid of dumping, customs wars, etc., to expand onto foreign markets (see the section on the development of trade). Finally, international integration plans and treaties were formed with the aim of creating the largest possible common market (the Central European plans conceived in the 1880s and during 1914–1918 made one of the military objectives of the central powers, namely the concept of *Mitteleuropa* promoted by Friedrich Naumann, a member of parliament in the German Reich, and referred to in the Habsburg Monarchy as "economic rapprochement").

The concentration of production, more often known in the latest economic theory as functional integration, was not unknown even during the

---

80 For more details, see Křížek, J. *Die wirtschaftlichen Grundzüge des österreichisch-ungarischen Imperialismus in der Vorkriegszeit 1900–1914.* Praha, 1963; Mosser, A. "Raumabhängigkeit und Konzentrationsinteresse in der industriellen Entwicklung Österreichs bis 1914." *Bohemia* 17 (1976): 136–192.

early stages of industrialisation prior to March 1848, nor in the 1850s and 1860s (e.g., Around 1840 in Brno, the centre of the textile industry, factories were already on the scene employing almost a thousand workers, and a later example would be the creation of the Pražská železářská společnost or Prager-Eisen-Industrie-Gesellschaft [Prague Iron and Steel Company] in 1857). However, the concentration of production picked up pace during the boom of 1867–1873 and even more so after the crisis and depression of the 1870s, when financial losses, falling prices, and a lack of sales saw many small- and medium-sized companies go bankrupt and led the large companies to take rationalisation measures and reach agreements between themselves. Unfortunately, we cannot corroborate the course and pace of the concentration of production in the Austrian factory industry with precise figures, since the industrial censuses taken in 1880, 1885, 1890, and 1902 were based in different criteria and prior to 1902 were not even complete. For the sake of illustration, we can say that during two decades, from 1880–1902, the average number of workers per factory in the Czech lands rose approximately 2.6-fold and the deployment of propulsion units 5.6-fold. However, in this first stage (lasting until the end of the century), the focus of the concentration process was to be found more in an increase of technological equipment. As far as the workers were concerned, what was expected was an increase in productivity per unit of time. It was symptomatic of the entire process that it took place more easily and faster in sectors with smaller, more specialised production ranges and a relatively restricted number of large customers. Mass production gravitated towards mining, iron and steel, the chemical and paper industries, and power, followed by metallurgy, engineering, and the textiles and food industries. Ceramics, glass, leather, and printing were the domain of medium-sized companies, and production in the rest of industry was the preserve of small companies. An example of this would be the fact that in 1876 there were a total of 176 coalmines extracting 4.5 million tonnes of coal in the Czech lands. By 1913, the number of mines had dropped to 109, though their output had risen to 14.2 million tonnes. The trend is even more marked in the production of pig iron, and this time the data relates to the whole of Cisleithania. In 1872, 112 blast furnaces with an average output of approximately 28,000 quintals were responsible for production of around 3 million quintals of pig iron, whereas in 1913, only 13 factories were producing 17.5 million quintals (i.e., an average of 1.3 million quintals per blast furnace). In comparison, the sugar industry featured relatively low concentration. An increase in production of only 17% from 1876–1914 saw only a 15% reduction in the number of plants (i.e., the increase in output was only fractionally above the rise in production overall). This confirms a well-known fact that the process of concentration as applied to means of production takes place faster and attains greater volume than in the production of consumer goods. An analysis of the data provided by the census of 1902 offers a relatively accurate picture of the concentration of production in Cisleithanian industry (limited to factories employing more than 21 workers):

Table 25: The share of individual size groups in industrial production in Cisleithania in %

Factory by no. of workers	No. of factories	No. of people active in factory	No. of HP engines
21–50	54.0	16.6	small and medium total 20.3
51–100	22.4	15.2	
101–300	17.1	27.7	large companies and super entities total 79.7
301–1,000	5.7	27.7	
more than 1,000	0.8	12.7	
total	13,110=100	1,341,040=100	1,017,518=100

Source: Jindra, Z. "Průmyslové monopoly v Rakousko-Uhersku." ČsČH, vol. 4, no. 2, (1956): 235.

The table makes it clear that, though large corporations employing more than 100 workers comprised less than a quarter of all factory-based companies, they brought together more than two-thirds of all workers. Out of every 100 employees, an average of 68 worked in mass production. In the category of large corporations we find 750 companies employing more than 300 people, and a further 112 super entities employing more than 1,000 people. Though there were not many such massive organisations, they employed almost 13% of the factory workforce and used 16.5% of the power consumed. Although there were only eight such corporations in every thousand factories, they employed almost 13 people of every 100 employees. At first sight this would appear to be a relatively high concentration of industrial production. However, in Germany, for instance, the same degree of concentration was attained ten years earlier, if not at the end of the 1880s. At the start of the twentieth century, the share of small production enterprises in Cisleithania was high. Of a total of 970,000 plants that the census of 1902 reported in mining and all trade production, almost 95% belonged to the category of small enterprise (employing up to five workers) employing 46% of the entire workforce. However, for our purposes what is important is that in 1902, the Czech lands occupied first place as regards the concentration of industrial production in Cisleithania, ahead even of the Alpine countries.

The Czech lands not only dominated Cisleithanian industry in terms of the total number of factories, workers, and engines, but they also had the highest concentration of these production factors, a concentration especially

Table 26: The concentration of industry in the Alpine and Czech lands in 1902 (in %)

Region	No.	Total	Factories by no. of active persons		
			21–100	more than 100	more than 1,000
Alpine lands	factories	37.7	29.6	8.1	0.2
	active persons	33.1	12.0	21.0	3.6
	HP propulsion engines	37.2	8.7	28.5	5.4
Czech lands	factories	52.0	38.3	13.6	0.5
	active persons	56.9 (!)	16.3	40.5 (!)	7.1 (!)
	HP propulsion engines	54.7 (!)	10.7	44.0 (!)	8.4 (!)
Cisleithania	factories	100.0	76.2	23.7	0.8
	active persons	100.0	31.9	68.1	12.6
	HP propulsion engines	100.0	21.9	78.0	15.0

Source: Křížek, J. *Die wirtschaftlichen Grundzüge des österreichisch-ungarischen Imperialismus in der Vorkriegszeit 1900–1914*. Praha, 1963, p. 90.

remarkable in the category of large firms and super entities. In this respect, the Czech lands were the equal of neighbouring Germany, expressed in per capita terms naturally, since the Czech lands and indeed the entire monarchy still had nothing to match the Krupp steel, engineering, and armaments firm with its 81,000 workers and annual turnover of 406 million M (1914). However, this concentration was organised in the same way as in Germany and elsewhere, that is to say upon a horizontal axis (through the combination of companies operating on the same production base through merger or purchase), partly through creating vertical concerns combined under the joint management of an interlinked production level from the extraction of raw materials to their processing into semi-finished products and goods.

An example of the establishment of a large corporation by gradual merger is the concentration of iron and steel production in Bohemia under the wing of the Pražská železářská společnost / Prager Eisen-Industrie-Gesellschaft / Prague Iron and Steel Company (PŽS). First to be formed in 1848 was Kladenské kamenouhelné těžařstvo / Kladno Coal Mining, followed in 1851 by Kladenské železářské těžařstvo / Kladno Ironworks Mining, which in 1857, along with another two firms, merged with PŽS, which then in 1862 was transformed into a joint-stock company (with the majority participation of the leading Viennese bank Österreichische Creditanstalt). At that time, PŽS already employed several thousand workers and smelted almost 45% of all the pig iron produced in the Czech lands. PŽS expanded not only vertically by buying up coal, iron ore, and limestone mines, but it also grew horizontally by adding an engineering workshop, bridge-building works, and rolling mill for rail and metal profiling to its foundry, and later the Edgar Thomson Steel Works. Another milestone was reached in 1886, when under the direction of the renowned tycoon Karl Wittgenstein the three largest iron and steelworks in the Czech lands (PŽS; Teplická válcovna / Teplitzer Walzwerk / Teplice Mill; and Česká montánní společnost / Böhmische Montan-Gesellschaft / Czech Monatane Company) merged, thus bringing together 90% of all production of pig iron in the Czech lands. As general manager of PŽS, Wittgenstein then bought up other Czech steelworks, forced some to cease production in return for compensation, and reached an agreement with those remaining on the level of production and prices. In this way, he laid the foundations of the general Austrian iron and steel cartel (1886), which then proceeded (under the camouflage of high customs duties) to dictate the high price of iron to its customers until the end of the monarchy, thus slowing down economic development and becoming famous as the most powerful monopoly in Austria-Hungary ever. This was made possible by a high degree of concentration that the Cisleithanian iron and steel industry achieved prior to the First World War, when only five companies produced 97% of all pig iron, of which 55% were supplied by three corporations in the Czech lands (PŽS, the Vítkovice Mining and Iron Company, and the Austrian Mining and Metallurgical Company). In reality, this concentration was even higher, since even prior to the war, PŽS had acquired a strong capital position in Oesterreichisch-Alpine Montangesellschaft and in October 1913 even submitted the government in Vienna a plan for the merger of both companies (the plan was thwarted by the war), a move that would have created a colossus controlling the largest part of iron ore fields and 55% of all pig iron.

At the end of the century, the process of concentration in Cisleithania intensified and entered a second, more widespread phase in which it was joined by cartels and banks. Isolated cartel agreements had been recorded during the peak period of laissez-faire capitalism (the first syndicate in Bohemia for the sale of coal, the Buštěhradsko-kladenský spolek / Buštehrad-Kladno Association, was created in 1856), and after the crisis of 1873 other cartels were formed. However, we can only really speak of a large cartel movement in Austria from the second half of the 1880s onwards, when cartels grew in terms of number, stability, contractual duration, and above all the degree of control they exercised over the market: the number of cartels grew from four in 1880 to seven in 1886, eighteen in 1890, fifty-seven in 1900, and nearly tripling to over 200 by 1912. At the start of the twentieth century we therefore speak of the developmental phase of the cartel movement during which cartels infiltrated every corner of industry, became more aggressive and powerful, and established close ties with large banks, which they had often helped establish and whose activities they had supervised. In 1914, they created a special Control Bank for this very purpose. The spur to monopolize the market no longer came from the corporations themselves but from the large banks. This should not surprise us too much if we bear in mind the dimensions attained by the large industrial banking concerns and the connections between banks and industrial capital. The level of influence banks enjoyed in industry is clear from the distribution of cartels in the main manufacturing sectors in 1909: twenty-seven operated in textiles; nineteen in the iron, steel, and engineering industries; nineteen in ceramics; twelve in the chemicals industry; ten in the glass and paper industries; nine in foodstuffs; and fourteen in miscellaneous sectors. However, the number of cartels only partially indicated their real market power. We acquire a better idea of this from the organisational form and content of the cartel agreements, the percentage of cartel production, and the conditions agreed on to restrict mutual competition, which in every sector depended on the degree of concentration attained, the character of production, and sales opportunities. Cartelisation thus moved away from partial, local, short-term, and ineffective agreements to more comprehensive, national, long-term, and highly centralised coalitions. That is to say, it moved from the arrangement of sales conditions (conditional cartels, of which there were fifty in 1909) and the stipulation of agreed prices (price cartels, of which there were eighty-five) or the distribution of markets (twenty-four regional cartels) to the distribution of production amongst their members (fifty-six contingent cartels) or its reduction (five reduction cartels), and to the centralisation of sales (thirty-five syndicates). Certain cartels encompassed more than one of these forms. There were even examples of trusts that exerted monopoly control over an entire sector (e.g., in 1899 in the production of fezzes, and in 1903 in the production of matches and glue). Overall, leaving aside the difference in magnitude, cartelisation progressed in Austria to roughly the same extent as in Germany, which meant that prior to the First World War, Austria, along with Germany, found itself heading the table of the cartel movement, and Austrian or Austro-Hungarian cartels cooperated closely with many international cartels.[81]

At the end of this overview, it would be worth examining the overall dynamic of economic development in the Czech lands and Cisleithania from a quantitative perspective measured using several macroeconomic indicators. These include the industrial production indices worked on during the 1970s by the American historian Richard Rudolph, in the first phase for each year from 1880–1913, and in the second phase retrospectively back to 1830

---

81 Cf. Jindra, Z. "Průmyslové monopoly v Rakousku-Uhersku." ČsČH, vol. 4, no. 2 (1956): 231–270; Křížek. *Die wirtschaftlichen Grundzüge des österreichisch-ungarischen Imperialismus in der Vorkriegszeit*, p. 26 et seq.

in five-year intervals. Rudolph's indices are pretty reliable, since they were constructed on a numerical base of five representative production sectors (mining, the iron and steel industry, engineering, and the food and textile industries), which prior to the First World War represented approximately 70% of the total value of Austrian industrial production.

Table 27: The increase in Austrian industrial production during the First and Second Industrial Revolutions

Where 1880 = 100				Annual real increase per capita		
1830	44	1875	91	1830–1855	2.4	1.9
1835	49	1880	100			
1840	60	1885	129	1855–1890	2.1	1.3
1845	76	1890	165			
1850	69	1895	205	1890–1913	3.1	2.3
1855	80	1900	228			
1860	87	1905	247			
1865	69	1910	303	1830–1913	2.5	1.8
1870	75	1913	333			

Source: Rudolph, R. "The Pattern of Austrian Industrial Growth from the Eighteenth to the Early Twentieth Century." *Austrian History Yearbook* XI (1975), Table 1, p. 3.

These figures confirm that lasting economic growth in the Austrian region of the empire goes back to the pre–March Revolution period and that production fell somewhat during the crisis of 1847–1849 before picking up again in the 1850s. However, it was impacted severely by the monarchy's participation in three wars (falling by 20%) and needed the boom of 1867–1873 to regain lost ground. Surprisingly, growth continued, albeit at a slower rate, even during the great depression, and from 1895–1913 it more than doubled. During its eighty-three years of development, we find no great leap or clear take-off. However, if we leave aside the first half of the 1860s and the turmoil of 1873–1874, there is also no great interruption to the overall continuous, irreversible economic growth of Austrian industry, during which production increased more than sevenfold. However, was this growth uniform throughout? The best way to answer this question is to examine average annual increases in industrial production compared over three longer phases. This shows that the period from 1890–1913 had the highest increase, though according to Rudolph this is not very significant. Far more important is the gradual character of Austria's industrial growth and its similarity from one phase to another. However, the implications of such developments only really become clear when we compare them to similar figures in other countries. In this respect, it is interesting that at the end of the nineteenth century the rate of growth of Austrian industry outstripped that of even France and Great Britain, though these were ranked amongst the old industrial countries at that time. The dynamic and methods of modern capitalism and the Second Industrial Revolution were now being set by the new industrial countries. In Europe this above all meant Germany, whose industrial growth rates the Habsburg Monarchy had previously been unable to match, let along under the more demanding, higher phase of organised capitalism. The annual increase per capita was satisfactory largely because of the slowdown in the country's population growth.

An important new perspective on the secular economic development of Europe, including the Habsburg Empire, in the decisive century of industrialisation 1820–1913 (and brought right up to 1975 in the analysis) was offered in the mid-1970s by the Swiss historian Paul Bairoch. His calculations show that, compared to the slow average annual rise of gross national product (GNP) in Europe of around 0.2%–0.3% in the centuries 1500–1800, the industrialisation of 1830–1910 saw an acceleration of European economic growth to approximately 0.9% (less than previously thought). Europe diverged from this average only twice. The first time was from the 1840s–1860s, when the increase in per capita GNP was 1.2%, and the second time in the last two decades prior to the First World War, when the rate of growth was 1.5%. Interestingly, these periods coincide with the commencement and upswing of the Industrial Revolution in the Czech lands and with the second *Gründerzeit* of the Czech economy in the pre-war period. If we examine Rudolph's figures, we see that Austrian industrial development was basically in line with Europe as a whole.

Table 28: The volume of GNP in the Habsburg Empire compared to Germany and Europe 1830–1913 in market prices (billions of $ converted to US$ and 1960 price equivalents)

	1830	1850	1870	1890	1910	1913
Habsburg empire	7,210	9,190	11,380	15,380	23,970	26,050
Germany	7,235	10,395	16,697	26,454	45,523	49,760
Europe	58,152	77,937	114,966	146,723	231,550	256,845

Source: Bairoch, P. "Europe's Gross National Product 1800–1975." *Journal of European Economic History* 5 (1976), Tab. 4.

Bearing in mind that in 1913, the French national product was not much larger than that of Austria-Hungary, we might well conclude that the Habsburg Empire had nothing to be ashamed of. In fact, the highest GNP in Europe at the time was posted by Tsarist Russia. The explanation for this is simple. During the nineteenth century, both France and Austria-Hungary were characterised by relatively slow population development, while the size of the Russian GNP was due to the size of its population. In the end, what was crucial was the extent to which a state was able to include its population in the creation of national product by means of modern industrialisation. That Austria-Hungary was unable to undertake this successfully is shown by the fact that it increasingly lagged behind the absolute volume of GNP of Germany and the European average. From 1830–1913, Germany managed to increase GNP by almost 588% and Europe as a whole by an average of 342%; in the case of the Habsburg Monarchy this figure was only 261%. This resulted in a shift in economic power within Europe. The share of the Habsburg Empire of total European GNP fell from 12.4% in 1830 to 9.7% in 1880 and improved slightly to finish on 10.1% in 1913. During the course of these developments, the Habsburg Empire outwardly remained in fifth place, though in reality its economic position was seriously weakened. This is particularly visible compared with Germany, which around 1830 was a unit comparable to the Habsburg Empire in terms of economic output, yet by 1913 had increased its share of European GNP from 12.5%–19.4%. This slowdown of the Austro-Hungarian economy is even more apparent if we examine its growth and position on the European scale using a more precise indicator in the form of annual rate of increase of both absolute and per capita GNP. Of the nineteen European countries for which Bairoch collected data, for ease of comparison we have selected six countries with the status of great powers in the following table:

Table 29: Annual rate of growth of GNP in leading European countries 1830–1910 and 1860–1910

Country	GNP total		GNP per capita	
	1830–1910	1860–1910	1830–1910	1860–1910
Habsburg empire	(1.51)	(1.76)	(0.79)	(0.98)
Germany	2.33	2.57	1.33	1.39
Great Britain	(2.01)	1.87	1.21	0.97
France	1.44	1.41	1.18	1.25
Russia	(1.80)	2.25	(0.66)	0.96
Italy	1.03	1.05	0.40	0.39
Europe	1.74	1.88	0.92	0.96

Source: Bairoch, P. "Europe's Gross National Product," tab. 5. (The figures for the first and last year show the three-year averages and the figures in brackets do not exclude a certain margin of error.)

In both cases shown above, from 1860–1910 the Habsburg Empire posts an annual rate of GNP that is either below the European average or hovers

around it. Though its national economy rose in the last half-century prior
to the First World War at a somewhat faster rate than before, it nevertheless
stood no chance of catching up with the more advanced Western countries,
since its rate of growth during these years was slightly less than 1.8% GNP per
annum. This was low, not only compared with Germany, which after unifica-
tion grew fastest of all the European powers (2.6%), but meant that Austria-
Hungary was no better placed than the club of "young" industrial countries
of Europe, coming in below even Russia (2.2%). Though it outperformed Italy
(1%) and Balkan countries such as Serbia (1.6%) and Bulgaria (1.4%), it was
unable to keep up with Denmark (2.9%), Sweden (2.7%), Switzerland (2.1%),
or Belgium and the Netherlands (2%).

The Habsburg Empire does not show up in a better light even if we measure its economic activity in terms of GNP growth per capita (i.e., if we take
into account the parallel annual population growth). From 1860–1910, this
was only 0.78%, one of the lowest figures in Europe and well below the average annual rate (0.92%), and places the country sixth from bottom in Bairoch's index of nineteen countries. Using these figures, Bairoch identifies
three groups of countries in Europe with different annual GNP growth per
capita in the period 1860 and 1910:

(1) The first group, with an increase of at least 15% higher than the European
average, comprised Sweden (growth of 2%), Denmark (1.9%), Germany
(1.4%), Switzerland and France (1.3%), and possibly Finland.
(2) The second group, with an increase less than +/– 15% of the European
average comprised seven countries led by Belgium (1.1%) and followed by
Norway, Great Britain, Russia, the Netherlands, and possibly Romania—
the Habsburg Monarchy squeezes into this group with just less than 1%
growth.
(3) The remaining southern countries (Italy, the Balkan states, Spain, and
Portugal) had very low GNP per capita that was at least 15% lower than
the European average.

Bairoch's segmentation is interesting in that it overturns the widespread
myth of France's very slow economic growth in the nineteenth century and
does not even rank the German Empire at the head of the most rapidly developing European countries. However, it is far more important from the perspective of the Habsburg Monarchy, since it confirms more effectively than
the growth of global GNP that the country lagged behind other countries and
its citizens enjoyed only a relatively low level of wealth and welfare. Compared to previous numerical comparisons, although the Habsburg Empire
edges out Russia, it remains a slow-track European country. According to Bairoch's figures, the country only managed to maintain a respectable position

within Europe at the very start of the Industrial Revolution from 1830–1850, when its per capita GNP was approximately $250 to $283, not so different from the European average of between $240 and $283. The lead enjoyed by Great Britain, the first industrial power in the world, which the Habsburg Monarchy wished to eradicate, was at this time too large, and according to Bairoch did not diminish over the following decades, but on the contrary increased. Around 1850, the difference was $175, but this had risen to $467 by 1913. This means that for the whole of this period of time, the Habsburg Monarchy failed to show up amongst the handful of eight or nine richest states in Europe with above-average or at least average per-capita GNP. The example of the Habsburg Monarchy serves to confirm the well-known model of the modern global economy according to which the wealthier become even wealthier and the poor are not absolutely poor, but, with a few exceptions, remain relatively poor. On the threshold of the twentieth century and the eve of the First World War, when considerable weight was accorded economic strength and the dynamic development of states, the status of Austria-Hungary as one of the Great Powers has to be called into question.

At the same time, however, we know that Austria-Hungary was a state of great paradoxes economically speaking. In addition to the peripheral, backward lands and the regions in the east and southeast, it also included the relatively advanced regions of the northwest. After the collapse of the monarchy, the Alpine states became the basis of the Austrian Republic and the Czech lands became a key part of the Czechoslovak Republic. Though the material legacy that both republics acquired from the Habsburg Empire was not ideally distributed, generally speaking we can say that in 1918, they were the best placed economically of all the successor states. A few macroeconomic indicators will bear out this claim.

The first of these involves the now most authoritative estimates of GDP made not so long ago by the American historian David F. Good. His calculations are based both on a revision of national revenue estimates made from 1915–1928 for the final phase of the monarchy by the statisticians Ferdinand Fellner, Alfred Gürtler, and Ernst Waizner, and also draw on estimates made after the Second World War by the Israeli historian Nachum T. Gross and the Austrian Institute of Economic Research. However, most importantly of all, they expand our knowledge considerably, diversifying it into the monarchy's successor states while at the same time digging retrospectively deeper into the nineteenth century.

Good's new estimates give rise to several interesting conclusions. The first has relevance today, since the figures clearly show that the current economic backwardness of Czechoslovakia, the Czech Republic, Slovakia, and other countries of Eastern and Southeast Europe in comparison with the West is far from being simply a legacy of the communist era. Their roots stretch

Table 30: Level and growth rate of per capita GDP in the successor states of the Habsburg Empire 1870–1910 (in USD in 1980 equivalents)

State	1870	1880	1890	1900	1910	Growth rate
Czechoslovakia	803	913	1,077	1,296	1,491	1.59
present-day Czech Republic	896	1018	1,187	1,429	1,634	1.54
present-day Slovakia	503	572	721	866	1,030	1.85
Austria	1,045	1,161	1,334	1,623	1,813	1.44
Hungary	532	661	789	1022	1,253	2.15
Slovenia	584	683	785	913	1,137	1.62
Croatia	377	446	506	595	786	1.76

Source: Good, David F. "The Economic Lag of Central and Eastern Europe: Income Estimates for the Habsburg Successor States, 1870–1910." *Journal of Economic History* (1994), Table 3.

back into the nineteenth century, if not further back to the beginning of industrialisation. This can be seen from the initial data of 1870, when GDP per capita throughout the Habsburg Monarchy was $642, slightly more in the Czech lands ($896), yet still only a fraction of that in Great Britain ($1,993). The same West–East axis of decline is mirrored in regional differences in the Habsburg Empire itself. In 1870, GDP in the monarchy's western regions was two or three times higher than in the eastern regions. By 1914, these regional differences had diminished somewhat thanks to a higher rate of GDP growth in eastern countries, but in essence remained, substantially weakening the economies of the successor states.

To conclude this chapter, I would like to examine to what extent individual industrial sectors contributed to the economic performance of the Czech lands. Of particular importance were the advances in Czech engineering in response to the increased demand for propulsive engines in mining, textiles, and the iron and steel industry. The first steam engines for the textile industry in the monarchy, including the Czech lands, came from abroad or were built by foreign mechanics. Steam engines for pumping out pit water had been used in the Czech lands since the 1820s, for coal extraction in Kladno since the end of the 1830s, and in Ostrava from the start of the 1840s.

The importance of engineering in the Czech lands is borne out by the fact that from the 1880s, sugar-making machines were exported to Italy, Sweden, France, British Guiana, and Russia (by the companies Daňkova strojírna / Daněk Machine Factory in Prague; Českomoravská/Bohemian-Moravian Machine Works in Prague; and Škodovy závody / Škoda Works in Plzeň).

Škodovy závody manufactured crankshafts for marine engines, and Ring-hoffer's railway carriage factory in Prague exported its production to the Balkans, Bulgaria, Belgium, and Russia.

Similarly, machines for the textile industry were first imported (ille-gally at first, because of English bans) and copied. In the 1840s, the Habsburg Empire was one of the leading European manufactures of cotton fabrics, of which one-third was produced in the Czech lands.[82] Development of the machine press began in the 1820s. The 1830s saw the discovery of the block-printing machine, the *perrotine* (invented by Louis-Jerome Perrot) for three and four-colour printing, and the Czech *leitenbergina* (Eduard Leitenberger) for eight-colour printing.

The processing of large quantities of agricultural production was charac-teristic of the economic structure of the Czech lands. This applied mainly to what was known as "white gold" (i.e., sugar). Experiments were conducted with the refinement of sugar cane (in 1787 by the cane sugar refinery in Zbra-slav, Prague), and then with sugar beet (in 1801 the first sugar beet factor was opened in Hořovice in West Bohemia). By the mid-1830s, the Germans Karl Weinrich (1800–1860) and Friedrich Kodweiss (1803–1866) had perfected em-pirical technology for cleaning beet juice. The new procedure provided strong support for the development of the Czech sugar industry, and was applied abroad under the label "Czech work". The technology of sugar production continued to be improved by means of diffusion (the extraction of beet pulp: Julius Robert, 1864) and saturation (the clarification of the sugar juice using lime and its purification with carbon dioxide: Hugo Jelínek, Bedřich Frey Jr.). The production of sugar lumps is associated with the Czech lands. In 1843, the director of the Dačice sugar refinery in Moravia, Jakob Christoph Rad, obtained a patent to produce sugar lumps.

The development of brewing meant the abolition of the *propination* laws that ensured a monopoly on the production and sale of spirits for the land-owning nobility. In 1784, the propination laws applying to spirits and beer drunk by the peasants (obliging them to make purchases only in hostelries owned by the aristocracy) were abolished and competition was permitted under a declaration establishing the free purchase of spirits by serfs and innkeepers in 1788. However, until 1869, the production of spirits remained limited by the continuing monopoly on their production enjoyed by the no-bility and bourgeois with brewing rights or *Braurecht*. During the second half of the nineteenth century, Czech beer became known even beyond Europe. The technological codification and reform of brewing—including the intro-duction of beer controls during production using the thermometer, modified

---

82   Jindra, Z., Jakubec, I. et al. *Hospodářský vzestup českých zemí od poloviny 18. století do konce monar-chie.* Praha, 2015, p. 262.

hydrometer, etc., and not simply the senses—is associated with the name of the Czech brewer František Ondřej Poupě.

We should at least mention the type of beer known as Pilsen (lower fermentation in accordance with the Bavarian model), Pilsner Urquell (i.e., a golden beer, full of colour, medium bitter, with a distinctive aroma). The current international classification system distinguishes between Bohemian-style Pilsner, German-style Pilsner, and international-style Pilsner.

We also find in the Czech lands representatives of the new sectors, namely electrical engineering and the automobile industry. From the start of the 1880s, especially after the International Exposition of Electricity in Paris and the first International Electrical Congress in 1881, the electricity industry began to expand in the Czech lands particularly thanks to the efforts of František Křižík and Emil Kolben, and in Moravia thanks to Robert Bartelmus, Štěpán Doubrava, and Josef Donát. Four of Křižík's arches with Edison's light bulbs illuminated the main staircase at the International Exposition of Electricity in Paris in 1881. Schuckert exported to Germany under the terms of Křižík's patent (1880/1882), and this patent was further utilised in Britain, France, Belgium, and the USA. Kolben's electricity plant supplied turbo-alternators not only to the monarchy, but also to Great Britain (the Bankside Power Station in London, now Tate Modern), the Balkans, the Ottoman Empire, Italy, France, Spain, Persia, Argentina, etc.

The oldest carmaker in the Czech lands, now Tatra, was based in Kopřivnice and the largest in the monarchy was Laurin & Klement in Mladá Boleslav (now VW-Škoda), which produced mainly luxury vehicles for the Russian and Japanese courts along with utility vehicles for the postal authorities around Europe.

A hugely important company as regards the development of the chemical industry was the joint-stock Oesterreichischer Verein für Chemische und Metallurgische Produktion, founded in 1856 in Ústí nad Labem. From the end of the 1860s onwards, the scale of its production made it the largest chemicals manufacturer in the whole of the Habsburg Monarchy. At the start of the twentieth century, it was one of the four largest chemicals companies in Europe.

One of the most important discovers was the principle of blade rotation not only on a distributor wheel but turbine rotors. This was made by Professor Viktor Kaplan, a professor of German technology in Brno (patent no. 74244/1918), who began his research into this problem before the First World War.

4. DEVELOPMENT
OF THE TERTIARY SECTOR

DEVELOPMENT OF TRANSPORT AND COMMUNICATIONS

During the eighteenth and nineteenth centuries, major changes happened to the transport infrastructure in Central Europe that laid the foundations for the way it is organised at present.[83] The movement of people and goods changed dramatically and was both a symptom and catalyst of fundamental economic and social transformation. In the transport sphere, the modernisation process was manifest as follows:

(1) The construction and improvement of a road network of regional and supraregional importance and the commencement of automobile transport at the start of the twentieth century
(2) The creation of waterways and steam navigation
(3) The arrival of rail transport
(4) The laying of the foundations of modern urban public transport

In addition, during the latter half of the nineteenth century, the foundations were laid for a completely new communications network based on the latest technologies (above all the telegraph and telephone), and prior to the First World War the seeds were planted in the Czech lands of what later became regular air transport. These seismic changes in the sphere of transport and communications were not only an essential condition for the expansion of trade, but they had significant social and cultural knock-on effects.[84]

---

83 Merki, Ch. M. *Verkehrsgeschichte und Mobilität.* Stuttgart, 2008, pp. 9–11; Roth, R. "Verkehrsrevolutionen," in: Sieder, R. and Langthaler, E. (eds.). *Globalgeschichte 1800–2010.* Wien, 2010, pp. 471–501.

84 Roth, R. *Das Jahrhundert der Eisenbahn. Die Herrschaft über Raum und Zeit 1800–1914.* Ostfildern, 2005; Roth, R. and Schlögel, K. *Neue Wege in ein neues Europa. Geschichte und Verkehr im 20. Jahrhundert, Frankfurt am Main.* New York, 2009; Dinhobl, G. (ed.). Eisenbahn/Kultur, Railway/Culture (Mitteilungen des Österreichischen Staatsarchivs, Sonderband 7). Wien, 2004; Dienel, H. L. and Schmucki, B. *Mobilität für alle. Geschichte des öffentlichen Personennahverkehrs in der Stadt zwischen technischem Fortschritt und sozialer Pflicht.* Stuttgart, 1997; Popelka, P. and Dvořák, J. "Vývoj dopravy a komunikací," in: Jakubec, I. and Jindra, Z. *Hospodářský vzestup českých zemí od poloviny 18. století do konce monarchie.* Praha, 2015, pp. 305–350.

During the first half of the eighteenth century, we see the first wave of the modernisation of transport in the Habsburg Monarchy in the construction of a new type of road called *chaussée*.[85] In 1724, a court decree was issued under which work began on five main highways intended to link Vienna with Trieste, Bohemia, Moravia, Hungary, Upper Austria, and Silesia. Of most significance to the Czech lands was the main highway from Vienna via Znojmo and Jihlava to Prague, and from Vienna via Brno and Olomouc to Wrocław. The number of such road projects increased under Maria Theresa. At the end of the 1740s, a plan was drafted for the construction of 910 km of highway in Moravia and Silesia alone. However, for a number of reasons, the road works stretched on until 1780. Under Emperor Joseph II, major reforms were enacted in the sphere of highway construction that impacted on the road network in the Czech lands. Notwithstanding this, at the end of the eighteenth century the network of *chaussées* was still inadequate (it ran to 730 km in Bohemia and to 680 km in Moravia and Silesia).[86]

The situation started to improve in the aftermath of the Napoleonic Wars. From 1820–1840, a backbone road network was constructed, and by the end of the 1840s the Czech lands boasted one of the most dense road networks in the Habsburg Monarchy.[87] Better quality roads and technically more advanced vehicles made possible the significant expansion of both postal and private transport during the first half of the nineteenth century.[88]

By the end of the 1820s, transport systems had changed beyond recognition. The backbone of supraregional trade consisted of a small number of roads built and maintained by the state. Where natural conditions permitted, the navigable flow of important rivers played a similar role. However, from the 1830s onwards, a new transport system began making its presence felt. This was the railway, which rapidly came to assume a pivotal role. The character of the road infrastructure began to change rapidly. Long-distance transport by covered wagons and stagecoaches was quickly replaced by the railroad, the capacity of which in the nineteenth century outstripped that of roads. This was another reason why state participation in road building had

85 Dienel, H. L. and Schiedt, H. U. (eds.). *Die moderne Strasse: Planung, Bau und Verkehr von 18. bis zum 20. Jahrhundert.* Frankfurt am Main, 2010; Helmedach, A. *Das Verkehrssystem als Modernisierungsfaktor. Straßen, Post, Fuhrwesen und Reisen nach Triest und Fiume vom Beginn des 18. Jahrhunderts bis zum Eisenbahnzeitalter.* München, 2002; Müller, U. (ed.). *Infrastrukturpolitik in der Industrialisierung zwischen Liberalismus, Regulierung und staatlicher Eigentätigkeit.* Leipzig, 1996.
86 Popelka, P. "Die Hauptprobleme des Aufbaus eines modernen Straßennetzes in den böhmischen Ländern in der Zeit des aufgeklärten Absolutismus, Das Achtzehnte Jahrhundert und Österreich." *Jahrbuch der Österreichischen Gesellschaft zur Erforschung des Achtzehnten Jahrhunderts* 30 (2016): 171–190.
87 *Mittheilungen aus dem Gebiete der statistik, Dritter Jahrgang, VII. Heft.* Wien, 1854, p. 4; Hlavačka, M. *Dějiny dopravy v českých zemích v období průmyslové revoluce.* Praha, 1990, p. 27.
88 Hlavačka, M. *Cestování v éře dostavníků.* Praha, 1998.

already abated by the end of the 1840s. During the latter half of the century, modernisation of the road network was more about improving minor roads. This was mainly the remit of the emerging self-governing local governments. Under these new conditions, the road network acquired additional significance. If the railway was becoming the transport backbone, then the network of different categories of highway was to form a system of "capillaries" making accessible the trunk and later the branch railway stations.[89]

The latter half of the nineteenth century saw not only a boom in rail transport but also the completion and modernisation of the road network in the Czech lands. This network formed the foundation of the subsequent motorisation and individualisation of transport. Motorisation was hampered by the poor condition of many roads, the cost and scarcity of fuel, the heavy taxation imposed on motorised vehicles, and the price of cars.[90]

Since the Habsburg Monarchy was essentially landlocked, with only a few poorly situated ports at its disposal, and water transportation still underdeveloped, the railways were of major importance in the modernisation of the transport infrastructure in the Czech lands. Alongside the boom in the construction of state roads and the development of stagecoach transport, the first rail transport was horse-drawn on lines linking České Budějovice to Linz and Prague to Lány. Both projects featured the input of the outstanding mathematician František Josef Gerstner (1756–1832) and his son František Antonín (1795–1840).[91]

However, far more important in terms of the development of transport was the arrival of the steam train. During the 1830s and 1840s, many private railway initiatives were launched. Most important for the Czech lands was Rothschild's k.k. Kaiser Ferdinands-Nordbahn linking Vienna and Moravia, Silesia, Galicia, and Prussian Silesia.[92] In 1838, the banker Georg von Sina obtained permission to build a railway from Vienna to Rab and founded the k.k. Wien-Raaber Eisenbahn-Gesellschaft. In 1853, the company was nationalised and absorbed into the k.k. Südliche Staatsbahn.[93] In 1844, the private

89   Popelka, P. "The Transport Revolution and Austrian Silesia 1742–1914," in: Zářický, A. and Závodná, M. (eds.). *Creating an Interdisciplinary Paradigm Using the Example of Modernization in a Region (Austrian Silesia): Contributions for the XVIIth World Economic History Congress in Kyoto.* Ostrava, 2015, pp. 79–95.

90   Hlavačka, M. "Doprava a komunikace v českých zemích 1848–1914." ČsČH 37 (1989): 536–560 and 666–679.

91   Hons, J. *František Antonín Gerstner.* Praha, 1948.

92   Hons, J. et al. *Čtení o Severní dráze Ferdinandově.* Praha, 1990; Artl, G., Gürtlich, G., and Zenz, H. (eds.). *Allerhöchste Eisenbahn. 170 Jahre Nordbahn Wien – Brünn.* Wien, 2009; Popelka, P. *Zrod moderní dopravy. Modernizace dopravní infrastruktury v Rakouském Slezsku do vypuknutí první světové války.* Ostrava, 2013, pp. 87–97.

93   Artl, G., Gürtlich, G., and Zenz, H. (eds.). *Mit Volldamf in den Süden. 150 Jahre Südbahn Wien – Triest.* Wien, 2008.

company Ungarische Central-Eisenbahn was awarded a licence to construct and operate a railway line from Marchegg via Pressburg and Pest to Debrecen. In 1850, the company was bought by the state and formed the core of the k.k. Südöstliche Staatsbahn. An important project for Galicia was the Krakau-Oberschlesische Bahn built in the late 1840s. This line linked Kraków not only with Vienna but also with Prussia and Russia. In 1850 the Krakau-Oberschlesische Bahn was purchased by the state and formed the basis of the k.k. Östliche Staatsbahn.[94]

The state-financed construction of the backbone railway network lasted until the mid-1850s, during which time approximately 1,800 km of track had been built. A backbone network of rail links was created by means of state conceived initiatives and the nationalisation of private lines: k.k. Nordliche Staatsbahn (Olomouc – Prague – Podmokly – the Saxony border and Brno – Česká Třebová), k.k. Südliche Staatsbahn (Vienna – Trieste; Graz – Celje – Ljubljana; Katzelsdorf – Sopron and Mödling – Laxenburg), k.k. Südöstliche Staatsbahn (Marchegg – Pest – Cegléd – Szeged – Timişoara, Vienna – Rab – Komárno; Oraviczabanya – Bazias), k.k. Östliche Staatsbahn (Dębica – Kraków – Trzebinia – Szczakowa – the border of Prussia and Russia; Trzebinia – Oświęcim; Bieżanów – Wieliczka) and k.k. Lombardisch-venetianischen Staatsbahn (Venice – Padua – Verona – Milan; Verona – Mantua; Milan – Monza – Como).[95]

However, during the mid-1850s, the state began extricate itself from the railway sector, and under a new licensing act of 1854 offered incentives to private rail construction companies and sold off the state lines. By 1859, virtually all the state lines had been privatised, including the newly completed and strategically important line linking Vienna and Trieste. The state-guaranteed yield on investment enshrined in the licensing act provoked a rail fever from 1855–1859. However, in the early 1860s the state abandoned its system of generous guarantees and adopted a more frugal approach. This led to a temporary weakening of interest in rail investment, and from 1860–1863 no new railway initiatives were launched. The situation in Hungary was catastrophic, since no railway licences were awarded from 1861–1866.[96] At the same time, the Ministry of Commerce, responsible for railways, attempted to create an overarching concept of the development of the rail network across the length and breadth of the monarchy. This comprehensive plan was published in 1864 and contained

---

94 Dressler, S. "Der österreichische Eisenbahnbau von den Anfängen bis zur Wirtschaftskrise des Jahres 1873," in: Gutkas, K., and Bruckmüller, E. (eds.). *Verkehrswege und Eisenbahnen*. Wien, 1989, pp. 74–86.

95 Czedik, A. *Der Weg von und zu den österreichischen Staatsbahnen 1824–1854/8, 1882–1910, Bd. I.* Wien, Teschen, Leipzig 1913.

96 *Die Habsburgermonarchie 1848–1918, Bd. I.* p. 283–287; Hlavačka. *Dějiny dopravy v českých zemích*, p. 66.

a proposal for the creation of the fifty-five most important routes. In total, almost 7,000 km of track was to be laid costing an estimated 684 million gulden.[97]

During the late 1860s and early 1870s, interest in rail construction picked
up considerably. The short-lived economic upswing of that time was accompanied by the rapid construction of new track, and this completed the basic
network in the Czech lands. Activity was most frenzied from 1867–1873 and
resulted in an unprecedented 10,920 km of track being laid throughout the
monarchy. In 1875, the total track length was 10,920 km, and the Czech lands
hosted approximately a quarter of all railway connections with more than
3,300 km of track.[98]

Railway construction by private companies was affected in 1873 by economic crisis. As in other sectors, signs of the crisis had begun to appear
around 1871–1872, while railway construction was still in full swing. The
Viennese financial collapse of May 1873 began to impact rail construction
only the following year. Though the companies were hit by the crisis very
quickly, a certain momentum saw construction continue until the mid-1870s.
The problems experienced by many companies during the depression meant
the state had to take up the slack. Most of the new private lines built during
the previous years needed massive state support, while many new projects
fell by the wayside for lack of funds.[99]

In 1877, the rising cost to the state led to the Sequestration Act, which
allowed for the privatisation of stricken companies with a state guarantee.
By the First World War, there had been three waves of privatisation in the
Habsburg Monarchy (in 1881–1884, 1892–1895, and 1906–1908), at the end of
which only Southern Rail, Košice–Bohumín Railway, and a few industrial and
branch lines remained in private hands. In 1912, only 2,518 km of track was
held by private owners, of which 1,412 km was local.

In addition, from 1874 onwards, the state restarted its construction
programme, including the first local railway lines, as part of its attempt to
kick-start the economy by creating temporary jobs. From 1882–1910, a total of
2,273 km of new line was laid by the state, with the biggest projects in Galicia
(1,224 km or 53.8%); the Czech lands (406 km or 18%); Upper Austria, Styria,
Carinthia, and Carniola (332 km or 14.6%); and Tyrol and Vorarlberg (124 km
or 5.4%).[100]

---

97   *Denkschrift zu dem Entwurfe eines neuen Eisenbahnnetzes der österreichischen Monarchie.* Wien,
      1864.
98   Hlavačka. *Dějiny dopravy v českých zemích*, p. 102.
99   Popelka, P. "Hospodářská krize 70. let 19. století a její dopad na železniční společnosti v habsbur-
      ské říši," in: Kubů, E., Soukup, J., and Šouša, J. (eds.). *Fenomén hospodářské krize v českých zemích
      19. až počátku 21. století.* Praha and Ostrava, 2015, pp. 159–168.
100 Czedik, A. *Der Weg von und zu den österreichischen Staatsbahnen 1824-1854/8, 1882-1910,* Bd. I.
      Wien, Teschen, Leipzig, 1913, p. 150.

During the late 1870s and early 1880s, the attention of both the public and private sector turned to the support and construction of a new type of railway (i.e., local or branch lines). The construction of branch lines laid the foundation for the development of the economy of those regions that had not shared in the benefits of previous construction activities. Though initially regarded as an interim measure, this type of line soon became clearly advantageous. This was especially so in the 1870s, when the rail industry was severely affected by the economic crisis. Prior to branch lines being enshrined in law (i.e., before 1880), five routes had been built in the Czech lands that met the parameters of what were later to become branch lines under special laws.[101]

Act 56 of 25 May 1880 created a rail construction system in which routes were divided for the first time into trunk and branch lines. Fewer technical demands were placed on branch lines, which were tax exempt for up to thirty years. However, these regulations did not answer the question of financing. Funding for local lines from the crown land or state had to be secured by a special act for each case. This opened up a space for public-private partnerships. The local lines were built by both well-established companies and start-ups, and these enterprises focused exclusively on creating branch lines with guaranteed returns. During the 1890s and into the twentieth century, various groups comprising self-governing bodies, landowners, and local industrialists joined in the construction of local rail tracks.[102]

During the 1880s and 1890s, construction work was mostly the preserve of cash-rich companies keen on opening up a space for their own transport services. In the Czech lands there was k.k. Österreichische Staatseisenbahn-Gesellschaft (in 1882–1887, the company laid 359 km of local track and a purchased a further 72 km in Bohemia and Moravia), k.k. Kaiser Ferdinands-Nordbahn (which in 1888–1900 laid 261 km of local track, purchased 88 km, and oversaw operations on a further seven local routes owned by another company), and Österreichische Lokaleisenbahn-Gesellschaft (which in 1880–1892 laid 344 km of local track in Bohemia and Moravia). As far back as the 1880s several smaller companies had entered the market, including k.k. Böhmische Commercialbahnen, Mährische Westbahn, Actien-Gesellschaft der priv. Kremsierer Eisenbahn, and Brünner Local-Eisenbahn-Gesellschaft.[103]

Initially the state only provided limited direct support for the construction of new track. In 1880–1887, licences were awarded for 2,262 km of track, of which only 231 km enjoying direct state support was put into operation (mostly in Galicia and Bukovina). After the Branch-Line Support Act was

---

101 Pavlíček, S. *Naše lokálky. Místní dráhy v Čechách, na Moravě a ve Slezsku*. Praha, 2002.

102 Popelka, P. "Podíl zemské samosprávy na budování lokální železniční sítě a zemská železniční akce v Rakouském Slezsku (do roku 1918)." *Časopis matice moravské* 127 (2008): 35–66.

103 Pavlíček. *Naše lokálky*, pp. 27–66.

amended in 1887, the state share of support rose. In 1888–1894, licences were awarded for 1,264 km of local track, and only 220 km was laid without any public support whatever.[104]

As government spending spiralled, it became clear that some of the burden must be shared by the self-governing bodies of the crown lands and local businesspeople. The state now gave priority to projects enjoying multi-source financing. As a consequence, during the 1890s, most of the crown lands enacted special laws that amended the process of supporting branch lines in various different ways. The Crown Lands Branch-Line Support Act was passed in Bohemia in 1892 and in Moravia and Silesia in 1895. These laws supported the "self-help" construction of branch lines financed by both local interest groups (municipalities, entrepreneurs, etc.) and individual provinces or the state.

Following the promulgation of the crown land acts, there was a boom in the construction of branch lines. From 1893–1910, when work on new branch lines essentially came to a halt in Bohemia, fifty-four tracks were laid totalling in excess of 1,700 km. In Moravia and Silesia, more than thirty branch lines were laid from 1895–1914, supported by the state, the crown land, and local businesspeople. Only in exceptional cases in Moravia and Silesia was a branch line financed directly by the state with assistance from local groups.[105]

From 1877–1914, a total of 4,567 km branch lines were laid in the Czech lands, of which Bohemia accounted for 3,087 km (67.5%), Moravia 1,212 km (26.5%), and Silesia 268 km (5.9%). In Bohemia these routes were mostly in the hands of private owners backed by a guarantee from the state or crown land, while in Moravia they were built using the capital of large railway companies. Come the twentieth century, with the exception of suburban lines, few profitable projects remained for construction, and interest in investing in branch lines inevitably dropped. The First World War marked the definitive end to the process of building a network of branch lines.

The construction of a rail network in the Czech lands was completed prior to the war. Geographically speaking, the network was distinctly uneven in Cisleithania. The Czech lands boasted the densest network in terms of surface area, and along with Upper and Lower Austria were very well provided for in terms of infrastructure. However, northern and eastern Cisleithania lagged behind. The share of individual crown lands of the Cisleithanian railway network is shown in the table 31.

The fact that the region was landlocked and the character of its river network allowed for only limited development of river transport, usually on

104 Hodáč, F. *Finanční účast království a zemí při zřizování vedlejších železnic předlitavských.* Brno, 1910, pp. 56–67.
105 Pavlíček. *Naše lokálky,* pp. 107–109.

Table 31: Share of individual crown lands of the total length of the railway network in Cisleithania (1912)

Crown land	Track length (km)	Share of network (in %)	Metres of track per km²	Kilometres of track per 100,000 inhabitants
Bohemia	6,769	29.6	130	100.0
Moravia	2,119	9.3	95	80.8
Silesia	668	2.9	130	88.2
Lower Austria	2,477	10.8	125	70.1
Upper Austria	1,085	4.7	91	127.3
Salzburg	418	1.8	58	194.7
Styria	1,478	6.5	66	102.3
Carinthia	625	2.7	61	157.9
Carniola	508	2.2	51	96.5
Littoral	586	2.6	73	65.5
Tyrol and Vorarlberg	1,183	5.2	40	108.3
Galicia	4,131	18.1	53	51.5
Bukovina	602	2.6	58	75.2
Dalmatia	230	1.0	18	35.7

Source: *Die Habsburgermonarchie 1848–1918, Bd. I*, p. 301.

medium and lower river flows. River transport was traditionally by means of rafts and boats. In the Czech lands, rivers were most often used for log driving, both freely and bound together into rafts. Until the mid-nineteenth century, the rivers most often used for log driving in Bohemia were the Elbe, Otava, Vltava, Malše, Lužnice, Nežárka, Sázava, and Berounka, and in Moravia the Morava and Bečva.[106] Freight was also transported by river, especially on the Elbe. Thanks to the direction of its current, Elbe-driven trade mainly consisted of exports, including grain, glass, and coal. The goods imported into Bohemia on the river were mostly colonial.[107]

During the second half of the nineteenth century, waterways were impacted by the development of rail transport, which provided strong competition. However, the relationship between water and rail was more symbiotic than it might at first sight appear. Though demand shifted from water to rail,

106 Hubert, M. *Dějiny plavby v Čechách I, II*. Děčín, 1996–1997; Morávek, J. *Plavci na Sázavě*. Praha, 1965; Hons, J. "Schwarzenberský plavební kanál na Šumavě I-II." *Dějiny věd a techniky*, v. 24, no. 4 (1991): 193–208 and *Dějiny věd a techniky*, v. 25, no. 2 (1992): 111–119.

107 Hlaváčka. *Dějiny dopravy v českých zemích*, p. 37.

where conditions were favourable, railway companies would build wharfs and transit sheds that processed goods for transportation by water. River transport remained the cheapest mode of transport, even in the era of railways, and was particularly useful for goods that, due to their weight and relatively low price, were hit by the higher tariffs of rail companies, especially coal, timber, building supplies, and grain.

Until the mid-nineteenth century, water transport in the Czech lands remained on the same technical level as previous centuries. Vessels floated downstream under their own weight in the manner of rafts. Against the current they were towed by yoked horses or the crew themselves. The arrival of steam navigation revolutionised traditional water transportation. In 1841, the first steamboat began operations on the Elbe, linking Bohemia with Dresden. However, this inaugural route, designed exclusively for passenger transport, could not hold its ground against the arrival of trail transport in the Labe/Elbe region. Freight continued to be shipped in traditional form by Prager Segelschiffahrts-Gesellschaft (founded in 1822), which saw demand for its services increase sevenfold by the mid-nineteenth century.[108]

The further development of steam navigation on the Elbe and the Vltava took place only in the latter half of the 1850s. In 1856, Prager Segelschiffahrts-Gesellschaft started to use steamers (tugs) with towed dinghies in addition to sailboats, and as a consequence the company changed its name to Prager Dampf- und Segel-Schiffahrts-Gesellschaft. After the introduction of steam technology, the number of vessels travelling between Hamburg and river ports in Bohemia increased and journey times fell dramatically. Transport along the Elbe felt the positive impact of the expansion of the rail network. Many rail companies built wharfs and transit sheds at convenient locations (Ústí nad Labem, Děčín, Lovosice, Rozbělesy, Litoměřice, and Krásné Březno), and by the end of the nineteenth century Ústí nad Labem had become the busiest port in the whole of the Habsburg Monarchy in terms of volumes of goods shipped. From 1895–1900, 4.3% of Cisleithania's total imports and 18.3% of its exports passed through the city (i.e., more than through the monarchy's largest maritime port in Trieste).

Following the founding of the Prager Dampfschiffahrts-Gesellschaft in 1864, passenger steam transport expanded on the Vltava, though this was mainly significant in terms of the development of tourism. During the 1870s, traditional freight transport on the upper and middle Vltava was badly hit by the opening of the Emperor Franz Joseph Railway. The most important wharf on the Vltava was that in Karlín, joined from the 1890s onwards by newly built port in Holešovice.

---

108 Ibid., pp. 36–38.

The next stage in the development of steam navigation was the introduction of chain-boat navigation. Vessels called chain boats were used to haul strings of barges upstream by using a fixed chain lying on the bed of a river. The chain was raised from the riverbed to pass over the deck of the steamer, being hauled by a heavy winch powered by a steam engine. Team-boat navigation began in 1863 in Magdeburg and chain was gradually laid all the way to Hamburg (1874). As far back as 1871, the Prager Dampf- und Segel-Schiffahrts-Gesellschaft laid chain along the bed of the river from Ústí nad Labem to the border with Saxony. In the 1880s, more chain was laid (Štětí to Mělník, 1885–1888). The largest shipping company in the Czech lands operating on the Elbe at this time was Österreichische Nordwest-Dampfschiffahrts-Gesellschaft, which was affiliated with Österreichische Nordwestbahn. In 1881, Österreichische Nordwest-Dampfschiffahrts-Gesellschaft bought up Prager Dampf- und Segel-Schiffahrts-Gesellschaft, in the process becoming the only Austrian company operating on the Elbe. In addition to this corporate giant, from 1896 onwards Deutsch-Österreichische Dampfschiffahrts-AG transported Bohemian goods along the Elbe, and in 1907 was joined by Neue Deutsch-Böhmische Elbeschiffahrt-AG. In 1904, Österreichische Nordwest-Dampfschiffahrtsgesellschaft leased its entire vessel fleet to the imperial Vereinigte Elbeschiffahrts-Gesellschaften AG, headquartered in Dresden.[109]

The development of water transportation in the Czech lands was closely bound up with the problems of river navigation. The main problem was the non-navigability of rivers by fully loaded freight vessels during periods of low water levels. This was especially the case along the Vltava–Elbe route. In the eighteenth century, a long-term plan was launched that involved a shift away from the simple removal of obstacles from the riverbed and the creation of towpaths for comprehensive modifications to waterways aimed at improving navigation. During the reign of Maria Theresa and Joseph II, the state created the conditions necessary for the systematic care of important watercourses, and the first locks were built on the Vltava and Elbe, facilitating navigation around weirs. Extensive modifications were made to the flow of the River Morava at the start of the nineteenth century in the section between Hodonín and Děvín, where the river flowed into the Danube.[110]

During the latter half of the nineteenth century, in association with the development of steam navigation, the systematic regulation was initiated of selected river sections. This controlling the flow rate and the construction

109 Hubert, M. and Hlavačka, M. "Rakouský dopravní gigant: Rakouská severozápadní dráha a Rakouská severozápadní plavební společnost 1868–1922." *Dějiny vědy a techniky* (1992): 65–84; Hlavačka. *Dějiny dopravy v českých zemích*, pp. 128–134.
110 Hájek, J. "Návrhy na splavnění českých řek v 17. a 18. století," in: Pánek J. (ed.). *Vlast a rodný kraj v díle historika. Sborník prací žáků a přátel věnovaný profesoru Josefu Petráňovi*. Praha, 2004, pp. 447–472.

of locks and wharfs. It mainly affected the Vltava–Elbe waterways and was aimed at creating reliable trade links between the Czech lands and the port in Hamburg. During the 1850s, regulatory work was carried out on the lower Elbe and upper Vltava, financed from the state budget, and on the upper and middle flows of both rivers financed by the crown lands. The work intensified at the end of the 1860s, and in 1868 regulatory work commenced on the Vltava between Prague and Mělník. Of great importance for the development of the Elbe for navigation purposes was creation of the Elbeverein or Elbe Club in 1875 in Ústí nad Labem, which brought together Czech and German traders interested in developing the Elbe navigation channel. In the 1890s, the Adalbert Lanna company proposed the construction of a system of locks between Prague and Ústí nad Labem, and from 1897 onwards this was gradually completed. Regulatory work on the Vltava and Elbe picked up in pace in connection with the publication of the Waterway Construction Act in 1901, in which the state undertook to build a number of water structures.[111]

The process of canalisation also saw efforts made to connect up rivers and create a network of natural and man-made waterways. At the start of the eighteenth century, some old plans were revived for connecting up the Vltava basin with the Danube. This study, drafted during the reign of Maria Theresa, for a canal linking the Danube to the Vltava was intended to provide a cheap way of transporting timber to large cities, mainly Vienna and Prague. All that remained of the unrealised project was the almost 90-kilometre long Schwarzenberg Navigation Canal from the mouth of the River Mühl to the Danube along the path of the Zwettelbach stream, which was built in two stages between 1789 and 1822. The oldest plans for connecting up the Danube and the Odra go back to the mid-seventeenth century and were dusted down several times during the eighteenth century.[112]

The development of steam navigation saw a revival of the idea of canals linking important rivers. From 1870–1873, an ambitious plan was hatched for a canal between the Danube and the Oder for which the Anglo-Österreichische Bank was awarded a licence. However, the project came to naught as a result of the collapse of the Vienna stock exchange and the resulting economic crisis. At the end of the 1870s, the idea of a canal between the Danube and the Vltava was proposed once again, but failed to receive the support of the Cisleithanian government. A change of approach to the construction of waterways in the territory of Cisleithania was contained in Act 66/1901

---

111   Černá, M. "Komise pro kanalizování řek Vltavy a Labe v Čechách." *Hospodářské dějiny–Economic history*, vol. 29, no. 1 (2014): pp. 1–36.

112   Nožička, J. "Nejstarší projekty kanálu dunajsko-oderského a Slezsko." *Slezský sborník* 54 (1953): 473–488; Dvořák, J. "Putování krajinou Schwarzenberského plavebního kanálu (po proudu vody i času)," in: Chodějovská, E. and Šimůnek, R. (eds.). *Krajina jako historické jeviště. K poctě Evy Semotanové*. Praha, 2012, pp. 199–220.

on the construction of waterways and modifications to rivers of 1901. The act envisaged the construction of 1,600 km of waterways. The state undertook to build a ship canal between the Danube and the Oder and between the Danube and the Vltava and to canalise the Vltava in the section between Budějovice and Prague. There were also plans to build a connecting canal from the Danube-Oder canal to the middle Elbe, to canalise the Elbe between Mělník and Hradec Králové, and to link up the Danube-Oder canal and the Vistula with a connection all the way to the navigable part of the Dniester. Publication of the Waterways Act was seen as an attempt by the government in Vienna to placate the Czech lands, which had had their nose put out of joint by the plans for extensive infrastructural investment in other parts of the monarchy.[113]

Table 32: Network of navigable routes in Cisleithania in 1910 by country

Crown land	Timber rafting (in km)	Navigable (in km)	Steam navigation (in km)
Lower Austria Rakousy	–	319	202
Upper Austria	141	462	157
Salzburg	54	44	–
Styria	463	191	–
Carinthia	311	4	–
Carniola	19	138	22
Littoral	–	118	70
Tyrol and Vorarlberg	252	77	–
Bohemia	806	365	193
Moravia	200	33	–
Austrian Silesia	–	27	–
Galicia	1,288	815	637
Bukovina	346	–	–
Dalmatia	–	55	49

Source: *Österreichisches Statistisches Handbuch*, Vol. 30, 1911, Wien 1912.

During the nineteenth and early twentieth century, transport in Central European towns and cities was transformed beyond recognition. On the one

---

113   Jakubec, I. "Říšský vodocestný zákon č. 66/1901 jako fenomén hospodářských dějin a DVT?: Dějiny vědy a techniky 12." *Rozpravy Národního technického muzea v Praze* 189 (2004): 52–58; Jakubec, I. "Idea Dunajsko-oderského průplavu v 19. a 20. století a její proměny," in: Rossová, M. (ed.). *Integration und Desintegration in Mitteleuropa. Pläne und Realität.* Praha and München, 2009, pp. 235–256; Jakubec, I. "Velkorysá síť vodních cest jako 'všelék' předlitavské společnosti?" in: *Člověk a stroj v české kultuře 19. století.* Praha, 2013, pp. 32–42.

hand, there was an increase in the number and size of urban settlements and the creation of urban agglomerations, while on the other, changes in the structure of society made imperative the creation of effective transport systems capable of transporting growing numbers of people reliably and regularly within cities and the suburbs springing up around them.[114]

To begin with, transport in Central Europe was dominated by non-rail vehicles towed by horses. There was the droshky (a one-horse carriage for two persons), the fiacre (a two-horse carriage for four), and the omnibus (a simple horse-drawn vehicle capable of carrying twelve to sixteen persons). Fiacres and droshkies were common in the Czech lands in the eighteenth century, with omnibuses only appearing in the second third of the nineteenth century. The demand for omnibuses was triggered by the construction of the railways, when it became necessary to connect stations with distant city centres. This applied to Prague, Olomouc, Jablonec nad Nisou, Mariánské Lázně, Opava, České Budějovice, Jihlava, and Moravská Ostrava.

However, during the nineteenth century, traditional means of non-rail public transport were sporadically replaced and finally taken over by rail transport. Rail vehicles began to appear in towns and cities in the 1830s. To begin with, there was the horsecar, which spread around European states from 1850 onwards.[115] In the Czech lands we only encounter the horsecar in the two largest urban agglomerations: Brno (1869) and Prague (1875).

Soon, however, horsepower was replaced by other types of propulsion. The development of the steam engine enabled the construction of small, light tram locomotives in the 1870s, and this saw the gradual inclusion of steam into the transport systems of Moravian and Silesian cities. A steam tram was operated in Brno (the first attempts were made in 1879 and full operation began in 1884), Ostrava (1894), and Bohumín (1903). There were several plans to create steam trams in Prague, but none were realised. Instead, in 1894 preparations began for an electrical tram.

After a period during which alternative power sources were sought (cable lines and fire-and gas- and petrol-powered railway lines), electrical traction came out top. The first electrical tram line was put into operation in the Czech lands on the occasion of the Prague Jubilee Exhibition 1891 and was overseen by the leading Czech electrical engineer František Křižík. By 1894, when it was put into operation in Teplice, the electrical tram had become the standard means of transport in the Czech lands, and in 1896 the first electrified line was put into operation in Prague. From the late nineteenth century

114 Závodná, Město a koleje. Problematika městské kolejové dopravy ve vybraných moravských a slezských městech v letech 1850–1918, Ostrava, 2016.
115 Paris 1854, Liverpool 1859, London 1861, Geneva 1862, Copenhagen 1863, The Hague 1864, Berlin 1865, Vienna 1865, Warsaw 1865, Budapest 1866, Hamburg 1866, Brussels 1869.

onwards, we find electrical trams in many Bohemian, Moravian, and Silesian towns and cities: Liberec (1897), Most (1897), Pilsen (1899), Ústí nad Labem (1899), Olomouc (1899), Jablonec nad Nisou (1900), Brno (1900), Ostrava (1901), Mariánské Lázně (1902), Opava (1905), České Budějovice (1909), Jihlava (1909), and Těšín (1911).[116]

Prior to the First World War, other types of urban transport were slow to spread. The trolleybus, the prototype of which had been constructed by inventor Werner von Siemens at the start of the 1880s, was only to be found providing public transport in the Czech lands in České Budějovice (beginning 1909) and Gmünd (from 1907 onwards connecting the station in what is now České Velenice with the town centre). The first and only use of a bus for public transport purposes took place in Prague in 1908. In 1907, the first horseless carriages (i.e., early automobiles) began to appear on the streets of Prague, but did not catch on due to the high tariffs they were subject to.

As far as air transport is concerned, the foundations only had been laid prior to the First World War. Experiments with heavier-than-air aircraft had been conducted during the latter half of the nineteenth century, though success only came as the first decade of the twentieth century came to a close. An important pioneer of Czech aviation is Igo Etrich (1879–1967), a native of Trutnov. Inspired by pioneering aviator Otto Lilienthal, he and his partner Franz Wels (1873–1940) conducted experiments with gliders. When Wels was replaced by Karl Illner, the glider took on a new form. The culmination of the collaboration between Etrich and Illner was the Taube motorised aeroplane in which Illner made the first intercity flight in 1910 from Wiener Neustadt to Vienna and back. Etrich set up a firm producing military reconnaissance aircraft. In the Czech lands the first aircraft were built and tested by the engineer Jan Kašpar (1883–1927) and his cousin Evžen Čihák (1885–1958). In 1911, Kašpar took his first long flight between Pardubice and Velká Chuchle (now Prague), and in the same year founded the first school of aviation in the Czech lands in Pardubice.[117]

During the latter half of the nineteenth century, the foundations were laid for a new communications network in the Habsburg Monarchy. The traditional means of communication, namely the postal service and the periodical and non-periodical press, expanded rapidly. In addition, a new communications network was created based on the latest technology. The

---

116   Losos, L. "Městská hromadná doprava," in: Jílek, F. et al. *Studie o technice v českých zemích 1800–1918*, vol. IV, Praha 1986, pp. 324–334.

117   Hozák, J. "Letectví," in: Jílek, F. et al. *Studie o technice v českých zemích 1800–1918*, vol. IV, Praha 1986, pp. 384–417; Sviták, P. *První český letec inženýr Jan Kašpar a začátky českého letectví*. Pardubice, 2003.

telegraph and the telephone especially wrought major changes to the system of communication and the exchange of information.[118]

The electromagnetic telegraph essentially abolished spatial distance and set off a chain reaction that spread through the means of communication. However, the telegram was initially very costly and its price was slow to fall. Most telegraph lines were built parallel to railway lines, since it was the railway telegraph that was most popular to begin with. The first line in the monarchy was created in 1847 in tandem with the Emperor Ferdinand Northern Railway and linked Vienna with Brno. It was extended the following year via Olomouc to Prague. As far back as 1852, all the capital cities of the crown lands had a dedicated telegraph link with Vienna, with the exception of Zadar in Dalmatia.[119] By the time of the First World War, a dense telegraph network existed and the rapidly increasing number of telegraph stations, along with a drop in the price of telegraph services, led to an increase in the number of telegrams sent.[120] After the 1880s, the telegraph had to compete with a new invention, namely the telephone. However, the expansion of the telephone, patented in 1876 by Alexander Graham Bell, was held up by the bureaucracy of the Austrian Empire, partly because so much money had been invested by the state in the creation of a telegraph network. As a result, the first telephone lines in the Czech lands were very much a private affair. In the early 1880s, local telephone networks began operating in Prague, Brno, Plzeň and Liberec. During the 1890s, the first intercity lines were created. In its initial stages, the telephone network was restricted to a small circle around telephone exchanges, but in 1886 the first intercity telephone connection was created linking Brno and Vienna. At the same time, the first state telephone network was opened, along with the first public phone booth for intercity calls. In 1889, Prague acquired a telephone connection with Vienna. At the start of the twentieth century, the Prague intercity and international exchange already had seventeen intercity lines connecting it not only with cities in Austro-Hungary, but also in Germany. At the end of the 1880s, other, mainly industrial cities acquired the telephone thus forming an intercity line (Varnsdorf, Teplice, Ústí nad Labem).

At the start of the 1890s, important administrative changes were enacted. In 1892, the state bought out the licences of private telephone operators and

---

118 Hlaváčka, M. "Komunikační revoluce v Českých zemích," in: *Sborník Poštovního muzea v Praze.* Praha, 1986, pp. 194–213.
119 Nemrava, A. "Raný věk elektrického telegrafu," in: *Sborník Poštovního muzea v Praze.* Praha, 1983, pp. 47–77.
120 In 1914, there were 11,227 km of telegraph lines and 1,968 telegraph stations in Bohemia, 3,756 km telegraph lines and 656 telegraph stations in Moravia, and 1,042 km telegraph lines and 205 telegraph stations in Silesia. *Österreichisches Statistisches Handbuch, Jahrgang 33* (1914), Wien 1916, p. 204.

at the end of 1892, the Municipal Telephone Network Nationalisation Act was passed.[121] Compared with other crown lands, the Czech lands scored slightly lower in terms of telephone per capita of the population.[122]

DEVELOPMENT OF TRADE

DOMESTIC AND FOREIGN TRADE DURING THE MERCANTILE PERIOD

Mercantilism, the first comprehensive system of economic thinking, reacted to the economic problems of its time. While mercantilism was oriented more toward commercial profit, its Central European iteration, cameralism, was more administration based and it advocated a policy of strengthening the military, economic, and financial power of a state. At its core was the idea of population growth as a means of reinforcing the military and increasing the number of taxpayers and production. For cameralists, wealth was no longer associated with precious metals and money, as it was for mercantilists, but with the maximisation of revenue.[123]

This period saw the interlinking of the economic interests of both entrepreneurs and the imperial court. Merchants obtained privileges, support, and protection of their property, while the crown received income with which to fund the organisation and administration of the modern centralised state. The mercantile state was interested in expanding the industrial base and developing outlying areas as sources of food and raw materials. If the domestic environment was insufficient in terms of the sale of goods, the state moved into foreign markets and created colonies. A prerequisite was the removal of internal customs barriers and, on the other hand, the creation of barriers protecting domestic industry against foreign competition. Precious metals represented a means of expanding trade and industry. A favourable trade balance was regarded as the biggest indicator of success. The first phase of mercantilism (cameralism) ended with the arrival of Maria Theresa, and the

---

121 Nemrava, A. "Sdělovací technika," in: Jílek et al. *Studie o technice v českých zemích 1800–1918.* Praha, 1986, pp. 218–231; Hlavačka. "Vývoj dopravy a komunikací," in: Jakubec, I. and Jindra, Z. et al. *Dějiny hospodářství českých zemí od počátku industrializace do konce habsburské monarchie.* Praha, 2006, p. 270.

122 The most lavishly furnished with telephones of the crown lands was Lower Austria, with 211 subscriber stations per 10,000 of the populations, followed by Vorarlberg (101 stations), Salzburg (93 stations), and Austrian Littoral (81 stations). In Bohemia there were 54 stations per 10,000 of the population, in Moravia 44 stations, and in Silesia 40 stations. *Österreichisches Statistisches Handbuch, Jahrgang 33* (1914), Wien 1916, pp. 208–209.

123 Heckscher, E. F. *Mercantilism.* London, 1935; Klíma, A. "Merkantilismus in Habsburg Monarchy in Bohemian Lands." *Historica* 11 (1965): 95–119; Good, David F. *The Economic Rise of the Habsburg Empire, 1750–1914.* Berkeley, 1984.

second phase ended with Leopold II. These phases were characterised by support for domestic production and internal trade and restrictions on imports and population growth. A sign of the state's foreign trade ambitions was the creation of the Imperial Privileged Oriental Company in Vienna (1719) for trade with the Ottoman Empire, and the East India Company in Ostend (1718) for trade with East India and China. The second phase was the product of a concise and systematic state cameralist policy. The loss of the rich Silesian provinces prompted far-reaching administrative and economic reforms (the general commercial collegium or Kommerzkollegium in Vienna in 1746, the royal chambers in 1749). Foreign specialists and craftsmen were highly sought after, especially for their technological know-how (in the spheres of textiles, iron and steel production, and paper). Customs tariffs rose sharply on imported products. Support for the transport infrastructure (inland waterways, the construction of a seaport in Trieste and the construction of main roads) was of great importance.[124] The Czech lands were an important centre of industrial activity in the monarchy, especially as regards the production of textiles, and benefitted from injections of English business capital (Robert Allason).

The monarchy's trade policy was influenced by the ideas of the mercantilists and cameralists, including their protectionist strains, from the seventeenth century through to the 1830s. The role of foreign trade as one of the most important sources of wealth in the eyes of the mercantilists was slightly downplayed by the cameralists, who accorded greater significance to internal commerce and support for domestic industry. They also believed it was important to prevent the flight of capital and the export of precious metals.

The aim of an absolutist mercantile economic policy in shunting customs duties to the borders, simplifying the administration and tax system, improving national transport, simplifying rates and monetary values, and thus increasing the economic and tax power of as much of the population as possible encountered resistance from individual crown lands, which did not wish to lose their many privileges.[125]

The development of trade (both domestic and foreign) is bound up with the issue of customs. Under Maria Theresa, the compulsory stamping of all goods was introduced (with a customs stamp for foreign goods and a trade stamp for domestic goods). Exports were supported by premiums. At the start of the eighteenth century, duties and tolls were applied at more than seven hundred places in the Czech lands alone, which increased the price of transport and commerce. In 1775, internal customs borders were abolished

124   Good. *The Economic Rise*, pp. 24–34.
125   Wolfram, H. (ed.). *Österreichische Geschichte, Roman Sandgruber, Ökonomie und Politik*. Wien, 2005, p. 228.

between the Czech and Austrian crown lands (Lower Austria, Styria, Carinthia, Carniola, Gorica, Gradiška and the Austrian Littoral, Bohemia, Moravia, and Silesia). This represented the first important step towards the creation of a single customs territory and the liberalisation of commerce. From 1783–1796, customs barriers were abolished between Galicia and Salzburg (1819), Tyrol, Vorarlberg, Lombardy-Venetia (1825–1826), Hungary (1850), and the last territory, Dalmatia, (1879). Over two hundred years, the monarchy was gradually transformed into a customs union. At the start of the nineteenth century, liberal voices began demanding the relaxation of foreign trade. Attempts to introduce autarky and mercantilism were boosted by the announcement of the continental blockade of Great Britain in 1806. On the one hand the blockade supported domestic production (including the search for substitute products), but on the other it did not prevent the smuggling of British goods into Europe. In the monarchy, the blockade was epitomised by the tariffs of 1810–1812, often dubbed the peak of prohibition. Most affected by the blockade were traditional exports of glass and fabrics.

In 1835, the customs code of 1788 was replaced by a customs and state monopoly, which tightened up even further the prohibitive foreign trade policy.[126] In 1838, a single customs tariff was introduced that freed up considerably trade relations with foreign countries. In the 1840s, we see the emergence of more liberal tendencies, especially in light of the German Customs Union, or Zollverein, culminating in the promulgation of new customs tariffs at the start of the 1850s.

Foreign trade had a burden lifted with the end of the Napoleonic Wars and the adoption of the Elbe Navigation Act of 1821. Wood, grain, sheet and decorative glass, black coal from the mid-1830s, brown coal, iron, ash, bones, fresh and dried fruit, potash, horn, graphite, etc. was exported from Bohemia on the Elbe, while castor sugar, cotton, terracotta, stone, chalk, and colonial goods (coffee, cocoa, ginger, pepper, almonds, star anise, and rice) were imported into Bohemia. Most goods exported from Bohemia ended up in Saxony or Anhalt, and to a lesser extent in Hamburg.[127]

Brokers and middlemen played a major role in the Czech lands, especially in the textiles (foreign trade) and the glass industry (domestic trade). Brokerage firms remained important in the Czech lands until the end of the 1920s. To begin with, manufacturers had overseen sales of their products themselves.

126 Ibid. pp. 229–230.
127 Hlavačka, M. *Dějiny dopravy v českých zemích v období průmyslové revoluce*. Praha, 1990, pp. 35–37; the same, "Období 1815–1848: Vnitřní a zahraniční obchod" in Jakubec, I. and Jindra, Z. et al. *Dějiny hospodářství českých zemí. Od počátku industrializace do konce habsburské monarchie*. Praha, 2006, p. 275.

Prague became the natural centre of Czech trade with its close contacts to Saxony, Hamburg, Vienna, and Trieste. From the second third of the nineteenth century onwards, Hamburg in Germany and Trieste in Austria were increasingly important. In Moravia, the largest trade centre was Brno, while the significance of Těšín as gateway to the trade route to Eastern Europe fell. Similar products were exported from Moravia as from Bohemia. Moravia, thanks to its geographical features, was a more important transit territory than Bohemia, and this was both on a north/northeast–south axis (Krakow–Vienna) and west/northwest–south/southeast axis (Prague–Vienna–Pest/Budapest).[128] The monarchy was a closed economical unit importing raw materials until the start of the 1850s.[129]

DOMESTIC COMMERCE IN THE NINETEENTH CENTURY

In 1910, as the table below shows, the share of workers (including family members and dependents) in commerce and transport in Bohemia was 13.17% (active 10.8%), Moravia 10.80% (8.68%), and Silesia 11.18% (9.71%).

Table 33: No. of people dependent on and active in specific sectors in Bohemia in 1910 in %

	Bohemia no. of people		Moravia no. of people		(Austrian) Silesia no. of people	
	dependent	active	dependent	active	dependent	active
Primary sector Agriculture and forestry	32.29	36.64	41.28	45.83	29.17	35.06
Secondary sector Industry	41.08	36.73	35.00	30.09	46.31	39.46
Tertiary sector (without civilian or military service) Trade and transport	13.17	10.80	10.80	8.68	11.18	9.71

Source: *Ottův obchodní slovník, díl II/1, Praha 1913–1916*, p. 699, according to *Österreichisches statistisches Handbuch 1914*, vol. 33. Wien, 1916, pp. 14–30.

The wholesale industry was mainly in the hands of Austrian (Viennese) or local, mostly ethnic Jewish-German capital. Wholesale represented the most advanced organisation and division of labour, and included a range of operations from transport to marketing and forwarding, with high demands made on management. A medium-sized business needed a hired workforce often linked with local Jewish, German or Czech capital. The owner and co-

---

128   Hlaváčka. *Období 1815–1848. Vnitřní a zahraniční obchod*, p. 276.
129   Chylík, J. *Vývoj zahraničního obchodu v našich zemích*. Praha, 1947, pp. 36–38.

owners of medium-sized enterprises were active in the day-to-day running and management of the business, though some managerial functions were delegated to employees.

According to the census of business establishments taken in June 1902 in Cisleithania, the retail sector involved different structures ranging from the participation of only family members in trade (86.34% of employees were employed at companies employing up to five people) to business with six to ten employees (6.34% of employees).[130] This category featured both Czech and German capital, again with a significant share of Jewish capital. In general, Czech businesspeople did not focus on mass commercial activities to the same extent that German businesspeople did.

THE STATE'S TRADE POLICY

The state's economic policy was reflected in its own economic activities, in the stipulation of legal standards, and through active intervention, especially in the sphere of customs and foreign trade. The economic policy of Austria-Hungary from the start of the 1850s was one of gradual liberalisation in general and was a transition from a prohibitive system of customs tariffs to a merely protective system that culminated in the 1860s. Beginning in the mid-1870s, we note a retreat from a liberalistic concept of the relationship of the state to economic questions geared more towards active participation in an attempt to overcome production and sales difficulties. Business and trade affairs fell within the purview of the Ministry of Trade. The state policy included the creation of chambers of commerce, trade licensing offices, and trade associations. A network of private institutions (i.e., business museums and clubs on the level of empire or crown land of diverse activities) complemented this structure.

THE SALE OF GOODS

Depending on legal status, business was conducted at the owner's own liability or in the form of commission trading, where the owner of goods put their sale in the hands of a broker for a commission. This depended on the relationship to the consumer and often on the volume of purchases or turnover of commercial commodities, and the forms of retail and wholesale differed. Depending on type and territory, sales might be internal (domestic) or foreign (external), export (active) or import (passive), or fixed or travelling

---

130 Starzyczná, H. and Steiner, J. "Velikostní a sortimentní struktura obchodních podniků českých zemí v období první republiky." *Slezský sborník* 1 (1994): tab. 1, p. 25. zpracováno podle Österreichische Statistik, Bd. LXXV., 9. Heft (Böhmen), 10. Heft (Mähren) and 11. Heft (Schlesien), Wien 1905.

(door-to-door). The traditional forms of trade known since the Middle Ages included the marketplace. However, in the nineteenth century we observe a steady decline in the importance of weekly markets serving to supply the urban population especially. The function of market was to a large extent taken over by newly built marketplaces, central marketplaces, and retail marketplaces. Annual fairs for tools, clothing, household goods, etc. retained a certain significance. Wholesale activities with livestock and grain were concentrated in Vienna and Budapest, with textiles in Prague and Brno and with colonial goods in Trieste. Wholesalers in sugar included the Brno-based Alexander Schoeller of the Rhineland and the brothers Alfred and August Skene, originally from Scotland, who made a name for themselves by opening a wholesale outlet for kilts. The function of trade fair was taken over not only by world exhibitions (1873 in Vienna), but also regional exhibitions organised by various different organisations (e.g., the exhibitions in Prague in 1891, 1895, and especially 1908). Vienna became the most important centre of domestic trade in the monarchy.

THE DEVELOPMENT OF THE RETAIL INDUSTRY

During the latter half of the nineteenth century, the retail sector was in fierce competition with the wholesale industry. At the turn of the nineteenth and twentieth centuries, the number of retailers rose in line with the development of modern mass production, the decline of the small craftsman, and the expansion of the range of goods on offer. The traditional commodities sold by retailers included sugar, coffee, tea, spices, mineral oils, dyes, and spirits. Czech businesspeople were more active in retail sales, especially from the 1890s onwards, at the expense of the German-Jewish sector.

The retail industry in the monarchy was relatively sophisticated and specialised. It was usually conducted via a shop or store. Unlike consumer co-operatives, it did not operate branch (chain) stores. Nomadic (door-to-door, travelling) sales were undertaken largely on markets or on a small scale. For instance, in Prague, door-to-door sales were, with a few exceptions, banned under the regulation of the Ministry of Trade no. 49/1896. Even so, there were many exemptions (sugar, gingerbread, chocolate, imported goods, etc.). Temporary outlets were set up for sales (shop, store, room, or boat), clearance sales, and lotteries. Higher purchase, this is to say payment by instalment (e.g., for sewing machines, clocks, paintings, publications, automobiles, cleaning equipment, etc.), first took off in the monarchy. Another type of business was mail order, with goods sent in small consignments by post or train. A single postal tariff was applied in the monarchy to mail order goods, regardless of distance travelled (e.g., the Ferdinand Vondráček mail order coffee service based in Trieste).

THE DEVELOPMENT OF THE WHOLESALE INDUSTRY

The wholesale (bulk buying) sector represented a more advance form of business. Unlike the retail sector, it was focused on the relationship between the producer and the shopkeeper. For the wholesaler (*Grossist*), the share of gross sales of total revenue was more than two-thirds, while for the semi-wholesaler (*Demogrossist*), gross sales represented between one- and two-thirds. Like retail traders, wholesalers availed themselves of the services of travelling salesmen and agents, as well as mediation by means of commission agent or broker. Czechs were active in the wholesale sector only in the sale of sugar, machinery, iron goods, cement, raw materials, and colonial goods. Otherwise, the sector remained in the hands of German and German-Jewish capital.

Department stores competed with shopkeepers in the sale of small goods and more expensive items. Their sales strategy involved both specialisation and a combination of related goods, so as to customise their offer to the taste and convenience of buyers. Several department stores even offered a catalogue-based delivery service. The concentration of sales in one place reduced total unit costs, and this became an effective weapon against retailers. From 1871 onwards, Prague was home to a department store owned by the Vienna-based firm of Haas und Söhne, and from 1903 the department store U Nováků and the shop U města Paříže. Important department stores in Austrian Silesia included Breda & Weinstein (1898) in Opava, which up until 1914 had branches not only in Vienna but also in Kravaře in Prussian Silesia and in Solingen, Germany.

ATTEMPTS AT DISINTERMEDIATION

Attempts to cut out the middleman and to create a path straight from the producer to the consumer were aimed at both retailers and wholesalers. As regards retailers, efforts were made by factory owners to sell their products directly from their warehouses, by mail order (especially fabrics and canned goods), and by their own travelling salesmen. Small farmers did the same with food (butter, fruit, poultry, and cheese); producers organised agricultural and trade sales cooperatives, and consumers established basic consumer and purchasing cooperatives and associations. Measures against the exclusion of wholesalers included creating direct links between large manufacturers, urban warehouses, and travelling salesmen (including samples), and creating cartel sales offices.

COMMERCIAL DEPARTMENTS OF BANKS

An Austrian speciality was the creation of commodities trading departments in banks that compensated for the lack of trading networks and the circulation of goods. These departments arose from the close link banks had with the sugar industry. The emergency of cartels provided a new impetus for this form of trade. The banks became clearinghouses for the cartels, and the cartels' joint sales offices were affiliated with the trading departments. The banks began to undertake not only commission trades, but also the buying and selling of commodities at their own account. Živnostenská banka, for instance, oversaw the sale of the products of twenty-five sugar factories, most distilleries, and the ironworks based in the Hradec Králové region. In addition, it had an office for the sale of the products of several foundries, ceramics, covering boards, some of the output of the Ostrava mines run by the Rakouská báňská a hutní společnosti / Österreichische Berg- und Hüttengesellschaft (Austrian Mining and Metallurgical Company), Galician chemical companies, etc.

COOPERATIVES

Cooperatives or merchant cooperatives were part of the retail industry and set out to exclude wholesalers and middlemen. The emergence of purchasing cooperatives was driven by small traders needing to buy good quality raw materials, semi-finished products, tools, and machinery for an affordable price and resorting to buying in bulk. The same rationale lay behind the creation of agricultural purchasing cooperatives and, not long before the First World War, retailers' cooperatives (for the purchase of colonial goods, wine, etc.). These purchasing cooperatives mostly took the form of limited liability companies (under the act of 1873), and less often societies. They were either purchasing enterprises (acting on the basis of orders placed by their members) or storage cooperatives. There were also sales, machinery, and slaughterhouse cooperatives. Retailers and traders regarded them as serious competitors.

Consumer cooperatives (societies) differed from department stores in how they were organised. They were created in an effort to remove brokered business from what was known as the "second hand" and were used by the labouring classes above all. Even though they brought together consumers for the purpose of joint purchases of everyday consumer goods in bulk (food, fuel, lighting, etc.), the distribution of profits was done on the basis of the value of the sale and not capital. Consumer associations were able to combine and form larger cooperatives or wholesale companies, which allowed them both to negotiate directly with factory owners, importers, and other businesspeople, and to buy in bulk.[131]

THE EMANCIPATION OF CZECH TRADE

Any account of the culmination of the emancipation of ethnic Czech business must include its participation in the preparation and realisation of the General Land Centennial Exhibition in Prague 1891.[132] By the end of the nineteenth century, Czech business was basically emancipated on many levels, even though Czech-German and Jewish capital maintained its position in the wholesale sector. During the latter half of the nineteenth century, the share taken by the tertiary sphere increased and a number of associations were established at the regional, ethnic, and national level. Closer links were established between merchants and banks following the emergence of cartels and commercial banks. The social prestige of wholesalers in ethnically Czech and German society rose. During the 1860s, mutual savings banks, savings banks, and other banks were created within Czech business and commercial circles. Given the integrationist character of commercial activities, further research into the development of trade (including commerce) would increase our knowledge not only in the sphere of the tertiary sector but also in industry, banking, and other sectors.

A description of the transformation of the economic elites, especially the commercial elites in Prague during the latter half of the nineteenth century, was attempted by František Svátek. His work is worth quoting in more detail: The Prague (merchant class), which between 1860 and 1880 remained primarily German or German Jewish, was probably the most important professional corporation in the city. [...] In smaller towns and cities, the constraints on local markets were maintained by the mainly conservative bourgeoisie within the bounds of tradition. Their local elites comprised the owners of buildings and shops on squares and main streets. These small-town elites of the "pre-capitalist" period had a tendency to be inward looking, were intolerant of anything foreign, and were often anti-Semitic. As well as being closed off from the world, they were extremely aware of their rank and their place in the social hierarchy as decided by patrician origin, property, and prestige. The wealthiest masters of the food and textile industries (millers, brewers, bakers, farmers, weavers, etc.), grain traders, butchers, and draymen were sidelined until the end of the nineteenth century as a consequence of creeping industrialisation and urbanisation, which saw city centres being

---

131 *Ottův obchodní slovník, II/1, Praha–Bratislava 1913–1916*, p. 230.
132 City of Prague Archive (AMP). Merkur Business Association in Prague fonds. Records of the business association Merkur in Prague, Resoluce, kart. 67, sine.

surrounded by industrial peripheries. The "elites" were replaced by factory owners, the first founders of "technical offices" and suppliers of equipment to sugar factories, breweries, agricultural manufacturers, breweries, architects' building contractors, and land speculators.[133]

TRADE BETWEEN AUSTRIA AND HUNGARY

Under imperial regulations of 20/21 October 1849 and 5 March 1850, the customs border between the Austrian lands and Hungary was abolished, and as of 1 October 1850 the movement of goods became duty free. Austria signed another convention with Lichtenstein in 1852. At that time, the formation of a single customs territory was regarded on a foreign-policy level as the first step to achieving a customs union with the Zollverein (German Customs Union) led by Prussia, though in the event this never took place.

The Austro-Hungarian Compromise of 1867 did not bring about changes to the dimensions of the customs territory, but did impact on the creation and focus of customs policy. The eastern part of the monarchy, Transleithania, was only linked in a union with the western part, Cisleithania, by a customs and trade treaty with a ten-year duration conditional upon the principle of reciprocity. The result was that there was no permanent customs union between the two regions of the monarchy. A conference was called to draft trade treaties on which representatives of the ministries of foreign affairs, trade, and finance of Cisleithania and Transleithania sat alongside invited experts. Fraught negotiations were held on prolonging the customs and trade union between Austria and Hungary in 1878, 1887, 1899, 1907, and 1917. The talks were influenced not only by the different geographical conditions, but also by the different economic levels of both regions. Above all, the views of the Cisleithanian representatives of industry clashed with the demands of representatives of Hungarian estates, and from the end of the nineteenth century onwards, the interests of big business linked with agrarian estates. Although the Austro-Hungarian Empire was a single customs territory, it was by no means a unified internal market and single economy. The Czech lands did not comprise a separate economic entity within the framework of the monarchy.

During the 1880s, a policy of protectionism was applied rigorously in the spheres of industry and agriculture. The extraordinarily limited connections between the Austrian economy and global markets caused by this, along with attempts to achieve autarky (self-sufficiency), resulted in the monarchy becoming economically weak and isolated. Compared with advanced countries, Austria-Hungary lacked technology, specialists, and a strong technical base,

133   Svátek, F. *Politické a sociální elity*. Praha, 2003, pp. 56–57.

and it was uncompetitive on foreign markets. The individual parts of the monarchy had different interests. Commercially, the monarchy had close ties to Germany, its most important customer and supplier, though also its biggest competitor. Yet the monarchy represented a large market with fifty-two million inhabitants, all of whom had the option of buying Czech goods easily and safely. The mutual trade between Cisleithania and Transleithania can be regarded as a special case of internal and simultaneously interstate (i.e., foreign) trade.

Regional specialisations were reflected in trade between Austria and Hungary. While Transleithania exported commodities to Cisleithania in three categories, namely agricultural products (field crops, sugar, and flour), livestock and animal products, and food and beverages, Cisleithania exported to Transleithania industrial raw materials and fuels, fibres and textiles, iron and metals, salt, chemical products, artificial fertilisers, machinery, and other products. As far as value was concerned, field crops were most important for Transleithania and fabrics and textiles for Cisleithania, and this has led the American historian Scott Eddie to characterise the Dual Monarchy as a marriage of wheat and textiles.

Transleithania accounted for 35% of Cisleithanian exports, while more than 20% of Cisleithanian exports ended up in Transleithania. The Austrian share of Hungarian exports prior to the First World War was around 74.1%, while the Hungarian share of Austrian exports was only approximately 39.1%.[134] As regards trade between Austria and Hungary, we see a tendency on the part of Transleithania to restrict Austrian exports to Hungary and increase Hungarian exports to Cisleithania. As regards several commodities, Cisleithania was dependent on sales in Transleithania (fibres and textiles, as well as machinery) and Transleithania was dependent on the sale of agricultural products in Cisleithania.

THE FOREIGN TRADE OF THE DUAL MONARCHY IN THE NINETEENTH CENTURY

TRADE AND CUSTOMS POLICY

The monarchy can be characterised by its supply of both raw materials and industrial goods, as well as agricultural products. It enjoyed a considerable

---

134 Source: Pickl, O. "Das Wirtschaftswachstum der Habsburger Monarchie und ihre Verflechtung in den internationalen Handel im 19. Jahrhundert," in: Kellenbenz, H. (ed.). *Wirtschaftliches Wachstum, Energie und Verkehr vom Mittelalter bis ins 19. Jahrhundert*. Stuttgart and New York, 1978, tab. p. 196. Good, David F. *The Economic Rise of the Habsburg Empire, 1750–1914*. University of California Press: Berkeley, Los Angeles, London, 1984, tab. 13, p. 111. According to Eddie, S. "Economic Policy and Economic Development in Austria-Hungary, 1867–1913," in: *The Cambridge Economic History of Europe, Vol. 8*.

degree of self-sufficiency in the sphere of industrial production, raw materials for industry and the energy sector, and agrarian products.

The limited number and poor quality of foreign trade contacts enjoyed by the monarchy lasted until the mid-nineteenth century. The 1830s were characterised by a relatively stable balance between exports and imports, and the 1840s by a passive trade balance influenced by the growth in the imports of machinery from Great Britain, Belgium, and the German states, an increase in the purchasing power of the population (e.g., cane flour), and a change of economic policy (the abolition of import bans).[135] During the 1840s, the German Customs Union accounted for 30.2% of the total turnover of the Dual Monarchy, followed by Italy (21.6%), the Ottoman Empire (14.5%), and Switzerland (12%). No other state exceeded 6%.[136]

The economic hub of the Dual Monarchy was Vienna, and it was via this city and the department stores of Hamburg and Trieste that the country was connected economically to the world market. The Austro-Hungarian foreign trade policy is often deemed synonymous with its customs policy (Brusatti, 1973). Up until the Austro-Prussian war of 1866, its foreign trade (and hence its customs) policy was subordinate to the foreign policy orientation of the monarchy on the German question. Subsequently, there was a tendency to look after the monarchy's own economic interests.

Up until the early 1850s, Austrian trade policy could be described as prohibitive and highly protectionist (so-called pragmatic protectionism, Myška, 1999), though from the early 1840s onwards, voices were heard calling for an end to this policy. Karl Ludwig von Bruck (1798–1860), Minister of Trade, and later Finance Minister, became the official representative of the new liberal policy. The new customs tariffs valid as of 1852 (the general customs tariff of 1851) and 1853 (the tariff convention with the Zollverein) significantly reduced customs barriers. The high tariffs in place until then had prevented imports of raw materials. The new tariff represented the transition from a prohibitive to a protectionist system. However, this transition took place very suddenly, and from the view of power politics (rapprochement with Prussia and its allies) failed to take sufficient account of the need to protect domestic industry. Austrian goods failed to establish a position on the market of the German Customs Union, and were squeezed out by Prussian goods of not only the European market but also the domestic market.

The period beginning in the early 1850s and running through to the end of the 1870s saw the liberalisation of the customs system in the form of mild

---

135 Myška, M. "Zahraniční obchod železem a hutními výrobky v rakousko-uherské monarchii v období 1830–1914." *Historica*, 1999, sv. 7, Universitas Ostraviensis – Acta facultatis philosophicae, vol. 182, p. 53.

136 Ibid., p. 61.

protection offered to domestic producers. The tariff conventions (treaties) formed the basis of this process. The provisional tariff of 1865 and 1868 reduced rates still further. The free trade period was apparent in many treaties signed between the late 1860s and mid-1870s. These included trade agreements with France (1866), Italy (1867), Belgium (1867), the Netherlands (1867), Great Britain (1868), Switzerland (1868), the North German Confederation (1868), Spain (1870), Portugal (1872), Sweden and Norway (1873), and Romania (1875). Non-European countries included Siam, China, and Japan (1869), and countries in Latin America (1870).

However, the economy of the monarchy was not sufficiently prepared for the liberalisation of customs policy, and this was painfully apparent in the foreign trade balance. From 1869–1877, a surplus was transformed into a deficit.

The attempts made during the latter half of the 1870s to overcome production and sales difficulties found expression in efforts made by Austrian and Hungarian producers to monopolise the monarchy's internal market and to ensure suitable export conditions (protectionism combined with support for exports). During the mid-1870s, the monarchy pulled out of trade agreements with Great Britain (1875), France (1875), and Prussia (1876). The era of free trade ended and was replaced by a protectionist system (aggressive cartel protectionism, M. Myška) in the form of an autonomous customs tariff. The autonomous customs tariff, protectionist measures, and support for exports, including transport tariffs (the nationalisation of railways and the construction of new state railways, the construction of Adriatic ports and their support against North German seaports, and support for maritime and inland navigation) made possible the economic and industrial development of the monarchy.

Proposals for the establishment of customs unions at different levels had begun to appear from the end of the 1870s, and from the 1890s through to 1903 were at the forefront of the plan to create a broader economic unit (a European customs union) in Central Europe with its approximately 131 million inhabitants (Germany, Austro-Hungary, Italy) and to create a line of defence against France, the USA, and Great Britain (the plan proposed by Count Leo Caprivi, the Chancellor of the German Reich). During the 1890s, Austria-Hungary made new trade agreements with Germany, Italy, Belgium, Switzerland, Russia, Bulgaria, Japan, Serbia, and Romania valid until 1903, with an option to extend until 1905 or until new treaties were signed in 1905 and 1906 (with Germany, Belgium, Italy, Switzerland, and Russia), 1909 (Romania), and 1911 (Montenegro). Austria-Hungary thus reintroduced a double system of customs tariff, namely contractual (enshrined in conventions) with countries with which it had trade agreements, and general in respect of other trade partners.

The protectionism pursued by Austria-Hungary culminated in the years after 1906. In 1902, Germany increased import duties on agricultural and industrial products. The basis of the new Austro-Hungarian customs tariff in 1903 was an autonomous tariff expressing the common interest of Austrian and Hungarian landowners and iron industry entrepreneurs. However, the annexation of Bosnia and Herzegovina and the subsequent boycott of Austro-Hungarian goods meant the Dual Monarchy lost its economic foothold in the Balkans to Germany.

During the 1850s, Austria-Hungary reported a slightly active balance of trade (an average of 3 million florins per annum). During the 1860s, this grew (by an average of 52 million florins per annum), during the 1870s it was more passive (an average of 35 million per annum), during the 1880s extremely active (an average of 133 million florins per annum), and it culminated in an active balance of trade in the 1890s (with an average of 84 million florins per annum). From 1907, the balance of trade was very passive (from 1907–1913, an annual average of 471 million crowns). On the one hand, relatively high customs protection allowed for the consolidation of the Cisleithanian economy (e.g., the iron and steel industry) compared with its competitors. However, the profits acquired by the cartels were insufficient to stimulate technical innovation and the rationalisation of production. In 1912, Cisleithania accounted for 84% of Austria-Hungary's total net exports, and Transleithania 16%.

The Dual Monarchy's exports were aided by the establishment of large river and maritime transport companies, the development of maritime navigation, and the construction of the Trieste and Rijeka seaports. However, notwithstanding the Adriatic seaport, only one-tenth of goods were imported by sea and one-twentieth of goods exported by sea. The Austrian government's efforts to support exports included the nationalisation of Austrian rail in 1906–1908, and downward pressure was applied to railway tariffs.

The monarchy enjoyed its largest trade relations with its neighbours. In 1913, Germany accounted for 40% of the monarchy's exports, Great Britain 10%, and Italy almost 8%. In the same year, the most important importers included Germany at 40%, the USA at almost 10%, and the British Raj at almost 7 %.

Compared to the advanced economies, the Dual Monarchy's foreign trade was small, though beer and glass both enjoyed a share on world markets of almost 20%, and sugar 16.7%. Nevertheless, foreign trade rose, more than doubling from 1880–1910. Though from 1860–1880 the monarchy occupied fifth place in terms of European trade (with 7.2% in 1880), on a global scale from 1885–1908 it was in a similarly insignificant position to Italy (with 3.3% in 1908).[137] It is estimated that prior to the First World War, Austro-Hungary

---

[137] Chylík, J. *Vývoj zahraničního obchodu v našich zemích*. Praha, 1947, tab. I, p. 37; Pickl, O. "Das Wirtschaftswachstum der Habsburger Monarchie und ihre Verflechtung in den internationalen Handel

exported only 7% of its gross domestic product (GDP): the European average was around 12.3%, with Germany at 14.6% and France at 15.3%. Austro-Hungarian exports were in fierce competition with British and German on their natural markets, namely the Balkans and the Levant. The Austrian government's attempts to turn Trieste into a forwarding centre and Vienna into a trading hub for imports of American cotton were important in respect of European trade.

From the last third of the nineteenth century onwards, machinery, raw materials, and luxury goods entered the monarchy from the advanced European states, while the monarchy supplied these same states with glass, jewellery, sugar, raw materials, and semi-finished products. On the other hand, the monarchy exported consumer goods to the Balkan states and Russia, especially textiles, sugar, machinery, and equipment for sugar factories and distilleries. The composition of foreign trade thus reveals the ambivalent position of the monarchy vis-à-vis its more advanced partners in the West and its less advanced partners in Southern and Eastern Europe. The export of machinery from the monarchy (including the Czech lands) tended to rise during times of economic crisis and depression, while imports of machinery were stronger during economic upswings. This was most apparent during the first half of the 1870s.

The industrialisation of the monarchy is documented by the overall structure of foreign trade. At the end of the 1860s, foodstuffs and finished products predominated, while at the start of the twentieth century it was raw materials for industry and agriculture. The most dynamically growing imported commodities included textiles and grain, and from the 1890s onwards imports of anthracite or black coal in parallel with the development of heavy industry. Exports of traditional industrial and craft products fell, to be replaced by industrial and agricultural raw materials and products. In other words, imports of grain fell while exports rose, exports of finished products and industrial raw materials tripled, and in the engineering sector exports of machinery for sugar factories, breweries, and distilleries rose.

A relatively important role was played by middlemen, namely foreign exporters and wholesalers, especially in Hamburg. Exports were undertaken by both domestic Viennese parties as well as large industrial corporations, by means of their business reps, warehouses, and sales outlets abroad or their travelling salesmen (this applied to exports of glass, beer, malt, handcrafted furniture, machinery, canvas, etc.). In Prague there were no export stores.

---

im 19. Jahrhundert," in: Kellenbenz, H. (ed.). *Wirtschaftliches Wachstum, Energie und Verkehr vom Mittelalter bis ins 19. Jahrhundert*. Stuttgart and New York, 1978, p. 184, 194; Rudolph, R. L. "Quantitative Aspekte der Industrialisierung in Cisleithanien 1848–1914," in: *Die Habsburgermonarchie 1848–1918*, Vol. I: *Die wirtschaftliche Entwicklung*. Wien, 1973, p. 246.

However, exporters were based in Jablonec nad Nisou specialising in the purchase of local goods (jewellery). Imports were mostly undertaken by auction,
second hand, or at the agencies and representatives of foreign firms with
branches in Vienna, and only a small proportion of imports were direct. It
was not until the 1850s that banks were established in Vienna that dealt with
the transfer of remunerations to and from foreign countries. Prior to that,
purchases had been made for cash or using business loans, and transfers and
bond trading had been carried out by private bankers and wholesalers. The
limitations of the monarchy's efforts to create a single market were also apparent in economic contacts. Certain crown lands or regions enjoyed closer
cooperation with foreign countries than they did with other crown lands and
regions, and in some cases their economic and trade centres were located
beyond the borders of the monarchy (this applied especially to border regions). In professional circles it was often said that the business activity of
the monarchy did not correspond to its size, population, political status, and
natural wealth. The Austro-Hungarian market was confronted by a number
of affiliates, representatives, and agents of foreign firms. In 1891, the Hungarian part of the monarchy accounted for approximately one-third of industrial products and the Austrian part the remaining two-thirds. In terms of
commodities, the monarchy could boast no highly sought-after export goods.
The industrialisation of the monarchy can be inferred from the structure of
its foreign trade. At the end of the 1860s, imports of foodstuffs and finished
products predominated. By the start of the twentieth century, it was raw
materials for industry and agriculture. Exports of traditional industrial and
craft products fell, while those of industrial and agricultural raw materials
(including sugar, timber, and—until 1888—grain) rose. Industrialisation entailed a shift away from the traditional pillars of the agrarian sector, and in
foreign trade this was manifest in the way that grain was no longer exported
but imported and exports of finished products tripled along with exports of
industrial raw materials.

THE ORGANISATION OF AND SUPPORT FOR EXPORTS

The government of the monarchy provided various means of support for
exports (an active trade activity). These included export associations, trade
museums, the organisation of exports, warehouses of export samples and
trade warehouses abroad, the organisation of exhibitions, consulates and
foreign offices, chambers of commerce abroad, and export-oriented training
institutes. Exports were also given a boost not only by the activities of banks
(foreign and overseas banks), but also the transport tariff policy pursued by
Vienna (an export tariff policy, including groups of goods and destinations,
the construction of port facilities, subsidies to entrepreneurs, postal tariffs)

and economic measures (export bonuses, consumption tax refunds). Finally, exports were significantly affected by the trade and customs agreements entered into.

THE CZECH LANDS AND FOREIGN TRADE

Czech trade struggled with a lack of buyer intel, a lack of business confidence, insufficient organisation of exports overseas, and the non-existence of a Czech transport company linking the crown land with Hamburg via the Elbe. The sale of Czech goods also had to overcome another barrier in the monarchy, this time an ethnic barrier, since Czech merchants were not popular amongst consumers in the ethnically Germany regions (economic nationalism).

A basic problem was the lack of direct contacts, since for many producers the mediation of sales by department stores based in Hamburg and Vienna was more comfortable, albeit more expensive. In addition, the Hamburg stores were reluctant to accept goods that might represent competition with German goods.

Consulates were established in Prague and other Czech towns and cities (representing France, Belgium, Great Britain, Italy, Mexico, Germany, the Netherlands, Persia, Russia, Greece, Serbia, Switzerland, Turkey, and the USA). The sheer number of consulates in the Czech lands gives some indication of the contacts enjoyed abroad and of certain important commodities.

The economic heft of the Czech lands in industry and agriculture was also reflected in its trade relations. The closest links were forged within the monarchy with the Alpine countries, Galicia and Bukovina, and the Yugoslavian, Romanian, and Italian states of the former monarchy. From Galicia and Bukovina, the Czech lands imported kerosene, salt, eggs, pigs, spirits, and other produce. From the Alpine states came salt, pigs, magnesite, chemical raw materials, and industrial products. From the Yugoslav states came tannin, fats, wool, ferrosilicon, corn, and mercury. And from the Italian provinces came wine, single oils, and eggs. In turn, the Czech lands exported coal, agricultural and industrial products, sugar, machinery, textiles, etc. to these countries.

The Czech lands exported barley, malt (malt from Bohemia and Moravia accounted for as much as one third of world supplies), hops, seeds, chicory, vegetables, and fruits. They imported wheat, maize, rye, oats, feed barley, etc. from Hungary and other countries. Cattle was exported to Germany and light cattle imported for fattening, cows for both breeding and hauling, and fat pigs from Hungary. Czech carp was exported to the Alpine states and overseas.

Initially the Czech lands exported timber in the form of lumber, though logs predominated as a consequence of a German government measure. Brown coal was exported to the Alpine states and Germany, and coke was imported from Westphalia and Upper Saxony. Magnesite arrived from the Alpine states. Kaolin, Czech graphite, and other raw materials were exported. Kerosene was imported from Galicia. Sugar was exported to Hungary and overseas. Other exports included malt, beer, alcohol, liqueurs, smoked products (Prague ham), starch, syrups, confectionary, chocolate, coffee substitutes, vegetable and meat preserves, Žatec hops, Bohemian and Haná barley and malt, Pilsner beer, Carlsbad and Kysibel mineral water, Bohemian crystal, porcelain, fireclay goods, ceramic goods, furniture from handcrafted wood, matches, paper and paper goods, iron and metal goods, fezzes, hats, linen, pearl buttons and snap fasteners, Jablonec goods (jewellery), musical instruments, and other machinery and appliances.

For instance, the Kolbenka electrical plant in Prague exported more than 20% of its production. The Škoda plants in Pilsen supplied cannons and howitzer firearms not only to the Austro-Hungarian army, but also to Romania, Serbia, and Montenegro. Textiles from Bohemia found their way not only around the monarchy but also to the Balkans, the Near East, and Latin America, and delicate fabrics and lace to Germany and France. The produce of sugar refineries, breweries, malt houses, and distilleries were exported to Switzerland, Germany, Great Britain, and the Balkans. The monarchy took third place after Germany and Russia as regards the production of beet sugar. In the glass industry, the production of bottles (using the Owens automatic glass-forming machine) and sheet glass was so successful that two thirds of production was exported to Great Britain, Germany, Italy, the Netherlands, France, and the USA.

THE DEVELOPMENT OF THE MONETARY AND CREDIT SYSTEM

FINANCIAL INSTITUTIONS UP UNTIL THE MID-NINETEENTH CENTURY

From the end of the eighteenth century through the first half of the nineteenth century, the entrepreneurial spirit in the modern sense of the word was as yet underdeveloped in the Czech lands. The opportunities for financing both economically progressive manorial estates whose production (or at least part thereof) was intended for the free market, and already existing proto-industrial (or early industrial) plants, was limited. Financing of these enterprises was largely dependent on their owner's personal funds, and these came either from family assets or income from other activities. Only rarely were such funds accumulated from the operations of the enterprise itself.

A second, as yet not very widespread, method of raising funds was obtaining money from other private individuals. Those referred to as private bankers tended to be the ones who were involved in monetary transactions, though financial operations represented only one of their business activities. Most were involved in trade, which is why they were commonly referred to as wholesalers or moneychangers. In the financial sphere, their activities were restricted mainly to the provision of traditional consumer credit (either personal loans or pawn credit), the acceptance and safekeeping of deposits, and currency exchange services. However, the terms and conditions of credit services were often borderline usurious. Only a small part of the financial transactions of these "wholesalers" (i.e., in reality private banking firms) was devoted to supporting modern business.

As well as many Viennese bankers (e.g., Arnstein & Eskeles, Sina, or the famous Rothschild banking house),[138] many domestic banking families conducted financial transactions in the Czech lands. Virtually every larger town or city had its local banking ("wholesale") firms that met the local need for credit in a more or less transparent way. In Prague, the Lämmel family (father Šimon and son Leopold) and Zdekauers (Moritz) became more and more important. The significance of these two banking families extended beyond Prague and their business activities spread around the whole of the monarchy. Nevertheless, both firms looked at the Czech lands, especially Prague, as the buttress of their commercial operations and the base from which to expand.[139]

In Brno, the strengthening Moravian centre of textile production in particular, during the eighteenth century there had been the Johann Michael Köffiller banking house along with, for instance, the company Jakub "Dobruška" Moyses, while the start of the nineteenth century saw the appearance of the Gomperz family banks. From the middle of the century onwards, members of this family became involved in the creation and management of the first modern banking institutions in Brno. A feature particular to Brno was that many of the local bankers (wholesalers and money changers) were quite closely connected to the local textile industry.[140]

During the eighteenth century and into the nineteenth, several institutions operated in parallel with private bankers in the Habsburg Monarchy that we might deem proto-credit institutions. During their creation and subsequent activities, they still displayed signs of older mercantile thinking alongside activities more associated with the modern financial services sector. This would apply to Wiener Stadt-Banco (Viennese City Bank), founded in 1705, which during the 1760s began printing the oldest paper currency in

138 The literature is vast. For the latest on the subject, see Ferguson, N., The House of Rothschild, vol. I, New York 1999; Morton, F., Rothschildové. Portrét jedné dynastie, Praha – Litomyšl 2011.

139 Urfus, V., Peněžníci předbřeznové Prahy, Pražský sborník historický, 1972, vol. 7, pp. 107-128.

140 Janák, J., Úvěrování průmyslu na Moravě do počátku 60. let 19. století, Časopis Matice moravské, 1985, vol. 104, pp. 244-267.

the Habsburg Monarchy and thus became our first issuing (central) bank. In the Czech lands, the oldest proto-credit institution was Lehenbank (Lending Bank) in Brno, which opened its doors in 1751.[141] The Commerzial-, Leih- und Wechselbank (Commercial, Lending, and Exchange Bank), operating in Vienna from the end of the eighteenth century, also had an influence on the economic affairs of the Czech lands. This institution is also sometimes known as the Schwarzenberg Bank in light of its owners and management.[142]

In 1811, the disorderliness of state finances caused mainly by the wars with revolutionary and Napoleonic France culminated in state bankruptcy. One of the results of the subsequent monetary reforms was the emergence of the first modern financial institution in the monarchy, Privilegierte Österreichische National-Bank (Privileged Austrian National Bank).[143] This central issuing bank was founded in 1816 with a remit covering the entire monarchy. However, it did not exercise its right to open branches in other centres of the empire for more than thirty years, when in 1847 it opened its first branch in Prague. Branch offices in other large cities of the monarchy (e.g., in Budapest, followed by Brno, Opava, Olomouc, and Liberec in the Czech lands) were only opened in the first half of the 1850s.

During the first quarter of the nineteenth century, the first financial institutions of a somewhat different character, savings banks, were also founded in the monarchy. As in the case of the British Isles or the German states, right from the start these savings banks were seen mainly as philanthropic institutions intended to stabilise the social situation of the poorer sections of society. In 1819, Erste oesterreichische Sparkasse (First Austrian Savings Bank) was established in Vienna. In less than ten years, it extended its reach into Moravia, when during the latter half of the 1820s it opened branches in Brno, Znojmo, and Jihlava.[144]

The example of the Vienna savings bank was decisive in that it inspired the creation of similar institutions in a number of the larger towns and cities of the monarchy. The fifth in sequence of these was the Savings Treasury for the City of Prague and Bohemia, the name of which was later simplified to Česká spořitelna (or Böhmische Sparkasse—Bohemia Savings Bank). Of course, the word "Česká" in the title did not indicate the linguistic or national affiliation of the institution, but its territorial scope (i.e., the entirety of the Kingdom of Bohemia).[145]

141   Chylík, J., První obchodní banka u nás, Časopis Matice moravské, 1950, vol. 69, pp. 261–282.
142   Štefanová, D., Schwarzenberská banka 1787–1830. Firma období osvícenství, in: Brnovják, J. – Zářický, A. (eds.), Šlechtic podnikatelem – podnikatel šlechticem. Šlechta a podnikání v českých zemích v 18.–19. století, Ostrava 2008, pp. 69–92.
143   Silin, N., Rakousko-uherská banka, Praha 1920.
144   Fritz, H., 150 Jahre Sparkassen in Österreich, Bd. 1, Geschichte, Wien 1972.
145   Plecháček, I., K dějinám spořitelnictví v Československu, Praha 1983; Hájek, J., 180 let českého

At the start of the 1820s, some small local savings banks were also established in Bohemia (e.g., in Těchobuz, around 70 km southeast of Prague) on the initiative of the mathematician and philosopher Bernard Bolzano, and in Smečno near Kladno (around 30 km west of Prague) on the initiative of Jan Nepomuk Ochsenbauer, the forward-looking administrator of the aristocratic Clam-Martinic family.

Up until the middle of the nineteenth century, the monetary and credit system of the Czech lands relied mainly on private bankers, along with Česká spořitelna (Bohemia Savings Bank) in Prague, branches of the Vienna-based Erste oesterreichische Sparkasse (First Austrian Savings Bank) in Moravia, and the central Österreichische Nationalbank (Austrian National Bank). This system of financial institutions was supplemented by the activities of several domestic insurance companies, for instance the První česká vzájemná pojišťovna (First Czech Mutual Insurance Company), founded in 1827 in Prague, and the Moravsko-slezská vzájemná pojišťovna (Moravian-Silesian Mutual Insurance Company), founded in 1830 in Brno. The activities of the two domestic insurance companies were supplemented by insurance institutions from other Austrian lands (from Vienna, Trieste, and Budapest) and from abroad (above all from Munich).[146] This relatively poor, simple system of financial institutions basically corresponded to the nascent capitalist production relations in the Czech lands and reflected the immature state of the modern market economy.

THE DEVELOPMENT OF THE FINANCIAL SERVICES SECTOR FROM THE MID-NINETEENTH CENTURY TO 1914

A) SAVINGS BANKS

In the middle of the nineteenth century, there were around fifteen savings banks in Austria, most created during the 1820s (see above). However, for more than two decades Česká spořitelna in Prague remained the sole institution of its kind in the Czech lands (apart from three branch offices of the Viennese Erste oesterreichische Sparkasse in Moravia, two of which were closed down at the start of the 1840s). A new legal norm was created in Austria (referred to as the Sparkassenregulativ - the savings bank regulation) in an effort to stimulate the creation of more such institutions. The regulation formulated the general principles of the establishment and operations of sav-

spořitelnictví – 180 Years of the Czech Savings System – 180 Jahre des tschechischen Sparkassenwesens. Česká spořitelna 1825–2005, Praha 2005.

146 Marvan, M., a kol., Dějiny pojišťovnictví v Československu, 1. díl. Dějiny pojišťovnictví v Československu do roku 1918, Praha 1989.

ings banks. It was issued in 1844, though it was not followed by any noticeable increase in the number of new savings banks.[147] The only institution founded on the basis of this regulation in the Czech lands during the first half of the nineteenth century was a savings bank in the town of Aš, the westernmost city of Bohemia, in 1847.

It was only in the second half of the nineteenth century that savings banks began to spread. In the mid-1850s, new savings banks opened their doors to the populations of Brno, Cheb, Liberec, and České Budějovice (i.e., in large, still mostly German-speaking cities in the Czech lands). This was followed by another twenty or so institutions in several cities in the northern, mostly German speaking border regions. At the end of the 1850s and into the 1860s (i.e., after a short period of time), the first Czech-speaking savings banks had also been established in approximately twenty of the larger towns and cities of the Czech interior. The oldest Czech-speaking institution of this kind is reckoned to be the savings bank of the City of Plzeň, founded in 1857.[148]

In addition to the large increase in the number of savings banks, other important changes took place at this time. The savings institutions created in Austria in the first half of the nineteenth century were mostly associations. They were established by philanthropic societies, created on the initiative of the local aristocracy or leading members of the bourgeoisie. They were tasked with supporting thrift (and thereby creating an instrument for economic security), mainly amongst members of the lower classes. In other words, they arose upon the instigation of the elites of that time but were intended to serve the lowest social classes. Unlike these associational savings banks, however, most of the savings banks from the latter half of the nineteenth century were municipal institutions (i.e., they were established with the patronage of the local and regional authorities, the municipalities, the cities, and the counties).[149] However, they were no longer voluntary philanthropic institutions turning the attention of their elite founders to the opposite end of the social scale, but were created by bourgeois circles and intended to serve the interests of these circles. In other words, they were established by and for the middle classes.[150]

The municipal savings banks in the Czech lands soon began to be defined in terms of language (or nation). The graph in fig. 2 shows a remarkable aspect of savings banks newly created during the second half of the nineteenth

147   Schmidt, W., Das Sparkassenwesen in Österreich, Wien 1930.
148   Rauchberg, H., Die deutschen Sparkassen in Böhmen, Prag 1906; Klier, Č., České spořitelnictví v zemích koruny české do roku 1906, Praha 1908.
149   Albrecht, C., Savings banks in Bohemia 1852–1914: The Politics of Credit (unpublished PhD dissertation, Indiana University), 1986
150   Hájek, J., 180 let českého spořitelnictví; Hájek, J., Vývoj peněžní a úvěrové soustavy, in: Jakubec, I. - Jindra, Z., Dějiny hospodářství českých zemí. Od počátku industrializace do konce habsburské monarchie, Praha 2006, např. p. 359.

Fig. 2: The establishment of Czech and German savings banks in Bohemia 1853–1913

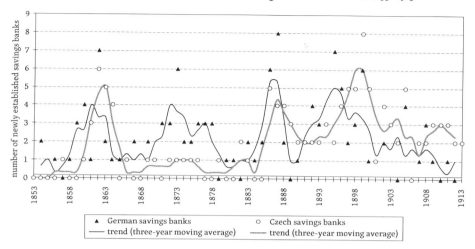

Source: Hájek, J., 180 let českého spořitelnictví, p. 38. Also Hájek, J., Vývoj peněžní, p. 445.

century. After the initial boom at the start of the 1860s, for the next approximately two decades, from the mid-1860s to the mid-1880s, there are almost no new savings banks created in Bohemia by Czech-speaking founders. One of the reasons for this fact was the competition represented by another type of small financial institution, the credit cooperative (see below). Indeed, savings banks as strictly urban institutions (created "by the middle classes for the middle classes"), initially arose primarily in larger, more advanced urban communities, of which most at this time were German-speaking. On the other hand, in Czech-speaking localities, smaller towns, craft market towns, and larger villages in the Czech interior, it was mutual credit cooperatives that were hugely popular. This created the impression amongst the Czech population that savings banks were "German" in character, while credit cooperatives were inherently "Czech".[151]

This relatively widespread opinion regarding national differences and the competition of both types of financial institution only began to change at the end of the century. A Czech author wrote at that time: "Only recently has it become clear that savings banks and credit cooperatives have *specific, fundamentally different tasks* in the economic organisation of a country" (emphasis added). The same author goes on to issue a challenge: "Large Czech municipalities where there is as yet no savings bank should consider whether

---

151 Hájek, J., Záložny a spořitelny – pilíře českého peněžnictví, in: Hájek, J. – Lacina, V., Od úvěrních družstev k bankovním koncernům, Praha 1999, pp. 121–158.

such an institution would not be of huge benefit to the town and a blessing for the entire region."[152]

This change of heart on the part of the Czechs was manifest in a new wave of savings banks created from the mid-1880s onwards. Another important milestone was reached at the turn of the century. Allowing for a certain time lag, up until then Czech savings banks had been created at the same pace as their German counterparts. However, from the end of the 1890s onwards, the rate at which new Czech savings banks opened increased, and as the new century began Czech institutions became the main driver of the savings banks movement in the Czech lands. In addition to the greater initiative shown by Czech founders, this was also because at the end of the nineteenth century the creation of the net total of German savings banks in the Czech lands reached its social and economic limit, since their spatial and financial capacities had been exhausted.

As the new century started, the Czech-speaking savings banks gradually caught up with their German counterparts. During the decade and a half prior to the First World War, the structure and national makeup of savings banks in the Czech lands was gradually transformed. In 1895, of the approximately 160 savings banks in operation in the Czech lands, only 60 were Czech-speaking (i.e., something over one-third). However, immediately prior to the war, around 120 Czech-run savings banks operated alongside 130 German institutions. In Moravia at the same time, the number of Czech-speaking savings banks (in excess of 50) even outnumbered German-speaking institutions (just less than 40).[153]

Despite the gradual equalizations in numbers, the older and more advanced German-speaking institutions still enjoyed significant capital supremacy. For instance, in 1897, total deposits in excess of ten million crowns were reported by only two Czech-run savings banks, Městská spořitelna pražská (Prague Municipal Savings Bank) and the oldest of all, Spořitelna města Plzně (Plzeň City Savings Bank), as opposed to sixteen German institutions. As well as the savings banks of large cities, such as Liberec (Reichenberg), Cheb (Eger), Karlovy Vary (Carlsbad), České Budějovice (Budweis), and Ústí nad Labem (Aussig), this included the financial institutions of many smaller German towns, such as in Aš (Asch), Loket (Elbogen), Česká Lípa (Böhmisch-Leipa) and Frýdlant (Friedland). At the end of the nineteenth century, in terms of capital, savings banks from even these relatively small German settlements outstripped their Czech counterparts operating in large

152 Fejfar, F., Peněžní ústavy v království Českém roku 1897, Praha 1899, p. 34.
153 Klier, Č., O spoření a spořitelnách, Praha 1914.

Czech cities such as Hradec Králové, Pardubice, Jičín, Písek, Chrudim, and other important Czech-speaking towns.[154]

However, with the arrival of the twentieth century, the Czech-run savings banks made up for lost time and began to increase the volume of assets under management at an ever-faster pace. This was especially true of the Prague Municipal Savings Bank referred to above, as well as the savings bank in the still independent city of Královské Vinohrady (now part of Prague) and savings banks in many other larger Czech cities. The capital strengthening of Czech savings banks was in part caused by the gradual transfer of deposits from German-run institutions to Czech ones.[155] This was largely due to the increased national awareness of the Czech population, which was turning inexorably in the direction of gradual economic emancipation. This tendency was sometimes connected with manifestations of economic nationalism.

Taken as a whole, the savings banks of the Czech lands represented an important segment of the financial and credit system of the monarchy. What is interesting is that several such institutions operated as subsidiary offices of the Viennese central (issuing) bank. In the rest of Cisleithania (leaving aside the Czech lands), this status was granted to only five savings banks. And yet in Moravia alone, eight savings institutions performed the function, while in Bohemia the same was true of more than twenty savings banks (six German and sixteen Czech).[156]

More money was deposited in the savings banks domiciled in the Czech lands than anywhere else in the western part of the empire. These sums represented more than one-third of the deposits of the savings banks of the whole of Cisleithania. The result was that shortly before the First World War, German-run savings banks in the Czech lands held approximately 1.3 billion crowns under management, while their Czech counterparts held around 1 billion crowns. For the sake of comparison, shortly before the outbreak of the war, the share capital of Czech-run commercial banks represented only one-fifth of the total funds of Czech savings banks, while the equity of all German commercial (joint-stock) banks in the Czech lands was only one-tenth of the deposits of German-run savings banks.

A short time into the twentieth century, locally dispersed savings banks created their own central association organised along both linguistic and

154 Rauchberg, H., Die deutschen Sparkassen; Klier, Č., České spořitelnictví.
155 Hájek, J., Bankovnictví v českých zemích před první světovou válkou jako základ bankovního systému meziválečného Československa, Hospodářské dějiny – Economic History, 1992, vol. 20, pp. 79–80.
156 Hájek, J., Zur Entwicklung der Sparkassen in den böhmischen Ländern bis 1914, in: Geld und Kapital. Jahrbuch der Gesellschaft für mitteleuropäische Banken- und Sparkassengeschichte, Bd.2, 1998 – Sparkassen in Mitteleuropa im 19. und 20. Jahrhundert , pp. 61–83; Hájek, J., 180 let českého spořitelnictví, p. 48.

territorial lines. These unions then instigated the creation of regular commercial banks in Prague to centralise the funds of the savings banks. This
involved the Central bank der deutschen Sparkassen in Prag (Central Bank
of German Savings Banks in Prague—created in 1901) and the Ústřední banka
českých spořitelen (Central Bank of Czech Savings Banks, which opened its
doors in 1903). These institutions incorporated the savings banks of the Czech
lands as a whole to a higher level of the financial services sector, which was
represented by joint-stock commercial banks.

B) CREDIT COOPERATIVES: MISCELLANEOUS SELF-HELP (MUTUAL) FINANCIAL INSTITUTIONS

One of the most pressing problems of the nascent capitalist economy in the
Habsburg Monarchy was the lack of liquidity. This was especially so in the
Czech lands and even more so in the Czech-speaking enclaves. Due to the particular circumstances of historical development, during which the political
and economic elites in the Czech lands became ethnically and linguistically
alienated from the Czech nation, business capital was not accumulated in the
traditional ways (i.e., through the development of traditional trade capital or
the gradual transformation of aristocratic capital). The third method (i.e., the
acquisition of the requisite funds with the aid of the concentration of small
or scattered resources, usually in the form of share capital) was also modified. And so in the Czech-speaking social environment the creation of the
financial resources necessary for the further development of the economy
took place mainly by means of small local financial facilities, self-help (or
mutual) credit institutions known as *záložny*—credit cooperatives.[157]

Self-help credit cooperatives offered credit mainly to small manufacturers, craftsmen, and small peasant farmers on the principles of capitalist
enterprise. They accumulated funds from small deposits, put them to productive use, and then, unlike the older savings banks with a more conservative outlook, usually reinvested them immediately. During the latter half of
the nineteenth century, several types of these small credit institutions were
formed in the Czech lands, for instance craft, contributory, district agricultural, and peasant cooperatives.

The first of an important group of what were known as civic (or craft)
credit cooperatives was in Vlašim (approximately 50 km southeast of Prague),
founded in 1857.[158] The impetus for its creation came partly from the ideas of

---

157 Schreyer, J., Dějiny svépomocných záložen českých, Praha 1891; Wenzl, F., Dějiny záložen a ostat-
     ního družstevního podnikání na Moravě do roku 1885, Praha 1937.
158 Pouzar, J., Historie první občanské záložny v Čechách, Sborník vlastivědných prací z Podbla-
     nicka, 1965, vol. 6, p. 169 et seq. Also Hájek, J., Počátky občanské záložny ve Vlašimi. Příspěvek

the German economist Franz Hermann Schulze-Delitzsch (1808–1883). This pioneering act on the part of the craftsfolk of Vlašim was soon copied in other Czech cities. The end of the 1850s and beginning of the 1860s saw the first phase of the extensive development of Czech self-help credit cooperatives in Bohemia (approximately 130 already existed by 1865), and a decade later this trend was further accelerated by the large increase of these institutions in Moravia.[159] Similar credit cooperatives were also created in the German-speaking enclaves of the Czech lands, though their significance was not as great.[160]

In their initial phase of development, the Czech credit cooperatives represented virtually the only examples of an indigenous Czech financial services industry. They were the first institutions providing credit to a nascent Czech entrepreneurial class still lacking the necessary financial resources. The relatively few small institutions scattered far and wide across the Czech lands felt an increasingly urgent need to combine forces. Therefore, at their first congress in Prague in 1865, the decision was taken to create some common institutions. Thus were created the first Czech-run commercial banks, the Záložní úvěrní ústav v Hradci Králové (Credit Institute in Hradec Králové, founded in 1868) and Živnostenská banka v Praze (Trade Bank in Prague, which opened its doors in spring 1869).[161]

The great economic boom of the 1860s and 1870s saw a sharp rise in the number of Czech credit cooperatives and their capital reserves. The cash resources of several of the largest credit cooperatives of the 520 such institutions in existence in the Czech lands around 1873 were comparable with many local joint-stock banks. The optimism that accompanied this period of economic growth meant that many of the credit cooperatives took an increasing interest in further entrepreneurial ventures. Unfortunately, these activities backfired on some of them during the subsequent economic crisis in the second half of the 1870s.

After recovering from the consequences of the economic recession, during which a number of civic credit unions paid heavily for the rash decisions of their reps and gradually disappeared from the scene, the capital differentiation of the remaining institutions continued to increase. The civic credit cooperatives holding the most capital began to be centred partly in Prague (these included Svatováclavská záložna / St. Wenceslas Credit Cooperative;

k 125. výročí založení první české záložny, Sborník vlastivědných prací z Podblanicka, 1983, vol. 24, pp. 259–283.

159 Hájek, J., Počátky a rozmach českého záloženského hnutí ve třetí čtvrtině 19. století, Hospodářské dějiny – Economic History, 1984, vol. 12, pp. 265–320; Janák, J., Počátky moravských záložen a úvěrování průmyslu do roku 1873, Sborník prací filozofické fakulty brněnské univerzity, C 34, 1987, pp. 71–81.

160 John, V., Die Vorschuss- und Credit-Verein in Böhmen, Prag 1870.

161 Živnostenská banka v Praze. 1869–1918, Praha 1919.

První občanská záložna v Praze / First Civic Credit Cooperative in Prague; and Občanská záložna v Karlíně / Civic Credit Cooperative in Karlín) and partly in some other cities in the fertile regions of Central Bohemia (Slaný, Roudnice, Nymburk, Čáslav, Chrudim). There was also as an important credit union that acted in Vysoké Mýto. The leading credit cooperatives managed relatively large amounts of money. In 1888, for instance, the seven largest Czech credit cooperatives each held more than three million florins in their vaults. This sum was equivalent to the total share capital of the largest Czech commercial bank, Živnostenská banka. And while the total share capital of all existing commercial joint-stock banks in the same year in the Czech lands, both Czech and German, was just under fourteen million florins, the amount held by only the largest ten Czech credit cooperatives (of the hundreds of institutions of this type) exceeded thirty million florins, i.e., more than double that figure.[162]

During the first half of the 1880s, another building block of the credit system was put in place in Bohemia. These were the district agricultural credit unions (Okresní hospodářské záložny – Landwirtschaftlichen Bezirks-vorschusskasse). Though their roots can be traced back to the second half of the eighteenth century, in the form of what were known as contribution funds attached to individual estates (i.e., stocks of grain that would cover taxes in the event of poor harvests), their real beginnings within the finan-cial-credit system can be found in the latter half of the nineteenth century. In 1864, the financial form of what had originally been natural grain funds was made possible by law. In this way, so-called contributory credit institutions could be created. Under a resolution of the Bohemian Diet of March 1882, it became possible to merge the resources of individual contribution-based credit unions into a single institution within the framework of a judicial pre-cinct, and thus arose the district agricultural credit unions.[163]

The establishment of such institutions was not compulsory, and this type of credit institution was not created in all judicial districts of Bohemia, but mainly in regions with a significant share of agricultural production. Their main task was to meet the credit requirements of agricultural enter-prises. After a sharp rise in their numbers immediately after the law was passed, during the mid-1890s the situation stabilised and remained almost unchanged until the beginning of the First World War. Thus in 1914, there were 165 district agricultural credit unions in operation in Bohemia. Three-quarters were Czech-speaking and the rest German-speaking.[164]

---

162 Hájek, J., Záložny a spořitelny – pilíře českého peněžnictví, in: Hájek – Lacina, Od úvěrních družstev k bankovním koncernům, pp. 121–158.
163 Plecháček, I., Zdroje zemědělského úvěru v Českých zemích ve druhé polovině 19. století, Hospodářské dějiny – Economic History, 1984, vol. 12, pp. 321–377.
164 See Okresní záložny hospodářské. Almanach vydaný na paměť padesátiletého jejich trvání, Praha 1932.

Around a quarter of the judicial precincts of Bohemia did not have this type of credit institution. This included chiefly German-speaking districts situated in mainly mountainous or non-agricultural border regions. District agricultural credit unions did not figure at all in Moravia and Silesia (nor indeed in the other parts of Cisleithania), though this was because the Provincial Diet (*Landtag*) failed to pass the necessary implementing regulation. In these parts of the Czech lands dozens of usually very small contributory credit unions continued to operate in the administrative headquarters of the former manorial estates.

At the end of the 1880s, further new financial institutions began operating in the agricultural regions of the Czech lands. These were small peasant (agrarian) credit cooperatives based on the principles propounded by the German politician and economist Friedrich Wilhelm Raiffeisen (1818–1888). Small financial institutions were created on the basis of neighbourhood reciprocity and voluntary work. The money deposited by members was guaranteed by the limited territorial range of each cooperative (all the members knew each other) and by the fact that members of what became known as the *raiffeisenkas* stood surety by means of their total property. In other words, these were basically unlimited liability associations, as opposed to many of the older civic (craft) credit cooperatives established by artisans and other tradesmen in cities from the end of the 1850s. A close neighbourly awareness of the economic situation of members' individual *raiffeisenkas* was the guarantee of a return on loans. The loans were cheap thanks to minimal operating costs, since almost all the work was unpaid and posts were honorary.

The first Raiffeisen-style credit cooperatives were established in the Moravian-Silesian German-speaking border region, and later in the German-speaking regions of North Bohemia. However, they spread rapidly to central, Czech-speaking regions. A wave of start-ups in the 1890s saw the total number of such small credit cooperatives in the Czech lands exceed one thousand by the end of the century. This rapid growth continued into the new century, when every year on average about 200 such institutions were created. In 1912, there were more than 3,700 such establishments in operation in the Czech lands.[165]

As far as loans to small agricultural enterprises and petty farmers were concerned, the *raiffeisenkas* became significant competitors of the administratively more cumbersome district agricultural credit unions. During the first decade of the twentieth century, the *raiffeisenkas* began to be called *kampeličkas* in the Czech-speaking regions of Bohemia. This was in honour of the Czech physician and national revivalist František Cyril Kampelík (1805–

---

165 Sedlák, J., České spořitelní a záložní spolky dle soustavy Raiffeisenovy, Praha 1902; Nožička, J., Jak vznikly naše kampeličky, Praha 1939.

1872). This new name was purely an expression of Czech linguistic nationalism, since Kampelík himself played no part whatsoever in the establishment
of these cooperatives.[166]

C) POSTAL SAVINGS BANK

The mid-1880s also saw the emergence of a financial institution that was to
become an established fixture within the financial system of the Czech lands
and indeed the whole of Cisleithania. This was the Postsparkassenamt (in Czech
Poštovní spořitelní úřad or *Poštovní spořitelna*—Post Savings Bank). It came into
being under the terms of an act of 1882 and commenced operations in January of the following year. It became an accepted part of life so quickly because
it had a readymade network of branch offices in the form of post offices. This
unrivalled network of outlets numbered several thousand payment locations.
Along with its simple operating regulations, this fact saw postal savings soon
catch on amongst the less wealthy of the population. Financial funds of these
socially weaker population groups, which had not proved sufficiently great
and so interesting to other financial institutions up until then, were very
quickly centralised by the postal savings system into unprecedented sums.
At the end of the nineteenth century, savings held by the Cisleithanian Post
Savings Bank exceeded the deposits held by both the largest savings banks
and commercial joint stock banks in the monarchy. This basic sphere of the
commercial activities of the domestic Post Savings Bank (deposits and savings) was based on similar institutions in England, Belgium, and elsewhere.[167]

The second, perhaps even more important sphere of operations of the
Cisleithanian Post Savings Bank was the organisation of non-cash payment
transactions, firstly through the introduction of cheques into everyday
money operations, and secondly through the creation of a clearing service
reciprocally settling receivables and debts. In short, while the deposit service saved money, the clearing activity saved cash. The cheque and clearing
services of the Cisleithanian Postal Savings Bank provided huge support for
the trade and industry sectors. In this respect they led the way in Europe and
provided a model for other states.[168]

The third sphere of activities of the domestic Post Savings Bank was the
management of state loans. In the early years of the twentieth century, it
made significant inroads into what had hitherto been the exclusive preserve

---

166 Hájek, J., Kampelička semper viva aneb Tři životy Františka Cyrila Kampelíka, in: Řepa, M. (ed.),
      19. století v nás. Modely, instituce a reprezentace, které přetrvaly, Praha 2008, pp. 355–368.
167 Hájek, J., Počátky činnosti Poštovní spořitelny v Předlitavsku a vývoj jejich úsporových obchodů
      do roku 1914, Sborník Poštovního muzea, 1989–90, vol. 11, pp. 40–70.
168 Hájek, J., Šekové a clearingové řízení předlitavské Poštovní spořitelny, Sborník Poštovního
      muzea, 1991, vol. 12, pp. 33–57.

of the Rothschild banking house and the so-called Rothschild group of banks (which included, e.g., the Viennese-based Credit-Anstalt). In the consortium that the Cisleithanian Post Savings Bank was tasked with establishing shortly before the First World War and which was to mediate the assignment of a new state loan, several mainly commercial banks from the Czech lands played an important role. This served as indirect proof that the banking sector of the Czech lands, especially Czech-speaking institutions, had gradually won a very important and generally respected position for itself within the whole of Cisleithania.[169]

D) COMMERCIAL (JOINT-STOCK) BANKS

From a political point of view, the turbulent years of 1848–1849 were followed by a relatively repressive decade. However, numerous administrative reforms smoothed the way for an economic upswing. The old credit system of the previous decades was incapable of meeting the evolving needs of industry. Private firms and family banking houses offering financial services were gradually replaced by new institutions in the form of commercial, joint-stock banks.

Around the mid-1850s, two new financial institutions of this new type appeared in Vienna: the somewhat conservative discount-deposit Niederösterreichische Escompte-Gesellschaft (1853) and the Österreichische Credit-Anstalt (1855), with its more active engagement with the economy at large.[170] Around ten years later, they were joined by another three joint-stock banks. Two of these modern financial institutions, Anglo-Österreichische Bank (founded in 1863) and Österreichische Boden-Credit-Anstalt (founded in 1864), were established with the participation of foreign capital (English and French). Most of the large Vienna banks, both those referred to above and banks that were formed later, played an active role in the economic life of the Czech lands for the lifetime of the monarchy.

During the first half of the 1860s, joint-stock banks began to be established even outside the confines of Vienna. Five new institutions were created, most of them relatively conservative in their activities, of which three were domiciled in the Czech lands. The oldest of these was the Mährische Escompte-Bank in Brno, founded in 1862.[171] A year later Böhmische Escompte-

169 See Jindra, Z., K rozvoji českého bankovního kapitálu před první světovou válkou, ČsČH, 1957, vol. 5, no. 3, p. 506 et seq.; Hájek, J., Nejrozšířenější peněžní ústav v našich zemích: Poštovní spořitelna 1883–1945, AUC Philosophica et historica 5, 1997, Studia historica XLVII, Praha, 2000, p. 79 et seq.
170 For more details see the jubilee publication Ein Jahrhundert Creditanstalt-Bankverein, Wien 1957.
171 Janák, J., Úvěrování moravského průmyslu od počátku šedesátých let 19. století do roku 1880, Časopis Matice moravské, 1986, vol. 105, pp. 63–90.

Bank, the first independent joint-stock bank in Bohemia, was opened. The last institution of this type, Warnsdorfer Escompte-Gesellschaft, established in 1864, was a smaller bank of local significance.[172]

In addition to the operations associated with overseeing the state finance and the provision of credit for railway construction, the third most lucrative commercial sphere of these banks was mortgage lending. In 1864, in order to expand the range of mortgage products on offer, the Hypothekenbank des Königreiches Böhmen was opened in Prague, the first provincial mortgage lending institution of this type in the entire monarchy.[173] According to its founding statute, the Prague-based Hypoteční banka was a not-for-profit institution under public law, which set it apart somewhat from commercial joint-stock banks.

All of these banks, and not only those based in Vienna but also those domiciled in the Czech lands, were German-speaking institutions. They were founded by more advanced and established German entrepreneurs and landowners in the process of becoming capitalists. A nascent Czech-speaking entrepreneurial class was reliant mainly on self-help mutual credit cooperatives. It was against this backdrop that an initiative arose that led to the creation of the first Czech-run commercial banks. These were Záložní úvěrní ústav v Hradci Králové (Credit Institute of credit cooperatives in Hradec Králové) and Živnostenská banka v Praze (Trade Bank in Prague—see above). At the same time, the Czech-German Landwirtschaftliche Credit-Bank für Böhmen (also Hospodářská úvěrní banka pro Čechy—Farming Credit Bank for Bohemia) was founded in Prague (1868), focused mainly on the agricultural sector. A year later, the business oriented Allgemeine Böhmische Bank (General Bohemian Bank, 1869) was founded.[174]

The creation of these banks was part of the economic boom in the late 1860s and early 1870s, during which time the number of joint-stock enterprises, including banks, rose sharply. At the beginning of 1867 there were only ten commercial banks in Austria: five in Vienna and five elsewhere. Five years later, in May 1873, more than 140 banking institutions were in operation in Cisleithania, of which 69 were based in Vienna and 72 in other cities. Though the number of institutions is similar, the Vienna banks held far higher capital resources.[175]

172　Hájek, J., Bankovnictví v českých zemích v 50. a 60. letech 19. století, Hospodářské dějiny – Economic History, 1999, vol. 22, pp. 83–106; Hájek, J. – Lacina, V., Multinacionální Böhmische Escompte-Bank (1863–1945), in: Hájek, J. – Lacina, V., Od úvěrních družstev k bankovním koncernům, Praha 1999, p. 191 et seq.

173　Ženíšek, B., Vznik a vývoj Hypoteční banky království Českého 1865–1915, Praha 1915.

174　Dějiny bankovnictví v českých zemích, Praha 1999, p. 114 et seq.

175　Hájek, J., Úvěrová soustava českých zemí do r. 1914, in: Hájek J. – Lacina, V., Od úvěrních družstev k bankovním koncernům, Praha 1999, p. 25 et seq.

This febrile atmosphere of economic boom and speculation was also apparent in the Czech lands. In Prague alone, 15 new banks were created in the early 1870s. New commercial, mortgage, construction, and brokerage banks were set up by either local business circles (both Czech and German-speaking) or older Prague-based banks. Around one-third of new banks were created as relatively independent subsidiaries of Viennese banks. Other new banks were launched in the administrative centres of the Czech lands, Brno and Opava, as well as in other large towns and cities (e.g., Plzeň, České Budějovice, and Olomouc).[176]

Several other medium-sized banks were created in the mainly Czech-speaking hinterland (e.g., in Klatovy, Lysá nad Labem, Kolín, and Kutná Hora). However, most of the new banks that appeared in Bohemia at the start of the 1870s were situated in the broad semicircle of German-speaking cities of the northern borderlands (Cheb, Karlovy Vary, Žatec, Teplice, Liberec, Trutnov, and Svitavy). Here they were supplemented by what was by the standards of that time a dense network of branches of the Prague-based Böhmische Escompte-Bank. The first branch of this bank was opened in Pilsen (1864), other branches were gradually established in Teplice, České Budějovice, Česká Lípa, Karlovy Vary, Trutnov and Litoměřice in the years 1868–73. The territorial distribution of most of the new banks and their branches thus aptly illustrates the state of the economy of the Czech lands at that time. The northern borderlands were home to the principle industrial sector at that time, i.e., primarily the textile industry.

The period of rapid economic growth was brought to an end with a bump by the collapse of the Vienna Stock Exchange in May 1873. This was followed by a long period of deep recession, and one of the worst hit areas of the economy was the banking sector. During the course of the 1870s, four-fifths of all banks in the Czech lands shut down. Of the twenty Prague-based banks, only five survived the crisis years: the older Böhmische Escompte-Bank, Hospodářská úvěrní banka and Živnostenská banka, along with Böhmische Union-Bank and Böhmische Boden-Credit-Gesellschaft among the newer banks. In Bohemia, outside of Prague only three banks survived (Kolínská úvěrní banka in Kolín, Záložní úvěrní ústav in Hradec Králové, and Reichenberger Bank in Liberec). The situation was even worse in Moravia and Silesia, where only the oldest Mahrische Escompte-Bank in Brno was able to ride out the crisis.

---

176 Dějiny bankovnictví, p. 120 et seq.; Hájek, J., Vývoj peněžní a úvěrové soustavy, in: Jakubec, I. – Jindra, Z., Dějiny hospodářství českých zemí. Od počátku industrializace do konce habsburské monarchie, Praha 2006, e.g., p. 333 et seq.; Janák, J., Nezdařené pokusy o založení českých akciových bank na Moravě v letech 1872–1873, Sborník prací filozofické fakulty brněnské univerzity, C 33, 1986, pp. 79–89.

This gloomy picture brightened up for a short period in the first half of the 1880s. In 1884, the bankruptcy of the Prague-based Böhmische Boden-Credit-Gesellschaft, prey to its own excessively close links to the sugar industry, brought to an end to the short-lived recovery.[177] What all of this meant was that for the second half of the 1870s and almost all of the 1880s, the remaining banks had to struggle to survive. They pared down their activities to the most basic operations. Credit transactions and other financial operations were reduced to a minimum, and dividends were paltry. After several banks went into liquidation, public confidence in such institutions was severely shaken, and many people turned their sights to other segments of the financial system (e.g., to savings banks).

The new business activities that began in Austria-Hungary from the late 1880s onwards saw a gradual recovery in the banking sector.[178] During the eighties and nineties, the downward trend of the previous fifteen years, both in terms of the number of banks and in the size of the capital they held, stopped. As the century drew to a close, the banks of Cisleithania rapidly put the setbacks of previous years behind them and consolidated their position at the forefront of the financial and credit system of the monarchy.

The nature of the banking sector in the Czech lands also changed. An important event in this respect was the creation of the Zemská banka království českého (Provincial Bank of the Kingdom of Bohemia) in 1890. Even though it was established by the Bohemian Diet and was therefore not a joint-stock company but more like a not-for-profit concern, it had a strong influence on many of the country's economic sectors by virtue of the provision of municipal loans, soil amelioration (drainage) loans, and local railway construction credit.[179]

Though the economic crisis of the first few years of the twentieth century saw the stagnation of the financial services sector, a new core of indigenous national Czech banking capital was taking shape in Prague. In addition to the older Živnostenská banka, in 1898 the Česká průmyslová banka (Czech Industrial Bank) was formed, in 1899 the Pražská úvěrová banka (Prague Credit Bank), and in 1903 the Ústřední banka českých spořitelen (Central Bank of Czech Savings Banks) already referred to. Ethnic Czech banking capital could now really take off.

The formation of the overall structure of the banking sector in the Czech lands was completed from 1907–1912, during which time ten new joint-stock

---

177 Horák, J., Přehled vývoje českých obchodních bank, Praha 1913.

178 Hájek, J., „Velká deprese" 19. století a peněžnictví v českých zemích, in: Kubů, E. – Soukup, J. – Šouša, J. (eds.), Fenomén hospodářské krize v českých zemích 19. až počátku 21. století, Praha 2015, pp. 141–158.

179 K Zemské bance nověji Novotný J. – Šouša, J, Samospráva a české banky druhé poloviny 19. a první poloviny 20. století, in: Malý, K. – Soukup, L. (eds.), Vývoj české ústavnosti v letech 1618–1918, Praha 2006, p. 668 et seq.

Fig. 3: Stages in the growth of share capital of national Czech banks 1890–1914

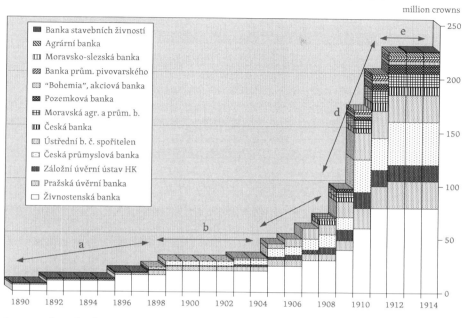

Source: Dějiny bankovnictví, p. 155.

banks were established. These included the the Česká banka (Czech Bank –
1907) in Prague, Moravská agrární a průmyslová banka in Brno (Moravian
Agrarian and Industrial Bank – 1908) and the Agrární banka in Prague (Agrarian Bank – 1911). The other new Prague banks, such as the Pozemková banka
(Land Bank – 1909), the Banka pro průmysl pivovarský (Bank for the Brewing
Industry – 1910), and Deutsche Agrarbank für Österreich (German Agricultural Bank for Austria – 1912), were smaller institutions oriented towards
a specific customer base or economic sector.

The ten years prior to the outbreak of war represented a period of extraordinarily dynamic growth for the Czech lands. Even more striking than
the rise in the number of joint-stock banks was the increase in their capital strength. The Czech-speaking institutions were at the forefront of this
tendency. From the end of 1898 to 1913, their share capital increased almost
tenfold, from 23 million crowns to 226 million crowns (see fig. 3). Despite the
strong capital growth of German banks in the Czech lands, in the years leading up to the First World War, national Czech banking outstripped the older
and originally more advanced institutions of domestic Germans.[180]

---

180 Dějiny bankovnictví, p. 150 et seq.; also Hájek, J., Rozvoj národnostně českých bank od konce
19. století do roku 1914, Praha 1986; Hájek, J., Vzájemný poměr a velikostní struktura českých

Fig. 4: Newly established domestic branches of national Czech banks 1895–1914

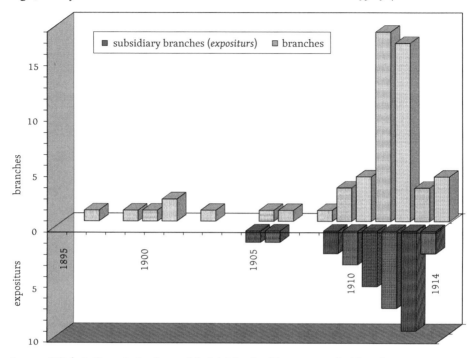

Source: Hájek, J., Rozvoj národnostně českých bank od konce 19. století do roku 1914, pp. 36–37.

This economic boom entailed a great need for liquidity, i.e., free money for business. It was the network of branches located in the smaller cities of the empire that were supposed to help banks in brokering loans for entrepreneurs. These branches also operated as the collection point for cash deposits. It is worth observing that it was the Czech lands, the most industrial region of the monarchy, that boasted the most densely spread network of bank branches. Of the 320 affiliates of Cisleithanian banks, more than half (around 170) were located in their territory. Shortly before the war, the national Czech banks played a significant role as far as this trend was concerned. The decisive phase in the creation of the network of their branches was in 1911–1912, both in the Czech lands and outside them (see fig. 4).

The greater need for cash reserves was reflected in several manifestations of Czech economic nationalism. As part of the drive for economic emancipation, the Czechs were encouraged not to deposit their funds in national Ger-

a národnostně německých akciových bank v českých zemích v letech 1900–1924. Příspěvek k metodice statistického srovnání, in: Pocta profesoru Zdeňku Jindrovi, AUC Philosophica et historica 3, 1998, Studia historica L, Praha 2003, p. 149–165.

man institutions (in banks, savings banks, and the Viennese Postal Savings Bank), but rather in Czech institutions. In the early years of the twentieth century, several large cash transfers were made from German to Czech institutions, e.g., from Böhmische Sparkasse to Městská spořitelna pražská (Prague Municipal Savings Bank) in spring 1903.[181]

The credit links between most of the major companies of the Czech lands had previously been associated with the older, more advanced German banks (either branch offices of large Viennese institutions or domestic German banks), which controlled a sizable chunk of the capital market of the Czech lands. The national Czech banking sector, which increased in size shortly prior to the First World War, therefore could not find many places to assert itself on the domestic money markets and so turned its sights to the export of capital. The capital expansion of Czech banks was directed to the industrially less developed eastern and southern regions of the monarchy, and beyond the borders of Austria-Hungary, especially to Southeast and Eastern Europe.[182]

The export of Czech capital was carried out in several ways. On the one hand it was accomplished via the establishment and financing of local industrial enterprises such as breweries, sugar refineries, and lumber mills. The creation of proper branches by individual Czech banks in these target regions then had a more lasting impact. The most tangible form by which Czech capital found its way into other countries was through the creation of subsidiaries. Though in name these institutions were independent, in practice they were highly dependent on their parent Czech banks.

Since the expansion of Czech capital beyond the borders of the country was directed mostly at the Slavic speaking region, this policy was justified on the grounds of nationalism and the concept of Slavic reciprocity, and also from the perspective of a non-governing nation through the declaration of the need for economic unity and solidarity on the part of oppressed nations in the monarchy. The Czech banks portrayed their expansionary strategy as David facing up to the Viennese Goliath and as being part of the struggle against the poverty that was to be found in the backward regions of the empire and which was, so it was claimed, mainly down to the policy of the Viennese government.[183]

---

181 See footnote 156. Also Hájek, J., Obchodní činnost předlitavské Poštovní spořitelny a projevy českého ekonomického nacionalismu, in: Hájek, J. – Jančík, D. – Kubů, E. (edd.), O hospodářskou národní državu. Úvahy a stati o moderním českém a německém hospodářském nacionalismu v českých zemích, AUC Philosophica et Historica 1/2005, Studia historica LIX, Praha 2009, p. 155 et seq.

182 Nečas, C., Na prahu české kapitálové expanze. Rozpínavost českého bankovního kapitálu ve střední, jihovýchodní a východní Evropě v období rakousko-uherského imperialismu, Brno 1987, and also, Podnikání českých bank v cizině 1898–1918, Brno 1993. Also Hájek, J., Rozvoj národnostně českých, p. 43 et seq.

183 Herman, K., Novoslovanství a česká buržoazie, in: Kapitoly z dějin vzájemných vztahů národů

A characteristic feature specific to the development of Czech banking sector was the fact that it was small ("folk") financial institutions that arose at the beginning, acting as midwives during the birth of some of the most important Czech banks. This can be said of the mutual civic credit cooperatives that during the 1860s initiated the foundation of the oldest national Czech commercial banks (Záložní úvěrní ústav in Hradec Králové and Živnostenská banka in Prague), as well as about the savings banks that prepared the fertile ground from which sprang one of the most predatory Czech banks prior to the First World War (Ústřední banka českých spořitelen—Central Bank of Czech Savings Banks), and also about hundreds of small agricultural credit institutions (i.e., both the district agricultural credit unions and peasant credit cooperatives—*raiffeisenkas* or *kampeličkas*), that provided the impetus for the creation one of the leading Czech banks of the interwar period (Agrární banka—Agrarian Bank).[184]

Despite their impressive expansion, the joint-stock banks of the Czech lands could not match the dimensions of the large Viennese banks. However, they made of Prague the second most important financial centre in Cisleithania. At this time national Czech financial institutions gradually overtook domestic German institutions in the Czech lands. Vienna could not afford to ignore the situation, so in 1910, when what had hitherto been the monopoly enjoyed by the Rothschild banking group on transactions involving sovereign bonds and the newly issued state koruna annuity was awarded to the Cisleithanian Post Savings Bank, the largest banks from Prague were invited to join the consortium tasked with undertaking this transaction. Of the German-speaking banks this meant the Böhmische Union-Bank, and of the Czech-speaking banks it included Zemská banka, Živnostenská banka, Ústřední banka českých spořitelen, and later the Česká průmyslová banka.[185]

We see a similar importance being assigned to Czech financial capital shortly before the First World War. The newly created Österreichische Kontrollbank für Industrie und Handel (Austrian Control Bank for Industry and Commerce) was to be the "central, supervisory authority for economic organisation" to oversee "the management of syndicates and central commercial offices and to supervise the contracts of industrial or commercial

---

ČSR a SSSR, sv. 1, Praha 1958, s. 235–312; Hájek, J., Novoslovanský sjezd a společenské akce v Praze v létě roku 1908, Documenta Pragensia, 1995, vol. XII, pp. 283–303.

184   Hájek, J., Bankovnictví v českých zemích před první světovou válkou jako základ bankovního systému meziválečného Československa, Hospodářské dějiny – Economic History, 1992, vol. 20, e.g. p. 85.

185   Jindra, Z., K rozvoji českého bankovního kapitálu před první světovou válkou, ČsČH, 1957, vol. 5, no. 3, p. 506, Proces koncentrace bankovního kapitálu v Předlitavsku, zvláště v českých zemích do r. 1914, Hospodářské dějiny – Economic History, 2009, vol. 24, pp. 49–110.

companies," etc.[186] This institution thus represented the culmination of monopolistic tendencies in Austrian banking. Among the ten largest banks of Cisleithania present at its creation and the only institution outside Vienna was the Czech Živnostenská banka.

E) THE INSURANCE INDUSTRY

An important yet often overlooked part of the financial services sector is the insurance industry. In Western Europe especially, this form of financial business had been developing since the dawn of the modern era as a way of reducing the risk involved in maritime trade. Under the conditions of the Czech lands, without a coastline, there was a more urgent need for the insurance of property (mainly buildings) against fire and the protection of agricultural activities (especially small farmers) against harsh weather (hailstones) and the sudden death of livestock. Over time, various forms of life assurance were added. The oldest of these arose at the end of the eighteenth century in the form of widows' and orphans' pension institutions (e.g., in Olomouc in 1793), which, however, were not an option available to the poorer off in society.

The first modern insurance institutions, based mainly on reciprocity, were created in the Czech lands in the 1820s and 1830s (see above, p. 189). Shortly before that large insurance companies were opened in Vienna and Trieste that quickly penetrated the insurance market in the Czech lands, for instance the first joint-stock insurance company in the monarchy, Azienda Assicuratrice Triestina (Insurance Company in Trieste, founded in 1819), and the Vienna-based Erste oesterreichische Brandversicherungs-gesellschaft (First Austrian Fire Insurance Company, established in 1824). Later on, another two institutions were opened in Trieste, the Assicurazioni Generali Austro-Italiche (General Austro-Italian Insurance Company, founded 1831), which exists to this very day, and Riunione Adriatica di Sicurta (established in 1838).[187]

Insurance remained in pretty much the same state until the middle of the century. Its further development followed basically the same trajectory as the banks. The first wave of the creation of new institutions began in the 1860s (the companies formed at this time mostly survived the crisis and depression following 1873), the second culminated at the start of the 1870s (though most of these enterprises soon succumbed to economic pressures). Among the firms established in the 1860s were some Czech-run institutions too.

---

186 Compass. Finanzielles Jahrbuch, XLVIII. Jg., 1915, I. Bd., Wien 1914, p. 513.
187 Marvan, M., a kol., Dějiny pojišťovnictví v Československu, 1. díl. Dějiny pojišťovnictví v Československu do roku 1918, Praha 1989.

At the start of 1865, the Pražská městská pojišťovna (Prager städtische Versicherungs-Anstalt, or Prague Municipal Insurance Institution) opened in Prague. Linguistically this was an Utraquist enterprise created on the principle of mutuality, and its purview was limited to the insurance of movable property and real estate within the perimeter of the Royal Capital City of Prague. The Vzájemná pojišťovací banka Slavia (Slavia Mutual Insurance Bank, founded in 1869) originally planned to only provide life insurance to Slavic clientele, but soon expanded its operations to include property insurance throughout the monarchy.[188] Pojišťovna Praha (Insurance Company Prague) offered life insurance, too. It was created at almost exactly the same time as Slavia, though its founders did not have such ambitious plans. Though Pojišťovna Praha never extended its coverage to property transactions, it became a prosperous Czech insurance company. Another property insurance company opened its doors in 1870 in Lysá nad Labem. In time it relocated to Prague and was gradually renamed Rolnická vzájemná pojišťovna, Praha (Agricultural Mutual Insurance Company Prague). The febrile atmosphere of 1872–1873 saw many other insurance companies founded. However, like the banks, almost all institutions created in the second wave of start-ups shortly before the Vienna Stock Exchange crash disappeared after the outbreak of the financial crisis in 1873 or a year later.

From the second half of 1870s through to the early 1890s, the insurance industry suffered a significant economic downturn. Property insurance was still dominated by fire coverage, though its focus was shifting from residential buildings and agricultural objects and outbuildings to the insurance of factories and workshops. Despite the existence of many domestic insurance institutions, companies based in Vienna, Trieste, and Budapest still occupied an important place on the insurance market of the Czech lands as regards both property insurance and life assurance.

At the end of the nineteenth and start of the twentieth centuries, the insurance industry again copied the developmental trajectory of joint-stock banking. We see new insurance companies opening right at the start of the new century and then in the second wave in 1910–1913.[189]

The Czech lands saw a real boom in life assurance right around 1910. Several older companies that had previously been involved solely in property insurance decided to dip their toes in this new sphere. The most successful of these was První česká vzájemná pojišťovna (founded 1827 – see above), which in 1910 opened up a Prague subsidiary company named Česká vzájemná

---

188 Peča, V, Banka Slavie 1869–1919, Praha 1919. Holec, R., Medzi slovanskou vzájomnosťou a podnikateľskou aktivitou (Pražská banka Slávia v Uhorsku v druhej polovici 19. storočia), Hospodárske dějiny – Economic History 21, 1995, pp. 145–172.

189 For more details see Marvan M., Dějiny pojišťovnictví, p. 194 et seq.

životní pojišťovna (Czech Mutual Life Assurance Company). Another older institute, Pražská městská pojišťovna (1865), followed a similar route and in the same year created Pražská městská pojišťovna životní a důchodová (Prague Municipal Life and Pensions Insurance Company). The network of insurance institutions in the Czech lands was completed in 1913, when landowners, unhappy with the existing offer of fire coverage, established Vzájemná pojišťovna statkářů a nájemců (Mutual Landowners and Tenants Insurance Company). However, this small firm never really took off on the already saturated insurance market of the Czech lands.

Attempts to form cartels within the monarchy found expression in the establishment of the nationwide Verband der Privatversicherungsanstalten (Association of Private Insurance Companies) in Vienna at the end of 1899.[190] This organisation brought together all insurance companies (joint-stock, mutual, and cooperative) domiciled in Austria-Hungary and lobbied for their interests, especially in the face of pressures from policyholders. Another feature of the insurance sector was the tendency for individual companies to become incorporated into the concern groups of the largest banks and the completion of individual groups of financial capital.[191] This was true of both Viennese and, albeit to a lesser extent, Czech banks and insurance companies. The tendency to export capital also appeared, again to a limited extent, in the Czech insurance industry.

DEVELOPMENT OF THE CURRENCY

The legal tender and currency system as a whole in the Czech lands underwent three fundamental changes shortly into the latter half of the eighteenth century. Firstly, what was known as a conventional currency was introduced, and it lasted more than a hundred years. Secondly, low-denomination credit coins were put into circulation for the first time. And thirdly, the era of paper money commenced. The last two innovations remain valid to this day.

Regarding the first point, agreement was reached in 1753 between Austria and Bavaria that slight modifications would be made to the main Austrian unit of payment to date, namely the tolar, in respect of its weight and precious metal content (silver). The aim was to make it possible to express the

---

190 For the latest on this topic see Pojar, V., Hospodářská krize – formativní činitel kartelizace pojišťovnictví na území Předlitavska, in: Kubů, E. – Soukup, J. – Šouša, J. (eds.), Fenomén hospodářské krize v českých zemích 19. až počátku 21. století, Praha 2015, pp. 169–178.

191 Jindra, Z., Proces koncentrace; ibid. Postup centralizace bankovního kapitálu v Předlitavsku, zvl. v Českých zemích do roku 1914, in: Z dějin českého bankovnictví 19. a 20. století, AUC Philosophica et historica 5, 1997, Studia historica 47, pp. 49–76. Also Hájek, J., Bankovnictví a pojišťovnictví v Rakousku do roku 1914, Praha 1987.

new tolar as an exact fraction of the two main units of weight of silver, namely the Viennese hryvnia used in the Austrian monarchy (that contained approximately 280.6 g of pure silver), and the Cologne hryvnia used in Bavaria and other German states (containing approximately 233.8 g of pure silver). Under the terms of the convention signed, the content of the precious metal in one new tolar would be 23.38 g of silver (i.e., 1/12 of the Vienna hryvnia and 1/10 of the Cologne hryvnia). The tolar was then divided into two *florins* (guldens), which was the basic nominal unit at that time of this new *conventional currency* (or *Konventionsmünzen*). One florin was then divided into 60 kreutzer (one tolar therefore had 120 kreutzers).[192] The main objective of this reform was to enable all the other states of the then Holy Roman Empire to enter into the currency valid in the countries of the Habsburg Monarchy without problem. This was arguably one of the earliest attempts to create a single currency in Central Europe. This ultimate goal was not reached. However, the conventional currency was valid in the Habsburg Monarchy without much variation for more than one hundred years, practically right up to 1857.

Regarding the second point, up until 1760, all coins in the Austrian monarchy were full-bodied currency. In other words, their value corresponded (or was supposed to correspond) to the value of the precious metal they contained. Kreutzers were therefore very small and usually had a silver content higher than would represent 1/120 of a tolar. In addition to practical problems (the tiny coins and the ease with which they wore out), this led to a speculative outflow of small coins abroad, which were then melted down into silver. The new credit coins (the value of which is assigned by government order) were cast from copper and intended to resolve all the negative effects mentioned above. The new copper coins of various denominations soon flooded the market and in 1765 low-value silver coins were definitively withdrawn.[193]

Regarding the third point, paper money was first introduced in the Czech lands in the 1760s. These so called *Bancozettels* were originally banknotes of the Wiener Stadt-Banco (Vienna City Bank) established at the start of the eighteenth century under the influence of mercantilist ideas. In 1762, the bank issued the first paper money with a total face value of twelve million florins. There were three further issues of *Bancozettels* in the second half of the eighteenth century. Originally, the circulation of paper currency had not been obligatory and its use entirely voluntary. It could be used to pay taxes and other financial obligations to the state. However, at the end of the eighteenth century, the free convertibility of banknotes for silver was abolished in

---

192 For more details see Vondra, R., Peníze v moderních českých dějinách, Praha 2012.
193 Regarding the development of legal tender in general see Staněk, J., Peníze v českých zemích. Přehled mincí a papírových peněz v dějinných souvislostech od 10. století dodnes, Praha 1995.

connection with the increased military expenditures of the state, and paper currency entered obligatory circulation.[194]

The increased financial needs of the state during the wars with revolutionary and Napoleonic France meant that the fourth issue saw the entry into circulation of banknotes with a total value of 141 million florins. The basis of this inflationary development was intended to result in a radical act, namely state bankruptcy. On 15 March 1811, a decree required all outstanding *Bancozettel* to be exchanged at one-fifth of their face value for "redemption certificates" (*Einlösungsscheine*), and later for "anticipation certificates" (*Anticipationsscheine*) in a proportion of five florins in *Bancozettels* for one florin in certificates. Both these new certificates ("scheines")were known as the *Viennese currency*.

The continuing precariousness of state finances contributed to the emergence of the first modern financial institution. In 1816, a central bank was created, the Privilegierte Österreichische National-Bank (Privileged Austrian National Bank).[195] The law emphasised that this was a private, joint-stock bank under state protection. It had the exclusive right to create branches throughout the empire and was granted a monopoly on issuance (i.e., the exclusive right to issue banknotes throughout the Austrian Empire). It was obliged to exchange banknotes for silver coinage and to withdraw gradually devalued paper money – so-called treasury notes (certificates of Viennese currency) – from circulation. However, the proclaimed convertibility of the conventional currency for silver coinage had to be suspended when the bank's stocks of precious metal ran out after a few months. Under an act published in 1820, the exchange rate of the two currencies in circulation was stipulated as follows: 1 florin of the *conventional currency* (*Conventions-Währung*, abbr. c.w., or *Konventionsmünzen*, abbr. k.m.) was equal to 2.5 florins of Viennese currency (*Wiener Währung*, abbr. w.w.). This essentially fixed exchange rate remained in force until both currencies expired at the very end of the 1850s.

During the course of the social and economic breakdown of the revolutionary years 1848–1849, small currency declined rapidly. The paper money in circulation began to be torn into halves and quarters and payment made with these pieces. Local financial institutions and town councils, and sometimes even individual tradesmen, craftsmen and merchants, began printing their own emergency tender.[196]

---

194 Staněk, J., Peníze v českých zemích, p. 60 et seq.

195 E.g. Silin, N., Rakousko-uherská banka, Praha 1920. Briefly also Bažantová, I., Centrální bankovnictví v české historii po současnost. Studie národohospodářského ústavu Josefa Hlávky 4, Praha 2005.

196 Ryant, J., Nouzové peněžní poukázky v Českých zemích v letech 1848–1850 (Příspěvek k ekonomické charakteristice), Hospodářské dějiny – Economic History, 2009, vol. 24, p. 25 et seq. Large

In the early 1850s, economic life and monetary relations gradually began to stabilise. At the start of 1857, a mintage agreement was signed between Austria and the other states of the German Confederation on the introduction of a unified silver metal currency. One custom pound (500 g) of silver was made into either 45 new Austrian currency units, now containing 11.11 g of silver, or 30 confederational tolars (valid in the remaining states of the German Confederation). The basic unit of this new Austrian currency, (or *österreichische währung*) valid as of 1 November 1858, retained its old name, the florin (gulden or *zlatý* in Czech). The new florin was exchanged in the proportion of one florin of *Konventionsmünzen* for 1.05 of the new florin. The new florin was divisible into one hundred kreutzers (formerly into 60), and so there was a problem with conversions of small coinage, since 60 kreutzers (1 florin) of *Konventionsmünzen* was equal to 105 kreutzers of Austrian currency, or 1 kreutzer of *Konventionsmünzen* was equal to 1.75 kreutzer of new Austrian currency.[197]

The aim of the reform was de facto currency union between Austria and the states of the German Confederation and the German Customs Union (*Zollverien*). The confederational tolar was thus freely convertible with the florin of the Austrian currency on the basis of a simple exchange rate in which 1 confederational tolar was equal to 1½ florins of Austrian currency. The result was perhaps the greatest currency chaos in the history of the Habsburg Monarchy when four different currencies (the *Konventionsmünzen*, Viennese, Austrian, and confederational currencies) were simultaneously valid. Even seasoned financiers found calculations in four different systems problematic. For instance, the Viennese currency was 2.5 lower than the *Konventionsmünzen*, which was 1.05 times higher in value than the Austrian currency, while the confederational currency was 1.5 the value of the Austrian. There were also problems when converting small change from a sexagesimal system to a centesimal one. The existence of four currencies operating in parallel placed a huge burden on the economy. Beginning 1859, the state recognised only two currencies, the Austrian and confederational.

After losing the war with Prussia in 1866, Austria ended its membership of the German Confederation and the German Customs Union. In mid-1867, the confederational currency was no longer valid in Austria and for the first time since 1811 (i.e., in fifty-six years), the Habsburg Monarchy had a single currency.

The Austro-Hungarian Compromise and the creation of the Dual Monarchy (Austria-Hungary) in 1867 impacted the Austrian National Bank (es-

---

number of samples of this emergency tender – see also Vostal, L. – Ryant, J., Nouzové peněžní poukázky v českých zemích v letech 1848–1850, Brno 2005.

197   Vondra, R., Peníze v moderních, p. 39 et seq.

tablished in 1816), now issuing the tender of the Austrian currency. In 1878, the bank was transformed into the Austro-Hungarian Bank and soon became a reliable, relatively modern issuing institution.[198] However, its relationship to Czech national and economic interests was in many cases clearly discriminatory. Periodic negotiations on extensions to the bank's "privilege" (after every ten years, the last were valid until 1917) were often accompanied by political wrangling. The bank usually issued currency in two languages (either German or Hungarian), and nevertheless this currency was valid throughout the entire territory of the empire.

Because of the increasing share of gold in the metal coverage by the issuing bank, it was decided at the start of the 1890s that the basis of the newly conceived currency of the Habsburg Monarchy would be gold.[199] In early August 1892, a law was passed on the new Austro-Hungarian currency. The new basic unit was the *koruna* (crown), divided into one hundred hellers. The relationship between the old and the new currency was simple—one florin of Austrian currency was equal to two crowns of Austro-Hungarian tender. In theory, this Austro-Hungarian crown currency was supposed to have become valid the following year. However, the gradual replacement of the old florins by new crowns lasted until the end of 1899.

The new currency, based purely on gold, thus came into effect definitively on 1 January 1900.[200] Several types of state notes were withdrawn after the turn of the century and the only paper money was the notes issued by the Austro-Hungarian Bank. The bank's gold reserves continued to increase. In the lead up to the First World War, only the gold reserves held by the central banks of Russia and France were larger than gold stocks of the issuing bank of the Habsburg Monarchy. Shortly after the collapse of the monarchy in 1918, the individual successor states adopted their own currency system with a different basic unit. Only the Czechoslovak Republic (despite the strong anti-Austrian and anti-monarchist tendencies of this new state) retained the same title of its new currency unit as that of the former monarchy—the crown (*koruna*).[201]

---

198 Bažantová, I., Centrální bankovnictví; též Kunert, J. – Novotný J., Centrální bankovnictví v českých zemích, Praha 2008, p. 22 et seq.
199 Cf. Vondra, R., Peníze v moderních, p. 47 et seq.
200 Staněk, J., Peníze v českých zemích, p. 143 et seq.
201 Vencovský, F., Vzestupy a propady československé koruny, Praha 2003; Šouša J. – Šůla, J., Peníze v proměnách moderní doby, Praha – Pelhřimov 2006.

5. THE CZECH CROWN LANDS IN THE AUSTRO-HUNGARIAN WAR ECONOMY 1914–1918

THE ECONOMIC SITUATION OF THE CZECH LANDS PRIOR TO THE FIRST WORLD WAR

Both contemporary witnesses and modern historians agree that prior to 1914, Austria-Hungary lagged behind other European countries economically. Though it acted as though it were one of the Great Powers, either because of tradition or its sheer size in terms of surface area and its population of fifty million, on an economic level it remained a largely agricultural society. The proportion of people working on the land (1910: 53%) placed it on the same level as Italy and Portugal. The causes of this situation stretch back a long time, but according to the Austrian economic historian Eduard März can be divided into roughly two groups:

(1) The country was severely handicapped by the legacy of its feudal, absolutist past and had failed to move on from economic, internal, and aggressive foreign policies set by the aristocracy, bureaucracy, and generals embroiling the country either in outright military conflicts in Italy (1859), Germany (1866), and the Balkans (1878, 1908, 1912, and 1914), or in protracted trade wars with Romania and Serbia. Successive governments sought palliative measures for the collapse of 1873, the prolonged depression that followed, and the profound agrarian crisis and abandonment of economic liberalism through prioritising the interests of large farmers (customs protectionism) and small merchants (amendments to the Trade Regulation Act, higher taxation of joint-stock enterprises, etc.). At the same time, there was considerable resentment of Jews and Jewish capital (supposedly to blame for the crisis and bankruptcy of the 1870s and 1880s) and an aversion on the part of the growing German bourgeoisie to the Austrian and Czech-German capital favoured by Vienna (the escalation of economic and political nationalism).

(2) Natural factors also impacted on the development of the monarchy. Firstly, basic mineral raw materials were either lacking or unevenly spread for the development of Austria's modern industry. In 1913, 63.4% of the monarchy's total imports were raw materials and semi-finished products for further processing (for the sake of comparison, Germany was extracting eleven times more black coal or anthracite, three times

more brown coal, eleven times more iron ore, twenty-two times more zinc ore, seventy-nine times more copper ore, and the list goes on). The monarchy excelled only in the extraction of magnesite, kaolin, graphite, and radium, with the last three being mined in the Czech lands. Secondly, from its very inception, the Habsburg Monarchy had been a conglomerate of naturally and ethnically diverse kingdoms and territories that the Habsburgs united either through war or marriages entered into for the sake of territorial expansion or to protect against expansion on the part of other states, especially the Turks. Thirdly, economic development was not encouraged by the distribution of energy sources (coking coal in the Czech lands, and high-quality iron ore in Styria) and natural transport routes (the Danube flowed east into the Black Sea, the Elbe was an excessively short link to the North Sea, and the trip to Trieste over the Alps was arduous). In addition, unlike Germany, Great Britain, and France, the country lacked large water canals and it had neither the will nor the funds to construct them. Fourthly, the internal market had insufficient purchasing power for the more systematic development of industry. This was the result of low levels of urbanisation, high rates of mortality, disproportionally high levels of emigration, and high numbers of people active in agriculture and living in traditional communities.

Nevertheless, regardless of these disadvantages, the economic and political unity of the Habsburg Monarchy was largely intact prior to the outbreak of the First World War. Figures from that time point to the undeniable and ongoing economic integration of the empire, the merging of local and regional markets in terms of commerce, finance, and communications, and the convergence of the price of goods, interest rates, and wages between the centre and the outlying areas.[202] And so no respectable economist or politician would seriously have contemplated calling for the breakup of this economic unit or the expulsion of one of its ethnic groups. Prior to 1914, not even Masaryk and Beneš had called for Czech independence, and only one small progressive party representing a small section of the petty bourgeois intelligentsia on the periphery of Czech politics (which in the elections to the Reich Council won but a single seat) spoke out in favour. Otherwise, maintaining the Habsburg Empire was a foreign policy axiom of all the European powers. It was considered to be a barrier to the expansion of Germany along the Berlin–Baghdad axis (France's interest) and to the rise of Russia (Britain's interest), and its

202 Cf. Fink, Krisztina Maria. *Die österreichisch-ungarische Monarchie als Wirtschaftsgemeinschaft.* München, 1968; Baltzarek, F. "Integration im Habsburgerreich," in: Schlermmer, E. (ed.). *Wirtschaftliche und soziale Integration in historischer Sicht (VSWG Beiheft 128).* Stuttgart, 1996, pp. 213–220.

existence was a buffer against the balkanisation of Central Europe, guaranteeing the retention of the traditional balance of forces in Europe.

To understand why this general perception of Austria-Hungary was overturned during the First World War, we must realise that, after one hundred years of successful cultural, political, and economic emancipation, the Czech lands in 1914 found themselves facing a dilemma: What stance should their representatives take to the new international order in order that the Czech nation might acquire greater influence and perhaps even statehood? In many respects, the status of the Czechs in the Habsburg Monarchy was more complex and sensitive than that of the other ethnicities, and the chances of improving it dropped considerably after the Austro-Hungarian Compromise of 1867, the subsequent expansion of Austro-Hungarian political and economic links to the German Empire, and after the last attempt at a Czech-German settlement shortly before the war. The unique situation of the Czech nation and the Czech lands is best illustrated as follows:

(1) Given their geographical location on the north-western edge of the Habsburg Monarchy, in the centre of Europe, and directly neighbouring the highly ambitious German Empire, the Czech crown lands were of crucial strategic importance for Vienna. After the thwarting of the Habsburgs' ambitions for Germany in the Austro-Prussian War of 1866 and the compromise with the Hungarians (1867), maintaining the Czech lands was the *sine qua non* of the continued existence of the monarchy under the Habsburgs.

(2) The political and military importance of the Czech lands during the nineteenth and early twentieth centuries was multiplied by their large, active participation in the modern industrialisation of the monarchy. Along with Lower Austria, including Vienna, the Czech lands became the main force driving progress in technology and the means of production, power, and productivity, as well as in the creation of a national income and wealth. More than any other region of the monarchy, the Czech lands boasted a higher number of people working in industry than in agriculture (in Bohemia the ratio was 41:32 and in Silesia even more favourable at 40:29). In addition, the region boasted higher birth rates and lower mortality rates, more people lived in cities, and in terms of cultural sophistication it was closer to the West. Not only did the traditional production of textiles flourish in the German-speaking borderlands, but also the sugar industry, distilleries, and starch industry were expanding rapidly in Bohemia and benefitting from the domestic agrarian base, along with "young" sectors linked with the second Industrial Revolution (chemicals, electrical engineering, engines, the arms industry, etc.).

(3) During the 1880s, after the introduction of the Thomas-Gilchrist process, the Czech lands took the lead in the metallurgical processing of basic

metals, pig iron, and steel. Drawing on huge deposits of phosphorous iron ore in Nučice, not far from Kladno and close to the place where coking coal was mined, the Czech lands became the main metallurgical base of the monarchy.

(4) Prague had been ascending since the 1890s as the second most important banking centre (after Vienna) in Cisleithania and in the empire as a whole.

(5) The Czech lands had completed a relatively dense network of railway lines and roads, and the Elbe connecting it with Hamburg represented the gateway for Austrian foreign trade to Germany and the world at large (outperforming the Danube River and Trieste).

(6) Before the war, the Czech lands had already achieved a relatively high level of urbanisation—of the forty-one Austrian cities with upwards of twenty-five thousand inhabitants, seventeen were to be found in the Czech lands. Literacy levels were high; of the eight Austrian universities, two were in Prague, and of the seven polytechnics, two were in Prague and two in Brno.

(7) Riding on the back of this all-round social, economic, and cultural boom, the Czech nation during the pre-war decade had succeeded in creating a comprehensive "Czech economy".[203] Though German businessmen in the Czech lands maintained their dominant capital stake thanks to the head start they had acquired during the initial phase of industrialisation, on the threshold of the twentieth century they found themselves on the defensive against a larger and more dynamically growing Czech bourgeoisie and resigned themselves to defending the status quo.

(8) Under the circumstances enumerated above, in the lead-up to the Great War, the historical composition of the population of the Czech lands, with its majority Czech-speaking and minority German-speaking peoples, increasingly acquired the character of a "community in conflict".[204] On the one hand, the Czechs demanded increasingly greater influence on government and power in the state, while on the other, the Czech Germans, relying on their economic clout and with strong support from Austrian Germans and the Viennese government, as well as nationalist circles in the German Empire, had no intention of surrendering so much as an inch of their political power. As a consequence they did their best to undermine efforts at a Czech-German settlement and fought against any concessions being made in the sphere of German as the official language. By the time war broke out, this protracted struggle between Czechs and

203 Mommsen, H. *Die Sozialdemokratie und die Nationalitätenfrage im habsburgischen Vielvölkerstaat*, Vol. I. Wien, 1963, p. 26.

204 Cf. Křen, J. *Konfliktní společenství*. Toronto, 1989.

Germans had become a serious problem undermining the very foundations of the monarchy and impeding further economic, cultural, and political progress in the Czech lands. As the only "nation without a state" in the Habsburg Monarchy, the Czechs increasingly felt that in spite of everything they contributed, they were discriminated against, lacked commensurate influence on the decision-making processes of the provincial and central authorities,[205] and ceased to be satisfied by Karel Kramář's so-called positive policy involving the negotiation of minor concessions. The First World War inevitably saw this entire situation unravel. The Czechs came face to face with the fact that the Habsburg Empire had slipped into the role of the German Empire's weaker partner and that the victory of the German-Austrian coalition would frustrate all Czech national aspirations and lead from the wartime persecution of all Czechs[206] directly to a programme of Germanisation (see the "Easter Demands" or *Osterbegehrschrift* of Czech and Austrian Germans published in 1915–1916), as well as the incorporation of the Czech lands into a huge *Mitteleuropa* that Germany had in its sights as a wartime objective and the path to which was being greased in Austria under the slogan "economic convergence".[207] Fortunately, Austrianised politicians (Bohumil Šmeral, Zdeněk Tobolka, and the Moravian Catholics) willing to negotiate this with the Germans were few and far between and did not last longer than the first two years of the war.[208] Otherwise, Czech newspapers and magazines, and above all the Maffia, a secret domestic resistance movement operating during the First World War, and Tomáš Garrigue Masaryk, came out against German expansionary plans, preferring to break with the Habsburgs and establish an independent state of Czechs and Slovaks.

205 Cf. Jindra, Z. "Národnostní složení úřednictva centrálních úřadů v habsburské monarchii a v Předlitavsku podle šetření k 1. lednu 1914," in: *Pocta Zdeňku Kárníkovi. Sborník k jeho 70. narozeninám, AUC-Philosophica et historica 1/1999, Studia historica LI*. Praha 2003, pp. 71-88.

206 Cf. Chování se vládních kruhů k českému národu za války. Dotaz poslanců F. Staňka, Z. Tobolky a soudruhů na jeho Excelenci pana ministerského předsedu, Praha s. d. [1917]; Tobolka, Z. *Politické dějiny československého národa, IV*. Praha, 1937.

207 See Jindra, Z. Rozpracování "'Středoevropského programu' Bethmanna Hollwega ve vládních resortech v prvním válečném roce 1914/15," in *Studie obecných dějin. Sborník k 70. narozeninám prof. Dr. J. Charváta*. Praha, 1975, pp. 141-167.

208 Cf. Jindra, Z. "Bohumír Šmeral a Friedrich Naumann. Důvěrné vztahy sociálně demokratického předáka s projektantem německého integračního cíle Mitteleuropa v prvním válečném roce 1914/15," in: Štemberk, J. and Manová, M., et al. *Historie a cestovní ruch perspektivní a podnětné spojení. Pocta prof. Vratislavu Čapkovi k 85. narozeninám*. Praha, 2008, pp. 49-70.

THE ECONOMIC SITUATION OF THE MONARCHY PRIOR TO THE FIRST WORLD WAR

The status of the Habsburg Monarchy on the international scene in 1914 was at odds with its political decision to enter the Great War. It was to have its military and economic strength tested in a conflict lasting years by the industrially advanced and democratically organised states of the West without even being properly prepared. Although from the mid-1890s onwards the economy had grown swiftly and important constitutional and political changes had been made, there was no way in such a short time the monarchy could match the more advanced industrial countries it was destined to do battle with. The extent to which the Habsburg Empire had lagged behind its competitors can be traced at least as far back as the middle of the nineteenth century, most obviously when compared to Germany, which over the course of generations became the dominant economic power of Europe.

Table 34: Gross domestic product per capita using the value of the US dollar 1960

	1840	1850	1860	1870	1880	1890	1900	1910	1913
Germany	(267)	308	354	426	443	537	639	705	743
Habsburg Empire	(266)	(283)	(284)	(305)	(315)	(361)	(414)	(469)	(498)
Difference	−1	−25	−70	−121	−128	−176	−225	−236	−245

Source: Z. Jindra. "Výchozí ekonomické pozice Československa," in *Střední a východní Evropa v krizi XX. století. K 70. narozeninám Zdeňka Sládka*. Praha, 1998, p. 201. The figures in brackets are approximate.

From 1840–1913, Germany increased its GDP by 178%; in the Habsburg Empire this figure was 87%. The monarchy was particularly sluggish in comparison with Germany in the peak years of the first Industrial Revolution from 1850–1870, and during the period of structural change and the emergence of new industrial sectors (engines, chemicals, electrical engineering, etc.) from 1880–1900. At a time when great importance was already accorded the economic power and dynamic development of states, this situation severely undermined the status of Austria-Hungary as one of the Great Powers. It is not by chance that the Austrian historian Eduard März characterises the country on the brink of the First World War as a "great underdeveloped [*unterentwickeltes*] economic sphere".[209]

---

209 März, E. *Joseph Alois Schumpeter: Forscher, Lehrer und Politiker*. München, 1983, pp. 93–94.

Above all, the monarchy was not sufficiently equipped with strategic raw materials and was dependent on imports for many goods ranging from non-ferrous metals to cotton. It was not even self-sufficient in the extraction of such basic raw materials as good quality coal. Though stone coal mining rose by 38% in the last ten years prior to the war, in 1913 Cisleithania had to import up to 43% of its consumption, mainly from Germany. The lack of stone coal was partly offset by the higher extraction of brown coal. However, in both cases the location of coal deposits was favourable to the needs of industry based in the Czech lands, but not to those of businesses located in other parts of the monarchy. Of the 18.1 million tonnes of stone coal mined in the monarchy in 1913, Bohemia and Moravia were responsible for more than 14 million tonnes, half of which was from the Ostrava-Karviná coal basin. More remote towns and cities, as well as factories, gasworks, and power stations, needed a readymade transport system for their supplies. However, the railroad wagons at that time did not meet their demands, and this had huge consequences throughout the war. The extraction of iron ore covered only approximately 83% of domestic requirements and was not optimally distributed throughout the territory, since its seams were too far from deposits of coking coal. With production of 2.3 million tonnes of pig iron and 2.6 million tonnes of crude steel, the monarchy was in sixth place behind the USA, Germany, Great Britain, France, and Russia before the war. However, output rose sharply by more than 70% at the start of the century, accompanied by the consolidation of more than nine-tenths of production in six large corporations, the largest of which was not far from the Czech anthracite regions (Kladno, Králův Dvůr, and Vítkovice). In general we can say that, in addition to its substantial agricultural production, the distribution of raw materials and industry favoured the Czech lands at the outbreak of the war. On the other hand, the non-German nations had to face the fact that with the exception of several smaller Czech and Polish enterprises, the arms and heavy industries that occupy a key role in a war economy were mostly to be found in the hands of German-Austrian capital, as well as that of the German Empire. Other sectors (leaving aside textiles and cellulose), which were not directly linked to the war effort and whose development was therefore limited, were, on the contrary, the main basis of the emerging national economy of the non-German peoples of the monarchy.

The harshest criticism of the monarchy's woeful lack of readiness for war is to be found in Karl Uhlirz's historical handbook: "There were neither adequate supplies of raw materials nor measures for the planned distribution of materials, the regulation of imports, and the rapid adaptation of a peacetime industry to wartime needs. The incredible ignorance and inexperience of commercial bodies, the army and the civic authorities meant that... the military authorities did not think that they would conduct the economic side of the war differently to how it had been conducted in 1866, 1859 and during the Napoleonic wars. They allowed agents... merchants, military suppliers, dealers and bankers to arrive... and outsourced to them the procurement of weapons and food for the army."[210] However, it is only fair to point out that the other powers cannot really be said to have been on a war footing either. Nor can we conclude that the Habsburg Monarchy, limping behind the West, was a priori condemned in advance to perish upon entering the war.

The monarchy entered the war in a state of disorganisation and instability. In Prague, an administrative commission sat in place of the Bohemian Diet, while in Vienna, Minister-President Karl von Stürgkh's cabinet had been ruling since March 1914 without the Reichsrat under the terms of emergency constitutional paragraph 14. The Czech political camp was being torn apart by the Šviha affair (in which Karel Šviha, an MP, was accused of being a secret, paid collaborator with the police in Prague). This unstable internal political situation was intensified by the dwindling integrative cohesion of the empire, caused on the one hand by national frictions and the appeal of economic nationalism to small businesses, and on the other the constitutional dualism that in 1917 was driving both parties back into a "compromise" crisis.

The emancipatory endeavours of individual peoples, above all the Czechs, to create their own national economy had a contradictory effect. In the short term it actually contributed to the development of the Austro-Hungarian economy, while in the long run it intensified the unequal development of individual countries. This, under certain circumstances, then created a centrifugal force in the monarchy. Hungarian efforts dating back to 1867 set a precedent. Nevertheless, the economy of Austria and Hungary and their peoples prior to 1914 was still functional. Austrian industry exported 46% of its goods to Hungary, while Hungary sold more than 80% of its food and raw materials and more than 70% of its industrial products to the Austrians. Both the industry and capital of the Czech lands were largely oriented on the wider market of the Habsburg Monarchy, and at their last congress before the war, even the Czechoslavonic social democrats made clear their interest in preserving the monarchy as a large economic area in Central Europe.

However, ongoing negative factors such as its economic backwardness in relation to the West, the dualist constitution, and the unresolved nationalist question weakened Austria-Hungary's status as a Great Power as well as its internal stability and military readiness. This comes as no surprise when one considers that, from the Badeni Crisis (involving an attempt to make a knowledge of both Czech and German necessary for civil servants throughout Bo-

---

210 Uhlirz, K. *Handbuch der Geschichte Österreichs und seiner Nachbarländer Böhmen und Ungarn, Bd. 3: Der Weltkrieg, Graz 1939.* p. 201 et seq.

hemia) onwards, voices had been raised questioning its very viability and calling it the "sick man" of Europe (after Turkey) or a "monarchy on notice" (a reference to the ten-year "compromise crisis" with the Hungarians). Even though in terms of population the country was third in Europe and second only to Russia in terms of surface area, over the course of one hundred years it had dropped to last place in the pentarchy of European powers established at the Congress of Vienna. As the age of imperialism dawned and wars were fought that re-divided the world, Austria-Hungary found itself in the situation of a second-rate country. It lacked significant exports of capital, its own colonies, and a large army and navy.

To the extent that Austria-Hungary nevertheless attempted to pursue an aggressive, imperialist policy in an effort to acquire spheres of influence, markets, and raw materials in its neighbouring areas, partly in the northeast (in the Russian part of Poland), but mainly in the Balkans, it had no choice but to hitch its wagon to the economically and militarily stronger Germany. From the concluding of the Dual Alliance in 1879, this foreign policy, strengthening the Austrian and Czech Germans internally and therefore often criticised by Czech politicians, was long underpinned by the extensive infiltration of capital from the German Empire into all parts of the national economy of the Danubian Monarchy:

Table 35: Imperial German capital in Austria-Hungary in 1914

Economic sphere	Indicators
State loans abroad	In 1912, of the approximately 5 billion crowns of Austro-Hungarian state IOUs in foreign hands, 2.75 billion crowns were held by Germans.
Share capital of business companies	In 1912, of the approximately 4.5 billion crowns in dividend securities in foreign hands, almost 2 billion crowns were held by Germans.
Banking	German bank capital had a holding in six of Vienna's eight large banks.
Enterprise	From 1892–1913, 173 joint-stock companies, limited partnerships, or limited liability companies from the German Empire were domiciled in Cisleithania.
Commerce	Germany was the monarchy's top imports and exports market: a share of 40% in both in 1910.
Transport and stock exchange	All larger private railway companies had German capital participation. Hamburg and Bremen were middlemen in commerce between Austria-Hungary and America and Australia. Their stock exchanges controlled the purchase and sale of the main raw materials and semi-finished products.

Source: Jindra, Z. "Německo a Rakousko-Uhersko na prahu červencové krize 1914." ČsČH, vol. 32, no. 4 (1984): 529.

As far as the expansion of capital from the German Empire to Austria-Hungary was concerned, it is significant that, though it was mainly invested in the industrially advanced Czech lands, like Viennese capital it did not find support for direct link-ups with national Czech capital. Mixed (Utraquist) enterprises were rare exceptions.

ECONOMIC PREPARATIONS FOR WAR

The monarchy was not known for its bellicosity prior to 1914. Although from the customs war with Serbia and the Bosnian crisis of 1908–1909 (the Annexation crisis) onwards it had pursued an aggressive foreign policy, it had not been one of the initiators or leading actors in the international arms race. Increased military spending on the enlargement of the armed forces (from 383,000 in 1908 to 443,000 in 1914) and on modernisation of military equipment and the construction of a navy, as well as on partial mobilisation in 1908 and 1912, only goes as far back as the annexation of Bosnia-Herzegovina in 1908, when the chief of the general staff was Field Marshal Franz Conrad von Hötzendorf. Between then and 1913, the monarchy's defence spending rose by 14%. Compare this with Germany's 69% increase, France's 86% increase, and Russia's 53% increase.[211] In 1913, the monarchy spent a total of $172 million USD on defence. Although per capita (3.3 USD) this was less than Western European countries, in relation to the national income it was higher than Germany or Great Britain. Whatever the case, it was more than a highly indebted state treasury could afford. "A state living beyond its means" is how it was described by the Austrian historian Eduard März.[212]

Legal measures in the event of war were partly based on Article 20 of the December Constitution (*Dezemberverfassung*) of 1867 and the Act of May 1869, which dealt with the declaration of a state of emergency and the suspension of fundamental civil rights. Shortly before the First World War, a new defence act was published that reduced the three-year national service to two years. In addition, at the start of 1913, partly following the example of Germany, France, Switzerland, and Italy, and also in light of the Balkan War, the monarchy adopted a special Military Operations Act, which was applied during the war by an implementing regulation of the Ministry of War from 14 November 1914.

An amendment to this act was the secret *mobilisation memorandum*, a set of extraordinary dictatorial measures in the civilian and military adminis-

---

211 Jindra, Z. *První světová válka*. Praha, 1984, pp. 31–32.
212 März, E. *Österreichische Bankpolitik in der Zeit der großen Wende 1913–1923*. München, 1981, pp. 43–51.

tration. However, by Austrian standards, the memo went far beyond the technical organisation of mobilisation and from the outset had a political subtext with short- and long-term aims. These aims were as follows: a) upon entering a war, to confront the anticipated reluctance of reservists from the Slavic nations to fight Russia and Serbia, and to counter pacifist demonstrations or acts of sabotage on the part of industrial workers; b) to grant the military and police forces unlimited powers in order to retain the dualist government of German centralism and Hungarian nationalism. However, the internal political nature of these preparations for war already lent the next war the character of a "struggle for the existence of the monarchy" in its old spirit, and a "desperate struggle" on the part of the states without full rights.[213]

In contrast to the previous "emergency powers of the state" in the form of the wartime requisitioning and utilisation of people, working animals, vehicle fleets, roads, and buildings only within the theatre of war, the Military Operations Act subordinated not only the civilian population throughout the territory of the state and in foreign occupied regions to military authority (in communication with the administrative authorities), but also allowed the militarisation of the entire economy. To this end, it used coercion and sequestration. In practice, this meant the almost complete militarisation of civil and economic life and a "decisive shift in power to the benefit of entrepreneurs".[214] The bill laid upon non-combatants aged up to fifty a duty to work, withdrew many freedoms and employment rights, and yet made no claims upon private ownership (i.e., if movable property and real estate was subordinate to the needs of the army and state, compensation was provided). This paved the way for a state-controlled war economy as well as for absolute military and police government with the aid of consolidating dualism and the old Austrian, German-inflected bureaucratic centralism. In addition, this law pursued another militarily important objective, namely the establishment of social peace in society. Under the act, the workforce in selected militarised enterprises was subject to military discipline and divested of the freedoms of assembly, movement, and employment. The military commanders of such establishments, acting alongside the civilian management as a kind of "workplace police force", were not obliged to obey employment protection regulations and could impose punishments upon the workers. And since they permitted company owners to reduce wages, extend working hours, and impose other such measures, the owners initially welcomed them. It was only in March 1917, when social unrest was on the rise and the political influence of the army was waning, that the government eased off on the militarisation of workplaces with the establishment of a Complaints Commission made up

---

213   Redlich, J. *Österreichische Regierung und Verwaltung im Weltkriege.* Wien, 1925, pp. 88–93.
214   Grandner, M. *Kooperative Gewerkschaftspolitik in der Kriegswirtschaft.* Wien, 1992, pp. 435–436.

of representatives of management and workers that assessed all wage demands, changes to working conditions, and job vacancies.

It turns out that all the preparations of the ruling classes of the Habsburg Monarchy for war also had, more than any other country involved in the conflict, a domestic conservative subtext. For this reason, the Military Operations Act encountered stubborn opposition on the part of Czech, southern Slavic, and social democratic MPs during its passage through parliament. All of them were justifiably concerned that it would be abused to suppress civil liberties and the rights of non-German peoples and seriously threaten the progress made thus far in respect of Czech economic emancipation.

This suspicion was confirmed at the very start of the war in the *special acts of 25 and 31 July 1914*, which not only transferred to the military some of the powers of the political administration, the judiciary, and press supervision, but also made all means of communication subordinate to the army and placed huge restrictions on foreign trade (in the form of lists of goods that could not be imported, exported, or held in transit). In addition, the Cisleithanian cabinet arrogated to itself the powers of the legislature for almost three years of the war by not convening parliament upon war being declared and by governing until May 1917 on the basis of Section 14 of the constitution with the assistance of *imperial regulations*, of which approximately 170 were published from the start of the war to the end of May 1917. However, the attempt made by the government in Vienna to create a nationwide supervisory and managerial body to implement these special acts and regulations (including those relating to the economy) failed. According to the Imperial and Royal (*kaiserlich und königlich*) Ministry of War, this role would be taken by the War Surveillance Office, the *Kriegsüberwachungsamt*, which had been set up shortly after the outbreak of war and headed by a general who had been assigned the plenipotentiaries of the joint ministry of foreign affairs and finance, as well as their Austrian and Hungarian counterparts. He was granted military, almost dictatorial powers, and was to operate as a central body common to both states of the monarchy. However, the government in Budapest objected to the plan, and so the competence of this office remained restricted to Transleithania and Bosnia-Herzegovina. Inevitably, the Czechs perceived this measure as reinforcing German centralism. The Habsburg Monarchy thus went into its last and most complex war without a joint executive body overseeing the economic management of the war. It goes without saying that less was known of the requirements and consequences of modern war in Austria-Hungary than in Germany.

This was because in respect of war the ideas of the military, political, and economic elites of Austria-Hungary remained fossilised on the level of experience from the nineteenth century. Although the Russo-Japanese War had already dragged on for a year and four months, the leaders of the monarchy still assumed that war would last but a few months and be essentially a local campaign. At the same time, businesspeople, mindful of the interconnectedness of the world economy, were unable to conceive of a multilateral war lasting so long. Preparations for the mobilisation of the Imperial-Royal Army, some 1.4 million men strong, had assumed a worst-case scenario of a two-year long war. In fact, the army was at full strength only in September 1914, after Russia joined the war. Nobody anticipated that a state with a population of some 52 million would have to mobilise almost eight million men (i.e., 74% of the male population of recruitment age—in Germany the figure was 81%, in France 79%, in Italy 72%, in Great Britain 50%, and in Russia 39%) during the course of a war lasting an unimaginable four years. The dogma of a short war, like the obstinate liberal idea that a market economy would regulate itself in an emergency, had a detrimental influence not only on the strategic planning of the state, but also on economic preparations. The government did not deem it necessary to accumulate large stocks of weapons or strategic raw materials in advance, and did not even have a plan in place for the total reconstruction of the peacetime economy around wartime needs. In the event of war, only a few dozen industrial establishments or business consortia selected in advance and with which contracts on military supplies had been signed during peacetime were to be co-opted into the manufacture of arms. Under the terms of these contracts, military suppliers were to increase their supplies of matériel two to threefold if required, with the help of subcontractors if necessary. Indicative of the underdevelopment of large-scale industry in the monarchy at that time is the fact that some of these military orders were to be entrusted to small-scale producers and even domestic producers (e.g., up to 50% of all contracts in the case of boots and saddlery. (This, for example, was what enabled the small Zlín-based shoe company T&A Baťa to win large military contracts on the threshold of war, despite never having been previously part of the military supplies consortium of Austrian leather manufacturers.) The government left it up to the manufacturers and suppliers by what means and for how long they would supply the necessary raw materials. As a result, nobody ensured that the monarchy was pre-stocked with overseas raw materials (especially cotton, wool, leather, non-ferrous metals, etc.) in the event of war and naval blockade.

THE ESTABLISHMENT, CHARACTER AND DEVELOPMENT OF THE WAR ECONOMY

A "war economy", a concept hitherto largely unknown, is spoken of for the first time in connection with the First World War. What made this war different was not only its unprecedented duration and territorial dimensions (involving the participation of 38 states and 70 million mobilised men), but also the huge economic, specifically industrial potential that was deployed in the struggle (almost half of global industrial production was concentrated in the states of the Triple Alliance and the Triple Entente—four-fifths, if the USA is included). Unlike previous, mainly bilateral, local, and peripheral conflicts, the main stage of the First World War was the very centre of the global economy: Europe. In addition, the war took place during the era of the second Industrial Revolution. This was the age of machine warfare, what German historian Michael Geyer calls a period of "material-intensive armament" (1914–1945), in which new rapid fire weapons often replaced soldiers and equipment became more important than the size of an army.[215] It is for this reason, too, that the war of 1914–1918 could be described as "industrialised [...], factory made, with the mass production and mass consumption of weapons".[216] It is also why the problems of the first industrial war in history could only be resolved by a "war economy" adapted to it, the creation of which basically took the entire first year of the war.

The war showed that vast, populous empires such as Austria-Hungary and Russia, previously believed to be predestined for military success, could not stand the test of a modern, economically driven war, because they were not sufficiently developed industrially. This had fatal consequences. The Austro-Hungarian war economy was ultimately incapable of rising to the occasion in the same way as industrial Britain or Germany and was therefore exhausted far earlier and more deeply. This then resulted in the extreme physical and psychological debilitation of the population and eventually the military and political collapse of the monarchy.

What were the aims and basis of the war economy? In essence, the First World War was a positional or trench war in which the general staff attempted to overcome the strategic advantage always enjoyed by the defender by deploying the largest number of soldiers and equipment. Material battles ensued. The rapid technical and physical wear and tear of combat technology and its high losses in these battles, along with the greater demands of the army on the quantity, quality, and range of weapons, inevitably transformed this war into an encounter whose outcome was decided not only by solders on the front, but by the civilian population, its moral and political spirit, and above all the economic potential it embodied. The military campaign thus acquired a second dimension, becoming an "economic war" that placed gigantic demands on central management and planning with a two-pronged objective—to mobilise all the economic resources available in order to prosecute the war, and to sap the enemy's economic strength as much as possible. At the same

---

215 Geyer, M. *Deutsche Rüstungspolitik 1860–1980*. Frankfurt am Main, 1984, p. 13.
216 Caspary, A. *Wirtschafts-Strategie und Kriegsführung*. Berlin, 1932, p. 128.

time, within the war economy the balance of forces between the main social and economic factors changed within the tripartite: Organised labour was almost completely suppressed in the first half of the war (up until 1916), heavy industry (especially armaments) acquired a highly privileged position, and the state entered the economy as the main mediating and determining agent.

The state's economic policy was the first to change. To save the capitalist system itself, the state had to intervene both in the distribution of products and supplies (the introduction of rationing) and in the national economy itself, its decision-making powers and ownership rights (in the spheres of production, sectors, investment, raw materials, and foreign affairs, as well as in the deployment and supervision of the workforce and the establishment of state-owned companies). The intervention of the state in the economy was so huge, and the restrictions placed on market forces in production and commerce and on the capital and jobs markets so drastic, that contemporary commentators spoke (depending on their political orientation) either of the transformation of the liberal market system into "war capitalism" or "war socialism" as part of the "etatisation [*Durchstaatlichung*] of the economy" (Karl Renner). In reality, however, no change to the system took place. The wartime economy never abandoned the sphere of private property relations and in principle did not even question the right of businesspeople to turn a profit. Faced with a state of emergency, businesspeople and the state simply adapted to the extraordinary demands made by the war by modifying the existing system in respect of its internal and external functioning.

Massive state intervention was not, when all was said and done, so surprising. From 1914–1918, in the "long shadow of the state" as we have known it throughout the twentieth century (E. Hainisch), trends came to a head that had emerged at the end of the nineteenth century in association with the formation of organised capitalism. The war simply accelerated the transformation underway of the liberal market economy into a system in which production and the capital potential of large corporations, banks, and monopolies (cartels, syndicates, etc.) were closely intertwined institutionally and in terms of human resources with the highly organised power of the state. Unlike previously, this was not about a higher level of cooperation between the state and the economy as between two equal partners: "It was more about individual interested parties receiving a privileged position in relation to the rest of the economy through their close links with the state apparatus [...]. The state and the private economy did not stand as opposite poles. The state apparatus was dependent on the economy as regards both human resources and ideology, especially on individual groups within the economy."[217]

---

217 Hardach, G. *Der erste Weltkrieg 1914–1918 (Geschichte der Weltwirtschaft im 20. Jahrhundert, Bd. 2)*. München, 1973, pp. 69–70.

In Austria-Hungary organised capital went so far as to change relations on the market: Instead of partial regulation, it basically suppressed the function of the market both inside and outside.

The first significant intervention on the part of the state in the external market functioning of the pre-war economic system involved the severing of international economic ties. Instead of free commercial competition and the "peaceful penetration" of the internal market, all the warring countries employed the weapons of economic war (blockade, embargo, protectionism, unrestricted submarine warfare, the looting of occupied regions, etc.) against their enemies. The objective was to cut the enemy off from foreign supplies, make it more difficult for him to manufacture weapons, and to grind down and starve his population. The encircled Central Powers, under the influence of naval blockade, had to resort to strictly autarkic (self-sufficient) economic measures and find replacements for scarce raw materials. To this end, the state also transformed the internal market. The main measures were as follows: the recording and requisitioning of supplies; the centralisation of procurement and sales; rationing; and price regulation. In practice this led to the creation of two markets: the official and the black.

These internal structural changes mostly affected industrial production. In the war industry, not only was the dividing line blurred between the arms and the peacetime or civilian industry, but also the sense and purpose of economic activities changed. As a new category of mass-produced goods, military matériel did not return into the reproductive process but disappeared irrevocably from it—destroyed, shot, sunk, or decimated in battle. Prior to the war, only a few selected branches of industry (e.g., mechanical engineering, shipbuilding, and the chemicals industry) had been involved in the arms industry, and even then only partially. These sectors were now joined by the power, auto, and aerospace industries. Although the arms trade was already a lucrative business at the time, success and sales were reserved for the most technically and capital-rich large corporations as well as the state aresenals (e.g., in Cisleithania the Škoda works, Österreichische Waffenfabriks-Gesellschaft, and Hirtenberger Patronenfabrik; in Hungary Ungarische Kanonenfabrik [Győr]; in Germany Fried. Krupp [Essen], Rheinmetall [Düsseldorf], and Deutsche Waffen- und Munitionsfabriken; in Britain Vickers-Armstrongs; and in France, Schneider-Creusot), which were able to monopolise the domestic market, conquer foreign markets, and combine arms production with peacetime activities. However, during the war, the standard budgetary allocation and the existing state arsenal were insufficient to cover the army's insatiable needs, and the situation could not be saved, even by the established private arms manufacturers.

We might characterise the main elements of the Austro-Hungarian war economy as follows. First, there was extraordinary military expenditure by the state exceeding peacetime levels many times over, and this spending was financed partly from increased consumer and income taxes, but also by means of internal and foreign debt (loans) combined with the free printing of banknotes not covered by gold (inflation). Second, the public administration became the general contracting authority of most work and supplies. Third, the state took over the centralised management of the economy and used non-economic means of coercion and organisation to do so. Fourth, in order to cover wartime needs, all civilian industry was requisitioned if it had or could acquire the appropriate machines and labour. During this technically and organisationally challenging process of reorganisation, businesspeople were incentivised by several state measures, above all by favourable price and grant policies, the promise of shared investment, extraordinary profits, tax write-offs, and various guarantees, as well as the establishment of special organisations for the central management and preferential allocation of raw materials, and lastly by a state system for allocating the workforce to the most important wartime enterprises, or by having these enterprises and their workforces placed under military control.

When undertaking this extensive reorganisation, the military administration looked to Germany for inspiration. The German Empire had created the most sophisticated organisation and a huge wartime economic base. It was at this time the leading industrial country in Europe and so well placed to take these measures. Upon entering the war it boasted the largest arms industry in the world and the largest, most up-to-date metallurgy, engineering, chemical, and electrical industries on the continent. Its only weakness was its dependence on imports of essential raw materials. In addition, its status as a Great Power added impetus to Germany's efforts. It had to fight on two fronts and had megalomaniac objectives (the integration of Central Europe, continental hegemony, a desire to occupy the role of global number one) that demanded the maximum concentration of all forces. Walther Rathenau, director of the electrical company AEG, was the main organiser of the German war economy, and it was upon his initiative that, as early as August 1914, a department was created at the Ministry of War for military raw materials. This was the famous materials-supply division or Kriegsrohstoffabteilung (KRA), with departments and affiliates for every scarce resource. These hybrid companies, established with the capital participation and support of the state and managed by hugely influential businesspeople and managers, operated as compulsory cartels, and had a duty to record and manage inventory, procurement, and the distribution of all strategic raw materials.

The economically weaker Austria-Hungary lacked these foundations and objectives. And though it had its own skilled entrepreneurial figures, none had acquired such an exclusive position and influence on the creation of economic policy as Walther Rathenau and many other businesspeople in Germany. Consequently, the Habsburg Empire was obliged to yield much of the economic decision-making to its ally soon after the outbreak of war. Under the terms of the September contract signed at a conference in Berlin (24 September 1914) it undertook to imitate the German Kriegsrohstoffabteilung (i.e., to establish centralised organisations on the German model for managing foreign, and later domestic, raw materials at the cost of freeing up trade and the transport of raw materials and goods from Hamburg, Bremen and from neutral countries).

Typical, however, of the monarchy's wartime economy was an excessively bureaucratic and complex network of institutions, of which there were five types: a) military economic unions (34 of them) representing essentially state-imposed cartels for individual sectors; b) commissions (19), such as those that collected and managed old iron and paper, made up of government-appointed representatives of the relevant sectors; c) specialist committees (14) set up by the government for consultative purposes and also consisting of representatives of the different sectors; d–e) economic control centres for managing the main raw materials, of which twenty-one operated as private companies and three enjoyed the status of state head offices (for grain, fodder, and vegetables).

Of all of these wartime organisations, the greatest powers were granted the *military control centres*. Created at the suggestion of the German Empire and based on the German model, these were tasked with taking receipt of and distributing raw materials released under the September contract for the purposes of mutual trade. Soon, however, they went their own way. First of all, this meant that, given the growing calls for the emancipation of Hungary (from early 1915), they were not established on a nationwide basis but as dualistic institutions, and this greatly weakened their effectiveness. Unlike their German counterparts they acquired the status of private joint-stock companies or limited liability companies managed by businesspeople and banks that operated under the supervision of the state and could only pay out low dividends, while otherwise working without the direct capital participation or financial guarantees of the state. Only the central offices for the management of grain and food, in which the state retained direct supervisory powers, were an exception (e.g., the Military Corn Institute). On the other hand, as in Germany, the state granted all control centres the status of monopoly that in its organisational structure and personnel resembled or linked directly to the existing cartels. This significantly reinforced the system of "organised capital" in the country. In October and November 1914, the first control offices were established for managing raw materials of foreign origin (cotton, wool, and non-ferrous metals, still operating on a nationwide basis). Under the shadow of a munitions crisis, similar centres were created for oil and fats, which were essential for producing nitro-glycerine and explosives.

When shortly afterwards the monarchy's ability to import was squeezed by the tightening up of naval blockades and Italy's entry into the war, the centres began to shift over to the recording, procurement, collection, and distribution of scarce domestic raw materials and consumer goods (leather, flax, hemp, corn, sugar, spirits, malt, sulphuric acid, kerosene, etc.). In addition, commissions for the collection of old materials (rags and bones, paper, old iron, etc.) were created that operated similarly to the state control centres. In all, around sixty such special-purpose organisations were created during the war employing almost two thousand people, mainly women.

However, the work of the military control centres suffered from various shortcomings and problems. Often they were set up only after it had become too late to pass more than an emergency measure for the market regulation of the raw material in question. They were not granted sufficient powers and were not subject to integrated supervision, since their activities were entrusted to branches of the public administration—sometimes civilian, sometimes military. Their headquarters were not in the crown lands and regions where the relevant production activities were based, but usually in Vienna and Budapest, as close as possible to the ministries and banks with which they were in daily contact. It comes as no surprise that this wartime military centralisation in the capital city, similar to the pre-war tendencies (relocating the headquarters of joint-stock companies and cartels to Vienna), rubbed salt in the wound of Czech economic circles. This is clear, for instance, from the protest by the Prague Chambers of Trade and Commerce against the transfer of the branch office of a distillery syndicate from Prague to Vienna at the end of 1915. In March 1917, various shortcomings in the management of the wartime control centres were suddenly open to public scrutiny in the Viennese lawsuit against Josef Kranz, the leading representative of the distillery cartel, in which a number of prominent people were implicated. Following the reopening of the Imperial Council in summer and autumn 1917, these deficiencies were investigated by a special parliamentary commission. Impetus for establishing the commission came, inter alia, from the interpellation of Czech MPs, who offered the following testimony regarding the control centres:

"It was a common occurrence that if a 'control office' had not been set up for a particular sector, goods were at least available, but from the day such a centre was established, they disappeared from the market. The distribution of goods was not always efficient and fair. [...] Many of the centres were taken control of by [...] persons that saw them simply as organisations suitable for maintaining a high standard of living for themselves and their friends and relatives or party members and for generating large profits for individuals and entire communities. The huge overheads [...] and the pursuit of exorbitant profits meant that, after the establishment of the centres, not only was there no reduction in prices, but many goods actually rose sharply in price. [...] The best evidence of the detrimental effect of these centres are the outstanding balance sheets reported by certain other centres. [...] The profits are usually so high that their leading bodies should be brought to justice for price gouging."[218]

For the whole of the war, because of Hungary, the Habsburg Monarchy's war-management system suffered a duplication of activities and even, during the first half of the war (i.e., at a time when the army enjoyed extraordinary political and economic authority) triplication. This gave rise to frequent disputes regarding competencies between national, Hungarian and Austrian, and civilian and military bodies. It is no wonder that this complex, improvised organisation, created under pressure without proper preparation, faced problems. Sometimes these took the form of proverbial Austrian sloppiness (*Schlamperei*) and tardiness (*Zu-spät-kommen*), other times the protectionism and nationalist motivated actions of the omnipotent German-Austrian bureaucracy. These organisational activities not only limped along months behind Germany, but also were carried out inconsistently and unsystematically, sometimes without any knowledge of the facts of a case, and even worse, were applied inconsistently throughout the monarchy and with various exceptions in individual crown lands. The bloated organisation of these centres was too complex, cumbersome, and chaotic, and thus difficult to control. In practice this led to the further centralisation of state power in Vienna in the hands of the German-Austrian bureaucracy. This then meant that food and other scarce goods were distributed differently depending on territory or nationality. The closure of the Cisleithanian council in the first three years of the war prevented any form of parliamentary control of this wartime economic policy or its influence by other nations of the monarchy, specifically by the Czechs.

The periodization of the war economy in the Habsburg monarchy distinguishes four phases in this development. The military and economic milestones sometimes, but not always, overlap. It is difficult to stipulate the economic milestones with precision.

Phase one began with military mobilisation, which shook the entire economy and provoked uncertainty, chaos, and panic. This led to a transitional period characterised by widespread unemployment, and to stagnation and a decline in productivity in many sectors. The hope that the economy would right itself in accordance with liberal market ideas disappeared as soon as Germany's strategic plans for a short, offensive war foundered (the German retreat at Marne and the Austrian retreat in Galicia and Serbia). The transi-

---

218 *Obzor národohospodářský, 1917, y. XXII. Praha, 1917*, pp. 320–321.

tion to war of attrition accompanied by huge human and material losses on the front, along with the unexpected dwindling of military stocks culminating in a munitions crisis, eventually led the army and government to increase and expand all military contracts. This immediately revived one part of the national economy and indirectly caused its second part to reorient itself on the war. The change of military strategy soon necessitated a change in the state's economic policy. It was six months before all of these changes came to fruition. Phase one continued through the summer and entire autumn of 1914.

Phase two of the wartime economic development began with the onset of the first winter of the war in 1914–1915. The prospect of a long war, the insufficient production of munitions and weapons, difficulties in supplying the population with food, and problems with raw materials caused by the naval blockade of the Central Powers, obliged leaders in Vienna to look to Germany and reappraise the role of the economy in modern warfare. This led during 1915–1916 to a complete reorientation and restructuring of the national economy for war purposes, with the extensive assistance and intervention of the state in the sphere of production, trade, and distribution. It was only in this way that an economic upswing could be encouraged in many sectors, and for a time this created a balance between the needs of the army and the possibilities of producers. However, right from the start this upswing was unstable and unilateral. It did not boost the national economy but in fact undermined it. Capital was pumped into non-productive military purposes, people and their products were used to devastate and destory national assets, and a shrinking national income was redistributed to a small group of arms manufacturers and speculators. The economy became autarkic and inward looking, foreign trade fell, the internal market struggled with rising prices and a lack of consumer goods, inflation and the state debt became a headache, and industry recorded the first symptoms of overheating and a lack of certain raw materials and articles. Phase two of the wartime economy came to an end in autumn 1916, at the same time as the situation in the Habsburg Empire was deteriorating sharply both militarily and politically (the Brusilov Offensive on the Russian front, exhausting battles on the Italian front on the Sochi River, Romania's entry into the war on the side of the Allied powers, the assassination of the Cisleithanian Minister-President Stürgkh, and the death of Emperor Franz Joseph). During the first and second phases of the wartime economy, both the army and the war ministry intervened jointly in economic matters.

Phase three lasted from winter of 1916 to summer 1918. The economic upswing came to an end and the army and the government faced an uphill struggle in the form of exhausted supplies of food, raw materials, and other articles important for the war effort, labour, etc. If we consider this as a process advancing in three stages, from initial difficulties via a squeeze on resources to an undeniable state of emergency regarding individual articles and factors, then 1916 is the initial stage, 1917 the period of transition from shortages to emergency, and 1918 a genuine state of extreme emergency. Contemporary witnesses describe the situation as a "tragedy of depletion". This tragedy began to apply to individual articles in phase two (e.g., to honey from spring 1915 and to wool, cotton, shoes, and iron from spring 1916), was manifest in 1917–1918 in increased labour shortages and a lack of active soldiers, and culminated in the "spiritual exhaustion" of the population (a haemorrhaging of enthusiasm for the war and a desire for peace, and a move away from passive acceptance towards mass expressions of dissatisfaction, demonstrations, and strikes).[219] Under the influence of these difficulties, the civilian and military authorities were obliged to develop a comprehensive system of central state management, restrict the power of the army over the civilian population, return to parliamentary forms of government (by convening the Reichsrat), and sign a separate peace agreement with Bolshevik Russia.

The fourth and final phase, like the first, was short and dynamic. It was characterised by a perilous lack of industrial raw materials and agricultural products that appeared to be insoluble. The "tragedy of exhaustion" that could no longer be contained or alleviated by any government measures intensified in the summer and autumn of 1918 into a state of general emergency, a decline in production and productivity, and the collapse of the war economy. Simultaneously, the state that had introduced this economy and regulated it began to decompose from within. The central government could no longer ensure that the population had access to food or cover the most urgent need for munitions, weapons, and clothing for the army. This in turn undermined what remained of the economic and political cohesion of the empire. "The more exhaustion manifested itself, the more every geographical region of the monarchy tried to acquire as many scarce articles for itself, and this exhaustion helped turn individual regions of the monarchy against each other."[220]

THE MOBILISATION CRISIS AND THE TRANSITION TO A WAR ECONOMY

What were the immediate consequences of mobilisation in 1914? In terms of military organisation, the special bills and imperial regulations undoubtedly served their purpose, and the mobilisation of the imperial and royal army,

---

219   Cf. Gratz, G. and Schüller, R. *Der wirtschaftliche Zusammenbruch Österreich-Ungarns. Die Tragödie der Erschöpfung*. Wien, 1930.
220   Ibid., p. 199.

in the Czech lands and elsewhere, took place smoothly and without political excesses bearing in mind the manifestations of Slavic sympathies on the part of Czech reservists during the partial mobilisations of 1912–1913. The railway and transport infrastructure in general contributed most to the effective mobilisation, though at the price of relegating civilian needs, a state of affairs that lasted until the start of September. Not even then were railway services in territories behind the front restored to their pre-war extent. The effect of mobilisation on other sectors was more negative. In addition, it came at a highly inopportune moment, when the monarchy was only just becoming to recover from the economic depression of 1912–1913.

The economic crisis caused by mobilisation was partly triggered by the element of surprise, though the main role was played by the lack of readiness for a long and multilateral war. In practice this meant an inadequate raw materials base and a narrowly profiled, low capacity economy. The crisis and subsequent rebuilding of the economy was prompted by the severe lack of ammunition, gunpowder, weapons, and equipment that the imperial and royal army suffered from (a situation that placed it in a similar situation to other warring countries) during autumn and winter of the first year of the war and that was the cause of huge human, material, and territorial losses. Many divisions were armed with three thousand to five thousand rifles instead of the usual twelve thousand to fifteen thousand, and in addition mostly had only the now largely obsolete model dating back to 1888. The country had fewer cannon than the Russians and Serbs, and many had been manufactured in the state arsenal from "steel bronze" (i.e., using the now obsolete production process of General Uchatius from the 1870s).

Above all, mobilisation set in motion a crisis in agriculture, since it coincided with harvest time. This was especially onerous for the Czech lands, which, after the transformation of Galicia into a theatre of war, were promoted to being an important granary and main supplier of potatoes for Cisleithania. With the army's retreat from Galicia, Cisleithania lost one-third of its arable land and thus approximately 9% of its expected grain harvest. Though the army requisitioned many teams of horses and wagons, agriculture lost a substantial part of its male labour force, as thousands of peasants had to beat their ploughshares into swords, so to speak, and this placed the course of harvesting in serious jeopardy. This critical situation led the Ministry of Agriculture to be the first department to intervene directly in the organisation of the job market. On 5 August, it established harvest commissions in the municipalities, to which the local and non-resident, male and female workforces were forcibly assigned. These commissions continued to operate in subsequent years of the war overseeing springtime and harvest related tasks. Since farmers did not have access to rail transport during mobilisation and the army was the largest consumer of bread and flour, the distribution of basic foodstuffs to towns and cities also became bogged down. The market reacted by closing the crop markets and by raising the price of basic food-stuffs, flour, bread, and meat. In Prague in December 1914, wheat cost 61% more than in July. The first victim of this hike in prices was the state treasury on the one side, initially willing to pay its suppliers any prices, and on the other the small urban consumers, who reacted to this situation by going on a shopping spree and who could only look on helplessly as the cost of liv-ing rose inexorably with every month the war dragged on. This was why the very first protests against the war took place in October 1914. In the industrial region around Teplice there were open riots, and the Austrian and Czechoslo-vak social democrats conveyed their concerns and opinions regarding these developments in special memoranda sent to the government.

The first supply crisis, which hit the population of Cisleithania and the Czech lands in autumn 1914, was influenced by several factors. First, the grain harvest was down 10% in both halves of the empire compared with previous years. Second, the army bought up large quantities of grain at next to noth-ing. Third, there was the trade embargo, i.e., the suspension or restriction on imports into Cisleithania that even before the war had applied to cereals and meat from Hungary, Romania, and Serbia. Cisleithania suffered most under the illiberal agricultural policy pursued by Hungary, which first vetoed the abolition of cereal duties and then prioritised supplies to its domestic market over exports to Austria. Fourth, there was a lack of meat, and what little was available was overpriced. The causes for this situation can be seen in Prague wholesale statistics: In 1914, only 14,437 beef cattle were slaughtered in the local slaughterhouses, down by 18,472 on the previous year, mainly because of the sharp decrease in imports of cattle destined for slaughter from Gali-cia and Bukovina. Fifth, there was an unprecedented lack of salt, and many Czech rural towns sometimes remained without it for up to two weeks, alleg-edly because of a lack of wagons and sacks, though in fact mainly because the Galician salt works were to be found in the military operational area.

The government in Vienna attempted to counter this supply crisis with a number of measures. For instance, it set up local *procurement commissions*, banned food exports, and abolished cereal duties, and at the end of November 1914 set a cap on the price of grain and flour and, in the lead-up to Christmas, on potatoes too. However, in many cases these measures proved to be double-edged. According to the Prague Chamber of Commerce, the blanket ban on food exports, for instance, seriously damaged the producers of Prague ham, which up till then had largely been exported to France, Belgium, Germany, etc. The relaxation of imports of grain, to which the Hungarian government acceded in November, was too late and failed to prevent an overall deterio-ration in the quality of bread in Cisleithania. According to a regulation of November 1914, it was permitted to use up to 70% of wheat and rye flour in the production of bread, and to replace the rest with various surrogates (barely, corn, potatoes, and potato flour).

Industry was similarly affected by mobilisation and the suspension of civilian transport and trade. Unforeseen and in some cases catastrophic difficulties compelled many business to slash their production. A questionnaire on this topic organised for 13 August 1914 by the Prague Chamber of Commerce, which represented the most extensive industrial and commercial region in the Czech lands, showed that the 730 factories that participated had had to release more than 13,000 workers for military service (i.e., approximately one-fifth of all staff). In the centre of the Czech lands alone, 210 plants had to be decommissioned and another 244 placed on limited operations. The statistics show that in mid-September, across the whole of Bohemia, there were a total of 1,410 plants, with a further 3,046 operating on a go-slow basis. The causes of this situation were listed as follows: In 443 cases enlistment was to blame, in 490 cases a lack of coal, and in 863 cases a lack of other production requirements, with 1,414 plants having no liquidity or bank loans. In 2,618 cases, transport repairs were to blame, and in the end 3,496 factories had to suspend or restrict production because of reduced demand.[221]

This all created a paradoxical, almost chaotic situation on the labour market. While in some places jobs abounded, in others there was full, partial, or temporary unemployment as job opportunities decreased. Agriculture and the thus-far small number of industrial enterprises looking after government contracts fared well, while other businesses, all heavily represented in the Czech lands, came off badly. These included hotels, shops, workshops, the construction industry, fashion, and luxury goods (e.g., Prague gloves, Bohemian crystal, and porcelain), as well as agricultural machinery, textiles, and the logging, diesel, paper, and printing industries, plus, obviously, all exporting industries. However, in its short-sightedness the military administration had not given thought, on the very brink of war, to ensuring important military production. It later came to light that it had requisitioned 14% of miners from anthracite mines and 19% of miners from brown coalmines, which again were situated mainly in the Czech lands.

The result was mass unemployment that even in the early months of the war surpassed the dismal numbers of the jobless over the previous two years. Hundreds of thousands of workers found themselves without jobs in the industrial regions of Bohemia, Moravia, Silesia, and Lower Austria: In mid-August, their number was estimated in Vienna to be 150,000 and in the Czech lands in mid-September to be 200,000. Unemployment peaked in Vienna in mid-September, while in the Czech lands it remained a significant phenom-

---

221   Grandner. *Kooperative Gewerkschaftspolitik in der Kriegswirtschaft*, p. 61.

enon at the start of October. In the administrative and commercial centres such as Vienna, a large proportion of the unemployed were civil servants and shopkeepers, while in the industrial regions of the Czech lands they were mainly skilled workers. The government therefore had to resort to counter-measures above and beyond the policy it had till then been pursuing, such as public or military emergency works (earthworks, construction and fortification), and in addition to providing public or charitable soup kitchens had to establish central *employment offices*. These were created under the aegis of the government and were represented equally by businesspeople and trade unions in all the Austrian crown lands. They continued in operation until the start of 1915, until the war industry had absorbed most of the unemployed. However, in North and East Bohemia, where the exports and luxury goods industries were located (namely glass, jewellery, and porcelain), the problem of unemployment remained, excepting those workers who were willing to relocate to the centres of the war industry and accept a change to their social status (e.g., from foreman to unskilled labourer).

During the first months of the war, the economic depression caused by mobilisation and the unexpected loss of labour forces, along with the disruption to credit, supplier, and customer relations, led directly to stagnation and a drop in industrial production. The Czech lands were particularly hard hit. This can be seen indirectly from figures applying to the whole of Austria, which show that, at the end of 1914, when the wartime economic boom was beginning, production in the glass industry was down by 90%, in the agricultural machinery sector by 80%, in cement works by 60%, in cotton spinning mills by 55%, and in the brewing industry by 40%. First to be affected were the mining and metallurgical sectors.

Table 36: The drop in output of heavy industry in the Czech lands 1913–1914 (in millions of tonnes)

	Anthracite	Brown coal	Iron ore	Pig iron
1913	14.0	23.1	0.9	1.0
1914	13.4	20.0	0.6	0.7

Source: Coal: Batovcův almanach – Politický kalendář Čsl. republiky na rok 1929, p. 99. Iron ore and pig iron: Retrospektivní statistika čs. hutnictví železa, vol.1: České země před rokem 1918, Praha TEVÚH 1973, tabs. 1 and 5.

The monarchy's foreign trade also found itself in a blind alley after the outbreak of war. Trade with countries with which the monarchy was at war, including its ally Germany, were severely restricted and various prohibitions applied to the export, import and transit of raw materials and goods. A similarly negative effect was caused by the cessation of civilian transport, the increased risk of maritime transport, and payment and credit difficulties. Just how deeply these interventions affected the export-oriented members of the Prague Chamber of Commerce can be seen indirectly in the severe drop in its sectoral figures. In the first and second quarters of 1914, the export sector reported 11,494 business items, yet by the third and fourth quarters this was down to only 3,750 items. The overall drop in Austro-Hungarian foreign trade and the further increase in its passive trade balance due to the war is clearly shown in the table 37:

Table 37: The Habsburg Monarchy's exports and imports on the eve of war (in millions of crowns)

	August 1913	August 1914	September 1913	September 1914
exports	215.0	30.4	242.3	61.8
imports	268.6	94.7	261.9	111.4
passive trade balance	53.6	64.3	19.6	49.6

Source: Národní listy no. 292 of 24. October 1914 and no. 310 of 11 November 1914.

The sheer size of the passive trade balance had an extremely detrimental effect on the country's balance of payments, and this trend continued during the next phase of the war. On the one hand, large quantities of war material and food had to be imported, mainly from Germany, while on the other the exports of Austrian industry and agriculture fell sharply. This resulted in the even greater economic dependence of Austria-Hungary on Germany, both commercially and financially.

To begin with, the industry of the Czech lands and the rest of Austria was affected by the closure of the German border, since most exports flowed through Germany and its ports, and even prior to the war Germany had been the most important trade partner of the Habsburg Monarchy. And so, for instance, overseas consignments of cotton that were to be transported via Hamburg and Bremen to Czech textile factories fetched up in Germany. The Prague Chamber of Commerce contacted the imperial and royal embassy in Berlin and the Minister of Commerce in Vienna in an attempt to discover what had happened. The chamber opposed with equal vigour the boycott of goods originating from hostile countries that was being advocated by the central organisation of Austrian merchants in Vienna. This was in part but not only because of the serious lack of raw materials for the Czech textile industry, reliant on imports of cotton from America, flax from Russia, wool from Britain and France, and jute from the British Raj. There were similarly urgent difficulties in the sugar industry, another characteristically Czech sector, whose production was largely geared towards exports to Britain.

The financial markets reacted especially sensitively and quickly to the July international crisis and even more so to the mobilisation and declaration of war. The main barometer was the Vienna Stock Exchange, where, according to the Prague *Peněžní revue* (*Money Review*) of 25 July 1914, "A sad spectacle unfolded of a severe crisis unseen in our country since the Panic of 1873. Over the course of ten days, four or five sharp fluctuations, in which shares dropped by dozens of crowns, followed by several days of recovery and then at the start of the following week yet more precipitous drops that again saw shares fall to their lowest ever level and create rates the like of which have not been seen for many years. [...] Thousands and thousands of small and large speculators have had their fingers badly burned, and hundreds of them, for whom the crisis was a trauma, will never really recover." This stock market crisis directly impacted many companies in the Czech lands whose shares were quoted on the Viennese or Prague exchanges. It was therefore in response to their entreaties that on 26 July the Vienna Stock Exchange opted to suspend trading for three days. A similar measure was taken by the exchanges in Prague, Budapest, and Trieste. The influence of subsequent events was to see this temporary intervention prolonged for the whole of the first half of the war.

Tensions on the financial markets escalated after the handover of the ultimatum to Serbia. The Austro-Hungarian issuing bank (or Rubka, as it was known) experienced the first inklings in the form of an alarming reduction in foreign receivables and foreign exchange reserves, and an outflow of foreign currency and gold. There was a sudden run on banks and credit unions, and a panicked population began to withdraw their savings and hoard gold and silver coins. Production companies again saw orders decrease, along with the cash with which to pay wages, since the financial institutions were no longer acting with such largesse and had tightened up their terms and conditions. Rubka first tried to get a grip on this precarious situation on the money markets by means of standard banking instruments such as a gradual increase in the discount rate from 4%–8%, and then by suspending payments of foreign exchange and currency. However, it was unable to confront the strangulation of loans with sufficient Lombard credit. It extended it to other types of security or debentures issued against warehoused goods (warranties) at the end of August, and only then when begged to do so by interested parties, including the Prague Chamber of Commerce. The money markets only stabilised when the government announced a moratorium on the day of general mobilisation (31 July), under which all payments and receivables in excess of 200 crowns were suspended for fourteen days. Five more moratoria, albeit somewhat less dramatic, followed until summer 1915, though served best to highlight what huge problems the monarchy's financial market encountered when rejigging the economy to wartime conditions.

The credit market only really calmed down to any extent at the end of October, when Rubka, under the aegis of the government, two months after Germany and again at the request of the Prague Chamber of Commerce, established a *war loan treasury* or *Kriegsdarlehenskasse* as a state institution providing cheap, short-term loans to small merchants and tradesmen hit worst by the war, who in return provided a guarantee in the form of their stocks, securities, and mortgages. These treasuries were usually opened at branches of Rubka. Thirty-four of them were spread around the whole of Cisleithania, and one of them remained open in Prague throughout the war.

The imperial regulation of 4 August suspending Rubka's deed of foundation had even more serious consequences. In the interest of the unfettered printing of banknotes and the financing of war expenses, the reserve requirement of at least two-fifths gold for the issuance of paper banknotes was abolished, along with the duty to publish public statements on the bank's activities. As a consequence, by December 1914 the country was swamped by more than 6.5 billion crowns in paper banknotes (including giro receivables) as compared with just under 2.5 billion crowns in the period prior to the submission of Austria-Hungary's ultimatum to Serbia. The Austro-Hungarian currency was thus firmly on the path to wartime inflation, and the rapid increase in prices and the drop in the purchasing power of money was accompanied by a growing shortage of commodities on the market, with all the social consequences ensuing therefrom. The privy Imperial Council had but one supervisory body, the State Debt Oversight Commission, on which the Czech lands were represented by the young Czech MP and entrepreneur Jindřich Maštálka. However, even the commission yielded to the wishes of the government and countersigned its loans, which led to parliament passing a motion of no confidence in it immediately after it reconvened in summer 1917.

THE WAR BOOM

The boom that the Austro-Hungarian economy experienced at the turn of 1914–1915 exhibited some peculiar features. Not only did it rest on the problematic foundations of a war and was relatively short, but it also strangely skirted the agricultural sector and had its centre of gravity firmly in industry (and was not manifest in other sectors), along with, to a lesser extent, commerce, transport, and banking in cases where financial institutions were linked with militarily prosperous companies or participated in the state's financial operations. Not all corporations of a given sector benefitted equally, since the military administration gave precedence to wholesalers when it came to their large-scale and short-term contracts, and in this respect the war boom provided a strong impetus to the further concentration of Austrian industry. This was also influenced by the fact that the boom took place within the context of industry divided into three groups. While category I companies, the war industry, were given preferential treatment and reported unprecedented growth, category II companies (i.e., the civil industry, including many trades), which produced consumer, fashion, and luxury items, was hampered to such an extent that category III companies (i.e., industry working for both the civil and military sectors) could at least eke out a living. This differentiated development inevitably impacted the overall dynamic of industrial production during the war. Production volumes fell in the European countries at war by more than one-third and in Germany they fell to the level they had reached at the start of the century. In the case of the Habsburg Empire we have to factor in an even greater fall that estimates put at a half in comparison with the levels of 1913.

The war industry soon surpassed the narrow confines of the arms industry in its pre-war composition. Companies began—some enthusiastically, others reluctantly—to re-orientate part of their activities on wartime production when they could no longer find demand for the items they sold during peacetime. The companies that achieved this least painfully were those that already had the technology and labour in place. What was important was not so much *what* a company had until then produced as *how* it had produced it (i.e., what machinery and human resources it had used). This meant, for instance, that anyone who owned or could lay their hands on a lathe began to churn out grenades. The wartime industry was therefore sometimes born of strange combinations. For instance, in central Bohemia (according to the Prague Chamber of Commerce), the restructuring of industry looked like this:

peacetime production	wartime production
machinery	ammunition
agricultural machinery	sappers' tools
narrow-gauge railways	field beds
carpentry workshops	ammunition crates
pianos	rifle stocks
haberdashery	gear for tents
gloves	rucksacks, haversacks

There was great interest shown in the Czech lands in participating in the wartime boom. The prevailing feeling of insecurity and the sudden increase in unemployment, as well as the feeling that big profits were there for the taking, meant that during the first months of the war, the Prague Chamber of Commerce was overwhelmed by verbal and written requests that it broker military contracts. The chamber dutifully passed these on to the relevant authorities, provided information regarding a firm's balance sheet, attached samples of its production and letters of recommendation, and lobbied on its behalf. It managed to arrange many military contracts for small central Bohemian manufacturers to produce munitions as well as several textile, foodstuff, leather, and medical goods (e.g., 250,000 pairs of army boots and 460,000 items of saddlery and bridles). Nevertheless, the results were somewhat disappointing. A year into the war, the chamber informed Vienna that the method by which military contracts were being awarded to individual crown lands or industrial groups was subject to countless complaints in Bohemia. Notwithstanding all of this, the Czech lands were adjudged to have played a major role in the war economy of the monarchy since most of the heavy industry was situated here.

Coalmining, crucial to the war effort and a pivotal industry in the Czech lands, was one of the few sectors in which the drop in production during the war years was maintained within reasonable limits. Even though supply-chain failures had risen by the end of the war to the level of "severe", they had not deteriorated to such an extent as to qualify for the description "exhausted". The coal industry suffered its first blow immediately after mobilisation, when between the end of July and mid-August the number of miners fell from 140,913 to 112,407. Almost one-quarter of the workers of the most important Ostrava coalmining district enlisted during the first months of the war. Later attempts by the military administration to correct this mistake and reclaim experienced miners for the mines failed, since so many had in the meantime died in the trenches. Their place had to be taken in part by women, children, and POWs, or inexperienced labourers reassigned to the mines from other sectors. Even so, the number of people working down in the pits rose to a maximum of 120,000 in 1917, which was far below pre-war numbers. By comparison, the total output of coalmines in the monarchy during this period did not drop much; its index fell from one hundred points in 1913 to approximately eighty-eight points in 1917 (i.e., from 57 million tonnes to 50.1 million tonnes). The government in Vienna, under the impression that there was a smaller supply of coke from Upper Silesia, attempted to maintain and possibly increase its production in the Czech lands even at the cost of a drop in the production of the less calorific brown coal. It was fairly successful in this endeavour until 1916, after which coalmining output in the Czech lands dropped below its pre-war level; in 1918, its index fell to 76 points compared to 1913. In 1917, Austrian industry and households had 15.5% less coal at their disposal than in the last peacetime year, and in the first half of 1918 this deficit rose to one-fifth. The development of coalmining in individual years and the degree of concentration in the Czech lands is shown in the table 38:

Table 38: Coalmining during the war (in million tonnes)

Year	Anthracite		Brown coal	
	Austria-Hungary	Czech lands	Austria-Hungary	Czech lands
1913	16.3	14.0	27.4	23.1
1914	15.4	13.4	23.7	20.0
1915	16.0	14.3	22.0	18.3
1916	17.6	15.4	23.1	19.4
1917	16.7	14.5	21.6	18.2
1918	–	11.9	–	16.3

Source: Wegs, R. J. *Die österreichische Kriegswirtschaft 1914–1918.* Wien, 1979, pp. 84–85; *Batovcův almanach: Politický kalendář Čs. republiky na r. 1929,* p. 99. Data covering the entire monarchy is only available for the first half of 1918.

Unlike other sectors of the war industry, supervising the extraction and distribution of coal remained for most of the war a matter for the civilian authorities, specifically the Ministry of Public Works (headed from 1911–1917 by Otakar Trnka) and the coal supplies commission it founded, from which an independent Hungarian commission was established in 1915. Coal and transport wagons were allocated mainly to mining companies grouped into three categories of importance. In addition, as workers performing heavy duties, miners received extra food rations. Nevertheless, this level of care and organisation was unable to prevent the proliferation of coal short-ages, beginning with the calamity of the winter of 1916–1917. This disruption, which had a huge impact on the population in cities and industrial centres, resulted in gas and power plants being shut down, restrictions on transport, factory operations and the opening hours of shops and pubs, the closure of schools, theatres, and museums, and last but by no means least, inadequate heating for households. There were many causes, though most of the blame was pinned on the transport system, specifically the inability of the railways to provide mines with the requisite number of wagons. For instance, in 1917, Czech coalmining districts only received 64% of the rolling stock they had requested, with no account taken of whether it was summer or winter. Fur-thermore, the drop in output was caused by a noticeable reduction in the productivity of miners, which fell from 1,238 kg/day in 1913 to 1,032 kg/day in 1917. The miners were forced to work under difficult conditions for longer periods of time and, notwithstanding their extra rations, to contend with in-creasingly worse supply conditions. For example, in July 1918, shortly before harvest time, the Duchcov-Chomutov-Teplice-Falknov-Loket coal district had no bread for two weeks. It is no wonder that during the last two years of the war, the miners increasingly resorted to strike action, which inevitably led to a drop in output and economic performance as a whole. This was so in the case of the large strikes by miners of the Ostrava coalmining district in January 1918, when the extraction of coal remained below normal for two weeks.

Ironworks, struggling as of the summer of 1913 with a crisis in demand, also received a much-needed shot in the veins from the war. Iron and steel were the key raw materials for producing war equipment. Prior to the war, 5% at most of Austria-Hungary's steel production was used for military purposes, a figure that in 1917 shot up to 85%, of which 1 million tonnes went on the production of munitions, 850,000 tonnes were allocated to the railways, 250,000 tonnes on barbed wire and fortifications, and 400,000 tonnes on miscellaneous items. In practice this meant reducing civilian iron consumption per capita from 50 kg during peacetime to 0.5 kg at the end of the war. The ironworking sector went through three phases during the war. During mobilisation it was negatively affected by the loss of almost one-third of its workers (i.e., of the 15,000 workers at the Vítkovice ironworks, approximately 5,000 men joined the army), as well as disruption to civil transport and sales. As a consequence, the drop in iron ore and blast furnace production appeared on the face of it to be a continuation of the previous crisis caused by overproduction. And so in the summer of 1914, of the eight blast furnaces at Pražská železářská společnost (Prager Eisenindustrie-Gesellschaft or Prague Ironworks), only two were in operation, and only one of these upon the outbreak of war at the beginning of August. When in February 1915 the second furnace was fired up in Kladno, this indicated that the iron industry was entering its second wartime phase. This lasted without serious supply and production problems until approximately the start of winter 1917, and the Austro-Hungarian iron and steel industry attained outstanding results; for most of the war years, it managed to cover the wartime demand for iron and steel of the entire monarchy. After the significant drop in production in 1914, there was a modest revival during 1915, followed by record results the next year, with the pre-war production figures surpassed by more than a quarter. However, notably this often took place at the cost of the unscrupulous looting of raw materials and machinery, as well as the imposition of forced overtime. Even so, there was still not enough iron and steel on the market, partly because they had been replaced by scarce non-ferrous metals, but above all because in autumn 1916, the imperial and royal military administration, following the model of the Hindenburg Programme in Germany, set itself the task of massively increasing the production of munitions and weapons. As a result, the Ministry of War had to place strict restrictions on civil supplies and the exportation of iron, and in October 1916 it took over full management of the industry. In fact, divided four ways in its decision-making into both the Austrian and Hungarian and the military and civilian authorities, the Ministry of War never actually fulfilled this aim completely. Increasing difficulties led in 1917 to a drop in the production of pig iron. Only steel production remained above 1914 levels through the increased use of scrap iron. However, the third and final phase in 1918 was marked by an irreversible decline in production of around 50% in comparison with 1913, despite the fact that demand for both iron and steel on the part of the military continued to grow. The overall weakness of the metalworking industry was caused partly by a rise in production costs (prices, wages, and social benefits), and partly by reduced productivity and production failures ensuing from strikes and a lack of manganese ore, coal, coke, and wagons. In absolute figures, this development appeared as follows:

Table 39: Production of pig iron and steel during the war (in millions of tonnes)

Year	Pig iron			Crude steel		
	Austria-Hungary	Czech lands	%	Austria-Hungary	Czech lands	%
1913	2.4	1.0	42.7	2.6	1.1	42.5
1914	1.8	0.7	41.2	2.1	0.9	42.0
1915	1.8	0.8	45.4	2.6	0.8	31,5
1916	2.2	1.1	50.3	3.3	1.5	47.4
1917	1.9	0.9	49.3	2.9	1.4	50.7
1918 (I–IX)	1.1	0.5	49.6	1.4	0.7	51.4

Source: 1913–1915: *Dějiny hutnictví železa v Československu*, vol. 2, appendices 1 and 4; *Retrospektivní statistika čs. hutnictví železa*, vol. 2, Praha, 1977, tab. 7, vol. 3, Praha, 1986, tab. 2. 1916–1918: Mejzlík, H. *Die Eisenbewirtschaftung im 1. Weltkrieg.* Wien, 1977, tabs. 198–204. Percentage share of Czech lands according to Z. J.

If the Cisleithanian iron industry boasted output twice that of the Hungarian, then most of the credit, dating back before the war, goes to the Czech lands. At the height of the war boom on the eve of 1917, all the Austrian production of foundry, hematite, Thomas-method, puddling, and ferro-manganese iron was concentrated in the Kladno and Ostrava regions. During the same period, half of the smelted steel in Cisleithania came from the Czech lands, and the Czechs were not only the exclusive suppliers of Bessemer and Thomas steel and the biggest producers of electrosteel, but also, along with Moravian and Silesian steelworks, manufactured the largest share of Martin steel, at that time the biggest mass-produced converter with a range of applications in the arms industry. Right up until 1917, this provided ironworks in the Czech lands an opportunity for unprecedented expansion and big wartime profits, while leaving them the worst affected in the 1918 downturn. An example is the wartime development of the Pražská železářská společnost (PŽS) or Prague Ironworks, which through its interest in the Austrian Alpine-Montangesellschaft (PŽS not only held 50,000 shares in the company, but also chaired and occupied several positions on the board of directors) dominated the Austrian iron industry and thus controlled the all-powerful iron cartel. Increasing its workforce from a peacetime figure of 15,300 to 16,700 in 1917, this large corporation was able to exceed the pre-war production of pig iron by more than one-fifth and by the end of the war generated more than 150 million crowns in gross earnings, of which more than 50 million crowns was net profit. Yet not even this state-supported enterprise escaped the general economic downturn of 1918 (reporting a year-on-year fall in pig iron of 22.6% and in crude steel of 28.6%). Allocated less coal, it had to shut down its steelworks for three months.

The situation was different in the case of non-ferrous metals such as copper, nickel, lead, chrome, tungsten, and aluminium, which were indispensible in the production of ammunition, cannon, artillery, armour, cutting tools, etc., either in the form of separate components or additives for alloyed steels. Meeting the increased needs of these strategic raw materials was a thorny problem, since with the exception of aluminium, lead, and zinc, the monarchy was for the most part reliant on imports, which had virtually dried up during the war. And so during the first year of hostilities, the Ministry of War seized all domestic stocks of these metals, alloys, and metal products, and as of March 1915, with the help of Kovoústředna (Metallzentrale A.G.), kept centralised records and supervised mining activities and imports and the collection of scrap iron, along with its distribution to individual factories. The testimony of two senior civil servants regarding a single metal well illustrates what drastic measures the government resorted to in order to meet at least some of the military's demands:

"As far as copper was concerned, before the war the monarchy was almost completely reliant on foreign imports. [...] By mid-May 1915, around 1,000 tonnes of copper had been collected, but it was getting harder and harder to get our hands on it. And so a raft of measures was taken. [...] Mining activities recommenced in abandoned copper mines. [...] The navy was told to surrender its reserves of old copper. Electrolyte refining plants were established using brass copper. [...] The copper dividers in the furnaces of locomotives were requisitioned for the needs of the army and were replaced by iron boxes. [...] In 1915, a decision was taken to take [...] brass from apartments, trams, windows, doors, handles, railways, kitchen utensils, etc., and copper roofs on private and state buildings were also plundered. At the end of 1915, preparations were underway for the replacement of bronze gun barrels with steel. [...] The military authorities held out for a long time against the re-placement of copper parts in ammunition with steel and iron. [...] However, at the end of 1916 they were forced to concede and the measure was passed. There was also a demand for copper components in factory machinery. In 1916, church bells and lightening conductors were seized. However, because the army's monthly requirements in 1917 were estimated to be 4,590 tonnes and all the available sources could only come up with a figure of 3,400 tonnes, the shortage of copper became more and more acute and led to serious errors being made during the manufacture of ammunition."[222]

Under these circumstances, the limited supplies of copper from Germany and the occupied areas were weak and provided only temporary respite. And because the situation was similar as regards stocks of other non-ferrous metals, come 1918 the monarchy's exhaustion in this production sphere was far more drastic than in the iron industry, and this was to have far-reaching consequences for arms production.

Even at the start of the war, the arms and ammunition industry lacked production capacity and was not prepared for a long conflict, and within a few months it was showing signs of exhaustion. It was represented by a small number of large corporations in the hands of German-Austrian and Hungarian capital and was for the most part situated outside the Czech lands. Artillery was manufactured by Škoda works / Plzeň state arsenal / Vienna, and in 1912–1913 at the newly established Győri Állami Ágyúgyár in Győr (State Cannon Factory). The production of small arms was dominated by Österreichische Waffenfabriks-Gesellschaft in Steyr and the Budapest Arms Factory and Engineering Works, and heavy machine guns were also produced by Škoda works (a failing rifle trade in the Czech lands, especially in Vejprty, specialising in the production of hunting weapons, was only allowed to sup-ply rifle components). As well as Škoda works and Győri Állami Ágyúgyár, ammunition was produced in several factories in Vienna, Budapest, Hirten-berg, and Wöllersdorf (the Czech firm Sellier & Bellot was permitted to start producing complete infantry ammunition only because it fell under the in-fluence of the arms factory in Steyr). As well as at Dynamit Nobel in Prešpurk (one of the names by which Bratislava was known in the past), gunpowder and explosives were also produced by state factories situated in the Alpine states of Austria, and the Czech lands were not involved in the production of explosives until the creation of the Republic of Czechoslovakia. After the out-break of war, the military authorities were forced to involve other companies in arms production, including many engineering works in the Czech lands.

---

222 Gratz, G. and Schüller, R. *Der wirtschaftliche Zusammenbruch Österreich-Ungarns.* Wien, 1930, pp. 106–108.

At the end of 1916, there were 575 arms factories in operation in Cisleithania employing almost 230,000 workers.

If these arms factories were to function efficiently, it was important that state regulation was not thrown into confusion because of authorisation disputes between Hungary and Austria. It had to remain in the hands of the military bodies, which resorted to direct state control of companies only in exceptional cases (Steyr and Wöllersdorf). This meant that the arms industry could in essence retain its profit-motivated private character whilst being given preference by the state during the allocation of contracts, raw materials and labour, and the provision of surcharges, subsidies, guarantees, and investment loans allowing firms to expand their operations or initiate new projects. From November 1916–April 1917, for instance, the Ministry of War offered Škoda works a loan of three million crowns as part of the Hindenburg arms programme, in addition to support totalling 11.3 million crowns for necessary investment and a further 12.9 million crowns for the production of howitzers.

For an industrialised war of the modern era, the characteristic predominance of military technology, particularly artillery and other firearms, over sheer numbers of foot soldiers, was most evident in the prodigious consumption of ammunition and gunpowder, creating a demand that factories in the monarchy, no matter how hard they tried and despite a highly respectable increase in production from 1915–1917, were never able to meet. This disconnect intensified catastrophically in the last phase of the war, and in autumn 1918 the monarchy had used up almost all its reserves. A similar tendency can be seen in the production of guns, rifles, and machine guns, as the table 40 shows.

At first sight, the results up to 1917 seem so impressive that one is tempted to conclude that the main reason Austria-Hungary was defeated in the war had nothing to do with a lack of weaponry so much as poor military leadership

Table 40: Arms production of Austria-Hungary

Type of weapon	1914	1915	1916	1917	1918 (I–IX)
rifle	149,183	905,832	1,197,117	1,091,117	237,148
machine gun	1,187	3,730	6,335	15,436	12,201
cannon	–	1,730	6,948[a]	7,700	2,064
rifle rounds[b]	2.5	3.5–4.0	4.0	3.0	1.5–2.0
cannon ammunition[c]	0.3	1.3	2.0	1.4	0.75

[a] 1916–1918 the production of cannon and gun carriages, [b] daily production in millions of units, [c] monthly production in millions of units.

Source: Wegs, R. J. *Die österreichische Kriegswirtschaft 1914–1918.* Wien, 1979, p. 120.

and transport failure. However, these figures must be set in context. Firstly, as far as countries at war were concerned, the monarchy's productivity was comparable at most with that of Russia and Italy, but not with the advanced industrial countries. Had it not been for its alliance with Germany, which managed to produce two and a half times as many rifles, seven times more machine guns, four times more cannon, and far more in the way of ammunition, mortars, aeroplanes, and cars, the Habsburg Empire would undoubtedly have caved in well before 1918. Secondly, from 1917 the productivity of the Austro-Hungarian war industry could not be increased. Its hands were tied by a lack of raw materials and assets, rising production costs, and the physical depletion of its labour force. The situation was so grave that the expansion of arms production under the Hindenburg programme, on which the Ministry of War spent almost half a billion crowns, was treated with scepticism by the governments in both Vienna and Budapest and only implemented in part and for a short time. This programme was already beyond the economic power of the monarchy and rendered it even more dependent on Germany's support.

The part played by the Czech lands in the valiant war effort of the monarchy cannot be determined in detail. We have only a list of 132 Austrian firms that, up until December 1917, according to the records of the Ministry of War, participated in more ambitious military contracts (worth more than twenty million crowns). Only 32 of these were firms with their main operations or headquarters in the Czech lands, and only twelve ranked among the large suppliers (above one hundred million crowns). Of these twelve firms, only a small number belonged to the actual arms industry as producers of metal for weaponry or as machine processors. It was significant that most of the large military suppliers from the Czech lands were producers of food, boots, and leather goods, textiles, and chemicals, etc., among which Czech capital was represented only by Baťa.[223]

Other Czech firms were able to participate in the wartime boom at most as medium to large suppliers (overseeing contracts worth twenty to fifty million crowns up to December 1917) or small suppliers (up to twenty million crowns). These included the První českomoravská továrna na stroje in Prague (First Bohemian-Moravian Machinery Factory), Elektrotechnická akciová společnost Kolben & spol. in Prague (Electrotechnical joint-stock company), Spojené strojírny (formerly Škoda, Ruston, Bromovský, Ringhoffer) in Prague (United machine tools), and the young Czech auto manufacturers Laurin & Klement in Mladá Boleslav, Walter in Prague, and a factory for lorries in Kopřivnice. Up until 1917, the medium-sized suppliers produced military equipment worth around 140 million: the same information on small

223 For more details, see Jindra, Z. *Váleční dodavatelé c. a k. ministerstva války v letech 1914–1917, zvláště v českých zemích, Na pozvání Masarykova ústavu*, vol. 3, Praha, 2007, pp. 11–25.

Table 41: The largest military contractors in the industry of the Czech lands (more than one hundred million crowns)

Firm	Total value of contracts up until 31 December 1917 in crowns
Škoda works, Plzeň	543.5 million
Horní a hutní těžířstvo, Vítkovice	224.7 million
K. Budischowsky & Söhne (kůže), Třebíč	162.4 million
T. & A. Baťa, Zlín	140.3 million
Mannesmannröhrenwerke, Chomutov	139.3 million
Poldina ocelárna, Kladno	133.3 million
Tuchindustrie-Ges. Schumpeter a spol., Trieste	105.2 million

Source: Winkler, W. *Die Einkommensverschiebungen während des Krieges*. Wien, 1930, pp. 189–191.

suppliers is unavailable. However, they would undoubtedly have included the Ústí nad Labem–based Spolek pro chemickou a hutní výrobu (Österreichische Verein für Chemische und Metallurgische Produktion) and a chemical plant in Kolín that commenced production of poison gas.

The company Škoda works provides a microeconomic perspective on the expansion of the Austrian war industry. It was no accident that Škoda found itself in the vanguard of military suppliers from the ranks of Austrian industry. As a joint-stock company mainly controlled by Viennese capital, it had prior to the war been the largest ammunition works in the monarchy, known abroad for its wide range of technically advanced artillery ranging from field cannon to the heaviest fortifications, siege and naval cannons, and ammunition. Before the war broke out, it consolidated its position firstly by increasing its share capital from twenty-five to forty-two million crowns and with a deposit of almost thirty million crowns in its production facilities, and secondly by procuring a share in the construction of Győri Állami Ágyúgyár and acquiring decisive influence over the Prague merger of Spojené strojírny (formerly Škoda, Ruston, Bromovský a Ringhoffer). After the outbreak of war, the firm was inundated with orders, and as a result increased its share capital to 72 million crowns (1916), made further capital investments and initiated construction projects worth almost 123 million crowns, in the process taking on more employees. At the end of 1913, Škoda works employed 9,059 workers, of which 3,800 men worked in the actual factory. At the height of the war boom towards the end of 1917, the firm employed more than 32,000 people, of which almost 5,000 were women, of whom all either directly or indirectly, working day and night shifts, were involved in the production of weapons. The company expanded laterally too. It bought up land and mines, a share in the Austrian firm Daimler-Motoren-Gesellschaft (1915) and the Berlin-based Imperator-Motoren-Werke (1916), and participated in the establishment of a new aeroplane factory in Wiener Neustadt (1915) and the Skodawerke-Wetzlar AG gunpowder factory (1916). This is visible in its year-on-year productivity improvements: In addition to the many million units of ammunition it turned out, in 1915 it supplied the imperial and royal army with approximately 1,500 different calibre weapons, a figure that rose to 3,800 in 1916, then 4,500 in 1917, and roughly 2,120 in the last year of the war. It retained a monopoly over the production of large calibre guns, and it was only in the production of field cannon that, leaving aside Győri Állami Ágyúgyár and the Vienna arsenal, a new competitor appeared in the form of Böhler's works in Kapfenberg. This unprecedented wartime boom saw other winners, including all the shareholders in Škoda works headed by Karel Škoda and the Viennese company Creditanstalt für Handel und Gewerbe. From 1915–1917, Škoda's net profits rose to 15.3 million crowns compared to an average profit of 5.6 million crowns over the final three years of peace.[224]

However, despite the impressive results posted by Škoda works, we must not forget that, as the list above shows, the Ministry of War awarded many more war contracts to German-Austrian arms firms outside the Czech lands. And other companies supplying the army included the Böhler plant in Kapfenberg, the Roth Pulverfabrik in Vienna, the largest rifle works in Steyr, the Krupp Metallwarenfabrik in Berndorf, Dynamit Nobel in Vienna and Bratislava, and the munitions factory in Hirtenberg. In the same period up to December 1917, these companies supplied the army with equipment worth approximately 1,775 million crowns (i.e., three times the value of the contracts awarded Škoda works).[225]

The decline of light industry working for civilian requirements and mass consumption, specifically the consumer and exports industry (glass and porcelain, etc.), and a reliance on imports of raw materials (cotton, jute, leather, etc.), was the inevitable downside of the one-sided boosting of the war industry. As the war dragged on, this led to a deformation of the economic structure that the Czech lands could not escape. Since the nineteenth century the country had been strong in the textile, ceramic, glass, timber, paper, leather, and food industries. Unlike the war industry, this sector had to tackle the problem of unemployment for the duration of the war and emerged from the experience with obsolete machinery, since it lacked the resources for new investment. Companies awarded military contracts were few and far

---

224 For more details, see Jíša, V. *Škodovy závody 1859–1919*. Praha, 1965; Janáček, F. *Největší zbrojovka monarchie*. Praha, 1990.

225 Winkler, W. *Die Einkommensverschiebungen während des Krieges*. Wien, 1930, pp. 189–190.

between. For most of these companies, the war was a story of closure and rationalisation, either caused by dwindling sales (e.g., of beer and glass) or insufficient raw materials and human resources. The structural shifts can be seen in the figures pertaining to insured persons at occupational injury insurance companies in the Czech lands, which from 1914–1917 reported an increase in policies in the mining industry (up by 47%), chemical industry (46%), and engineering (38%), but a drop in the construction industry (down by 61.5%), stone and earth sector (59%), textiles (53%), food (38.5%), timber (35.5%), and paper and leather industries (12%). An example of the sharp decline in production suffered by the food industry in the Czech lands would be sugar, which fell from 12.7 million quintals (q) in 1913–1914 to 5.2 million q (i.e., to 41%) in 1917–1918, along with beer, production of which fell from 9.3 million to 1.3 million hectolitres (i.e., to as low as 14% of its peacetime levels). Cotton production was in an even worse situation. A critical lack of basic raw materials saw a reduction in production volumes of cotton yarn throughout the monarchy in the last year of the war to 0.8% of pre-war figures. The crisis in the textile industry and the resulting unemployment (especially amongst women) hit the Czech lands hard. This was reflected in the figures of individual regions at the end of 1915.

Table 42: Drop in production of light industry after one year at war

Operations	Bohemia	Moravia	Tyrol/Vorarlberg	Lower Austria
halted	57	4	8	2
reduced	82	2	5	6

Source: Grandner, M., Kooperative Gewerkschaftspolitik in der Kriegswirtschaft, Wien 1992, p. 128.

Overall, industry in the Czech lands suffered more than it benefitted during the war. The wartime economy milked it for supplies of fuel, raw materials and metallurgical semi-finished products, while arms production was limited to Škoda works, headquartered in Vienna. Other firms operating in this region participated in the war either selectively or insignificantly, either being awarded relatively small contracts or acting only as subcontractors for components. The stimulus to expand that the Czech automobile industry received during the war was undermined by the weakening of the light consumer and exports industry. This was hit not only by a slump in sales and a raw materials crisis, but also by government restrictions, including the disassembly of its equipment as part of the requisition of non-ferrous metals for the arms industry. Finally, of course, there was the collapse of the broad market the monarchy represented. Light industry in the Czech lands never recovered from these losses, not even in the interwar period. The predominance of light over heavy industry typical of the Czech economy prior to 1914 was dealt a serious blow.

AGRICULTURE AND SUPPLIES TO THE POPULATION

The weaknesses of the agrarian economy in Austria-Hungary, a hangover of its feudal past and manifest most clearly in the unequal distribution of land to the benefit of the nobility and farmers, was the cause of the relatively low output of agricultural production prior to the war. However, each state complemented the other's production; Cisleithania suffered a grain deficit in relation to its consumption that was covered by Hungary's surplus. However, the war caused great hardship and friction between the two countries, as despite extraordinary demand, the production of bread cereals (wheat, rye) declined inexorably, in Cisleithania year-on-year to 41% and in Hungary at the end of the war to 57% of the peacetime figures. In the Czech lands, too, up until 1917, the years for which we have information, the production of cereals declined by more than 48% of the last pre-war harvests). The same information shows that the main cause was related to poor soil cultivation. For instance, in the Czech lands the yield per hectare of wheat dropped over three years from 17.7 q to 8.2 q, and of rye from 16.1 q to only 7.5 q.

Table 43: Grain production in Austria-Hungary in the war years (in millions q)

	1914	1915	1916	1917	1918
Cisleithania	46.5	24.4	20.3	18.6	19.0
Transleithania	43.7	55.0	42.6	43.6	34.1
Czech lands	19.4	12.9	10.9	8.7	–
Bohemia	12.5	8.0	6.6	5.2	6.1

Source: Gratz, G. and Schüller, R. *Zusammenbruch*, pp. 42–46. *České země: Statistická příručka Republiky československé*, I. Praha, 1920, p. 47, tab. VII/11. *Čechy: Zprávy Zemského statististického úřadu království Českého*. Praha, 1923, XXV. 4: 168a.

The monarchy's cereal deficit (i.e., the difference between its aggregate production and consumption) increased dramatically from a just-about tolerable 9.8 million q (1914) to a completely intolerable 47.3 million q (1918). The situation was made all the worse by the fact that it was impossible to compensate by means of imports or to replace the cereals with other foodstuffs such as meat, potatoes, rice, barley, corn, and pulses, of which there was also significantly less on the market and for higher prices. Bohemia suffered a poor potato harvest, along with the flour the bedrock of the population's diet. The harvest fell from 32.2 million q (1914) to 10.4 million q (1918). In the same pe-

riod, pea production fell from 193,000 q to 16,000 q and the production of lentils from 21,000 q to 500 q. The growing difficulties experienced in supplying
the Austrian and Czech populations with meat is visible indirectly from the
fact that, according to the census of April 1918, the cattle inventory in Austria
was down from its 1910 level by 20%, pigs by 60% and sheep by 15%. In the
Czech lands, the cattle inventory was down by more than 846,000 (by 32.4%),
and the situation was made worse by the fact that the live weight of the cattle
fell by almost a half. Austria-Hungary was unable to withstand a fifth year
of war in which the cereal deficit was already calculated as approximately
23 million q (as opposed to 14 million q the year before).[226]

What were the causes and consequences of this situation? The reduction
in plant and livestock production that affected Cisleithania and the Czech
lands more than Hungary was the result of wartime factors such as the loss of
the male labour force (only replaceable in part by prisoners of war), a reduction in arable land and an increase in fallow land, the requisition of towing
animals and the depletion of fertile cattle for lack of feed, a drop in the yield
per hectare of land because of a lack of manure and artificial fertiliser, less
use made of agricultural machinery, and the devastation of Galicia and Transylvania by war operations. In addition, the weather was inclement in the last
two years of the war, and there was passive resistance on the part of peasant
farmers to the forced and inefficient management of agricultural products
by the state, which did nothing to prevent prices from rising and the black
market from being created. Over the long term, this drop in the primary economic sphere inevitably intensified what had, even prior to the war, been
the uneven development of agriculture and industry. Though this shunted
the social and economic structure of the monarchy away from an agrarian
towards an industrial state, this came at a high price. From the second year
of the war onwards, Cisleithania felt the consequences of this development
in the deterioration of supplies to the population (especially the inhabitants
of towns and cities), with all the concomitant effects on physical and mental
health. And yet it remained largely self-sufficient. Hungary, which had taken
over supplying the army, gradually cut supplies of grain and flour to Austria
to only 2.5% of the volume of the last year of peace. It was therefore no accident that at the end of their war the exhaustion experienced by Cisleithania
was nowhere as complete and deep as in bread supplies. Thus, agriculture can
be seen as the weakest link in the monarchy's wartime economic potential.

Government countermeasures were first aimed against rises in the price
of food. It began by stipulating maximum prices, which in turn necessitated
the seizure and recording of all production. It specified quotas for individual

---

226 Loewenfeld-Russ, H. *Die Regelung der Volksernährung im Kriege*. Wien, 1926.

crown lands, before opting to distribute purchased grain by means of a system of rationing featuring the notorious bread vouchers. This system allocated the highest rations to the army while dividing the civilian population into self-sufficient farmworkers and the mostly dependent urban population. However, the method by which the agricultural sector was managed in Austria-Hungary was never as thoroughgoing and efficient as the German method. The government tended to take the necessary measures too late and indecisively, and then applied them inconsistently around the monarchy, allowing for differences and exceptions between states and crown lands. This in turn made both the implementation of this system as represented by the War Grain Distribution Institution (Kriegs-Getreide-Verkehrsanstalt, founded in February 1915) and the "headquarters" for other agricultural products, and the state administration as managed by the Office for the Nutrition of the People in Vienna and Budapest and the Imperial and Royal Joint Nutrition Committee, excessively complex, dispersed, and cumbersome. The purchase of grain was divided by nationality, and so in the Czech lands, for instance, two branches performed the function of general commissioner of the War Grain Distribution Institution, namely the Czech and German Central Union of Economic Associations, each of which had several hundred commercial sub-commissioners for the Czech and German settlements. It is no wonder that this organisation was constantly delayed, ineffective, and unable to overcome dualistic and nationalistic prejudices even in such a sensitive area as supplying the civilian population and the army. The Hungarian government's policy of restricting imports and increasing the price of agricultural products meant that the Austrians were considerably worse off during the war than the Hungarians. The government in Vienna managed to offset partially the drop in supplies from Hungary by passing the burden for supplying Cisleithania over to the Czech lands. And when Czech peasant farmers objected and hid their grain or sold it on the black market, the government resorted to the violent seizure of stocks using soldiers and the police. However, not even this prevented a gradual reduction in official flour rations. Prior to the war, the monarchy-wide consumption of flour had been 380 g per person per day on average. From January 1918, the official (rarely attained) ration to the Austrian dependent population was 165 g, which was reduced in emergencies, such as in Vienna one month before harvest time, sometimes by as much as a half.[227]

The sharp deterioration of supplies in 1917–1918 was all the more punishing for the population of Cisleithania because, in addition to the waning of

---

227 For a detailed examination of the entire supply chain problem at the end of the war, see Jindra, Z. *Ekonomický úpadek habsburské monarchie v závěrečné fázi 1. světové války*, in *Československo a střední Evropa v meziválečném období (AUC – Philosophica et historica 3, Studia historica XL)*, pp. 29–60.

the monarchy's economic powers, it was accompanied by long harsh winters, a coal crisis, and transport difficulties. And then in 1917, the Russian
Revolution took place, which, in addition to the political ripples it created,
boosted the movement for peace in the Habsburg Monarchy. All this led the
government in Vienna to submit to Germany in that very month an urgent
request for a swift termination of the war, explaining that the monarchy was
at the end of its tether and could not continue in the war beyond autumn
1917. Shortly thereafter, the same bleak picture was painted by the Austro-
Hungarian Minister for Foreign Affairs Ottokar Czernin in a famous memorandum of April 1917 to Emperor Charles I,[228] a clear echo of which can be
discerned in the peace mission undertaken at the same time by Prince Sixtus
of Bourbon-Parma to France, as well as in the subsequent reconvention of
the Austrian Reichsrat and the resignation of the Austrian cabinet of Clam-
Martinic and the Hungarian cabinet led by Count István Tisza. Notably, this
political turnaround coincided with a supply chain crisis in Cisleithania
before the new harvests in which the government reduced daily rations of
grain and flour by more than one-fifth, and bread and flour were sometimes
unavailable for days, even weeks. This prompted mass strikes and demonstrations against hunger and high prices in many places of the Czech and Alpine lands, which were on occasion only suppressed by troops firing directly
at the demonstrators (Prostějov 26 April and Ostrava 2–8 July). For the same
reasons, in mid-June workers at arms factories in Vienna went on strike,
and at the end of June were followed by the thirty thousand workers of the
Škoda works in Plzeň, even though the state administration ensured that the
employees of munitions factories received higher rations, were better paid,
and were given priority during the planning of supplies. The radicalisation
of the Plzeň workers picked up pace with the explosion at the Škoda works
ammunition factory in neighbouring Bolevec on 25 May, during which two
hundred people, mostly workers, were killed.

The state of emergency and the hunger of the population in the Czech
and Alpine lands reached its peak in the last year of the war, which went
down in history for the complete and utter collapse of Austrian agricultural
production, the failure of its state regulation, and the escalation of tensions
between Austria and Hungary regarding supplies. The meeting of governors
of the Austrian lands after the poor harvest of 1917 (20 September) revealed
clear evidence of the complete breakdown of state authority in this area,
a fact particularly evident in the sabotage of all attempts to requisition larger
quantities of grain in the Czech lands. However, internal reserves were waning too and the transport situation created discrepancies between better and

---

228 Czernin, O. *Im Weltkriege*. Berlin–Wien 1919, p. 198 et seq.

worse supplied agricultural and industrial regions that heightened Czech-German tensions. For this reason, in November 1917, the government in Vienna announced seventeen industrial and coalmining regions in Northwest Bohemia as a single "emergency area" headed by an inspectorate for nutrition tasked with protecting the local, mainly non-agrarian and German population against the local emergency that many Germans attributed to the "evil intentions of the Czechs" from agricultural regions in the Czech interior who were holding back food supplies.

The general strike of January 1918, which the Austrian prime minister called the most serious crisis faced by the monarchy since the beginning of the war, was also seemingly related to the supply situation. Before the strike broke out on 17 January, there were only sufficient stocks of grain and flour in the crown lands and cities of Cisleithania for a few days. Though the government took measures to reduce rations, it remained unable to guarantee supplies. The mass strikes and demonstrations that first broke out in Vienna and Lower Austria spread to all the industrial centres and cities (in Plzeň 35,000 people took to the streets, in Prague 60,000, and in Kladno 27,000), but now, in addition to economic causes, had a social, political, and nationalist subtext. This was manifest in demands for the democratisation of public life and the termination of the militarisation of arms factories, in what is known as the Three Kings Declaration (the call for a united Czechoslovakia free from Habsburg rule made on 6 January 1918 or Three Kings Day), in the uprising by sailors in the Bay of Kotor, and above all in strident calls for immediate peace talks without annexation and reparations with Bolshevik Russia. Taken en masse, these events gave the impression that this was no ordinary failure of the state and criticism of the government, but that a genuine "state crisis" affecting the entire empire had begun, as the German ambassador in Vienna put it in February 1918.[229]

This state crisis, which ultimately culminated in the collapse of the monarchy, developed in close parallel with Austria's supply crisis. The first, during 1918, was accompanied, complicated, and intensified by the second, which grew from an isolated internal political problem into a serious foreign policy issue in which the monarchy was more reliant than it had been previously either on German assistance and uncertain imports of grain requisitioned from Ukraine or Romania. This was reflected in the Brest-Litovsk "bread peace" negotiations with Ukraine, during which the need for massive assistance in the form of grain from Ukraine became the leitmotif of Austrian politics. The monarchy was at the mercy of Germany, which was responsible for collecting Ukrainian and Romanian grain and allocated to the monarchy only the most

---

229   Bundesarchiv, Berlin, Stellvertreter des Reichskanzlers, Nr. 2539b, Bl. 1.

urgent or what the Austrians themselves seized out of desperation (a famous incident took place on 30 April 1918 in which German railway and maritime consignments of Romanian corn were confiscated). Even so, the final balance of foreign cereal supplies for the starving Cisleithians was modest. In the 1917–1918 harvest, Austrian imports of grain totalled 43,680 wagons, which covered barely a quarter of Austrian needs. Disappointingly, it was Ukraine and Germany that supplied the smallest number of wagons (2,348 and 2,619 respectively), with the rest coming from Hungary (10,185 wagons), along with Romania and Bessarabia (28,528). However, the situation on the ground was far worse than average annual figures reveal.

The deterioration of the supply situation recorded in April, May and June of 1918 prior to the last wartime harvest saw the complete and utter agrarian collapse of Cisleithania. The needs of the Austrian crown lands at that time were covered with the aid of requisitions and imports of grain only to the tune of between 42% and 48%. Government procurement was based on improvisation on a week-to-week basis, and the crown lands with low official supplies were literally to starve until the new harvest. As a consequence, violent "hunger revolts" broke out in Lviv, Kraków, Duchcov, Most, and elsewhere, which had to be forcibly put down by armed troops. At the start of April, an announcement arrived from the Czech lands: "For four weeks no flour has been distributed in Prague whatsoever, inadequate amounts of potatoes [...] and there is no fat at all. There is little meat, and what there is is so expensive that not even the wealthy can buy it. [...] The only way of alleviating the situation is through taking a bag and heading for the countryside [...], so as to buy whatever is to hand for high prices."[230]

However, reserves in the countryside diminished considerably when the government ordered that self-sufficient farmworkers were to have two months of rations and in other crown lands one month of their own grain and flour confiscated. Even this drastic measure bought the government only a few weeks' grace. In June, when imports of grain almost dried up and adverse weather conditions delayed Austria's harvest for another two weeks, Cisleithania was buffeted by another supply-chain crisis that impacted negatively on the last offensive of the imperial and royal army on the Italian front. Strikes, demonstrations, riots, and the looting of shops and transport conveys provoked by a reduction in the already-low rations of bread to a half of their previous level became a daily occurrence in many cities, as did military intervention, martial law, and the shooting of protesters. An average harvest allowed for the bread ration of 165 g daily for dependents to be revived as of 15 August, but the price of bread rose by more than 100%. Right up until the end

---

230 Ibid., Reichskanzlei, Nr. 2461/2, Bl. 192.

of the war there were long queues for bread and it was best not to dwell on its poor quality, the result of a high ratio of milled flour (80%–94% compared to 70% during peacetime) combined with potatoes or barley, oat, bean, pea and corn flour, and in extreme cases with beet. In autumn 1918, this was the critical state that supplies of food to the population were in.[231]

All of this had serious consequences for health and demographics. By the end of the war, long-term malnutrition and excessive physical and psychological pressures were visible even at a glance (in the form of physical decrepitude, dullness of wit and depression), especially in rapidly increasing rates of injury and sickness (especially tuberculosis and gastric, intestinal, and nervous disorders), and an increased number of disabled and deceased (especially babies, children, women, and the elderly). These pressures also impacted on many legal and ethical norms of human relationships. There was an unprecedented rise in economic criminality (the theft of food, domestic livestock, coal, items in post offices, and railway stations, poaching, etc.), often perpetrated by persons who had until then been of stainless character, especially women and young people. This, too, was an indirect consequence of the intolerable suffering, both physical and mental, which, along with economic exhaustion and the military and internal breakdown of the state, characterised the decline of the Habsburg Empire at the end of the war.

FINANCING OF THE WAR AND THE DEVELOPMENT OF BANKING

The financial cost of the First World War far exceeded the forecasts and all the yardsticks of previous wars. For instance, in 1870–1871, the Franco-Prussian War came to approximately 8.8 billion dollars (using the prices of 1900), whereas the First World War (leaving aside the loss of human life, property, production, etc.) is estimated to have cost a total of 208.5 billion dollars at current dollar prices or 82.4 billion dollars using 1913 prices. Of this sum, the Central Powers spent 61.5 billion dollars in nominal prices or 24.7 billion in pre-war dollars, of which Austria-Hungary spent 13.4 billion in current and 4.7 billion in pre-war prices. In current Austrian crowns this represents at least 81 billion (Wilhelm Winkler) and at most 90 billion (Janos Teleszky). Through this sum is not even a quarter of what the German Empire spent, this was not a sign of thriftiness on the part of Austria Hungary, but testament to its limited material resources and the early depletion of its financial strength. After all, the final wartime budget for 1917–1918 alone was for

---

231   Opočenský, J. *Konec monarchie rakousko-uherské*. Praha, 1928, pp. 486–495.

approximately 24 billion crowns, which was roughly six times more than state spending in the last peacetime year.[232]

As in other countries, the method of financing the war was based on the ruthless exploitation of the very bases of national product and income and the redistribution of these assets. If we assume on the basis of pre-war prices that the direct and indirect expenditure of Austria-Hungary on the war was 30 billion crowns, this would mean the war absorbed one and a half times its national income from 1910 (estimated by Fellner to be 19.3 billion crowns) and approximately one-quarter of its national assets (estimated by Fellner to be 126.2 billion crowns).[233] This means that the enormous wartime expenses exceeded the budgetary possibilities of the state. While during peacetime the state was able to cover its expenses mainly using direct and indirect (consumer) taxes, these only covered on average around 17% of its wartime needs, and even less in the case of the Habsburg Monarchy (12.6%). Austro-Hungarian fiscal policymakers long weighed up the pros and cons of applying this instrument more vigorously, on the one hand convinced that the war would be short, and on the other concerned not to disturb the fragile social and national peace. It was only in the second third of the war that the state began to provide assistance in the form of tax surcharges and, in exceptional cases, new taxes, such as the tax on wartime profits and the transport tax on railway companies.

Under these circumstances, the state had to find ways of covering its enormous military expenses and growing budget deficits by other means. It relied on the banking sector led by the central reserve bank Rubka, and financed the war from three basic sources:

(1) It suspended Rubka's basic rights and systematically drew down hundreds of millions—partly in credit, partly in debt—thus opening the way to the printing of uncollateralised banknotes. This meant that Rubka's metal reserves fell from 1,269 million crowns at the start of the war to a half that that figure by 1918, while the nominal amount of banknotes in circulation increased by almost 20 billion from 3.4 billion to 33.5 billion (i.e., almost tenfold, most of all in 1917–1918). At the end of the war, the monarchy owed Rubka alone a total of 39.3 billion crowns, the largest part of which (25 billion) was owed by Cisleithania, which had drawn down more than Transleithania. The huge increase in payment instruments without a commensurate increase in goods on the market could only have one outcome, namely a drop in the purchasing power of money and severe

232 Jindra, Z. *První světová válka*, pp. 198–199; Hardach, G. *Der Erste Weltkrieg 1914–1918*, p. 166; *Die Habsburgermonarchie 1848–1918, Bd. I. Die wirtschaftliche Entwicklung*. Wien, 1973, p. 101.

233 Fellner, F. "Das Volkseinkommen Österreichs und Ungarns." *Statistische Monatsschrift* 42 (1916): 485–625.

inflation that impacted broad swathes of the civilian population. This can be seen in the rapid growth in the cost of living, which in indexical figures (July 1914=100) were as follows: June 1915 – 153, June 1916 – 317, June 1917 – 650, June 1918 – 1,082, and October 1918 – 1,285 points.

(2) The most effective instrument for covering wartime requirements and redistributing national income amongst the widest swathes of the population was for the state to issue internal public loans. Austria-Hungary, isolated from the international financial markets, was reliant on this source and issued the highest number (21) of such loans of all the countries at war, eight of which in Cisleithania had a total yield in excess of 35 billion crowns.

(3) As well as internal loans, which eventually covered 80% of Austria-Hungary's extraordinary wartime spending, the monarchy had to seek loans abroad, though these only covered 7% of its needs. During the war, this source was considerably restricted, both by the number of countries willing to extend credit and by the level of the loans. Neutral Netherlands, Denmark, and Sweden helped the monarchy to the tune of only several million, basically so that the monarchy could buy their goods. The monarchy was more indebted to its ally Germany, from which it received a total of 1,336,000 crowns, enough to ensure that it economically and politically remained tied ever more tightly to the apron strings of its powerful neighbour.

A significant role in wartime finance was played by the large commercial banks in the three largest financial centres of the monarchy: Vienna, Budapest, and Prague. They were connected to the wartime boom on several levels. (1) Prior to the war they had extraordinarily close credit, capital, and personnel relations with the coal, metallurgy, engineering, chemical industries, etc., which now received a large proportion of wartime contracts and could not survive without new loans, investments, and the boosting of share capital. On the other hand, the close contact between industry and the banks allowed for a rapid reorientation on wartime production. (2) Thanks to expanded commission trade with goods and their leading role in cartels, the large banks had an important say in the state-run bodies of the war economy. (3) The banking sector led by Rubka played a key role in the state borrowing transactions and financing of the war. However, these operations were complicated by the fact that banks in Austria-Hungary lacked an integrated policy and were driven by both competing interests and nationalist considerations.

At first sight, the total extent and increase in banking transactions during the war is borne out by the unusual increase in the balance sheet (including equity and deposits) of the large banks, even though inflation is in part responsible. The two leading banks in Vienna and Prague that illustrate this development also represent the different growth dynamic of the commercial turnover of Austrian and Czech banks.

Table 44: Balance sheet of Österreichische Creditanstalt in Vienna and Živnobanka in Prague (in millions of crowns)

	1913	1914	1915	1916	1917	1918	% increase
Creditanstalt	1,181	1,365	1,626	2,188	2,913	3,174	168.7
Živnobanka	416	438	487	603	820	1,779	327.6

Source: Creditanstalt: März, E. *Österreichische Bankpolitik in der Zeit der großen Wende 1913–1923.* München, 1981, p. 226. Živnobanka: Pimper, A. *České obchodní banky za války a po válce.* Praha, 1929, p. 125; Živnostenská banka v Praze 1869–1918, s. d., appendix.

An interesting feature of the development of banking in the war years was that the enormous increase in turnover (leaving aside inflation and surplus liquidity) involved completely different types of operations than before the war. On the liabilities side there was a shift in the ratio between equity and deposits (e.g., in the case of all Prague-based joint-stock banks) from a relatively healthy 1:3 before the war to 1:8 in 1918. This alarming decline in equity or the reserve requirements only slowed down during the last two years of the war, when the banks increased their equity significantly. This was an important sign of the further centralisation of banking capital, this time with far-reaching consequences for the Prague banking centre, since the Czech national banks in Prague had issued 141 million crowns in new shares, thus boosting considerably their position in respect of both German-owned local banks and Viennese capital. At the same time, there was a 4.5-fold increase in the second largest item in the liabilities column of Prague-based banks caused by the war, namely creditors (i.e., business current accounts, the creditors of goods departments, deposits from other financial institutions, etc.), a problematic item illustrating the accumulation of cash for which neither companies nor banks could find a satisfactory place. We observe another equally significant transformation of banking transactions on the side of assets. Credit and currency trading waned in significance and this led to the relaxation of what before the war had been the relatively close relationships of dependence between industrial joint-stock companies and banks. State controls saw forex and currency transactions fall too, and after the closure of the stock exchange (until March 1916) there was a temporary squeeze on what had until then been the large and profitable purchase and sale of dividend securities. Wartime banking found a replacement for these regular transactions in the issuance of war loans and Lombard banking, the financing of arms supplies, and trading in goods. This last form of trading was especially popular with the indigenous Czech banks, partly because it had been used extensively before the war and so the banks had their own commodities departments, and also because in the first years of the war (until stocks ran out and the distribution of the items in question was banned by central offices) they were very lucrative. Agrární banka in particular became wealthy on the back of these transactions, in their case involving agricultural products.[234]

In addition, Czech-controlled banks and thrift institutions were invited from the first year of the war onwards to participate in the issuance and subscription of war loans. These were enormous transactions that every six months injected billions into the market in the form of treasury bonds, brought tens of thousands of institutional and individual subscribers to the bank counters, and offered financial institutions high interest rates, tax relief, and many other advantages. However, equally unquestionable was the purpose of these transactions, namely the procurement of cash with which to finance the war. By virtue of their active, lukewarm, or passive approach to state loans, notably during the great wars, the financial institutions and all subscribers offered a clue as to how they viewed the state and war. Even the authorities appealed to patriotic duty during the issuance of these loans. However, to the unpleasant surprise of the Czech governors, the results of the first three loans of 1914–1915 highlighted the disproportion between what the Czech and German savings banks had subscribed. For instance, during the second war loan, every Sudeten German deposited an average of 222 crowns, whereas every Czech averaged 28 crowns, well below the Austrian average of 92 crowns per capita. In certain cases, the imperial and royal authorities had to resort to repeatedly reprimanding the Czech savings banks before attaining a certain increase in subscriptions of the next loans. Disobedient firms were threatened with the withdrawal of their wartime contracts and allocation of raw materials, or with the conscription of their executives. The leading indigenous Czech banks subscribed to the first three wartime loans far less money than their Sudeten German counterparts even though they had far higher reserves, or discouraged their clients from subscribing. When they did buy government bonds, they were keen to offload them as soon as possible, and these facts made them subject to official investigations and pressure. Živnostenská banka, a relative newcomer, aroused the attention of the authorities for precisely this reason, and shortly after the arrest of Karel Kramář was labelled a "saboteur" of state loans. The language was even stronger in the case of Živnobanka, which was called "treacherous" in order to justify an investigation into the bank (December 1915) and to press charges against its top management (Jaroslav Preiss, Antonín Tille, Rudolf Pilát, and Ladislav Šourek) before a military court in Vienna. Wartime relations—already made brittle by governmental, German-Austrian centralism—was to be used for an unusual cause, namely the direct persecution of Czech bank-

---

234 For more details regarding these banking transactions, see: Jindra, in Venkovský, Jindra, Novotný. *Dějiny bankovnictví v českých zemích*.

ing capital. The compendious warrant against Živnobanka had already been compiled (February 1917) and only awaited the initiation of legal proceedings (May 1917), when a series of political events (the accession of Emperor Charles, the March Revolution in Russia and the break-up of military absolutism in the monarchy), led the government to suspend the criminal proceedings it had planned (April 1917) and to hold out the offer of an amnesty to the main bank officials headed by Dr Preiss (July 1917).

6. CONCLUSION: PREPARATIONS FOR ECONOMIC INDEPENDENCE

Regarding the motivation behind the wartime actions of the indigenous Czech banks, specifically Živnobanka, which the Austrian state prosecutor ascribed to political causes when preparing legal proceedings against the bank, even today we still cannot offer an exhaustive explanation. There was clearly a combination of reasons, with political and nationalist motives going hand in hand with economic considerations, with one or another gaining ascendency depending on circumstances. In 1918, this ambivalent relationship was still attempting to cling on to the protection of narrowly nationalist political interests with which economic interests were in alignment. The tendency was encouraged by the ongoing disintegration of the monarchy both internally and externally, partly caused by the Czechs themselves and many of their actions, such as the Three Kings Declaration in January 1918, the national oath taken by representatives of Czech culture and public in April of the same year, the fiftieth anniversary of the National Theatre and the Rumburk Uprising in May, the establishment of the Ústřední svaz českých průmyslníků (Central Union of Czech Industrialists), etc., and less specifically the general strike called in January, the mutiny at the Kotor naval base at the start of February, the Treaty of Brest-Litovsk with Soviet Russia in March, the fall of foreign minister Ottokar Czernin in April, and the definitive turnaround in July and August on the Western Front in favour of the Entente.

Prior to the war, leading Czech politicians and business representatives had sought to assert Czech nationalist interests in administrative and parliamentary bodies of the Habsburg Monarchy and fulfil their economic objectives on its broader market. However, the Great War, with its hallmark German campaign against the Slavs and the gloomy outlook of complete economic and political integration of the Habsburg Monarchy into Germany (by means of a process officially called the "economic convergence" of both countries or within the framework of the German military goal of Mitteleuropa), forced Czech economic and political elites to accept that there would be no dignified room in such a power structure for the free development of Czech capital and the Czech nation. And so, under the pressure of military developments at home and on the fronts, a new anti-Austria, Entente-oriented policy began to take shape, most obviously represented at home by the secret committee of the Maffia and in foreign exile headed by Tomáš Garrigue Masaryk and Edvard Beneš and Czechoslovak legions in Russia, France, and Italy. What is interesting is how swiftly many personalities of Czech economic life, especially those associated with Živnostenská banka, became involved with the activities of the Maffia.

The links between the Czech political and business elites were considerable even before the war.[235] However, the unusual situation pertaining during the war led to these relationships deepening, while also seeing the emergence of hitherto less well known personalities such as Přemysl Šámal and others, who later became known as the "28 October men". An important part of the Maffia's activities right from the start involved intelligence work on the side of the Entente, within which they occupied an important place in terms of economic news reports. The general secretary of the Young Czech Party, František Sís, who oversaw this work, relied when collecting information on contacts with trustworthy members of the party and VIP clients of Živnobanka active in industry, commerce, finance, and public administration. The employees of Živnostenská banka played a key role in the collection of information, according to Milada Paulová: "An important centre where economic, financial, technical, and industrial information was gathered was Živnostenská banka in Prague, headed by the nationalist trio: Bohdan Bečka, member of the executive committee of Živnostenská banka, the director Jaroslav Preiss, and František Malínský. Bečka was the link to Sís."[236] Just how beneficial this information was within the framework of the Entente was borne out by Beneš, a leading member of the Prague National Council during the war: "Right from the start, the Maffia sent valuable reports abroad on Austro-Hungarian political, economic, and military affairs that were often used by the Allied powers for the furtherance of military operations, political considerations, and economic and financial measures. This helped us catch the ear of many allied official circles."[237] In comparison, the influence enjoyed by Karel Kramář, prior to the war a leading Czech politician and wealthy industrialist, waned considerably. Though he was decorated with the aureole of Vienna 1915–1917 as an imprisoned national martyr, he was damaged by his unwillingness to pay heed to Masaryk's call to exile and remained politically focused on Russia. His place in his own party (after his release from prison) was taken by Preiss, Alois Rašín, and other business figures with strong links to Živnobanka.

---

235 Cf. ibid, 200 et seq.

236 Paulová, M. Dějiny Maffie. *Odboj Čechů a Jihoslovanů za světové války 1914–1918*, Vol. I. Praha, 1937, p. 158–159.

237 Beneš, E. *Světová válka a naše revoluce. Vzpomínky a úvahy z bojů za svobodu národa*, Vol. I. Praha, 1928, p. 89–90.

However, the Maffia did not restrict its activities to intelligence gathering. Another important point to bear in mind was the fact that this circle of people soon began to give consideration to the necessary first executive and legislative measures that any future independent Czechoslovak state would have to take in the economic sphere. According to the eyewitness testimony of Vilém Pospíšil, director of the Municipal Savings Bank in Prague and later governor of the Czechoslovak National Bank, meetings of important Czech financiers were already being held to that end from 1916. After his release from prison, Jaroslav Preiss, CEO of Živnobanka, became one of the leading lights of group. In October 1917, Preiss presented a paper entitled "On the Economic and Social Issues of Czech Politics" at a meeting of the Young Czech Party, in which he addressed some of the basic pillars of a national Czech economy in the immediate future. Even though he conceded certain social reforms, he rejected socialism and gave his full support to a system of private ownership. However, "in the interest of the nation" he was not averse to state intervention in the excessive ownership positions of the German bourgeoisie and nobility (e.g., through the nationalisation of the railways, iron and steelworks, mines, mineral springs, and land reform). (This was a precursor of the nostrification process of the 1920s.) At the same time, there was a convergence of opinions and institutions in the group. In September 1917, indigenous Czech banks agreed on the joint protection of their interests and created the Union of Czech Banks to do just that. It is testament to the strange atmosphere pertaining that even the two main banking rivals, Živnostenská and Agrární banka, reached agreement at the end of the war on wartime loans and the Habsburg Empire. This was largely the work of the CEO of Agrární banka, Karel Svoboda.

This secret cooperation of radical economic agents gave rise in the first six months of the war to the first economic programme of a liberated Czechoslovakia. Discussions took place and the first measures were jointly prepared of the Czechoslovak government in the administrative and political sphere within the framework of a special commission formed in April 1918 comprising members of the Maffia and the National Committee. Kramář, Rašín, Šámal, Franta, and Scheiner were joined by the two bank managers, Preiss and Pospíšil. The core of the group comprised representatives of the urban industrial, commercial, and financial bourgeoisie that came together in February 1918 to form the party Czech State Democracy. To begin with, representatives of Agrární banka were not involved in these meetings and the social reform parties headed by the social democrats were not informed of them. Meetings were held in private, mostly in Scheiner's apartment, sometimes at Rašín's or Preiss's, and around September 1918 draft laws and regulations were ready. In September, Ferdinand Pantůček of the Supreme Administrative Court in Vienna was invited to the final meeting of the editorial board of the basic

political legal code of the Czechoslovak state. In contrast, the economic programme was the work of Preiss and, after long informal discussions both
within the commission and without, underwent three drafts with the cooperation of Pospíšil. The eventual outcome was a considered conceptual set of
concrete measures setting forth the powers of a Czechoslovak government in
the economic sphere. In contrast to the principle of legal and administrative
continuity enshrined in the draft political bill, these measures were more
concerned with the short-term measures enabling a break with Vienna and
the filling of important economic positions in a future Czechoslovak state.
All Austrian state assets were to be taken over, an independent financial sector established (tax, revenue, currency, etc.), and the entire organisational
agenda of the war economy (controls of exchange rate, prices and wages,
foreign trade relations, the ration system, economic centres, and associations) placed under state supervision. In the longer term, the plan included
the nostrification of industrial and other enterprises, insurance companies
and banks with factories in the Czechoslovak republic and headquarters in
Vienna (with no intervention in ownership rights except in the case of railways and arms manufacturers), and the implementation of land reform on
the basis of the compulsory purchase of aristocratic farms and land.

Favourable conditions were already in place for the implementation of
this economic and political programme at the end of October 1918, when
the Habsburg Monarchy was beyond hope of saving. There was an uprising
in Prague and the eight-member delegation of prominent representatives
of the Czech resistance headed by Kramář set off for Geneva, where from
28–31 October they held discussions with Beneš regarding the problems involved in creating a free Czechoslovakia. During these talks, representatives
of the interim Parisian government "passed resolutions that the commission
of the National Committee had drafted for the transition from being part of
Austria-Hungary to being the new state of Czechoslovakia."[238]

This decision was taken with the direct, active participation of two economic experts that were deemed members of the Prague delegation to the
Geneva talks. These were Messrs Preiss and Svoboda, the former the manager
of Živnostenská bank and the latter of Agrární banka, representing the two
leading financial groups of Czech capital, which after 1918 played a central
role in the economy of the new republic. Virtually all the finance ministers
in the first years of the republic abided by the economic policy agenda agreed
on in Geneva.

---

238 Opočenský, J. "Cesta českých politiků do Švýcar v říjnu 1918." *Naše revoluce* IV (1926/27): 392.

7. SELECTED BIBLIOGRAPHY

OVERVIEWS AND GENERAL WORKS

Agnew, H. L., Origins of the Czech National Renascence, Pittsburgh, 1993.

Aubin, G., Kunze, A., Leinenerzeugung und Leinenabsatz im östlichen Mitteldeutschland zur Zeit der Zunftkäufe, Stuttgart, 1940.

Bairoch, P., "Europe's Gross National Product 1800–1975", The Journal of European Economic History, Vol. 5, 1976.

Baltzarek, F., "Zu den regionalen Ansätze der frühen Industrialisierung in Europa. Mit Überlegungen zum Stellenwert der frühen Industrialisierung im Habsburgerstaat des 18. and 19. Jahrhunderts", in: Knittler, H. (Ed.), Wirtschafts- und Sozialgeschichte. Festschrift Alfred Hoffmann zum 75. Jahrestag, Wien 1979, pp. 334–355.

Bělina, P., Kaše, J., Kučera, J. P., Velké dějiny zemí Koruny české, Vol. X, Praha – Litomyšl, 2001.

Bérénger, J., A History of the Habsburg Empire II, 1700–1918, London, 1997.

Brňovják, J., Zářický, A. (Eds.), Šlechtic podnikatelem, podnikatel šlechticem, Ostrava, 2008.

Brňovják, J., Županič, J. (Eds.), Changes of the noble society: aristocracy and new nobility in the Habsburg Monarchy and Central Europe from the 16th to the 20th century: a collection of studies from sections P69 and P80 of the 11th Congress of the Czech Historians (14th–15th September 2017, Olomouc, Czech Republic), Ostrava, 2018.

Bruckmüller, E., Sozialgeschichte Österreichs, Wien–München, 2001.

Butschek, F., Industrialisierung. Ursachen-Verlauf-Konsequenzen, Wien–Köln–Weimar, 2006.

Cameron, R. E., A concise economic history of the world: from Paleolithic time to the present, New York–Oxford, 1993.

Dějiny Rakouska, Praha, 2002.

Efmertová, M., České země v letech 1848–1918, Praha, 1998.

Freudenberger, H., Die proto-Industrielle Entwicklungsphase in Österreich. Proto-Industrialisierung als sozialer Lernprozeß, in: Matis, H. (Ed.), Von der Glückseligkeit des Staates. Staat, Wirtschaft und Gesellschaft in Österreich im Zeitalter des aufgeklärten Absolutismus, Berlin, 1981, pp. 351–381.

Freudenberger, H., Lost Momentum. Austrian Economic Development 1750s–1830s, Wien–Köln–Weimar, 2003.

Freudenberger, H., Redlich, F., The Industrial Development of Europe. Reality, Symbols, Images, Kyklos, 1964, Vol. 17, pp. 372–403.

Friedmann, G., Krise pokroku, Praha, 1937.

Gerschenkron, A., Wirtschaftliche Rückständigkeit in historischer Perspektive, in: Wehler, H.-U. (Ed.), Geschichte und Ökonomie, Köln, 1973, pp. 121–139.

Gešlová, J., Sekanina, M., Lexikon našich hospodářských dějin 19. a 20. století v politických a společenských souvislostech, Praha, 2003.

Good, D. F., National Bias in the Austrian Capital Market before World War I, Explorations in Economic History, 1977, Vol. 14, pp. 141–166.

Good, D. F., The Economic Rise of the Habsburg Empire, 1750–1914, Berkeley–Los Angeles–London, 1984; German: Der wirtschaftliche Aufstieg des Habsburgerreiches 1750–1914, Wien–Köln–Graz, 1986.

Die Habsburger Monarchie 1848–1918. Vol. I. Die wirtschaftliche Entwicklung, Wien, 1973; Vol. II., Verwaltung und Rechtswesen, Wien, 1975; Vol. VI. Die Habsburgermonarchie im System der internationalen Beziehungen, Wien, 1989; Vol. VII. Verfassung und Parlamentarismus, Wien 2000; Vol. XI. Die Habsburgermonarchie und der Erste Weltkrieg, Wien, 2014–2016.

Hájek, J., Jančík, D., Kubů, E. (Eds.), O hospodářskou národní državu. Úvahy a stati o moderním českém a německém nacionalismu v českých zemích, AUC, Philosophica et Historica 1–2005, Studia historica LIX, Praha, 2009.

Hájek, J., Kubů, E., Ekonomický nacionalismus českých zemí sklonku 19. a první poloviny 20. století jako středoevropský "model", ČCH, 2006, Vol. 104, no. 4, pp. 783–820.

Hammer-Luza, E., Economic and Social History, in: Wallnig, T., Frimmel, J., Telesko, W. (Eds.), 18th Century Studies in Austria, 1945–2010, Bochum, 2011 (= Das Achzehnte Jahrhundert und Österreich, Internationale Beihefte, ed. Wolfgang Schmale), Vol. 4, pp. 71–89.

Heckscher, E. F., Mercantilism, London, 1935.

Heppner, H., Urbanitsch, P., Zedinger, R. (Eds.), Social Change in the Habsburg Monarchy, Les transformations de la société dans la monarchie des Habsbourg: l'époque des Lumières, Bochum, 2011 (= Das Achzehnte Jahrhundert und Österreich, Internationale Beihefte, ed. Wolfgang Schmale, Vol. 3, Pt. 3).

Hlavačka, M., Zlatý věk české samosprávy. Samospráva a její vliv na hospodářský, sociální a intelektuální rozvoj Čech 1862–1913, Praha, 2006.

Hlavačka, M. et al., České země v 19. století, Vol. 2, Praha, 2014.

Hroch, M., Social Precondition of National Revival in Europe. A Comparative Analysis of the Social Composition of Patriotic Groups among the Smaller European Nations, Cambridge, 1985.

Janáček, F., Největší zbrojovka monarchie. Škodovka v dějinách, dějiny ve škodovce 1859–1918, Praha, 1990.

Janák, J., Dějiny Moravy III/1: Hospodářský rozmach Moravy 1740–1918, Brno, 1999.

Jančík, D., Kubů, E. (Eds.), Nacionalismus zvaný hospodářský. Střety a zápasy o nacionální emancipaci/převahu v českých zemích (1959–1945), Praha, 2011.

Jetschgo, J. et al., Österreichische Industriegeschichte: 1848 bis 1955: die verpasste Chance, Wien, 2004.

Jílek, F. (Ed.), Studie o technice v českých zemích 1800–1918, Vols. I–IV, Praha 1983–1986.

Jindra, Z., Die Triebkräfte u. Entwicklungslinien des tschechischen wirtschaftlichen Aufstiegs im 19. Jahrhundert (bis 1918), in: Henning F.-W. (Ed.), Die Regionen des ehemaligen Habsburgerreichs und ihre heutigen Wirtschaftsbeziehungen, Frankfurt a. M.–Berlin–Bern–New York–Paris–Wien, 1998, pp. 42–79.

Jindra, Z., Výchozí ekonomické pozice Československa. Odhady národního jmění, důchodu a hrubého národního produktu Rakousko-Uherska a českých zemí před 1. světovou válkou, in: Střední a východní Evropa v krizi XX. století. K 70. narozeninám Zdeňka Sládka, Praha, 1998, pp. 183–204.

Jindra, Z., Ekonomický úpadek habsburské monarchie v závěrečné fázi války, in: Československo a střední Evropa v meziválečném období, Praha, 1996, pp. 29–60.

Jiránek, T., Projevy hospodářského nacionalismu v obchodních a živnostenských komorách v Českých zemích 1850–1918, Pardubice, 1994.

Klíma, A., Agrarian Class Structure and Economic Development in Pre-Industrial Bohemia, Past & Present, 1979, No. 85, pp. 49–59.

Klíma, A., Die Länder der Böhmischen Krone 1648–1850, in: Fischer, W. et alii (Ed.), Handbuch der Europäischen Wirtschafts- und Sozialgeschichte. Vol. 1, Stuttgart, 1993, pp. 688–719.

Klíma, A., Domestic Industry, Manufactory and Early Industrialization in Bohemia, The Journal of Economic History, 1989, Vol. 18, 509–527.

Klíma, A., Economy, Industry and Society in Bohemia in the 17th–19th Centuries, Praha, 1991.

Klíma, A., Mercantilism in the Habsburg Monarchy – with special reference to the Bohemian Lands, Historica, 1965, Vol. 11, 95–119.

Klíma, A., The Domestic Industry and the Putting-out-System (Verlagssystem) in the Period of Transition from Feudalism to Capitalism, in: Deuxième Conférence International d'Histoire Économique Aix-en-Provence 1962. Congrès et colloques 8/2, Paris, 1965, pp. 477–481.

Klíma, A., Macurek, J., La question de la transitiv du féodalism au capitalism en Europe Centrale, 16e–18e siècles, in: Rapports du XIe Congrès International des Sciences Historiques, Stockholm, 1960, pp. 85–140.

Komlos, J., Die Habsburgermonarchie als Zollunion. Die Wirtschaftsentwicklung Österreich-Ungarns im 19. Jahrhundert, Wien, 1986.

Křížek, J., Die wirtschaftlichen Grundzüge des österreichisch-ungarischen Imperialismus in der Vorkriegszeit 1900–1914, Praha, 1964.

Kubů, E. et al., Ve znamení svépomoci a solidarity: družstva, družstevní elity a politika ve střední Evropě druhé poloviny 19. a první poloviny 20. století. In the sign of self-help and solidarity: cooperatives, cooperative elites, and politics in Central Europe in the second half of the 19th century and the first half of the 20th century, Praha, 2023.

Kubů, E., Soukup, J., Šouša, J. (Eds.), Fenomén hospodářské krize v českých zemích 19. až počátku 21. století. Cyklický vývoj ekonomiky v procesu gradující globalizace, Praha–Ostrava, 2015.

Kuczynski, J., Mendels, F. F., Zum Problem der Protoindustrialisierung. Ein Briefwechsel, Jahrbuch für Wirtschaftsgeschichte, 1984, No. 2, pp. 151–160.

Kula, W., Przewrot przemyslowy. Historia i perspektywy. Klasifikacja udanych procesów industrializacyjnych, Kwartalnik Historyczny, 1963, Vol. 70, pp. 3–22.

Kutnar, F., Přehled dějin Československa v epoše feudalismu IV, Doba národního obrození 1740–1848, 2nd Ed., Praha, 1963.

Lacina, V., Hospodářství českých zemí 1880–1914, Praha, 1990.

Liška, V. et al., Ekonomická tvář národního obrození, Praha, 2005.

Lněničková, J., České země v době předbřeznové 1792–1848, Praha, 1999.

Macartney, C. A., The Habsburg Empire 1790–1918, 2nd Ed., London–New York, 1971.

Macartney, C. A., The House of Austria: The Later Phase 1790–1918, Edinburgh, 1978.

Machačová, J., Matějček, J., Nástin sociálního vývoje českých zemí 1781–1914, Opava, 2002.

Matis, H., Österreichs Wirtschaft 1848–1913, Berlin, 1972.

Matis, H., Wirtschaftswachstum als ReVolutionsprophylaxe. Das Kaisertum Österreich im Vormärz, Wien, 1996.

Mendels, F. F., "Proto-Industrialization: The First Phase of the Industrialization Process", The Journal of Economic History, 1972, Vol. 12, 241–261.

Mendels, F. F., Proto-Industrialization: Theory and Reality, in: Eight International Congress of Economic History. Budapest, 1982.

Mokyr, J. (Ed.), The Oxford Encyclopedia of Economic History, Vols. 1–5, Oxford, 2003.

Myška, M., Pre-Industrial Iron Making in the Czech Lands: the Labour Force and Production Relations circa 1350–circa 1840, Past & Present, 1979, No. 82, pp. 44–72.

Myška, M., Problémy a metody hospodářských dějin. Část 1: Metodické problémy studia dějin sekundárního sektoru, Ostrava, 1995.

Myška, M., Proto-industrialization in Bohemia, Moravia and Silesia, in: Sheilagh C. Ogilvie, Cerman, M., European proto-industrialization, Cambridge, 1996, pp. 188–207.

Myška, M., Průmyslová reVoluce z perspektivy historiografie 70. a 80. let, ČsČH, 1991, Vol. 89, No. 4, pp. 533–546.

Myška, M., Rytíři průmyslové reVoluce. Šest studií k dějinám podnikatelů v českých zemích, Ostrava, 1997.

Myška, M., Un caso speciale o un diverso modello? La protoindustrializzazione in Bohemia, Moravia e Slesia, in: Fontana, G. L. [cura di], Le vie dell'industrializzazione europea. Sistemi a confronto, Bologna, 1997, pp. 405–437.

Okey, R., The Habsburg Monarchy c. 1765–1918. From Enlightenment to Eclipse, London, 2001.

Ottův obchodní slovník, díl. I–II/2, J. Otto, Praha–Bratislava, 1913–1925.

Paulinyi, Á., Industrielle reVolution. Vom Ursprung der modernen Technik, Reinbek bei Hamburg, 1989.

Pickl, O., Das Wirtschaftswachstum der Habsburger Monarchie und ihre Veflechtung in den internationalen Handel im 19. Jahrhundert, in: Kellenbenz, H. (Ed.), Wirtschaftliches Wachstum, Energie und Verkehr vom Mittelalter bis ins 19. Jahrhundert: Bericht über die 6. Arbeitstagung der Gesellschaft für Sozial- und Wirtschaftsgeschichte, Stuttgart-New York 1978, pp. 183-203.

Pierenkemper, T., Umstrittene ReVolutionen. Die Industrialisierung im 19. Jahrhundert, Frankfurt a. M., 1996.

Plecháček, I., Zdroje zemědělského úvěru v Českých zemích ve druhé polovině 19. století, Hospodářské dějiny - Economic History, 1984, Vol. 12, pp. 321-377.

Počátky českého národního obrození. Společnost a kultura v 70. až 90. letech 18. století, Praha, 1990.

Prinz, F. (Ed.), Deutsche Geschichte im Osten Europas, Berlin, 1993.

Propyläen der Technikgeschichte, 2. Ed., Vol. 5, Berlin, 1997.

Průmyslové oblasti českých zemí za kapitalismu, Vol. I., 1780-1918, Opava, 1987.

Půlpán, K., Nástin českých a československých hospodářských dějin do r. 1990, Vols. I-II., Praha, 1993

Purš, J., Průmyslová reVoluce. Vývoj pojmu a koncepce, Praha, 1973.

Rudolph, R. L., Banking and Industrialization in Austria-Hungary. The Role of Banks in the Industrialization of the Czech Crownlands, 1873-1914, Cambridge-London-New York-Melbourne, 1976.

Rumpler, H., Eine Chance für Mitteleuropa. Bürgerliche Emanzipation und Staatsverfall in der Habsburgermonarchie. (Wolfram, H. [ed.], Österreichische Geschichte 1804-1914, Vol. 1), Wien, 1997.

Sandgruber, R., Ökonomie und Politik. Österreichische Wirtschaftsgeschichte vom Mittelalter bis zur Gegenwart, Wien, 2005.

Sandgruber, R., Wirtschaftswachstum, Energie und Verkehr in Österreich 1840-1913, in: Kellenbenz, H. (Ed.), Wirtschaftliches Wachstum, Energie und Verkehr vom Mittelalter bis ins 19. Jahrhundert: Bericht über die 6. Arbeitstagung der Gesellschaft für Sozial- und Wirtschaftsgeschichte, Stuttgart-New York 1978, pp. 67-93.

Schlumbohm, J., Kriedte, P., Medick, H., Industrialisierung vor der Industrialisierung. Gewerbliche Warenproduktion auf dem Land in der Formationsperiode des Kapitalismus, Göttingen, 1977.

Schröder, W. H., R. Spree (Ed.), Historische Konjunkturforschung, Stuttgart, 1980.

Šedivý, I., Češi, české země a velká válka 1914-1918, 2nd Ed., 2014.

Seibt, F. (Ed.), Böhmen im 19. Jahrhundert. Vom Klassizismus zur Moderne, München-Berlin-Frankfurt (M), 1995.

Semotanová, E., Atlas českých dějin. 2 Vols., 3rd Ed., Praha, 2020-2023.

Semotanová, E., Cajthaml, J. (Eds.), Akademický atlas českých dějin, Praha, 2014.

Štaif, J. (Ed.), Moderní podnikatelské elity. Metody a perspektivy bádání, Praha, 2007.

Tapié, V.L., The Rise and Fall of Habsburg Monarchy, London, 1971.

Taylor, A. J. P., The Habsburg Monarchy 1809-1918. A History of the Austrian Empire and Austria-Hungary, 2nd Ed., London, 1969.

Teich, M., Porter, R. (Eds.), Industrial Revolution in national Context, Cambridge, 1996.

Tinková, D., Osvícenství v českých zemích. I., Formování moderního státu (1740-1792), Praha, 2022.

Válka, J., "Le grand domaine féodal en Bohème et en Moravie du 16e au 18e siècle. Un type d'économie parasitaire", in: Gunst, P., Hoffmann, T. (Eds.), Grands domaines et petites exploitations en Europe au moyen age et dans les temps modernes, Budapest, 1982, pp. 289-315.

Velková, A., Krutá vrchnost, ubozí poddaní?: proměny venkovské rodiny a společnosti v 18. a první polovině 19. století na příkladu západočeského panství Šťáhlavy, Praha, 2009.

Uhlirz, K., Handbuch der Geschichte Oesterreichs und seiner Nachbarländer Böhmen und Mähren, Vol. II. 1848-1914, Graz-Wien-Leipzig, 1941.

Urban, O., Die tschechische Gesellschaft 1848 bis 1918, Wien-Köln-Weimar, 1994.

Urbanec, V., Příspěvek k dějinám akciových společností v českých zemích, Praha 2005, doctoral dissertaion FF UK.

Wallerstein, I., Das moderne Weltsystem. Kapitalistische Landwirtschaft und die Entstehung der europäischen

Wegs, R. J., Die österreichische Kriegswirtschaft 1914–1918, Wien, 1979.

Zanden, van J., L., The Long Road to the Industrial Revolution. The European Economy in a Global Perspective 1000–1800, Leiden–Boston, 2009.

Županič, J., Židovská šlechta podunajské monarchie. Mezi Davidovou hvězdou a křížem, Praha, 2012.

Županič, J., Nová šlechta Rakouského císařství, Praha, 2006.

Županič, J., Fiala M., Nobilitas iudaeorum: židovská šlechta střední Evropy v komparativní perspektivě, Praha, 2017.

INSTITUTIONAL AND LEGAL FRAMEWORK

Boldt, H., Deutsche Verfassungsgeschichte, Vol. 2, München, 1990.

Gruber, J., O vývoji živnostenského zákonodárství v Rakousku a o cílech reformy živnostenské, Praha, 1904.

Gruber, J., Obchodní a živnostenská komora v Praze v prvním půlstoletí svého trvání 1850–1900, Praha, 1900.

Grulich, P., Obchodní a živnostenské komory 1918–1938, Hradec Králové, 2006.

Jindra, Z., Národnostní složení úřednictva centrálních úřadů v habsburské monarchii a v Předlitavsku podle šetření k 1. lednu 1914, in: Štaif, J. (Ed.), Pocta profesoru Zdeňku Kárníkovi. Sborník příspěvků k jubilantovým sedmdesátinám, AUC Philosophica et historica /1999, studia historica LI, Praha, 2003, pp. 71–88.

Jiránek, T., Projevy hospodářského nacionalismu v obchodních a živnostenských komorách v Českých zemích 1850–1918, Pardubice, 2004.

Krameš, J., Kameralismus a klasická ekonomie v Čechách, Praha, 1998.

Malý, K. et al., Dějiny českého a československého práva do roku 1945, 2. Ed., Praha, 1999

Myška, M., "Celní politika rakousko-uherské monarchie (se zvláštním zřetelem k hutnímu železářskému průmyslu) 1850 až 1914", Časopis Matice moravské, 1999, Vol. 98, No. 118, 48–50.

Nevšímal, A. V., Jaké a jak velké jsou nové daně?, Praha, 1897.

Randa, A., Soukromé obchodní právo rakouské, Praha, 1908.

Skřejpková, P., K dějinám obchodu a vzniku obchodního práva, Právněhistorické studie, 1997, Vol. 34, pp. 183–198.

Urfus, V., Zdomácnění směnečného práva v českých zemích a počátky novodobého práva obchodního, Praha, 1959.

Zápas o většinu v pražské obchodní a živnostenské komoře, Praha, 1905.

100 Jahre im Dienste der Wirtschaft, Wien, 1961.

DEMOGRAPHIC DEVELOPMENT

Bachinger, K., Hemelsberger-Koller, H., Matis, H. (Ed.), Grundriss der österreichischen Sozial- und Wirtschaftsgeschichte von 1848 bis zur Gegenwart, Wien, 1987, pp. 8–39.

Bruckmüller, E., Sozialgeschichte Österreichs, Wien–München, 2001.

Dlouhodobé populační trendy na území ČSR (předstatistické období), Acta demographica IV, Praha, 1981.

Englová, J., "Women's Working Activities in the Austrian Industrial Production in the Seventies and Eighties of the 19th Century", Hospodářské dějiny – Economic History, 1990, Vol. 18, pp. 185–209.

Horská, P. et al., Dějiny obyvatelstva českých zemí, 2. Ed., Praha, 1998.

Horská, P., Maur, E., Musil, J., Zrod velkoměsta. Urbanizace českých zemí a Evropa, Praha–Litomyšl, 2002.

Hubbard, W. H., Der Wachstumsprozess in den österreichischen Gross-Städten 1869–1910. Eine historisch-demographische Untersuchung, in: Ludz, P. Ch. (Ed.), Soziologie und Sozialgeschichte. Aspekte und Probleme, Kölner Zeitschrift für Soziologie und Sozialpsychologie, 1972, Sonderheft 16.

K novověkým sociálním dějinám českých zemí, Vols. II–IV, Praha, 1998–2001.

Kárníková, L., Vývoj obyvatelstva v českých zemích 1754–1914, Praha, 1965.

Kořalka, J., Češi v habsburské říši a v Evropě 1815–1914. Sociálněhistorické souvislosti vytváření novodobého národa a národnostní otázky v českých zemích, Praha, 1996.

Kořalka, J., Crampton, R. J., Die Tschechen, in: Wandruszka, A., Urbanitsch, P. (Ed.) Die Habsburgermonarchie 1848–1918, Vol. III/1, Wien, 1980, pp. 489–521.

Machačová, J., Matějček, J., Nástin sociálního vývoje českých zemí 1781–1914, Opava, 2002.

Melinz, G., Zimmermann, S. (Ed.), Wien – Prag – Budapest. Blütezeit der Habsburgermetropolen. Urbanisierung, Kommunalpolitik, gesellschaftliche Konflikte (1867 –1918), Wien, 1896.

Srb, V., Tisíc let obyvatel českých zemí, Praha, 2004.

Šubrtová, A., Dějiny populačního myšlení a populačních teorií, Praha, 1989.

Urbanisierung, Kommunalpolitik, gesellschaftliche Konflikte (1867 –1918), Wien, 1996.

DEVELOPMENT OF THE PRIMARY SECTOR – AGRICULTURE

Albert, E., Ekonomika moravského zemědělství v druhé polovině 19. století, Prameny historie zemědělství a lesnictví, Vols. 8–9, Praha, 1970.

Bairoch, P., Landwirtschaft und Industrielle ReVolution 1700–1914, in: Cipolla, C. M., Borchardt, K. (Ed.), Europäische Wirtschaftsgeschichte, Vol. 3, Stuttgart, 1977, pp. 203–235.

Balcarová, J., Kubů, E., Šouša, J., (Eds.), Venkov, rolník a válka v českých zemích a na Slovensku v moderní době, Praha, 2017.

Černý, B., Vývoj lihovarnictví v českých zemích. (Příspěvek k dějinám zemědělství), ČsČH, 1957, Vol. 5, No. 4, pp. 688–727.

Franěk, R., Základní tendence vývoje zemědělské výroby v Čechách na konci 19. a na počátku 20. století, Sborník historický 20, 1973, pp. 55–105.

Hanslian, A., Dějiny vývoje užitkových domácích zvířat, Praha, 1925.

Jeleček, L., Zemědělství a půdní fond v Čechách ve 2. polovině 19. století, Praha, 1985.

Křivka, J., Výnosy zemědělských plodin a sklizňová statistika v Čechách v letech 1870–1913, Prameny a studie, Vol. 32, Praha, 1989.

Kubačák, A., Dějiny zemědělství v českých zemích, 2 Vols., Praha, 1994–1995.

Kubačák, A., Společenské a hospodářské poměry po roce 1848 ve spojení s činností Františka Horského, Tradice, vzdělávání a pokrok, Vol. 3, Praha, 1993.

Kubačák, A., Beranová, M., Dějiny zemědělství v Čechách a na Moravě, Praha, 2010.

Kubů E. et al., Za německou hroudu a zrno: agrární hnutí Němců v českých zemích období habsburské monarchie: od hospodářských společností, odborných i politických spolků a exkluzivních politických reprezentací k agrárnímu stranictví (1848–1918), Praha, 2023.

Kutnar, F., Cesta selského lidu ke svobodě, Praha, 1948.

Lom, F., Československé zemědělství od roku 1848, Věstník Československé akademie zemědělské, 1939, Vol. 15.

Lom F., Dějinný vývoj změn organizační struktury zemědělských podniků v letech 1750–1914 v Čechách, Vědecké práce Československého zemědělského muzea, Vol. 16, Praha, 1978.

Lom, F., Přehled dějin zemědělské výroby v českých zemích, Praha, 1972.

Purš, J., Die Entwicklung des Kapitalismus in der Landwirtschaft der böhmischen Länder in der Zeit von 1849 bis 1879, Jahrbuch für Wirtschaftsgeschichte, 1963, pp. 31–96.

Reich, E., Základy organisace československého zemědělství, Praha, 1934.

Roubík, F., K vyvazení gruntů v Čechách v letech 1848–1853, Sborník archivních prací, 1959, Vol. 9.

Šmelhaus, V., Základní problémy vývoje zemědělství v Českých zemích v období 1750–1850, Vědecké práce zemědělského muzea, Vol. 19, Praha, 1979.

Šouša, J., K vývoji českého zemědělství na rozhraní 19. a 20. století, AUC Philosophica et Historica, XCVII, Praha, 1986, pp. 124–132.

Šouša, J., Miller, D. E., Hrabik Samal, M. (Eds.), K úloze a významu agrárního hnutí v českých a československých dějinách, Praha, 2001.

Tempír, Z., Zemědělství, in: Jílek, F. (Ed.), Studie o technice v českých zemích, díl I.–II., 1800–1918, Praha, 1983–1984.

Verbík, A., Zemědělské instituce v letech 1848–1900 v českých zemích, Vědecké práce Zemědělského muzea, Vol. 18, Praha, 1979.

Vilikovský, V., Dějiny zemědělského průmyslu v Československu od nejstarších dob až do vypuknutí světové hospodářské krise, Praha, 1936.

DEVELOPMENT OF THE SECONDARY SECTOR – INDUSTRY

Bednář, K., Rozmístění průmyslu v českých zemích na počátku 20. století (1902), Praha, 1970.

Brousek, K. M., Die Großindustrie Böhmens 1848–1918, München, 1987.

Dějiny hutnictví železa v Československu, sv. 2. Od průmyslové reVoluce do konce 2. světové války, Praha 1986.

Dílo sedmi generací. 150 let Spolku pro chemickou a hutní výrobu v Ústí nad Labem, Ústí nad Labem, 2008.

Dudek, F., Vývoj cukrovarnického průmyslu v českých zemích do roku 1872, Praha, 1979.

Dudek, F., Vývoj struktury průmyslu v českých zemích za kapitalismu, Slezský sborník, 1988, Vol. 86, No. 4, pp. 252–269.

Efmertová, M., Elektrotechnika v českých zemích a v Československu do poloviny 20. století. Studie k vývoji elektrotechnických oborů, Praha, 1999.

Englová, J., Spolek pro chemickou a hutní výrobu v Ústí nad Labem, in: Kaiserová, K., Kaiser, V. (Eds.), Dějiny města Ústí nad Labem, Ústí nad Labem, 1995, pp. 110–115.

Englová, J., Základní podmínky úspěšného velkopodnikání Spolku pro chemickou a hutní výrobu v Ústí nad Labem v letech 1857–1873, Sborník Severočeského muzea, Historia, 1986, Vol. 8, PP. 45–53.

Hlavačka, M., Kopáček, J. (Eds.), Lanna et Lanna: rodina a podnikání, Praha, 2022.

Hlavačka, M. et al., Fenomén Ringhoffer: rodina, podnikání, politika. 2. Ed., Praha, 2021.

Horská-Vrbová, P., Český průmysl a tzv. druhá průmyslová reVoluce, Praha, 1965.

Horská-Vrbová, P., Počátky elektrisace v českých zemích, Praha, 1961.

Hwaletz, O., Die österreichische Montanindustrie im 19. und 20. Jahrh., Wien–Köln–Weimar, 2001.

Jakubec, I., Zur Einführung des Thomas-Verfahrens in den böhmischen Ländern, in: Rasch, M. - Mass, J. (Ed.) Das Thomas-Verfahren in Europa. Entstehung – Entwicklung – Ende, Essen 2009, pp. 213–240.

Janák, J., Hospodářský rozmach Moravy 1740–1918, Dějiny Moravy díl 3/1, Vlastivěda moravská, Země a lid, Nová řada, Vol. 7, Brno, 1999.

Jílek, F. (Ed.), Studie o technice v českých zemích 1800–1918, Vol. I–IV, Praha, 1983–1986.

Jindra, Z., Průmyslové monopoly v Rakousko-Uhersku (Některé hlavní rysy vývoje do počátku světové války.), ČsČH, 1956, Vol. 4, No. 2, pp. 231–270.

Kárníková, L., Vývoj uhelného průmyslu v českých zemích do r. 1880, Praha, 1960.

Kořan, J., Vývoj výroby železa v českých zemích v údobí průmyslové reVoluce, Praha, 1978.

Křížek, J., Krize cukrovarnictví v českých zemích v 80. letech minulého století a její význam pro vzrůst rolnického hnutí, ČsČH, 1956, Vol. 4, pp. 270–298; 1957, Vol. 5, pp. 473–506; 1958, Vol. 6, pp. 46–59.

Mrázek, O., Vývoj průmyslu v českých zemích a na Slovensku od manufaktury do roku 1918, Praha, 1964.

Myška, M., Die mährisch-schlesische Eisenindustrie in der Industriellen ReVolution, Praha, 1970.

Myška, M., Založení a počátky Vítkovických železáren (1828–1880), Ostrava, 1960.

Myška, M. et al., Historická encyklopedie podnikatelů Čech, Moravy a Slezska do poloviny
    XX. století, 2 Vol., Ostrava, 2003 a 2008 (HEP).
Otruba, G., Kvantitative, strukturelle und regionale Dynamik des Industrialisierungsprozesses
    in Österreich-Ungarn vom Ausgang des 18. Jahrhunderts bis zum Ausbruch des Ersten Welt-
    krieges, in: Winkel, H. (Ed.), Vom Kleingewerbe zum Grossindustrie, Berlin, 1975.
Popelka, P., Zrod moderního podnikatelstva. Bratři Kleinové a podnikatelé v českých zemích
    a Rakouském císařství v éře kapitalistické industrializace, Ostrava, 2011.
Purš, J., Průmyslová reVoluce v českých zemích, Praha, 1960.
Purš, J., Struktur und Dynamik der industriellen Entwicklung in Böhmen im letzten Viertel des
    18. Jahrhunderts, Berlin, 1965.
Smrček, O., Kapitoly z dějin strojírenství, Praha, 1992.
Smutný, B., Šest studií k dějinám lnářství na Trutnovsku, in: Lnářský průmysl. Supplementum,
    Vol. 3., 1983
Uhelné hornictví v ČSSR, Ostrava, 1985.
Vrbová, P., Hlavní otázky vzniku a vývoje českého strojírenství do roku 1918, Praha, 1959.
Zářický, A., Rothschildové a ti druzí aneb dějiny velkopodnikání v Rakouském Slezsku před
    první světovou válkou, Ostrava, 2005.

DEVELOPMENT OF THE TERTIARY SECTOR – TRANSPORT
AND COMMUNICATIONS

Artl, G., Gürtlich, G., Zenz, H., Sisi auf Schienen. 150 Jahre Westbahn Wien–Linz, Wien, 2008.
Artl, G., Gürtlich, G., Zenz, H. (Ed.), Allerhöchste Eisenbahn. 170 Jahre Nordbahn Wien–Brünn,
    Wien, 2009.
Artl, G., Gürtlich, G., Zenz, H. (Ed.), Mit Volldamf in den Süden. 150 Jahre Südbahn Wien –
    Triest, Wien, 2008.
Bek, P. et al., Historie státních drah = História štátnych dráh: 1918–2018, Praha, 2018.
Brunner, J., Hajn, I., Lexikon koněspřežních železnic, České Budějovice, 2007.
Čtvrtník, P., Galuška, J., Tošnerová, P., Poštovnictví v Čechách, na Moravě a ve Slezsku, Liberec,
    2008.
D'Elvert, Ch., Geschichte der Verkehrs-Anstalten in Mähren und Oesterr. Schlesien, Brünn,
    1855.
Denkschrift zu dem Entwurfe eines neuen Eisenbahnnetzes der österreichischen Monarchie,
    Wien, 1864.
Die ersten fünfzig Jahre der Kaiser Ferdinands-Nordbahn 1836–1886, Wien, 1886.
Dušek, P., Encyklopedie městské dopravy v Čechách, na Moravě a ve Slezsku, Praha, 2003.
Eder, A., Die Eisenbahnpolitik Oesterreichs nach ihren finanziellen Ergebnisse, Wien, 1894.
Geschichte der Eisenbahnen der Österreichisch-Ungarischen Monarchie, Vols. I – VI, Wien-
    Teschen–Leipzig, 1898–1913.
Gutkas, K., Bruckmüller, E. (Ed.), Verkehrswege und Eisenbahnen. Beiträge zur Verkehrs-
    geschichte Österreichs aus Anlaß des Jubiläums „150 Jahre Dampfeisenbahn in Österreich",
    Wien, 1989.
Haberer, T., Geschichte des Eisenbahnwesens, Wien, 1884.
Hajn, I., Koněspřežní železnice České Budějovice - Linec - Gmunden, České Budějovice, 2004.
Helmedach, A., Das Verkehrssystem als Modernisierungsfaktor. Strassen, Post, Fuhrwesen
    und Reisen nach Triest und Fiume vom Beginn des 18. Jahrhunderts bis zum Eisenbahnzeit-
    alter, München, 2002.
Hlavačka, M., Cestování v éře dostavníku. Všední den na středoevropských cestách, Praha,
    1996.
Hlavačka, M., Dějiny dopravy v českých zemích v období průmyslové reVoluce, Praha, 1990.
Hons, J., Dějiny dopravy na území ČSSR, Bratislava, 1975.
Hons, J., František Antonín Gerstner, Praha, 1948.
Hons, J. et al., Čtení o severní dráze císaře Ferdinanda, Praha, 1991.

Hubert, M., Dějiny plavby v Čechách I.-II., Děčín, 1996–1997.
Jakubec, I., Idea Dunajsko-oderského průplavu v 19. a 20. století a její proměny, in: Rossová, M. (Ed.), Integration und Desintegration in Mitteleuropa. Pläne und Realität, Praha–München 2009, pp. 235–256.
Kladiwa, P., Elektrifikace municipalit na Moravě a v Rakouském Slezsku do první světové války, in: Kladiwa, P., Zářický, A. (Eds.), Město a městská společnost v procesu modernizace 1740–1918, Ostrava, 2009, pp. 342–358.
Komlosy, A., Bůžek, V., Svátek, F. (Eds.), Kulturen an der Grenze. Waldviertel, Weinviertel, Südböhmen, Südmähren, Wien–Waidhofen an der Thaya, 1995.
Krejčiřík, M., Kleinové. Historie moravské podnikatelské rodiny, Brno, 2010.
Krejčiřík, M., Po stopách našich železnic, Praha, 1991.
Losos, L., Dějiny městské hromadné dopravy, Praha, 1983.
Mechtler, P., Die österreichische Eisenbahnpolitik in Italien (1835–1866), Mitteilungen des Österreichischen Staatsarchives, 1961, Vol. 14, pp. 424–451.
Merkl, Ch. M., Verkehrsgeschichte und Mobilität, Stuttgart, 2008.
Pavlíček, S., Naše lokálky. Místní dráhy v Čechách, na Moravě a ve Slezsku, Praha, 2002.
Popelka, P., Zrod moderní dopravy. Modernizace dopravní infrastruktury v Rakouském Slezsku do vypuknutí první světové války, Ostrava, 2013.
Popelka, P., Závodná, M., Nacionální, politické a integrační faktory městské dopravy v moravských městech do roku 1914, Časopis Matice moravské, 2012, Vol. 131, pp. 341–366.
Pošvář, J., Dopravní politika na Moravě a ve Slezsku v 18. a 1. polovině 19. století, Studie o Těšínsku, 1973, Vol. 2, pp. 286–309.
Reisinger, N., Franz Riepl und die Anfänge des österreichischen Eisenbahnwesens, in: Ebner, H. (Ed.), Forschungen zur Geschichte des Alpen-Adria-Raumes, Graz, 1997, pp. 307–332.
Reisinger, N., Franz Riepl und seine Bedeutung für die Entwicklung des österreichischen Eisenbahnwesen, Graz, 1999.
Říha, Z., Fojtík, P., Jak se tvoří město. Vývoj dopravního systému Prahy v období průmyslové reVoluce, Praha, 2012.
Roth, R., VerkehrsreVolutionen in: Sieder, R., Langthaler, E. (Ed.), Globalgeschichte 1800–2010, Wien, 2010, pp. 471–501.
Roubík, F., Od nosítek k trolejbusu, Praha, 1956.
Roubík, F., Silnice v Čechách a jejich vývoj, Praha, 1938.
Šmoldas, Z., Naše první křídla, Praha, 1955.
Šmoldas, Z., Průkopníci českého letectví, Hradec Králové, 1984.
Statuten der k. k. priv. Kaiser Ferdinands-Nordbahn, Wien, 1886.
Štemberk, J., Automobilista v zajetí reality. Vývoj pravidel silničního provozu v českých zemích v první polovině 20. století, Praha, 2008.
Štemberk, J., Podnikání v automobilové dopravě v českých zemích v první polovině 20. století, Acta Universitatis Carolinae Philosophica et Historica – Monographia CLXV/2007, Praha, 2010.
Štěpán, M., Přehledné dějiny československých železnic 1824–1948, Praha, 1958.
Sviták, P., První český letec inženýr Jan Kašpar a začátky českého letectví, Pardubice, 2003.
Wagner, T., Entstehung, Wesen und Betrieb der auf der Karl Graf von Buquoyschen Domäne Gratzen in Böhmen bestehenden künstlichen Trift und Flösserei des Brenn- und Rundholzes, Gratzen, 1913.
Žákavec, T., Lanna. Příspěvek k dějinám hospodářského vývoje v Čechách a v Československu, Praha, 1936.
Závodná, M., Koleje a město. Problematika městské kolejové dopravy ve vybraných moravských a slezských městech v letech 1850–1918, Ostrava, 2016.
Železnice, Čech, Moravy a Slezska, Praha, 1995.
Ziegler, D., Eisenbahnen und Staat im Zeitalter der Industrialisierung, Stuttgart, 1996.

DEVELOPMENT OF THE TERTIARY SECTOR – TRADE

Albrecht, C., Chambers of Commerce and Czech-German Relations in the Late Nineteenth Century, Bohemia, Vol. 38 (1997), pp. 298–310.
Brodesser, S. et al., Celnictví v Československu, Praha, 1982.
Čechura, J., Hlavačka, M., Handel und Kommunikationen in den böhmischen Ländern vom Mittelalter bis zur industriellen ReVolutionen, in: Gyimesi, S. (Ed.), Der Binnenhandel und die wirtschaftliche Entwicklung, Budapest, 1989, pp. 200–240.
Chylík, J., Vývoj zahraničního obchodu v našich zemích, Praha, 1947.
Gruber, J., Obchodní a živnostenská komora v Praze v prvním půlstoletí svého trvání 1850–1900 k oslavě jejího padesátiletého jubilea, Praha, 1900.
Gruß, O., Ein Jahrhundert österr. Binnenhandel, in: Mayer, H., Hundert Jahre österr. Wirtschaftsentwicklung 1848–1948, Wien 1948, pp. 310–359.
Hotowetz, R., Zahraniční obchod československého státu, Praha, 1920.
Jakubec, I., Bildung der Handelseliten am Beispiel der Prager Handels- und Gewerbekammer, Prager wirtschafts- und sozialhistorische Mitteilungen/Prague economic and social history papers, 2007/2008, Vol. 8, pp. 21–31.
Jakubec, I., K problematice zahraničního obchodu rakousko-uherské monarchie v letech 1850–1914, in: Harna, J., Prokš, P. (Ed.), Studie k moderním dějinám. Sborník prací k 70. narozeninám Vlastislava Laciny, Praha, 2001, pp. 33–50.
Janda, J., O podmínkách exportu, zvláště českého, Praha s.a. (1913)
Meyer, Ch., Exportförderungpolitik in Österreich, Wien-Köln-Weimar, 1991.
Myška, M., Breda & Weinstein. (Kapitoly z dějin opavského obchodního domu 1898–1998), Opava, 1998.
Myška, M., "Celní politika rakousko-uherské monarchie (se zvláštním zřetelem k hutnímu železářskému průmyslu) 1850 až 1914", Časopis Matice moravské, 1999, Vol. 98, no. 119, 27–96.
Myška, M., Zahraniční obchod železem a hutními výrobky v rakousko-uherské monarchii v období 1830–1914, Historica, 1999, Vol. 7, Universitas Ostraviensis – Acta facultatis philosophicae, Vol. 182, pp. 37–109.
Rendoš, L., Kapitoly z vývoja obchodu, Bratislava, 1979.
Starzyczná, H., Steiner, J., Maloobchod v českých zemích v proměnách let 1918–2000, Karviná, 2000.
Tessner, M., Der Aussenhandel Österreich-Ungarns von 1867 bis 1913, Köln, 1989.
Třicet let české zemědělské družstevní práce, Praha, 1928.

DEVELOPMENT OF THE TERTIARY SECTOR – MONEY AND CREDIT SYSTEM

Chylík, J., "První obchodní banka u nás", Časopis Matice moravské, 1950, Vol. 69, 261–282.
Corti, E. C., Rothschildové, Praha, 1931.
Ein Jahrhundert Creditanstalt-Bankverein, Wien, 1957.
Fejfar, F., Peněžní ústavy v království Českém roku 1897, Praha, 1899.
Ferguson, N., The House of Rothschild, Vol. I, New York, 1999.
Fritz, H., 150 Jahre Sparkassen in Österreich, Vol. 1, Geschichte, Wien, 1972.
Hájek, J., Bankovnictví v českých zemích před první světovou válkou jako základ bankovního systému meziválečného Československa, Hospodářské dějiny – Economic History, 1992, Vol. 20, pp. 75–86.
Hájek, J., Bankovnictví v českých zemích v 50. a 60. letech 19. století, Hospodářské dějiny – Economic History, 1999, Vol. 22, pp. 83–106.
Hájek, J, Nejrozšířenější peněžní ústav v našich zemích: Poštovní spořitelna 1883–1945, AUC – Philosophica et historica 5/1997, Studia historica XLVII, Praha, 2000, pp. 79–92.
Hájek, J., Počátky a rozmach českého záloženského hnutí ve třetí čtvrtině 19. století, Hospodářské dějiny – Economic History, 1984, Vol. 12, pp. 265–320.

Hájek, J., Rozvoj národnostně českých bank od konce 19. století do roku 1914, Praha, 1986.

Hájek, J., Vzájemný poměr a velikostní struktura českých a národnostně německých akciových bank v českých zemích v letech 1900-1924. Příspěvek k metodice statistického srovnání, in: Pocta profesoru Zdeňku Jindrovi, AUC Philosophica et Historica 3 - 1998, Studia historica L, Praha, 2003, pp. 149-165.

Hájek, J., 180 let českého spořitelnictví - 180 Years of the Czech Savings System - 180 Jahre des tschechischen Sparkassenwesens. Česká spořitelna 1825-2005, Praha, 2005.

Hájek, J., Lacina, V. Od úvěrních družstev k bankovním koncernům, Praha, 1999.

Horák, J., Přehled vývoje českých obchodních bank, Praha, 1913.

Jakubec, I., Hospodářské výsledky Ústřední jednoty hospodářských družstev v prvním čtvrtstoletí jejího trvání (1896-1918), in: Půl století hospodářských dějin. Sborník k 75. narozeninám prof. Ing. Václava Průchy, CSc., Acta Oeconomica Pragensia, 2007, Vol. 15, No. 7, pp. 176-193.

Janák, J., Moravské záložny od vydání družstevního zákona v roce 1873 do roku 1880, Sborník prací filozofické fakulty brněnské univerzity, C 35, 1988, pp. 71-85.

Janák, J., "Spořitelny na Moravě a úvěrování průmyslu a živností v 19. století", Časopis Matice moravské, 1994, Vol. 113, 145-155.

Jindra, Z., Das Bankwesen in Ost- und Mitteleuropa 1914-1945, in: Das Bankwesen in Ost- und Mitteleuropa. Beiheft 24 des Bankhistorischen Archivs, Frankfurt a. M., 1993, pp. 34-47.

Jindra, Z., Ekonomická krize a sanace Záložního úvěrního ústavu v Hradci Králové v letech první světové války, Hospodářské dějiny - Economic History, 2010, Vol. 25, pp. 41-62, 125-148.

Jindra, Z., Proces koncentrace bankovního kapitálu v Předlitavsku, zvláště v českých zemích do r. 1914, Hospodářské dějiny - Economic History, 2009, Vol. 24, pp. 49-110.

John, V., Die Vorschuss- und Credit-Verein in Böhmen, Prag, 1870.

Juřík, P., Historie bank a spořitelen v Čechách, na Moravě a ve Slezsku, Praha, 2011.

Klier, Č., České spořitelnictví v zemích koruny české do roku 1906, Praha, 1908.

Kratochvíl, K., Bankéři, Praha, 1962.

Kubů, E., Za sjednocenou nacionálně českou bankovní frontu (Založení Svazu českých bank a jeho činnost v období rakousko-uherské monarchie), in: Z dějin českého bankovnictví v 19. a 20. století, Praha, 2000, pp. 139-162.

Kubů, E., Šouša, J. (Eds.), Finanční elity v českých zemích (Československu) 19. a 20. století, Praha, 2008.

Lacina, V., Živnostenská banka před a během první světové války (1907-1918), ČČH, 1990, Vol. 88, pp. 276-303.

Marvan, M. et al., Dějiny pojišťovnictví v Československu, 1. Vol. Dějiny pojišťovnictví v Československu do roku 1918, Praha, 1989.

Morton, F., Rothschildové. Portrét jedné dynastie, Praha - Litomyšl, 2011.

Nečas, C., Český finanční kapitál a česká buržoazní politika před r. 1914, Sborník prací filozofické fakulty brněnské univerzity, series C 33, 1986, pp. 71-78.

Nečas, S., Podnikání českých bank v cizině 1898-1918. Rozpínavost českého bankovního kapitálu ve střední, jihovýchodní a východní Evropě v období rakousko-uherského imperialismu, MU, Spisy FF, Vol. 295, Brno, 1993.

Novotný, J., Šouša, J., Banka ve znamení zeleného čtyřlístku. Agrární banka 1911-1938 (1948), Praha, 1996.

Nožička, J., Jak vznikly naše kampeličky, Praha, 1939.

Plecháček, I., K dějinám spořitelnictví v Československu, Praha, 1983.

Prokš, P., Pozice českého kapitálu v Rakousko-Uhersku v letech 1890-1914, in: Harna, J., Prokš, P. (Eds.), Studie k moderním dějinám. Sborník prací k 70. narozeninám Vlastislava Laciny, Praha, 2001, pp. 51-78.

Rauchberg, H., Die deutschen Sparkassen in Böhmen, Prag, 1906.

Růžička, O., Banky, jejich vývoj, funkce a politika, Praha, 1924.

Schmidt, W., Das Sparkassenwesen in Österreich, Wien, 1930.

Schreyer, J., Dějiny svépomocných záložen českých, Praha, 1891.

Sedlák, J., České spořitelní a záložní spolky dle soustavy Raiffeisenovy, Praha, 1902.

Silin, N., Rakousko-uherská banka, Praha, 1920.

Slávík, J. E., Spořitelnictví a jeho snahy opravné, Praha, 1908.

Somary, F., Die Aktiengesellschaften in Österreich, Wien, 1902.

Šouša, J., Jindra, Z. (Ed.), Z dějin českého bankovnictví v 19. a 20. století, Praha, 2000.

Vencovský, F., Jindra, Z., Novotný, J. aj., Dějiny bankovnictví v českých zemích, Praha, 1999.

Vondra, R., Peníze v moderních českých dějinách, Praha, 2012.

Wilson, D., Rothschildové. Příběh bohatství a moci, Praha, 1993.

Ženíšek, B., Vznik a vývoj Hypoteční banky království Českého 1865–1915, Praha, 1915.

Živnostenská banka v Praze 1869–1918, Praha, 1919.

ECONOMIC AND TECHNICAL CULTURE

Birk, A., Die deutsche Technische Hochschule in Prag 1806–1931, Prague, 1931.

Boehm, J. J., Die Deutsche Technische Hochschule in Prag und ihre Vorstufen. Zweieinviertel Jahrhunderte akademische deutsche Ingenieurausbildung (1718–1945), München, 1991.

Dějiny Univerzity Karlovy, sv. 3, Praha, 1997.

Efmertová, M., Jakubec, I., Josefovičová, M., Vývoj pražské německé techniky (1863–1945), Moderní dějiny, Praha, 2006, Vol. 14, pp. 5–50.

Farský, F., Stručný přehled vývoje školství a vyučování hospodářského vůbec v království Českém do roku 1918. Období 1728–1884, Praha, 1922.

Franěk, O., Dějiny české vysoké školy technické v Brně do roku 1945. 2 Vols., Brno, 1969–1975.

Jílek, F., Horská-Vrbová, P., Lomič, V., Dějiny ČVUT, Vol. 1., Pt. 2, Praha, 1973, 1978.

Mansfeld, B. (Ed.), Průvodce světem techniky, Praha, 1937.

Mikeš, J., Efmertová, M., Elektřina na dlani. Kapitoly z historie elektrotechniky v českých zemích, Praha, 2008.

Nešpor, V., Dějiny university olomoucké, Olomouc, 1947.

Petráň, J., Nástin dějin Filozofické fakulty Univerzity Karlovy, Praha, 1983.

Pokorný, J., Novotný, J. (Eds.), Česká akademie věd a umění 1891–1991, Praha 1993.

Sedmdesát let technické práce, Praha, 1935.

Schejbal, C. et al., Historie a současnost báňského školství v českých zemích, Ostrava, 1996.

Tayerlová, M. et al., Česká technika = Czech Technical University, 2. přeprac. vyd., Praha, 2004.

Velflík, A. A., Dějiny ČVUT, Praha, 1906.

STATISTICAL SOURCES AND LITERATURE

Bráf, A., Geschichte und Ergebnisse der zentralen amtlichen Statistik in Österreich 1829–1979.

Beiträge zur österreichischen Statistik, Heft 550, Wien, 1979.

Großmann, H., Die Anfänge und geschichtliche Entwicklung der amtlichen Statistik in Österreich, Statistische Monatschrift, 1916, pp. 331–423.

Krejčí, D., Statistika v publikacích sněmu a zemského výboru král. českého v l. 1895–1900, Sborník věd právních a státních, 1902, Vol. 2, pp. 253–256.

Laník, J., Počátky městské statistiky v Rakousku, ČsČH, 1989, Vol. 37, no. 2, pp. 235–250.

Lišková, M., Manufakturní tabely v Čechách a jejich využití, Hospodářské dějiny – Economic History, 1989, Vol. 16, pp. 183–210.

Mašek, F., Pozemkový katastr, Praha, 1948.

Podzimek, J., Vývoj čs. statistiky do vzniku Státního úřadu statistického, Praha, 1974.

Rauchberg, H., Der nationale Besitzstand in Böhmen, Leipzig, 1905.

Rauchberg, H., Die Bevölkerung Österreichs auf Grund der Ergebnisse der Volkszählung vom 31. Dezember 1890, Wien, 1895.

Sandgruber, A., The Decline and Fall of the Habsburg Empire 1815–1918, London-New York, 1989.

Stabilní katastr. Obraz zemědělství v Čechách v polovině 19. století z pohledu oceňovacího operátu, Praha, Geodetický ústav 1979, 2. Ed., 1988.

Weber, L., Die zahlenmäßige Entwicklung der Völker Österreichs 1846–1910, Statistische Monatschrift, 1915, pp. 589–721.

Zur Geschichte der amtlichen Statistik in Österreich: Denkschrift der k. k. Statistischen Zentralkommission zur Feier ihres fünfzigjährigen Bestandes, Wien, 1913.

8. APPENDICES

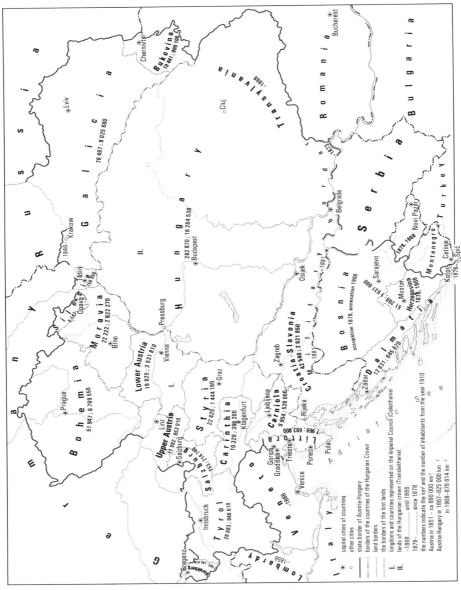

Map showing the administrative organisation of Austria-Hungary

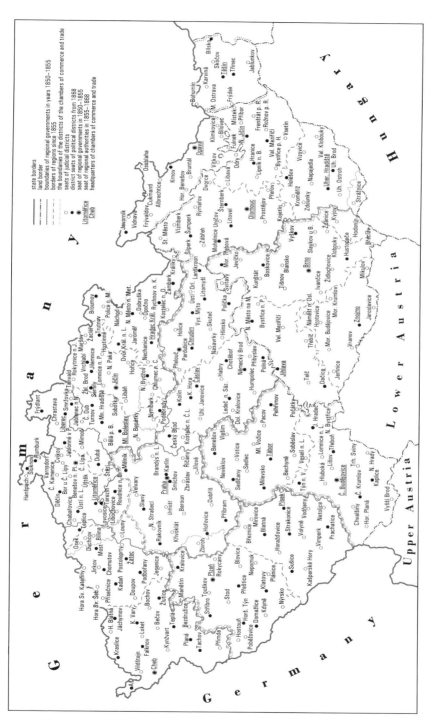

Map of the territorial scope of the chambers of trade and commerce in the Czech lands

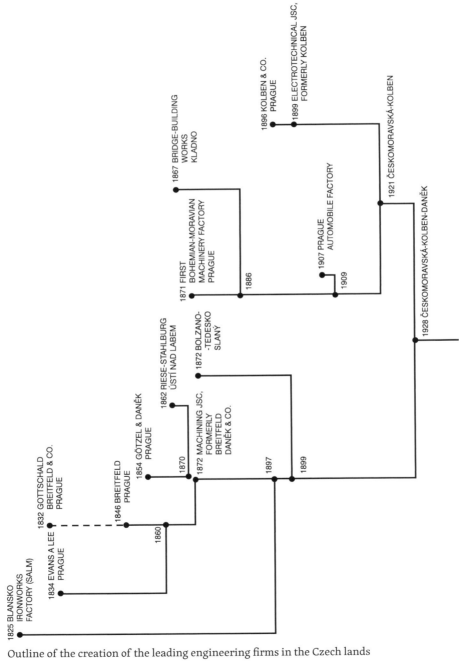

Outline of the creation of the leading engineering firms in the Czech lands

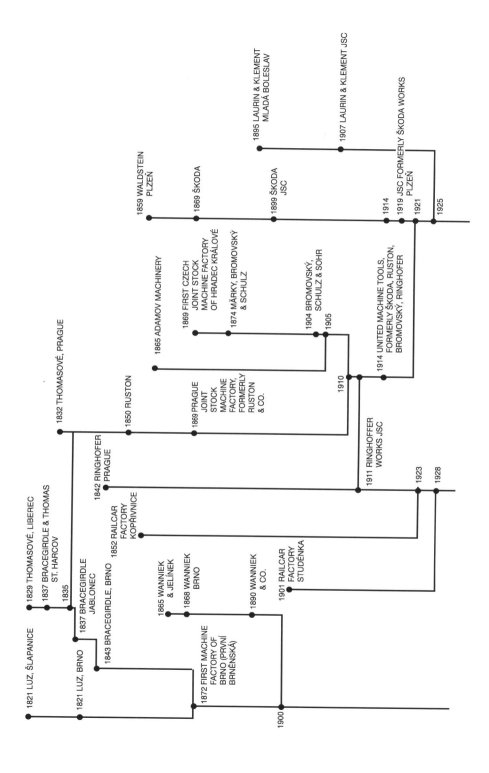

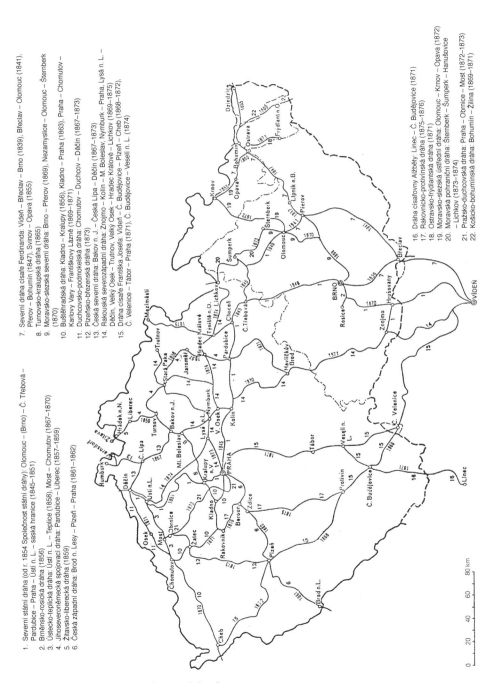

1. Severní státní dráha (od r. 1854 Společnost státní dráhy): Olomouc – (Brno) – Č. Třebová – Pardubice – Praha – Ústí n. L. – saská hranice (1845–1851)
2. Brněnsko-rosická dráha (1856)
3. Ústecko-teplická dráha: Ústí n. L. – Teplice (1858), Most – Chomutov (1867–1870)
4. Jihoseveroněmecká spojovací dráha: Pardubice – Liberec (1857–1859)
5. Žitavsko-liberecká dráha (1859)
6. Česká západní dráha: Brod n. Lesy – Plzeň – Praha (1861–1862)

7. Severní dráha císaře Ferdinanda: Vídeň – Břeclav – Brno (1839), Břeclav – Olomouc (1841), Přerov – Bohumín (1847), Svinov – Opava (1855)
8. Turnovsko-kralupská dráha (1865)
9. Moravsko-slezská severní dráha: Brno – Přerov (1869), Nezamyslice – Olomouc – Šternberk (1870)
10. Buštěhradská dráha: Kladno – Kralupy (1856), Kladno – Praha (1863), Praha – Chomutov – Karlovy Vary – Františkovy Lázně (1869–1871)
11. Duchcovsko-podmokelská dráha: Chomutov – Duchcov – Děčín (1867–1873)
12. Plzeňsko-březenská dráha (1873)
13. Česká severní dráha: Bakov n. J. – Česká Lípa – Děčín (1867–1873)
14. Rakouská severozápadní dráha: Znojmo – Kolín – M. Boleslav, Nymburk – Praha, Lysá n. L. – Děčín, Velký Osek – Trutnov, Velký Osek – Hradec Králové – Lichkov (1869–1875)
15. Dráha císaře Františka Josefa: Vídeň – Č. Budějovice – Plzeň – Cheb (1868–1872), Č. Velenice – Tábor – Praha (1871), Č. Budějovice – Veselí n. L. (1874)

16. Dráha císařovny Alžběty: Linec – Č. Budějovice (1871)
17. Rakovnicko-protivínská dráha (1875–1876)
18. Ostravsko-frýdlantská dráha (1871)
19. Moravsko-slezská ústřední dráha: Olomouc – Krnov – Opava (1872)
20. Moravská pohraniční dráha: Šternberk – Šumperk – Hanušovice – Lichkov (1873–1874)
21. Pražsko-duchcovská dráha: Praha – Obrnice – Most (1872–1873)
22. Košicko-bohumínská dráha: Bohumín – Žilina (1869–1871)

The main railway lines in the Czech lands

9. INDEX